Python for Data Analysis

Wes McKinney

Beijing · Cambridge · Farnham · Köln · Sebastopol · Tokyo

Python for Data Analysis

by Wes McKinney

Published by O'Reilly Media, Inc., 1005 Gravenstein Highway North, Sebastopol, CA 95472.

O'Reilly books may be purchased for educational, business, or sales promotional use. Online editions are also available for most titles (*http://safaribooksonline.com*). For more information, contact our corporate/institutional sales department: 800-998-9938 or *corporate@oreilly.com*.

Editors: Julie Steele and Meghan Blanchette
Production Editor: Melanie Yarbrough
Copyeditor: Teresa Exley
Proofreader: BIM Publishing Services

Indexer: BIM Publishing Services
Cover Designer: Karen Montgomery
Interior Designer: David Futato
Illustrator: Rebecca Demarest

October 2012:   First Edition.

Revision History for the First Edition:

2012-10-05	First release
2013-05-17	Second release
2014-12-12	Third release

See *http://oreilly.com/catalog/errata.csp?isbn=9781449319793* for release details.

ISBN: 978-1-449-31979-3

[LSI]

1418305833

Table of Contents

Preface

The scientific Python ecosystem of open source libraries has grown substantially over the last 10 years. By late 2011, I had long felt that the lack of centralized learning resources for data analysis and statistical applications was a stumbling block for new Python programmers engaged in such work. Key projects for data analysis (especially NumPy, IPython, matplotlib, and pandas) had also matured enough that a book written about them would likely not go out-of-date very quickly. Thus, I mustered the nerve to embark on this writing project. This is the book that I wish existed when I started using Python for data analysis in 2007. I hope you find it useful and are able to apply these tools productively in your work.

Conventions Used in This Book

The following typographical conventions are used in this book:

Italic
> Indicates new terms, URLs, email addresses, filenames, and file extensions.

`Constant width`
> Used for program listings, as well as within paragraphs to refer to program elements such as variable or function names, databases, data types, environment variables, statements, and keywords.

`Constant width bold`
> Shows commands or other text that should be typed literally by the user.

`Constant width italic`
> Shows text that should be replaced with user-supplied values or by values determined by context.

 This icon signifies a tip, suggestion, or general note.

This icon indicates a warning or caution.

Using Code Examples

This book is here to help you get your job done. In general, you may use the code in this book in your programs and documentation. You do not need to contact us for permission unless you're reproducing a significant portion of the code. For example, writing a program that uses several chunks of code from this book does not require permission. Selling or distributing a CD-ROM of examples from O'Reilly books does require permission. Answering a question by citing this book and quoting example code does not require permission. Incorporating a significant amount of example code from this book into your product's documentation does require permission.

We appreciate, but do not require, attribution. An attribution usually includes the title, author, publisher, and ISBN. For example: "*Python for Data Analysis* by William Wesley McKinney (O'Reilly). Copyright 2012 William McKinney, 978-1-449-31979-3."

If you feel your use of code examples falls outside fair use or the permission given above, feel free to contact us at *permissions@oreilly.com*.

Safari® Books Online

Safari Books Online (*www.safaribooksonline.com*) is an on-demand digital library that delivers expert content in both book and video form from the world's leading authors in technology and business.

Technology professionals, software developers, web designers, and business and creative professionals use Safari Books Online as their primary resource for research, problem solving, learning, and certification training.

Safari Books Online offers a range of plans and pricing for enterprise, government, and education, and individuals.

Members have access to thousands of books, training videos, and prepublication manuscripts in one fully searchable database from publishers like O'Reilly Media, Prentice Hall Professional, Addison-Wesley Professional, Microsoft Press, Sams, Que, Peachpit Press, Focal Press, Cisco Press, John Wiley & Sons, Syngress, Morgan Kaufmann, IBM Redbooks, Packt, Adobe Press, FT Press, Apress, Manning, New Riders, McGraw-Hill, Jones & Bartlett, Course Technology, and hundreds more. For more information about Safari Books Online, please visit us online.

How to Contact Us

Please address comments and questions concerning this book to the publisher:

O'Reilly Media, Inc.
1005 Gravenstein Highway North
Sebastopol, CA 95472
800-998-9938 (in the United States or Canada)
707-829-0515 (international or local)
707-829-0104 (fax)

We have a web page for this book, where we list errata, examples, and any additional information. You can access this page at *http://oreil.ly/python_for_data_analysis*.

To comment or ask technical questions about this book, send email to *bookquestions@oreilly.com*.

For more information about our books, courses, conferences, and news, see our website at *http://www.oreilly.com*.

Find us on Facebook: *http://facebook.com/oreilly*

Follow us on Twitter: *http://twitter.com/oreillymedia*

Watch us on YouTube: *http://www.youtube.com/oreillymedia*

## CHAPTER 1

Preliminaries

What Is This Book About?

This book is concerned with the nuts and bolts of manipulating, processing, cleaning, and crunching data in Python. It is also a practical, modern introduction to scientific computing in Python, tailored for data-intensive applications. This is a book about the parts of the Python language and libraries you'll need to effectively solve a broad set of data analysis problems. This book is *not* an exposition on analytical methods using Python as the implementation language.

When I say "data", what am I referring to exactly? The primary focus is on *structured data*, a deliberately vague term that encompasses many different common forms of data, such as

- Multidimensional arrays (matrices)
- Tabular or spreadsheet-like data in which each column may be a different type (string, numeric, date, or otherwise). This includes most kinds of data commonly stored in relational databases or tab- or comma-delimited text files
- Multiple tables of data interrelated by key columns (what would be primary or foreign keys for a SQL user)
- Evenly or unevenly spaced time series

This is by no means a complete list. Even though it may not always be obvious, a large percentage of data sets can be transformed into a structured form that is more suitable for analysis and modeling. If not, it may be possible to extract features from a data set into a structured form. As an example, a collection of news articles could be processed into a word frequency table which could then be used to perform sentiment analysis.

Most users of spreadsheet programs like Microsoft Excel, perhaps the most widely used data analysis tool in the world, will not be strangers to these kinds of data.

Why Python for Data Analysis?

For many people (myself among them), the Python language is easy to fall in love with. Since its first appearance in 1991, Python has become one of the most popular dynamic, programming languages, along with Perl, Ruby, and others. Python and Ruby have become especially popular in recent years for building websites using their numerous web frameworks, like Rails (Ruby) and Django (Python). Such languages are often called *scripting* languages as they can be used to write quick-and-dirty small programs, or *scripts*. I don't like the term "scripting language" as it carries a connotation that they cannot be used for building mission-critical software. Among interpreted languages Python is distinguished by its large and active *scientific computing* community. Adoption of Python for scientific computing in both industry applications and academic research has increased significantly since the early 2000s.

For data analysis and interactive, exploratory computing and data visualization, Python will inevitably draw comparisons with the many other domain-specific open source and commercial programming languages and tools in wide use, such as R, MATLAB, SAS, Stata, and others. In recent years, Python's improved library support (primarily pandas) has made it a strong alternative for data manipulation tasks. Combined with Python's strength in general purpose programming, it is an excellent choice as a single language for building data-centric applications.

Python as Glue

Part of Python's success as a scientific computing platform is the ease of integrating C, C++, and FORTRAN code. Most modern computing environments share a similar set of legacy FORTRAN and C libraries for doing linear algebra, optimization, integration, fast fourier transforms, and other such algorithms. The same story has held true for many companies and national labs that have used Python to glue together 30 years' worth of legacy software.

Most programs consist of small portions of code where most of the time is spent, with large amounts of "glue code" that doesn't run often. In many cases, the execution time of the glue code is insignificant; effort is most fruitfully invested in optimizing the computational bottlenecks, sometimes by moving the code to a lower-level language like C.

In the last few years, the Cython project (*http://cython.org*) has become one of the preferred ways of both creating fast compiled extensions for Python and also interfacing with C and C++ code.

Solving the "Two-Language" Problem

In many organizations, it is common to research, prototype, and test new ideas using a more domain-specific computing language like MATLAB or R then later port those ideas to be part of a larger production system written in, say, Java, C#, or C++. What people are increasingly finding is that Python is a suitable language not only for doing research and prototyping but also building the production systems, too. I believe that more and more companies will go down this path as there are often significant organizational benefits to having both scientists and technologists using the same set of programmatic tools.

Why Not Python?

While Python is an excellent environment for building computationally-intensive scientific applications and building most kinds of general purpose systems, there are a number of uses for which Python may be less suitable.

As Python is an interpreted programming language, in general most Python code will run substantially slower than code written in a compiled language like Java or C++. As *programmer time* is typically more valuable than *CPU time*, many are happy to make this tradeoff. However, in an application with very low latency requirements (for example, a high frequency trading system), the time spent programming in a lower-level, lower-productivity language like C++ to achieve the maximum possible performance might be time well spent.

Python is not an ideal language for highly concurrent, multithreaded applications, particularly applications with many CPU-bound threads. The reason for this is that it has what is known as the *global interpreter lock* (GIL), a mechanism which prevents the interpreter from executing more than one Python bytecode instruction at a time. The technical reasons for why the GIL exists are beyond the scope of this book, but as of this writing it does not seem likely that the GIL will disappear anytime soon. While it is true that in many big data processing applications, a cluster of computers may be required to process a data set in a reasonable amount of time, there are still situations where a single-process, multithreaded system is desirable.

This is not to say that Python cannot execute truly multithreaded, parallel code; that code just cannot be executed in a single Python process. As an example, the Cython project features easy integration with OpenMP, a C framework for parallel computing, in order to to parallelize loops and thus significantly speed up numerical algorithms.

Essential Python Libraries

For those who are less familiar with the scientific Python ecosystem and the libraries used throughout the book, I present the following overview of each library.

NumPy

NumPy, short for Numerical Python, is the foundational package for scientific computing in Python. The majority of this book will be based on NumPy and libraries built on top of NumPy. It provides, among other things:

- A fast and efficient multidimensional array object *ndarray*
- Functions for performing element-wise computations with arrays or mathematical operations between arrays
- Tools for reading and writing array-based data sets to disk
- Linear algebra operations, Fourier transform, and random number generation
- Tools for integrating C, C++, and Fortran code to Python

Beyond the fast array-processing capabilities that NumPy adds to Python, one of its primary purposes with regards to data analysis is as the primary container for data to be passed between algorithms. For numerical data, NumPy arrays are a much more efficient way of storing and manipulating data than the other built-in Python data structures. Also, libraries written in a lower-level language, such as C or Fortran, can operate on the data stored in a NumPy array without copying any data.

pandas

pandas provides rich data structures and functions designed to make working with structured data fast, easy, and expressive. It is, as you will see, one of the critical ingredients enabling Python to be a powerful and productive data analysis environment. The primary object in pandas that will be used in this book is the DataFrame, a two-dimensional tabular, column-oriented data structure with both row and column labels:

```
>>> frame
    total_bill  tip   sex     smoker  day  time    size
1   16.99       1.01  Female  No      Sun  Dinner  2
2   10.34       1.66  Male    No      Sun  Dinner  3
3   21.01       3.5   Male    No      Sun  Dinner  3
4   23.68       3.31  Male    No      Sun  Dinner  2
5   24.59       3.61  Female  No      Sun  Dinner  4
6   25.29       4.71  Male    No      Sun  Dinner  4
7   8.77        2     Male    No      Sun  Dinner  2
8   26.88       3.12  Male    No      Sun  Dinner  4
9   15.04       1.96  Male    No      Sun  Dinner  2
10  14.78       3.23  Male    No      Sun  Dinner  2
```

pandas combines the high performance array-computing features of NumPy with the flexible data manipulation capabilities of spreadsheets and relational databases (such as SQL). It provides sophisticated indexing functionality to make it easy to reshape, slice and dice, perform aggregations, and select subsets of data. pandas is the primary tool that we will use in this book.

For financial users, pandas features rich, high-performance time series functionality and tools well-suited for working with financial data. In fact, I initially designed pandas as an ideal tool for financial data analysis applications.

For users of the R language for statistical computing, the DataFrame name will be familiar, as the object was named after the similar R `data.frame` object. They are not the same, however; the functionality provided by `data.frame` in R is essentially a strict subset of that provided by the pandas `DataFrame`. While this is a book about Python, I will occasionally draw comparisons with R as it is one of the most widely-used open source data analysis environments and will be familiar to many readers.

The pandas name itself is derived from *panel data*, an econometrics term for multidimensional structured data sets, and *Python data analysis* itself.

matplotlib

matplotlib is the most popular Python library for producing plots and other 2D data visualizations. It was originally created by John D. Hunter (JDH) and is now maintained by a large team of developers. It is well-suited for creating plots suitable for publication. It integrates well with IPython (see below), thus providing a comfortable interactive environment for plotting and exploring data. The plots are also *interactive*; you can zoom in on a section of the plot and pan around the plot using the toolbar in the plot window.

IPython

IPython is the component in the standard scientific Python toolset that ties everything together. It provides a robust and productive environment for interactive and exploratory computing. It is an enhanced Python shell designed to accelerate the writing, testing, and debugging of Python code. It is particularly useful for interactively working with data and visualizing data with matplotlib. IPython is usually involved with the majority of my Python work, including running, debugging, and testing code.

Aside from the standard terminal-based IPython shell, the project also provides

- A Mathematica-like HTML notebook for connecting to IPython through a web browser (more on this later).
- A Qt framework-based GUI console with inline plotting, multiline editing, and syntax highlighting
- An infrastructure for interactive parallel and distributed computing

I will devote a chapter to IPython and how to get the most out of its features. I strongly recommend using it while working through this book.

SciPy

SciPy is a collection of packages addressing a number of different standard problem domains in scientific computing. Here is a sampling of the packages included:

- `scipy.integrate`: numerical integration routines and differential equation solvers
- `scipy.linalg`: linear algebra routines and matrix decompositions extending beyond those provided in `numpy.linalg`.
- `scipy.optimize`: function optimizers (minimizers) and root finding algorithms
- `scipy.signal`: signal processing tools
- `scipy.sparse`: sparse matrices and sparse linear system solvers
- `scipy.special`: wrapper around SPECFUN, a Fortran library implementing many common mathematical functions, such as the gamma function
- `scipy.stats`: standard continuous and discrete probability distributions (density functions, samplers, continuous distribution functions), various statistical tests, and more descriptive statistics
- `scipy.weave`: tool for using inline C++ code to accelerate array computations

Together NumPy and SciPy form a reasonably complete computational replacement for much of MATLAB along with some of its add-on toolboxes.

Installation and Setup

Since everyone uses Python for different applications, there is no single solution for setting up Python and required add-on packages. Many readers will not have a complete scientific Python environment suitable for following along with this book, so here I will give detailed instructions to get set up on each operating system. I recommend using the free Anaconda distribution provided by Continuum Analytics. At the time of this writing, Anaconda includes Python 2.7, though this might change at some point in the future.

At some point while reading, you may wish to install one or more of the following packages: statsmodels, PyTables, PyQt (or equivalently, PySide), xlrd, lxml, basemap, pymongo, and requests. These are used in various examples. Installing these optional libraries is not necessary, and I would would suggest waiting until you need them. For example, installing PyQt or PyTables from source on OS X or Linux can be rather arduous. For now, it's most important to get up and running with the base Anaconda distribution.

For information on each Python package and links to binary installers or other help, see the Python Package Index (PyPI, *http://pypi.python.org*). This is also an excellent resource for finding new Python packages.

Windows

To get started on Windows, download the Anaconda installer from *http://continuum .io/downloads*, which should be an executable named like `Anaconda-2.1.0-Windows-x86_64.exe`. Run the installer and accept the default installation location `C:\Python27`. If you had previously installed Python in this location, you may want to delete it manually first (or using Add/Remove Programs).

Next, you need to verify that Python has been successfully added to the system path and that there are no conflicts with any prior-installed Python versions. First, open a command prompt by going to the Start Menu and starting the Command Prompt application, also known as `cmd.exe`. Try starting the Python interpreter by typing `python`. You should see a message that matches the version of Anaconda you installed (here, 2.1.0).

If you see a message for a different version of Anaconda or it doesn't work at all, you will need to clean up your Windows environment variables. On Windows 7 you can start typing "environment variables" in the program's search field and select `Edit environment variables for your account`. On Windows XP, you will have to go to `Control Panel > System > Advanced > Environment Variables`. On the window that pops up, you are looking for the `Path` variable. It needs to contain the following two directory paths, separated by semicolons:

    C:\Python27;C:\Python27\Scripts

If you installed other versions of Python, be sure to delete any other Python-related directories from both the system and user `Path` variables. After making a path alternation, you have to restart the command prompt for the changes to take effect. To verify that everything is set up properly, fire up the command prompt and run the following command:

    C:\Users\Wes>ipython

You can also check that the IPython Notebook can be successfully run by typing:

    C:\Users\Wes>ipython notebook

Apple OS X

Download the OS X Anaconda installer which should be named something like `Anaconda-2.1.0-MacOSX-x86_64.pkg`. Double-click the `.pkg` file to run the installer. When the installer runs, it automatically appends the Anaconda executable path to your `.bash_profile` file. This is located at `/Users/your_uname/.bash_profile`.

To verify everything is working, launch IPython in the shell:

    $ ipython

GNU/Linux

 Some, but not all, Linux distributions include sufficiently up-to-date versions of all the required Python packages and can be installed using the built-in package management tool like apt. I detail setup using Anaconda as it's easily reproducible across distributions. I recommend it for all new users.

Linux details will vary a bit depending on your Linux flavor, but here I give details for Debian-based GNU/Linux systems like Ubuntu. Setup is similar to OS X with the exception of how Anaconda is installed. The installer is a shell script that must be executed in the terminal. Depending on whether you have a 32-bit or 64-bit system, you will either need to install the x86 (32-bit) or x86_64 (64-bit) installer. You will then have a file named something similar to Anaconda-2.1.0-Linux-x86_64.sh. To install it, execute this script with bash:

```
$ bash Anaconda-2.1.0-Linux-x86_64.sh
```

After accepting the license, you will be presented with a choice of where to put the Anaconda files. I recommend installing the files in the default location in your home directory, for example /home/wesm/anaconda (with your username, naturally).

The Anaconda installer should attempt to prepend its executable directory to your $PATH variable. If you have any problems after installation you can do this yourself by modifying your .bashrc with something akin to:

```
export PATH=/home/wesm/anaconda/bin:$PATH
```

Obviously, substitute the installation directory you used for /home/wesm/anaconda/. After doing this you can either start a new terminal process or execute your .bashrc again with source ~/.bashrc.

Python 2 and Python 3

The Python community is currently undergoing a drawn-out transition from the Python 2 series of interpreters to the Python 3 series. Until the appearance of Python 3.0, all Python code was backwards compatible. The community decided that in order to move the language forward, certain backwards incompatible changes were necessary.

I am writing this book with Python 2.7 as its basis, as the majority of the scientific Python community has not yet transitioned to Python 3. The good news is that, with a few exceptions, you should have no trouble following along with the book if you happen to be using Python 3.2.

Integrated Development Environments (IDEs)

When asked about my standard development environment, I almost always say "IPython plus a text editor". I typically write a program and iteratively test and debug each piece of it in IPython. It is also useful to be able to play around with data interactively and visually verify that a particular set of data manipulations are doing the right thing. Libraries like pandas and NumPy are designed to be easy-to-use in the shell.

However, some will still prefer to work in an IDE instead of a text editor. They do provide many nice "code intelligence" features like completion or quickly pulling up the documentation associated with functions and classes. Here are some that you can explore:

- Eclipse with PyDev Plugin
- Python Tools for Visual Studio (for Windows users)
- PyCharm
- Spyder
- Komodo IDE

Community and Conferences

Outside of an Internet search, the scientific Python mailing lists are generally helpful and responsive to questions. Some ones to take a look at are:

- pydata: a Google Group list for questions related to Python for data analysis and pandas
- pystatsmodels: for statsmodels or pandas-related questions
- numpy-discussion: for NumPy-related questions
- scipy-user: for general SciPy or scientific Python questions

I deliberately did not post URLs for these in case they change. They can be easily located via Internet search.

Each year many conferences are held all over the world for Python programmers. PyCon and EuroPython are the two main general Python conferences in the United States and Europe, respectively. SciPy and EuroSciPy are scientific-oriented Python conferences where you will likely find many "birds of a feather" if you become more involved with using Python for data analysis after reading this book.

Navigating This Book

If you have never programmed in Python before, you may actually want to start at the end of the book, where I have placed a condensed tutorial on Python syntax, language features, and built-in data structures like tuples, lists, and dicts. These things are considered prerequisite knowledge for the remainder of the book.

The book starts by introducing you to the IPython environment. Next, I give a short introduction to the key features of NumPy, leaving more advanced NumPy use for another chapter at the end of the book. Then, I introduce pandas and devote the rest of the book to data analysis topics applying pandas, NumPy, and matplotlib (for visualization). I have structured the material in the most incremental way possible, though there is occasionally some minor cross-over between chapters.

Data files and related material for each chapter are hosted as a git repository on GitHub:

```
http://github.com/pydata/pydata-book
```

I encourage you to download the data and use it to replicate the book's code examples and experiment with the tools presented in each chapter. I will happily accept contributions, scripts, IPython notebooks, or any other materials you wish to contribute to the book's repository for all to enjoy.

Code Examples

Most of the code examples in the book are shown with input and output as it would appear executed in the IPython shell.

```
In [5]: code
Out[5]: output
```

At times, for clarity, multiple code examples will be shown side by side. These should be read left to right and executed separately.

```
In [5]: code          In [6]: code2
Out[5]: output        Out[6]: output2
```

Data for Examples

Data sets for the examples in each chapter are hosted in a repository on GitHub: *http://github.com/pydata/pydata-book*. You can download this data either by using the git revision control command-line program or by downloading a zip file of the repository from the website.

I have made every effort to ensure that it contains everything necessary to reproduce the examples, but I may have made some mistakes or omissions. If so, please send me an e-mail: wesmckinn@gmail.com.

Import Conventions

The Python community has adopted a number of naming conventions for commonly-used modules:

```
import numpy as np
import pandas as pd
import matplotlib.pyplot as plt
```

This means that when you see `np.arange`, this is a reference to the `arange` function in NumPy. This is done as it's considered bad practice in Python software development to import everything (`from numpy import *`) from a large package like NumPy.

Jargon

I'll use some terms common both to programming and data science that you may not be familiar with. Thus, here are some brief definitions:

Munge/Munging/Wrangling
Describes the overall process of manipulating unstructured and/or messy data into a structured or clean form. The word has snuck its way into the jargon of many modern day data hackers. Munge rhymes with "lunge".

Pseudocode
A description of an algorithm or process that takes a code-like form while likely not being actual valid source code.

Syntactic sugar
Programming syntax which does not add new features, but makes something more convenient or easier to type.

Acknowledgements

It would have been difficult for me to write this book without the support of a large number of people.

On the O'Reilly staff, I'm very grateful for my editors Meghan Blanchette and Julie Steele who guided me through the process. Mike Loukides also worked with me in the proposal stages and helped make the book a reality.

I received a wealth of technical review from a large cast of characters. In particular, Martin Blais and Hugh Brown were incredibly helpful in improving the book's examples, clarity, and organization from cover to cover. James Long, Drew Conway, Fernando Pérez, Brian Granger, Thomas Kluyver, Adam Klein, Josh Klein, Chang She, and Stéfan van der Walt each reviewed one or more chapters, providing pointed feedback from many different perspectives.

I got many great ideas for examples and data sets from friends and colleagues in the data community, among them: Mike Dewar, Jeff Hammerbacher, James Johndrow, Kristian Lum, Adam Klein, Hilary Mason, Chang She, and Ashley Williams.

I am of course indebted to the many leaders in the open source scientific Python community who've built the foundation for my development work and gave encouragement while I was writing this book: the IPython core team (Fernando Pérez, Brian Granger,

Min Ragan-Kelly, Thomas Kluyver, and others), John Hunter, Skipper Seabold, Travis Oliphant, Peter Wang, Eric Jones, Robert Kern, Josef Perktold, Francesc Alted, Chris Fonnesbeck, and too many others to mention. Several other people provided a great deal of support, ideas, and encouragement along the way: Drew Conway, Sean Taylor, Giuseppe Paleologo, Jared Lander, David Epstein, John Krowas, Joshua Bloom, Den Pilsworth, John Myles-White, and many others I've forgotten.

I'd also like to thank a number of people from my formative years. First, my former AQR colleagues who've cheered me on in my pandas work over the years: Alex Reyfman, Michael Wong, Tim Sargen, Oktay Kurbanov, Matthew Tschantz, Roni Israelov, Michael Katz, Chris Uga, Prasad Ramanan, Ted Square, and Hoon Kim. Lastly, my academic advisors Haynes Miller (MIT) and Mike West (Duke).

I received significant help from Philip Cloud and Joris Van den Bossche in 2014 to update the book's code examples and fix some other inaccuracies due to changes in pandas.

On the personal side, Casey Dinkin provided invaluable day-to-day support during the writing process, tolerating my highs and lows as I hacked together the final draft on top of an already overcommitted schedule. Lastly, my parents, Bill and Kim, taught me to always follow my dreams and to never settle for less.

## CHAPTER 2

Introductory Examples

This book teaches you the Python tools to work productively with data. While readers may have many different end goals for their work, the tasks required generally fall into a number of different broad groups:

Interacting with the outside world
Reading and writing with a variety of file formats and databases.

Preparation
Cleaning, munging, combining, normalizing, reshaping, slicing and dicing, and transforming data for analysis.

Transformation
Applying mathematical and statistical operations to groups of data sets to derive new data sets. For example, aggregating a large table by group variables.

Modeling and computation
Connecting your data to statistical models, machine learning algorithms, or other computational tools

Presentation
Creating interactive or static graphical visualizations or textual summaries

In this chapter I will show you a few data sets and some things we can do with them. These examples are just intended to pique your interest and thus will only be explained at a high level. Don't worry if you have no experience with any of these tools; they will be discussed in great detail throughout the rest of the book. In the code examples you'll see input and output prompts like In [15]:; these are from the IPython shell.

To follow along with these examples, you should run IPython in Pylab mode by running ipython --pylab at the command prompt.

1.usa.gov data from bit.ly

In 2011, URL shortening service bit.ly partnered with the United States government website usa.gov to provide a feed of anonymous data gathered from users who shorten links ending with .gov or .mil. As of this writing, in addition to providing a live feed, hourly snapshots are available as downloadable text files.[1]

In the case of the hourly snapshots, each line in each file contains a common form of web data known as JSON, which stands for JavaScript Object Notation. For example, if we read just the first line of a file you may see something like

```
In [15]: path = 'ch02/usagov_bitly_data2012-03-16-1331923249.txt'
```

```
In [16]: open(path).readline()
Out[16]: '{ "a": "Mozilla\\/5.0 (Windows NT 6.1; WOW64) AppleWebKit\\/535.11
(KHTML, like Gecko) Chrome\\/17.0.963.78 Safari\\/535.11", "c": "US", "nk": 1,
"tz": "America\\/New_York", "gr": "MA", "g": "A6qOVH", "h": "wfLQtf", "l":
"orofrog", "al": "en-US,en;q=0.8", "hh": "1.usa.gov", "r":
"http:\\/\\/www.facebook.com\\/l\\/7AQEFzjSi\\/1.usa.gov\\/wfLQtf", "u":
"http:\\/\\/www.ncbi.nlm.nih.gov\\/pubmed\\/22415991", "t": 1331923247, "hc":
1331822918, "cy": "Danvers", "ll": [ 42.576698, -70.954903 ] }\n'
```

Python has numerous built-in and 3rd party modules for converting a JSON string into a Python dictionary object. Here I'll use the json module and its loads function invoked on each line in the sample file I downloaded:

```
import json
path = 'ch02/usagov_bitly_data2012-03-16-1331923249.txt'
records = [json.loads(line) for line in open(path, 'rb')]
```

If you've never programmed in Python before, the last expression here is called a *list comprehension*, which is a concise way of applying an operation (like json.loads) to a collection of strings or other objects. Conveniently, iterating over an open file handle gives you a sequence of its lines. The resulting object records is now a list of Python dicts:

```
In [18]: records[0]
Out[18]:
{u'a': u'Mozilla/5.0 (Windows NT 6.1; WOW64) AppleWebKit/535.11 (KHTML, like
Gecko) Chrome/17.0.963.78 Safari/535.11',
 u'al': u'en-US,en;q=0.8',
 u'c': u'US',
 u'cy': u'Danvers',
 u'g': u'A6qOVH',
 u'gr': u'MA',
 u'h': u'wfLQtf',
 u'hc': 1331822918,
 u'hh': u'1.usa.gov',
 u'l': u'orofrog',
 u'll': [42.576698, -70.954903],
```

---

1. *http://www.usa.gov/About/developer-resources/1usagov.shtml*

```
u'nk': 1,
u'r': u'http://www.facebook.com/l/7AQEFzjSi/1.usa.gov/wfLQtf',
u't': 1331923247,
u'tz': u'America/New_York',
u'u': u'http://www.ncbi.nlm.nih.gov/pubmed/22415991'}
```

Note that Python indices start at 0 and not 1 like some other languages (like R). It's now easy to access individual values within records by passing a string for the key you wish to access:

```
In [19]: records[0]['tz']
Out[19]: u'America/New_York'
```

The u here in front of the quotation stands for *unicode*, a standard form of string encoding. Note that IPython shows the time zone string object *representation* here rather than its print equivalent:

```
In [20]: print records[0]['tz']
America/New_York
```

Counting Time Zones in Pure Python

Suppose we were interested in the most often-occurring time zones in the data set (the tz field). There are many ways we could do this. First, let's extract a list of time zones again using a list comprehension:

```
In [25]: time_zones = [rec['tz'] for rec in records]
---------------------------------------------------------------------
KeyError                                 Traceback (most recent call last)
/home/wesm/book_scripts/whetting/<ipython> in <module>()
----> 1 time_zones = [rec['tz'] for rec in records]

KeyError: 'tz'
```

Oops! Turns out that not all of the records have a time zone field. This is easy to handle as we can add the check if 'tz' in rec at the end of the list comprehension:

```
In [26]: time_zones = [rec['tz'] for rec in records if 'tz' in rec]

In [27]: time_zones[:10]
Out[27]:
[u'America/New_York',
 u'America/Denver',
 u'America/New_York',
 u'America/Sao_Paulo',
 u'America/New_York',
 u'America/New_York',
 u'Europe/Warsaw',
 u'',
 u'',
 u'']
```

Just looking at the first 10 time zones we see that some of them are unknown (empty). You can filter these out also but I'll leave them in for now. Now, to produce counts by time zone I'll show two approaches: the harder way (using just the Python standard library) and the easier way (using pandas). One way to do the counting is to use a dict to store counts while we iterate through the time zones:

```python
def get_counts(sequence):
    counts = {}
    for x in sequence:
        if x in counts:
            counts[x] += 1
        else:
            counts[x] = 1
    return counts
```

If you know a bit more about the Python standard library, you might prefer to write the same thing more briefly:

```python
from collections import defaultdict

def get_counts2(sequence):
    counts = defaultdict(int) # values will initialize to 0
    for x in sequence:
        counts[x] += 1
    return counts
```

I put this logic in a function just to make it more reusable. To use it on the time zones, just pass the time_zones list:

```python
In [31]: counts = get_counts(time_zones)

In [32]: counts['America/New_York']
Out[32]: 1251

In [33]: len(time_zones)
Out[33]: 3440
```

If we wanted the top 10 time zones and their counts, we have to do a little bit of dictionary acrobatics:

```python
def top_counts(count_dict, n=10):
    value_key_pairs = [(count, tz) for tz, count in count_dict.items()]
    value_key_pairs.sort()
    return value_key_pairs[-n:]
```

We have then:

```python
In [35]: top_counts(counts)
Out[35]:
[(33, u'America/Sao_Paulo'),
 (35, u'Europe/Madrid'),
 (36, u'Pacific/Honolulu'),
 (37, u'Asia/Tokyo'),
 (74, u'Europe/London'),
 (191, u'America/Denver'),
 (382, u'America/Los_Angeles'),
 (400, u'America/Chicago'),
```

```
 (521, u''),
 (1251, u'America/New_York')]
```

If you search the Python standard library, you may find the collections.Counter class, which makes this task a lot easier:

```
In [49]: from collections import Counter

In [50]: counts = Counter(time_zones)

In [51]: counts.most_common(10)
Out[51]:
[(u'America/New_York', 1251),
 (u'', 521),
 (u'America/Chicago', 400),
 (u'America/Los_Angeles', 382),
 (u'America/Denver', 191),
 (u'Europe/London', 74),
 (u'Asia/Tokyo', 37),
 (u'Pacific/Honolulu', 36),
 (u'Europe/Madrid', 35),
 (u'America/Sao_Paulo', 33)]
```

Counting Time Zones with pandas

The main pandas data structure is the *DataFrame*, which you can think of as representing a table or spreadsheet of data. Creating a DataFrame from the original set of records is simple:

```
In [17]: from pandas import DataFrame, Series

In [18]: import pandas as pd

In [19]: frame = DataFrame(records)

In [20]: frame.info()
<class 'pandas.core.frame.DataFrame'>
Int64Index: 3560 entries, 0 to 3559
Data columns (total 18 columns):
_heartbeat_    120 non-null float64
a              3440 non-null object
al             3094 non-null object
c              2919 non-null object
cy             2919 non-null object
g              3440 non-null object
gr             2919 non-null object
h              3440 non-null object
hc             3440 non-null float64
hh             3440 non-null object
kw             93 non-null object
l              3440 non-null object
ll             2919 non-null object
nk             3440 non-null float64
r              3440 non-null object
t              3440 non-null float64
```

```
tz              3440 non-null object
u               3440 non-null object
dtypes: float64(4), object(14)
In [21]: frame['tz'][:10]
Out[21]:
0    America/New_York
1     America/Denver
2    America/New_York
3    America/Sao_Paulo
4    America/New_York
5    America/New_York
6       Europe/Warsaw
7
8
9
Name: tz, dtype: object
```

The output shown for the `frame` is the *summary view*, shown for large DataFrame objects. The Series object returned by `frame['tz']` has a method `value_counts` that gives us what we're looking for:

```
In [22]: tz_counts = frame['tz'].value_counts()

In [23]: tz_counts[:10]
Out[23]:
America/New_York       1251
                        521
America/Chicago         400
America/Los_Angeles     382
America/Denver          191
Europe/London            74
Asia/Tokyo               37
Pacific/Honolulu         36
Europe/Madrid            35
America/Sao_Paulo        33
dtype: int64
```

Then, we might want to make a plot of this data using plotting library, matplotlib. You can do a bit of munging to fill in a substitute value for unknown and missing time zone data in the records. The `fillna` function can replace missing (NA) values and unknown (empty strings) values can be replaced by boolean array indexing:

```
In [24]: clean_tz = frame['tz'].fillna('Missing')

In [25]: clean_tz[clean_tz == ''] = 'Unknown'

In [26]: tz_counts = clean_tz.value_counts()

In [27]: tz_counts[:10]
Out[27]:
America/New_York       1251
Unknown                 521
America/Chicago         400
America/Los_Angeles     382
America/Denver          191
```

```
Missing                120
Europe/London           74
Asia/Tokyo              37
Pacific/Honolulu        36
Europe/Madrid           35
dtype: int64
```

Making a horizontal bar plot can be accomplished using the plot method on the counts objects:

```
In [29]: tz_counts[:10].plot(kind='barh', rot=0)
```

See Figure 2-1 for the resulting figure. We'll explore more tools for working with this kind of data. For example, the a field contains information about the browser, device, or application used to perform the URL shortening:

```
In [30]: frame['a'][1]
Out[30]: u'GoogleMaps/RochesterNY'

In [31]: frame['a'][50]
Out[31]: u'Mozilla/5.0 (Windows NT 5.1; rv:10.0.2) Gecko/20100101 Firefox/10.0.2'

In [32]: frame['a'][51]
Out[32]: u'Mozilla/5.0 (Linux; U; Android 2.2.2; en-us; LG-P925/V10e Build/FRG83G)
AppleWebKit/533.1 (KHTML, like Gecko) Version/4.0 Mobile Safari/533.1'
```

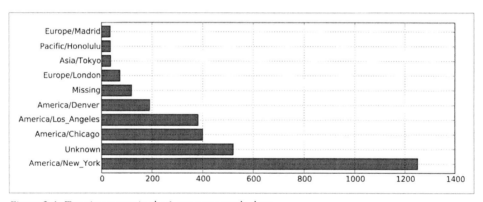

Figure 2-1. Top time zones in the 1.usa.gov sample data

Parsing all of the interesting information in these "agent" strings may seem like a daunting task. Luckily, once you have mastered Python's built-in string functions and regular expression capabilities, it is really not so bad. For example, we could split off the first token in the string (corresponding roughly to the browser capability) and make another summary of the user behavior:

```
In [33]: results = Series([x.split()[0] for x in frame.a.dropna()])

In [34]: results[:5]
Out[34]:
0              Mozilla/5.0
1    GoogleMaps/RochesterNY
```

```
2              Mozilla/4.0
3              Mozilla/5.0
4              Mozilla/5.0
dtype: object

In [35]: results.value_counts()[:8]
Out[35]:
Mozilla/5.0                   2594
Mozilla/4.0                    601
GoogleMaps/RochesterNY         121
Opera/9.80                      34
TEST_INTERNET_AGENT             24
GoogleProducer                  21
Mozilla/6.0                      5
BlackBerry8520/5.0.0.681         4
dtype: int64
```

Now, suppose you wanted to decompose the top time zones into Windows and non-Windows users. As a simplification, let's say that a user is on Windows if the string `'Windows'` is in the agent string. Since some of the agents are missing, I'll exclude these from the data:

```
In [36]: cframe = frame[frame.a.notnull()]
```

We want to then compute a value whether each row is Windows or not:

```
In [37]: operating_system = np.where(cframe['a'].str.contains('Windows'),
   ....:                             'Windows', 'Not Windows')

In [38]: operating_system[:5]
Out[38]:
array(['Windows', 'Not Windows', 'Windows', 'Not Windows', 'Windows'],
      dtype='|S11')
```

Then, you can group the data by its time zone column and this new list of operating systems:

```
In [39]: by_tz_os = cframe.groupby(['tz', operating_system])
```

The group counts, analogous to the `value_counts` function above, can be computed using `size`. This result is then reshaped into a table with `unstack`:

```
In [40]: agg_counts = by_tz_os.size().unstack().fillna(0)

In [41]: agg_counts[:10]
Out[41]:
                                Not Windows  Windows
tz
                                        245      276
Africa/Cairo                              0        3
Africa/Casablanca                         0        1
Africa/Ceuta                              0        2
Africa/Johannesburg                       0        1
Africa/Lusaka                             0        1
America/Anchorage                         4        1
America/Argentina/Buenos_Aires            1        0
```

```
America/Argentina/Cordoba          0     1
America/Argentina/Mendoza          0     1
```

Finally, let's select the top overall time zones. To do so, I construct an indirect index array from the row counts in `agg_counts`:

```
# Use to sort in ascending order
In [42]: indexer = agg_counts.sum(1).argsort()

In [43]: indexer[:10]
Out[43]:
tz
                                    24
Africa/Cairo                        20
Africa/Casablanca                   21
Africa/Ceuta                        92
Africa/Johannesburg                 87
Africa/Lusaka                       53
America/Anchorage                   54
America/Argentina/Buenos_Aires      57
America/Argentina/Cordoba           26
America/Argentina/Mendoza           55
dtype: int64
```

I then use `take` to select the rows in that order, then slice off the last 10 rows:

```
In [44]: count_subset = agg_counts.take(indexer)[-10:]

In [45]: count_subset
Out[45]:
                     Not Windows   Windows
tz
America/Sao_Paulo             13        20
Europe/Madrid                 16        19
Pacific/Honolulu               0        36
Asia/Tokyo                     2        35
Europe/London                 43        31
America/Denver               132        59
America/Los_Angeles          130       252
America/Chicago              115       285
                             245       276
America/New_York             339       912
```

Then, as shown in the preceding code block, this can be plotted in a bar plot; I'll make it a stacked bar plot by passing `stacked=True` (see Figure 2-2) :

```
In [47]: count_subset.plot(kind='barh', stacked=True)
```

The plot doesn't make it easy to see the relative percentage of Windows users in the smaller groups, but the rows can easily be normalized to sum to 1 then plotted again (see Figure 2-3):

```
In [49]: normed_subset = count_subset.div(count_subset.sum(1), axis=0)

In [50]: normed_subset.plot(kind='barh', stacked=True)
```

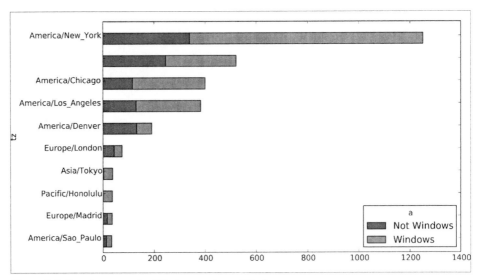

Figure 2-2. Top time zones by Windows and non-Windows users

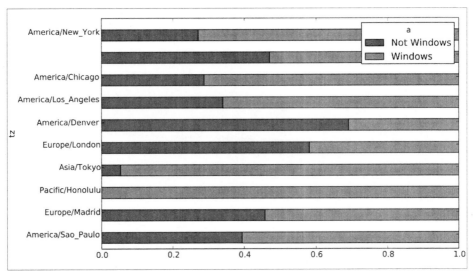

Figure 2-3. Percentage Windows and non-Windows users in top-occurring time zones

All of the methods employed here will be examined in great detail throughout the rest of the book.

MovieLens 1M Data Set

GroupLens Research (*http://www.grouplens.org/node/73*) provides a number of collections of movie ratings data collected from users of MovieLens in the late 1990s and early 2000s. The data provide movie ratings, movie metadata (genres and year), and demographic data about the users (age, zip code, gender, and occupation). Such data is often of interest in the development of recommendation systems based on machine learning algorithms. While I will not be exploring machine learning techniques in great detail in this book, I will show you how to slice and dice data sets like these into the exact form you need.

The MovieLens 1M data set contains 1 million ratings collected from 6000 users on 4000 movies. It's spread across 3 tables: ratings, user information, and movie information. After extracting the data from the zip file, each table can be loaded into a pandas DataFrame object using `pandas.read_table`:

```python
import pandas as pd

unames = ['user_id', 'gender', 'age', 'occupation', 'zip']
users = pd.read_table('movielens/users.dat', sep='::', header=None,
                      names=unames)

rnames = ['user_id', 'movie_id', 'rating', 'timestamp']
ratings = pd.read_table('movielens/users.dat', sep='::', header=None,
                        names=rnames)

mnames = ['movie_id', 'title', 'genres']
movies = pd.read_table('movielens/users.dat', sep='::', header=None,
                       names=mnames)
```

You can verify that everything succeeded by looking at the first few rows of each DataFrame with Python's slice syntax:

```
In [62]: users[:5]
Out[62]:
   user_id gender  age  occupation    zip
0        1      F    1          10  48067
1        2      M   56          16  70072
2        3      M   25          15  55117
3        4      M   45           7  02460
4        5      M   25          20  55455

In [63]: ratings[:5]
Out[63]:
   user_id  movie_id  rating   timestamp
0        1      1193       5   978300760
1        1       661       3   978302109
2        1       914       3   978301968
3        1      3408       4   978300275
4        1      2355       5   978824291

In [64]: movies[:5]
Out[64]:
   movie_id                        title                      genres
0         1            Toy Story (1995)  Animation|Children's|Comedy
1         2              Jumanji (1995)  Adventure|Children's|Fantasy
2         3     Grumpier Old Men (1995)               Comedy|Romance
3         4    Waiting to Exhale (1995)                 Comedy|Drama
```

```
4            5  Father of the Bride Part II (1995)                    Comedy
```

```
In [65]: ratings
Out[65]:
          user_id  movie_id  rating  timestamp
0               1      1193       5  978300760
1               1       661       3  978302109
2               1       914       3  978301968
3               1      3408       4  978300275
4               1      2355       5  978824291
...           ...       ...     ...        ...
1000204      6040      1091       1  956716541
1000205      6040      1094       5  956704887
1000206      6040       562       5  956704746
1000207      6040      1096       4  956715648
1000208      6040      1097       4  956715569
[1000209 rows x 4 columns]
```

Note that ages and occupations are coded as integers indicating groups described in the data set's README file. Analyzing the data spread across three tables is not a simple task; for example, suppose you wanted to compute mean ratings for a particular movie by sex and age. As you will see, this is much easier to do with all of the data merged together into a single table. Using pandas's merge function, we first merge ratings with users then merging that result with the movies data. pandas infers which columns to use as the merge (or *join*) keys based on overlapping names:

```
In [66]: data = pd.merge(pd.merge(ratings, users), movies)
```

```
In [67]: data
Out[67]:
          user_id  movie_id  rating  timestamp gender  age  occupation    zip  \
0               1      1193       5  978300760      F    1          10  48067
1               2      1193       5  978298413      M   56          16  70072
2              12      1193       4  978220179      M   25          12  32793
3              15      1193       4  978199279      M   25           7  22903
4              17      1193       5  978158471      M   50           1  95350
...           ...       ...     ...        ...    ...  ...         ...    ...
1000204      5949      2198       5  958846401      M   18          17  47901
1000205      5675      2703       3  976029116      M   35          14  30030
1000206      5780      2845       1  958153068      M   18          17  92886
1000207      5851      3607       5  957756608      F   18          20  55410
1000208      5938      2909       4  957273353      M   25           1  35401
                                                title                genres
0                   One Flew Over the Cuckoo's Nest (1975)                 Drama
1                   One Flew Over the Cuckoo's Nest (1975)                 Drama
2                   One Flew Over the Cuckoo's Nest (1975)                 Drama
3                   One Flew Over the Cuckoo's Nest (1975)                 Drama
4                   One Flew Over the Cuckoo's Nest (1975)                 Drama
...                                               ...                   ...
1000204                           Modulations (1998)            Documentary
1000205                         Broken Vessels (1998)                 Drama
1000206                            White Boys (1999)                 Drama
1000207                      One Little Indian (1973)  Comedy|Drama|Western
1000208  Five Wives, Three Secretaries and Me (1998)            Documentary
```

```
[1000209 rows x 10 columns]

In [68]: data.ix[0]
Out[68]:
user_id                                              1
movie_id                                          1193
rating                                               5
timestamp                                    978300760
gender                                               F
age                                                  1
occupation                                          10
zip                                              48067
title         One Flew Over the Cuckoo's Nest (1975)
genres                                           Drama
Name: 0, dtype: object
```

In this form, aggregating the ratings grouped by one or more user or movie attributes is straightforward once you build some familiarity with pandas. To get mean movie ratings for each film grouped by gender, we can use the pivot_table method:

```
In [69]: mean_ratings = data.pivot_table('rating', rows='title',
    ....:                                 cols='gender', aggfunc='mean')

In [70]: mean_ratings[:5]
Out[70]:
gender                              F          M
title
$1,000,000 Duck (1971)       3.375000   2.761905
'Night Mother (1986)         3.388889   3.352941
'Til There Was You (1997)    2.675676   2.733333
'burbs, The (1989)           2.793478   2.962085
...And Justice for All (1979) 3.828571  3.689024
```

This produced another DataFrame containing mean ratings with movie titles as row labels and gender as column labels. First, I'm going to filter down to movies that received at least 250 ratings (a completely arbitrary number); to do this, I group the data by title and use size() to get a Series of group sizes for each title:

```
In [71]: ratings_by_title = data.groupby('title').size()

In [72]: ratings_by_title[:10]
Out[72]:
title
$1,000,000 Duck (1971)                  37
'Night Mother (1986)                    70
'Til There Was You (1997)               52
'burbs, The (1989)                     303
...And Justice for All (1979)          199
1-900 (1994)                             2
10 Things I Hate About You (1999)      700
101 Dalmatians (1961)                  565
101 Dalmatians (1996)                  364
12 Angry Men (1957)                    616
dtype: int64
```

```
In [73]: active_titles = ratings_by_title.index[ratings_by_title >= 250]
```

```
In [74]: active_titles
Out[74]:
Index([u''burbs, The (1989)', u'10 Things I Hate About You (1999)',
       u'101 Dalmatians (1961)', ..., u'Back to School (1986)',
       u'Back to the Future (1985)', ...], dtype='object')
```

The index of titles receiving at least 250 ratings can then be used to select rows from mean_ratings above:

```
In [75]: mean_ratings = mean_ratings.ix[active_titles]
```

```
In [76]: mean_ratings
Out[76]:
gender                               F          M
title
'burbs, The (1989)               2.793478   2.962085
10 Things I Hate About You (1999) 3.646552  3.311966
101 Dalmatians (1961)            3.791444   3.500000
101 Dalmatians (1996)            3.240000   2.911215
12 Angry Men (1957)              4.184397   4.328421
...                                 ...        ...
Young Guns (1988)                3.371795   3.425620
Young Guns II (1990)             2.934783   2.904025
Young Sherlock Holmes (1985)     3.514706   3.363344
Zero Effect (1998)               3.864407   3.723140
eXistenZ (1999)                  3.098592   3.289086
[1216 rows x 2 columns]
```

To see the top films among female viewers, we can sort by the F column in descending order:

```
In [78]: top_female_ratings = mean_ratings.sort_index(by='F', ascending=False)
```

```
In [79]: top_female_ratings[:10]
Out[79]:
gender                                                       F          M
title
Close Shave, A (1995)                                    4.644444   4.473795
Wrong Trousers, The (1993)                               4.588235   4.478261
Sunset Blvd. (a.k.a. Sunset Boulevard) (1950)            4.572650   4.464589
Wallace & Gromit: The Best of Aardman Animation (1996)   4.563107   4.385075
Schindler's List (1993)                                  4.562602   4.491415
Shawshank Redemption, The (1994)                         4.539075   4.560625
Grand Day Out, A (1992)                                  4.537879   4.293255
To Kill a Mockingbird (1962)                             4.536667   4.372611
Creature Comforts (1990)                                 4.513889   4.272277
Usual Suspects, The (1995)                               4.513317   4.518248
```

Measuring rating disagreement

Suppose you wanted to find the movies that are most divisive between male and female viewers. One way is to add a column to `mean_ratings` containing the difference in means, then sort by that:

```
In [80]: mean_ratings['diff'] = mean_ratings['M'] - mean_ratings['F']
```

Sorting by `'diff'` gives us the movies with the greatest rating difference and which were preferred by women:

```
In [81]: sorted_by_diff = mean_ratings.sort_index(by='diff')

In [82]: sorted_by_diff[:15]
Out[82]:
gender                              F         M        diff
title
Dirty Dancing (1987)            3.790378  2.959596 -0.830782
Jumpin' Jack Flash (1986)       3.254717  2.578358 -0.676359
Grease (1978)                   3.975265  3.367041 -0.608224
Little Women (1994)             3.870588  3.321739 -0.548849
Steel Magnolias (1989)          3.901734  3.365957 -0.535777
...                                  ...       ...       ...
French Kiss (1995)              3.535714  3.056962 -0.478752
Little Shop of Horrors, The (1960) 3.650000  3.179688 -0.470312
Guys and Dolls (1955)           4.051724  3.583333 -0.468391
Mary Poppins (1964)             4.197740  3.730594 -0.467147
Patch Adams (1998)              3.473282  3.008746 -0.464536
[15 rows x 3 columns]
```

Reversing the order of the rows and again slicing off the top 15 rows, we get the movies preferred by men that women didn't rate as highly:

```
# Reverse order of rows, take first 15 rows
In [83]: sorted_by_diff[::-1][:15]
Out[83]:
gender                                 F         M        diff
title
Good, The Bad and The Ugly, The (1966) 3.494949  4.221300  0.726351
Kentucky Fried Movie, The (1977)       2.878788  3.555147  0.676359
Dumb & Dumber (1994)                   2.697987  3.336595  0.638608
Longest Day, The (1962)                3.411765  4.031447  0.619682
Cable Guy, The (1996)                  2.250000  2.863787  0.613787
...                                         ...       ...       ...
Porky's (1981)                         2.296875  2.836364  0.539489
Animal House (1978)                    3.628906  4.167192  0.538286
Exorcist, The (1973)                   3.537634  4.067239  0.529605
Fright Night (1985)                    2.973684  3.500000  0.526316
Barb Wire (1996)                       1.585366  2.100386  0.515020
[15 rows x 3 columns]
```

Suppose instead you wanted the movies that elicited the most disagreement among viewers, independent of gender. Disagreement can be measured by the variance or standard deviation of the ratings:

```
# Standard deviation of rating grouped by title
In [84]: rating_std_by_title = data.groupby('title')['rating'].std()

# Filter down to active_titles
In [85]: rating_std_by_title = rating_std_by_title.ix[active_titles]

# Order Series by value in descending order
In [86]: rating_std_by_title.order(ascending=False)[:10]
Out[86]:
title
Dumb & Dumber (1994)                          1.321333
Blair Witch Project, The (1999)               1.316368
Natural Born Killers (1994)                   1.307198
Tank Girl (1995)                              1.277695
Rocky Horror Picture Show, The (1975)         1.260177
Eyes Wide Shut (1999)                         1.259624
Evita (1996)                                  1.253631
Billy Madison (1995)                          1.249970
Fear and Loathing in Las Vegas (1998)         1.246408
Bicentennial Man (1999)                       1.245533
Name: rating, dtype: float64
```

You may have noticed that movie genres are given as a pipe-separated (|) string. If you wanted to do some analysis by genre, more work would be required to transform the genre information into a more usable form. I will revisit this data later in the book to illustrate such a transformation.

US Baby Names 1880-2010

The United States Social Security Administration (SSA) has made available data on the frequency of baby names from 1880 through the present. Hadley Wickham, an author of several popular R packages, has often made use of this data set in illustrating data manipulation in R.

```
In [4]: names.head(10)
Out[4]:
        name sex  births  year
0       Mary   F    7065  1880
1       Anna   F    2604  1880
2       Emma   F    2003  1880
3  Elizabeth   F    1939  1880
4     Minnie   F    1746  1880
5   Margaret   F    1578  1880
6        Ida   F    1472  1880
7      Alice   F    1414  1880
8     Bertha   F    1320  1880
9      Sarah   F    1288  1880
```

There are many things you might want to do with the data set:

* Visualize the proportion of babies given a particular name (your own, or another name) over time.

- Determine the relative rank of a name.
- Determine the most popular names in each year or the names with largest increases or decreases.
- Analyze trends in names: vowels, consonants, length, overall diversity, changes in spelling, first and last letters
- Analyze external sources of trends: biblical names, celebrities, demographic changes

Using the tools we've looked at so far, most of these kinds of analyses are very straightforward, so I will walk you through many of them. I encourage you to download and explore the data yourself. If you find an interesting pattern in the data, I would love to hear about it.

As of this writing, the US Social Security Administration makes available data files, one per year, containing the total number of births for each sex/name combination. The raw archive of these files can be obtained here:

http://www.ssa.gov/oact/babynames/limits.html

In the event that this page has been moved by the time you're reading this, it can most likely be located again by Internet search. After downloading the "National data" file names.zip and unzipping it, you will have a directory containing a series of files like yob1880.txt. I use the UNIX head command to look at the first 10 lines of one of the files (on Windows, you can use the more command or open it in a text editor):

```
In [95]: !head -n 10 names/yob1880.txt
Mary,F,7065
Anna,F,2604
Emma,F,2003
Elizabeth,F,1939
Minnie,F,1746
Margaret,F,1578
Ida,F,1472
Alice,F,1414
Bertha,F,1320
Sarah,F,1288
```

As this is a nicely comma-separated form, it can be loaded into a DataFrame with pandas.read_csv:

```
In [96]: import pandas as pd

In [97]: names1880 = pd.read_csv('names/yob1880.txt', names=['name', 'sex', 'births'])

In [98]: names1880
Out[98]:
        name sex  births
0       Mary   F    7065
1       Anna   F    2604
2       Emma   F    2003
3  Elizabeth   F    1939
4     Minnie   F    1746
```

```
   ...        ...  ..   ...
1995    Woodie   M      5
1996    Worthy   M      5
1997    Wright   M      5
1998      York   M      5
1999 Zachariah   M      5
[2000 rows x 3 columns]
```

These files only contain names with at least 5 occurrences in each year, so for simplicity's sake we can use the sum of the births column by sex as the total number of births in that year:

```
In [99]: names1880.groupby('sex')['births'].sum()
Out[99]:
sex
F        90993
M       110493
Name: births, dtype: int64
```

Since the data set is split into files by year, one of the first things to do is to assemble all of the data into a single DataFrame and further to add a year field. This is easy to do using pandas.concat:

```
# 2010 is the last available year right now
years = range(1880, 2011)

pieces = []
columns = ['name', 'sex', 'births']

for year in years:
    path = 'names/yob%d.txt' % year
    frame = pd.read_csv(path, names=columns)

    frame['year'] = year
    pieces.append(frame)

# Concatenate everything into a single DataFrame
names = pd.concat(pieces, ignore_index=True)
```

There are a couple things to note here. First, remember that concat glues the DataFrame objects together row-wise by default. Secondly, you have to pass ignore_index=True because we're not interested in preserving the original row numbers returned from read_csv. So we now have a very large DataFrame containing all of the names data:

Now the names DataFrame looks like:

```
In [101]: names
Out[101]:
            name sex  births  year
0           Mary   F    7065  1880
1           Anna   F    2604  1880
2           Emma   F    2003  1880
3      Elizabeth   F    1939  1880
4         Minnie   F    1746  1880
...          ...  ..     ...   ...
```

```
1690779     Zymaire    M    5   2010
1690780      Zyonne    M    5   2010
1690781   Zyquarius    M    5   2010
1690782       Zyran    M    5   2010
1690783       Zzyzx    M    5   2010
[1690784 rows x 4 columns]
```

With this data in hand, we can already start aggregating the data at the year and sex
level using groupby or pivot_table, see Figure 2-4:

```
In [102]: total_births = names.pivot_table('births', rows='year',
     .....:                                 cols='sex', aggfunc=sum)

In [103]: total_births.tail()
Out[103]:
sex          F        M
year
2006   1896468  2050234
2007   1916888  2069242
2008   1883645  2032310
2009   1827643  1973359
2010   1759010  1898382

In [104]: total_births.plot(title='Total births by sex and year')
```

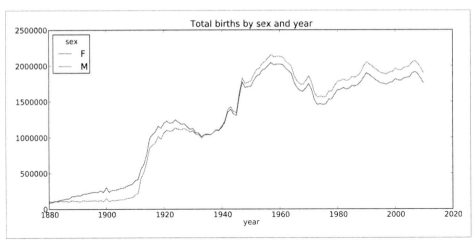

Figure 2-4. Total births by sex and year

Next, let's insert a column prop with the fraction of babies given each name relative to
the total number of births. A prop value of 0.02 would indicate that 2 out of every 100
babies was given a particular name. Thus, we group the data by year and sex, then add
the new column to each group:

```
def add_prop(group):
    # Integer division floors
    births = group.births.astype(float)
```

```
        group['prop'] = births / births.sum()
        return group
names = names.groupby(['year', 'sex']).apply(add_prop)
```

 Remember that because births is of integer type, we have to cast either the numerator or denominator to floating point to compute a fraction (unless you are using Python 3!).

The resulting complete data set now has the following columns:

```
In [106]: names
Out[106]:
               name sex  births  year      prop
0              Mary   F    7065  1880  0.077643
1              Anna   F    2604  1880  0.028618
2              Emma   F    2003  1880  0.022013
3         Elizabeth   F    1939  1880  0.021309
4            Minnie   F    1746  1880  0.019188
...             ...  ..     ...   ...       ...
1690779     Zymaire   M       5  2010  0.000003
1690780      Zyonne   M       5  2010  0.000003
1690781   Zyquarius   M       5  2010  0.000003
1690782       Zyran   M       5  2010  0.000003
1690783       Zzyzx   M       5  2010  0.000003
[1690784 rows x 5 columns]
```

When performing a group operation like this, it's often valuable to do a sanity check, like verifying that the prop column sums to 1 within all the groups. Since this is floating point data, use np.allclose to check that the group sums are sufficiently close to (but perhaps not exactly equal to) 1:

```
In [107]: np.allclose(names.groupby(['year', 'sex']).prop.sum(), 1)
Out[107]: True
```

Now that this is done, I'm going to extract a subset of the data to facilitate further analysis: the top 1000 names for each sex/year combination. This is yet another group operation:

```
def get_top1000(group):
    return group.sort_index(by='births', ascending=False)[:1000]
grouped = names.groupby(['year', 'sex'])
top1000 = grouped.apply(get_top1000)
top1000.index = np.arange(len(top1000))
```

If you prefer a do-it-yourself approach, you could also do:

```
pieces = []
for year, group in names.groupby(['year', 'sex']):
    pieces.append(group.sort_index(by='births', ascending=False)[:1000])
top1000 = pd.concat(pieces, ignore_index=True)
```

The resulting data set is now quite a bit smaller:

```
In [110]: top1000
Out[110]:
             name sex  births  year      prop
0            Mary   F    7065  1880  0.077643
1            Anna   F    2604  1880  0.028618
2            Emma   F    2003  1880  0.022013
3       Elizabeth   F    1939  1880  0.021309
4          Minnie   F    1746  1880  0.019188
...           ...  ..     ...   ...       ...
261872     Camilo   M     194  2010  0.000102
261873     Destin   M     194  2010  0.000102
261874     Jaquan   M     194  2010  0.000102
261875     Jaydan   M     194  2010  0.000102
261876     Maxton   M     193  2010  0.000102
[261877 rows x 5 columns]
```

We'll use this Top 1,000 data set in the following investigations into the data.

Analyzing Naming Trends

With the full data set and Top 1,000 data set in hand, we can start analyzing various naming trends of interest. Splitting the Top 1,000 names into the boy and girl portions is easy to do first:

```
In [111]: boys = top1000[top1000.sex == 'M']
```

```
In [112]: girls = top1000[top1000.sex == 'F']
```

Simple time series, like the number of Johns or Marys for each year can be plotted but require a bit of munging to be a bit more useful. Let's form a pivot table of the total number of births by year and name:

```
In [113]: total_births = top1000.pivot_table('births', rows='year', cols='name',
   .....:                                     aggfunc=sum)
```

Now, this can be plotted for a handful of names using DataFrame's `plot` method:

```
In [114]: total_births.info()
<class 'pandas.core.frame.DataFrame'>
Int64Index: 131 entries, 1880 to 2010
Columns: 6868 entries, Aaden to Zuri
dtypes: float64(6868)
In [115]: subset = total_births[['John', 'Harry', 'Mary', 'Marilyn']]
```

```
In [116]: subset.plot(subplots=True, figsize=(12, 10), grid=False,
   .....:             title="Number of births per year")
```

See Figure 2-5 for the result. On looking at this, you might conclude that these names have grown out of favor with the American population. But the story is actually more complicated than that, as will be explored in the next section.

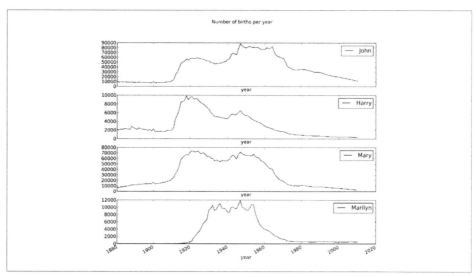

Figure 2-5. A few boy and girl names over time

Measuring the increase in naming diversity

One explanation for the decrease in plots above is that fewer parents are choosing common names for their children. This hypothesis can be explored and confirmed in the data. One measure is the proportion of births represented by the top 1000 most popular names, which I aggregate and plot by year and sex:

```
In [118]: table = top1000.pivot_table('prop', rows='year',
   .....:                            cols='sex', aggfunc=sum)

In [119]: table.plot(title='Sum of table1000.prop by year and sex',
   .....:            yticks=np.linspace(0, 1.2, 13), xticks=range(1880, 2020, 10))
```

See Figure 2-6 for this plot. So you can see that, indeed, there appears to be increasing name diversity (decreasing total proportion in the top 1,000). Another interesting metric is the number of distinct names, taken in order of popularity from highest to lowest, in the top 50% of births. This number is a bit more tricky to compute. Let's consider just the boy names from 2010:

```
In [120]: df = boys[boys.year == 2010]

In [121]: df
Out[121]:
            name sex  births  year      prop
260877     Jacob   M   21875  2010  0.011523
260878     Ethan   M   17866  2010  0.009411
260879   Michael   M   17133  2010  0.009025
260880    Jayden   M   17030  2010  0.008971
260881   William   M   16870  2010  0.008887
...          ...  ..     ...   ...       ...
```

```
261872   Camilo   M      194   2010   0.000102
261873   Destin   M      194   2010   0.000102
261874   Jaquan   M      194   2010   0.000102
261875   Jaydan   M      194   2010   0.000102
261876   Maxton   M      193   2010   0.000102
[1000 rows x 5 columns]
```

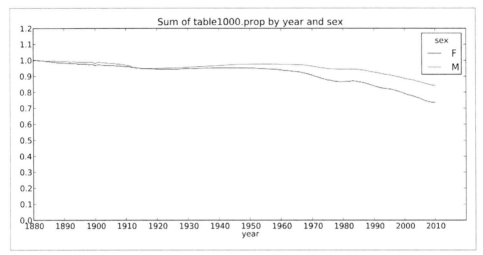

Figure 2-6. Proportion of births represented in top 1000 names by sex

After sorting prop in descending order, we want to know how many of the most popular names it takes to reach 50%. You could write a for loop to do this, but a vectorized NumPy way is a bit more clever. Taking the cumulative sum, cumsum, of prop then calling the method searchsorted returns the position in the cumulative sum at which 0.5 would need to be inserted to keep it in sorted order:

```
In [122]: prop_cumsum = df.sort_index(by='prop', ascending=False).prop.cumsum()

In [123]: prop_cumsum[:10]
Out[123]:
260877    0.011523
260878    0.020934
260879    0.029959
260880    0.038930
260881    0.047817
260882    0.056579
260883    0.065155
260884    0.073414
260885    0.081528
260886    0.089621
Name: prop, dtype: float64

In [124]: prop_cumsum.values.searchsorted(0.5)
Out[124]: 116
```

Since arrays are zero-indexed, adding 1 to this result gives you a result of 117. By contrast, in 1900 this number was much smaller:

```
In [125]: df = boys[boys.year == 1900]

In [126]: in1900 = df.sort_index(by='prop', ascending=False).prop.cumsum()

In [127]: in1900.values.searchsorted(0.5) + 1
Out[127]: 25
```

It should now be fairly straightforward to apply this operation to each year/sex combination; groupby those fields and apply a function returning the count for each group:

```
def get_quantile_count(group, q=0.5):
    group = group.sort_index(by='prop', ascending=False)
    return group.prop.cumsum().values.searchsorted(q) + 1

diversity = top1000.groupby(['year', 'sex']).apply(get_quantile_count)
diversity = diversity.unstack('sex')
```

This resulting DataFrame diversity now has two time series, one for each sex, indexed by year. This can be inspected in IPython and plotted as before (see Figure 2-7):

```
In [129]: diversity.head()
Out[129]:
sex    F   M
year
1880  38  14
1881  38  14
1882  38  15
1883  39  15
1884  39  16

In [130]: diversity.plot(title="Number of popular names in top 50%")
```

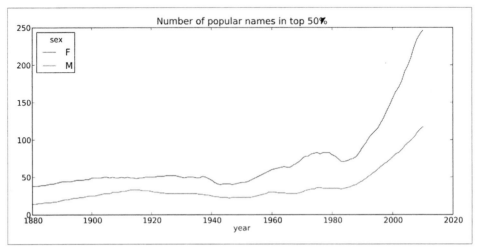

Figure 2-7. Plot of diversity metric by year

As you can see, girl names have always been more diverse than boy names, and they have only become more so over time. Further analysis of what exactly is driving the diversity, like the increase of alternate spellings, is left to the reader.

The "Last letter" Revolution

In 2007, a baby name researcher Laura Wattenberg pointed out on her website (*http://www.babynamewizard.com*) that the distribution of boy names by final letter has changed significantly over the last 100 years. To see this, I first aggregate all of the births in the full data set by year, sex, and final letter:

```
# extract last letter from name column
get_last_letter = lambda x: x[-1]
last_letters = names.name.map(get_last_letter)
last_letters.name = 'last_letter'

table = names.pivot_table('births', rows=last_letters,
                          cols=['sex', 'year'], aggfunc=sum)
```

Then, I select out three representative years spanning the history and print the first few rows:

```
In [132]: subtable = table.reindex(columns=[1910, 1960, 2010], level='year')
```

```
In [133]: subtable.head()
Out[133]:
sex               F                      M
year          1910    1960    2010    1910    1960    2010
last_letter
a           108376  691247  670605     977    5204   28438
b              NaN     694     450     411    3912   38859
c                5      49     946     482   15476   23125
d             6750    3729    2607   22111  262112   44398
e           133569  435013  313833   28655  178823  129012
```

Next, normalize the table by total births to compute a new table containing proportion of total births for each sex ending in each letter:

```
In [134]: subtable.sum()
Out[134]:
sex  year
F    1910     396416
     1960    2022062
     2010    1759010
M    1910     194198
     1960    2132588
     2010    1898382
dtype: float64
```

```
In [135]: letter_prop = subtable / subtable.sum().astype(float)
```

With the letter proportions now in hand, I can make bar plots for each sex broken down by year. See Figure 2-8:

```
import matplotlib.pyplot as plt

fig, axes = plt.subplots(2, 1, figsize=(10, 8))
letter_prop['M'].plot(kind='bar', rot=0, ax=axes[0], title='Male')
letter_prop['F'].plot(kind='bar', rot=0, ax=axes[1], title='Female',
                      legend=False)
```

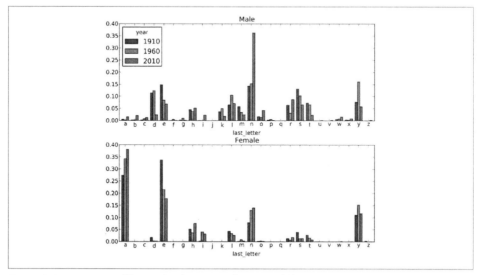

Figure 2-8. Proportion of boy and girl names ending in each letter

As you can see, boy names ending in "n" have experienced significant growth since the 1960s. Going back to the full table created above, I again normalize by year and sex and select a subset of letters for the boy names, finally transposing to make each column a time series:

```
In [138]: letter_prop = table / table.sum().astype(float)

In [139]: dny_ts = letter_prop.ix[['d', 'n', 'y'], 'M'].T

In [140]: dny_ts.head()
Out[140]:
             d          n          y
year
1880   0.083055   0.153213   0.075760
1881   0.083247   0.153214   0.077451
1882   0.085340   0.149560   0.077537
1883   0.084066   0.151646   0.079144
1884   0.086120   0.149915   0.080405
```

With this DataFrame of time series in hand, I can make a plot of the trends over time again with its plot method (see Figure 2-9):

```
In [142]: dny_ts.plot()
```

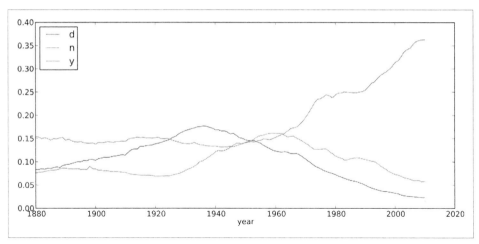

Figure 2-9. Proportion of boys born with names ending in d/n/y over time

Boy names that became girl names (and vice versa)

Another fun trend is looking at boy names that were more popular with one sex earlier in the sample but have "changed sexes" in the present. One example is the name Lesley or Leslie. Going back to the top1000 dataset, I compute a list of names occurring in the dataset starting with 'lesl':

```
In [143]: all_names = top1000.name.unique()

In [144]: mask = np.array(['lesl' in x.lower() for x in all_names])

In [145]: lesley_like = all_names[mask]

In [146]: lesley_like
Out[146]: array(['Leslie', 'Lesley', 'Leslee', 'Lesli', 'Lesly'], dtype=object)
```

From there, we can filter down to just those names and sum births grouped by name to see the relative frequencies:

```
In [147]: filtered = top1000[top1000.name.isin(lesley_like)]

In [148]: filtered.groupby('name').births.sum()
Out[148]:
name
Leslee      1082
Lesley     35022
Lesli        929
Leslie    370429
Lesly      10067
Name: births, dtype: int64
```

Next, let's aggregate by sex and year and normalize within year:

```
In [149]: table = filtered.pivot_table('births', rows='year',
   .....:                                  cols='sex', aggfunc='sum')

In [150]: table = table.div(table.sum(1), axis=0)

In [151]: table.tail()
Out[151]:
sex    F    M
year
2006   1  NaN
2007   1  NaN
2008   1  NaN
2009   1  NaN
2010   1  NaN
```

Lastly, it's now easy to make a plot of the breakdown by sex over time (Figure 2-10):

```
In [153]: table.plot(style={'M': 'k-', 'F': 'k--'})
```

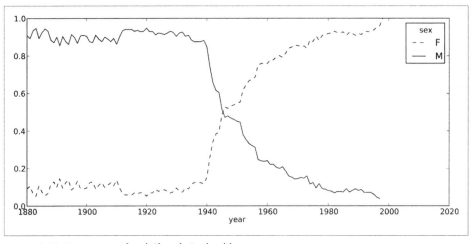

Figure 2-10. Proportion of male/female Lesley-like names over time

Conclusions and The Path Ahead

The examples in this chapter are rather simple, but they're here to give you a bit of a flavor of what sorts of things you can expect in the upcoming chapters. The focus of this book is on *tools* as opposed to presenting more sophisticated analytical methods. Mastering the techniques in this book will enable you to implement your own analyses (assuming you know what you want to do!) in short order.

## CHAPTER 3

IPython: An Interactive Computing and Development Environment

Act without doing; work without effort. Think of the small as large and the few as many.
Confront the difficult while it is still easy; accomplish the great task by a series of small
acts.

—Laozi

People often ask me, "What is your Python development environment?" My answer is almost always the same, "IPython and a text editor". You may choose to substitute an Integrated Development Environment (IDE) for a text editor in order to take advantage of more advanced graphical tools and code completion capabilities. Even if so, I strongly recommend making IPython an important part of your workflow. Some IDEs even provide IPython integration, so it's possible to get the best of both worlds.

The *IPython* (*http://ipython.org*) project began in 2001 as Fernando Pérez's side project to make a better interactive Python interpreter. In the subsequent 11 years it has grown into what's widely considered one of the most important tools in the modern scientific Python computing stack. While it does not provide any computational or data analytical tools by itself, IPython is designed from the ground up to maximize your productivity in both interactive computing and software development. It encourages an *execute-explore* workflow instead of the typical *edit-compile-run* workflow of many other programming languages. It also provides very tight integration with the operating system's shell and file system. Since much of data analysis coding involves exploration, trial and error, and iteration, IPython will, in almost all cases, help you get the job done faster.

Of course, the IPython project now encompasses a great deal more than just an enhanced, interactive Python shell. It also includes a rich GUI console with inline plotting, a web-based interactive notebook format, and a lightweight, fast parallel computing engine. And, as with so many other tools designed for and by programmers, it is highly customizable. I'll discuss some of these features later in the chapter.

Since IPython has interactivity at its core, some of the features in this chapter are difficult to fully illustrate without a live console. If this is your first time learning about IPython, I recommend that you follow along with the examples to get a feel for how things work. As with any keyboard-driven console-like environment, developing muscle-memory for the common commands is part of the learning curve.

 Many parts of this chapter (for example: profiling and debugging) can be safely omitted on a first reading as they are not necessary for understanding the rest of the book. This chapter is intended to provide a standalone, rich overview of the functionality provided by IPython.

IPython Basics

You can launch IPython on the command line just like launching the regular Python interpreter except with the `ipython` command:

```
$ ipython
Python 2.7.2 (default, May 27 2012, 21:26:12)
Type "copyright", "credits" or "license" for more information.

IPython 0.12 -- An enhanced Interactive Python.
?         -> Introduction and overview of IPython's features.
%quickref -> Quick reference.
help      -> Python's own help system.
object?   -> Details about 'object', use 'object??' for extra details.

In [1]: a = 5

In [2]: a
Out[2]: 5
```

You can execute arbitrary Python statements by typing them in and pressing <return>. When typing just a variable into IPython, it renders a string representation of the object:

```
In [541]: import numpy as np

In [542]: data = {i : np.random.randn() for i in range(7)}

In [543]: data
Out[543]:
{0: 0.6900018528091594,
 1: 1.0015434424937888,
 2: -0.5030873913603446,
 3: -0.6222742250596455,
 4: -0.9211686080130108,
 5: -0.726213492660829,
 6: 0.2228955458351768}
```

Many kinds of Python objects are formatted to be more readable, or *pretty-printed*, which is distinct from normal printing with print. If you printed a dict like the above in the standard Python interpreter, it would be much less readable:

```
>>> from numpy.random import randn
>>> data = {i : randn() for i in range(7)}
>>> print data
{0: -1.5948255432744511, 1: 0.10569006472787983, 2: 1.972367135977295,
3: 0.15455217573074576, 4: -0.24058577449429575, 5: -1.2904897053651216,
6: 0.3308507317325902}
```

IPython also provides facilities to make it easy to execute arbitrary blocks of code (via somewhat glorified copy-and-pasting) and whole Python scripts. These will be discussed shortly.

Tab Completion

On the surface, the IPython shell looks like a cosmetically slightly-different interactive Python interpreter. Users of Mathematica may find the enumerated input and output prompts familiar. One of the major improvements over the standard Python shell is *tab completion*, a feature common to most interactive data analysis environments. While entering expressions in the shell, pressing <Tab> will search the namespace for any variables (objects, functions, etc.) matching the characters you have typed so far:

```
In [1]: an_apple = 27

In [2]: an_example = 42

In [3]: an<Tab>
an_apple    and           an_example  any
```

In this example, note that IPython displayed both the two variables I defined as well as the Python keyword and and built-in function any. Naturally, you can also complete methods and attributes on any object after typing a period:

```
In [3]: b = [1, 2, 3]

In [4]: b.<Tab>
b.append   b.extend   b.insert   b.remove   b.sort
b.count    b.index    b.pop      b.reverse
```

The same goes for modules:

```
In [1]: import datetime

In [2]: datetime.<Tab>
datetime.date          datetime.MAXYEAR       datetime.timedelta
datetime.datetime      datetime.MINYEAR       datetime.tzinfo
datetime.datetime_CAPI datetime.time
```

Note that IPython by default hides methods and attributes starting with underscores, such as magic methods and internal "private" methods and attributes, in order to avoid cluttering the display (and confusing new Python users!). These, too, can be tab-completed but you must first type an underscore to see them. If you prefer to always see such methods in tab completion, you can change this setting in the IPython configuration.

Tab completion works in many contexts outside of searching the interactive namespace and completing object or module attributes. When typing anything that looks like a file path (even in a Python string), pressing <Tab> will complete anything on your computer's file system matching what you've typed:

```
In [3]: book_scripts/<Tab>
book_scripts/cprof_example.py          book_scripts/ipython_script_test.py
book_scripts/ipython_bug.py            book_scripts/prof_mod.py

In [3]: path = 'book_scripts/<Tab>
book_scripts/cprof_example.py          book_scripts/ipython_script_test.py
book_scripts/ipython_bug.py            book_scripts/prof_mod.py
```

Combined with the %run command (see later section), this functionality will undoubtedly save you many keystrokes.

Another area where tab completion saves time is in the completion of function keyword arguments (including the = sign!).

Introspection

Using a question mark (?) before or after a variable will display some general information about the object:

```
In [545]: b?
Type:       list
String Form:[1, 2, 3]
Length:     3
Docstring:
list() -> new empty list
list(iterable) -> new list initialized from iterable's items
```

This is referred to as *object introspection*. If the object is a function or instance method, the docstring, if defined, will also be shown. Suppose we'd written the following function:

```
def add_numbers(a, b):
    """

    Add two numbers together

    Returns
    -------
    the_sum : type of arguments
```

```
"""
    return a + b
```

Then using ? shows us the docstring:

```
In [547]: add_numbers?
Type:        function
String Form:<function add_numbers at 0x5fad848>
File:        book_scripts/<ipython-input-546-5473012eeb65>
Definition: add_numbers(a, b)
Docstring:
Add two numbers together
Returns
-------
the_sum : type of arguments
```

Using ?? will also show the function's source code if possible:

```
In [548]: add_numbers??
Type:        function
String Form:<function add_numbers at 0x5fad848>
File:        book_scripts/<ipython-input-546-5473012eeb65>
Definition: add_numbers(a, b)
Source:
def add_numbers(a, b):
    """
    Add two numbers together
    Returns
    -------
    the_sum : type of arguments
    """
    return a + b
```

? has a final usage, which is for searching the IPython namespace in a manner similar to the standard UNIX or Windows command line. A number of characters combined with the wildcard (*) will show all names matching the wildcard expression. For example, we could get a list of all functions in the top level NumPy namespace containing load:

```
In [549]: np.*load*?
np.load
np.loads
np.loadtxt
np.pkgload
```

The %run Command

Any file can be run as a Python program inside the environment of your IPython session using the %run command. Suppose you had the following simple script stored in ipython_script_test.py:

```
def f(x, y, z):
    return (x + y) / z

a = 5
```

```
b = 6
c = 7.5

result = f(a, b, c)
```

This can be executed by passing the file name to %run:

```
In [550]: %run ipython_script_test.py
```

The script is run in an *empty namespace* (with no imports or other variables defined) so that the behavior should be identical to running the program on the command line using `python script.py`. All of the variables (imports, functions, and globals) defined in the file (up until an exception, if any, is raised) will then be accessible in the IPython shell:

```
In [551]: c
Out[551]: 7.5

In [552]: result
Out[552]: 1.4666666666666666
```

If a Python script expects command line arguments (to be found in `sys.argv`), these can be passed after the file path as though run on the command line.

 Should you wish to give a script access to variables already defined in the interactive IPython namespace, use `%run -i` instead of plain `%run`.

Interrupting running code

Pressing `<Ctrl-C>` while any code is running, whether a script through `%run` or a long-running command, will cause a `KeyboardInterrupt` to be raised. This will cause nearly all Python programs to stop immediately except in very exceptional cases.

 When a piece of Python code has called into some compiled extension modules, pressing `<Ctrl-C>` will not cause the program execution to stop immediately in all cases. In such cases, you will have to either wait until control is returned to the Python interpreter, or, in more dire circumstances, forcibly terminate the Python process via the OS task manager.

Executing Code from the Clipboard

A quick-and-dirty way to execute code in IPython is via pasting from the clipboard. This might seem fairly crude, but in practice it is very useful. For example, while developing a complex or time-consuming application, you may wish to execute a script piece by piece, pausing at each stage to examine the currently loaded data and results. Or, you might find a code snippet on the Internet that you want to run and play around with, but you'd rather not create a new `.py` file for it.

Code snippets can be pasted from the clipboard in many cases by pressing <Ctrl-Shift-V>. Note that it is not completely robust as this mode of pasting mimics typing each line into IPython, and line breaks are treated as <return>. This means that if you paste code with an indented block and there is a blank line, IPython will think that the indented block is over. Once the next line in the block is executed, an IndentationError will be raised. For example the following code:

```
x = 5
y = 7
if x > 5:
    x += 1

    y = 8
```

will not work if simply pasted:

```
In [1]: x = 5

In [2]: y = 7

In [3]: if x > 5:
   ...:         x += 1
   ...:

In [4]:     y = 8
IndentationError: unexpected indent

If you want to paste code into IPython, try the %paste and %cpaste
magic functions.
```

As the error message suggests, we should instead use the %paste and %cpaste magic functions. %paste takes whatever text is in the clipboard and executes it as a single block in the shell:

```
In [6]: %paste
x = 5
y = 7
if x > 5:
    x += 1

    y = 8
## -- End pasted text --
```

 Depending on your platform and how you installed Python, there's a small chance that %paste will not work. Packaged distributions like EPDFree (as described in in the intro) should not be a problem.

%cpaste is similar, except that it gives you a special prompt for pasting code into:

```
In [7]: %cpaste
Pasting code; enter '--' alone on the line to stop or use Ctrl-D.
:x = 5
:y = 7
:if x > 5:
```

```
:   x += 1
:
:   y = 8
:--
```

With the %cpaste block, you have the freedom to paste as much code as you like before executing it. You might decide to use %cpaste in order to look at the pasted code before executing it. If you accidentally paste the wrong code, you can break out of the %cpaste prompt by pressing <Ctrl-C>.

Later, I'll introduce the IPython HTML Notebook which brings a new level of sophistication for developing analyses block-by-block in a browser-based notebook format with executable code cells.

IPython interaction with editors and IDEs

Some text editors, such as Emacs and vim, have 3rd party extensions enabling blocks of code to be sent directly from the editor to a running IPython shell. Refer to the IPython website or do an Internet search to find out more.

Some IDEs, such as the PyDev plugin for Eclipse and Python Tools for Visual Studio from Microsoft (and possibly others), have integration with the IPython terminal application. If you want to work in an IDE but don't want to give up the IPython console features, this may be a good option for you.

Keyboard Shortcuts

IPython has many keyboard shortcuts for navigating the prompt (which will be familiar to users of the Emacs text editor or the UNIX bash shell) and interacting with the shell's command history (see later section). Table 3-1 summarizes some of the most commonly used shortcuts. See Figure 3-1 for an illustration of a few of these, such as cursor movement.

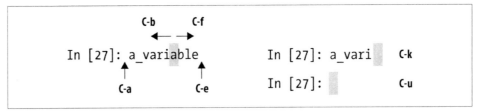

Figure 3-1. Illustration of some of IPython's keyboard shortcuts

Table 3-1. Standard IPython Keyboard Shortcuts

Command	Description
Ctrl-p or up-arrow	Search backward in command history for commands starting with currently-entered text
Ctrl-n or down-arrow	Search forward in command history for commands starting with currently-entered text
Ctrl-r	Readline-style reverse history search (partial matching)
Ctrl-Shift-v	Paste text from clipboard
Ctrl-c	Interrupt currently-executing code
Ctrl-a	Move cursor to beginning of line
Ctrl-e	Move cursor to end of line
Ctrl-k	Delete text from cursor until end of line
Ctrl-u	Discard all text on current line
Ctrl-f	Move cursor forward one character
Ctrl-b	Move cursor back one character
Ctrl-l	Clear screen

Exceptions and Tracebacks

If an exception is raised while %run-ing a script or executing any statement, IPython will by default print a full call stack trace (traceback) with a few lines of context around the position at each point in the stack.

```
In [553]: %run ch03/ipython_bug.py
---------------------------------------------------------------------------
AssertionError                            Traceback (most recent call last)
/home/wesm/code/ipython/IPython/utils/py3compat.pyc in execfile(fname, *where)
    176             else:
    177                 filename = fname
--> 178                 __builtin__.execfile(filename, *where)
book_scripts/ch03/ipython_bug.py in <module>()
     13     throws_an_exception()
     14
---> 15 calling_things()
book_scripts/ch03/ipython_bug.py in calling_things()
     11 def calling_things():
     12     works_fine()
---> 13     throws_an_exception()
     14
     15 calling_things()
book_scripts/ch03/ipython_bug.py in throws_an_exception()
      7     a = 5
      8     b = 6
----> 9     assert(a + b == 10)
     10
     11 def calling_things():
AssertionError:
```

Having additional context by itself is a big advantage over the standard Python interpreter (which does not provide any additional context). The amount of context shown can be controlled using the %xmode magic command, from minimal (same as the standard Python interpreter) to verbose (which inlines function argument values and more). As you will see later in the chapter, you can step *into the stack* (using the %debug or %pdb magics) after an error has occurred for interactive post-mortem debugging.

Magic Commands

IPython has many special commands, known as "magic" commands, which are designed to facilitate common tasks and enable you to easily control the behavior of the IPython system. A magic command is any command prefixed by the the percent symbol %. For example, you can check the execution time of any Python statement, such as a matrix multiplication, using the %timeit magic function (which will be discussed in more detail later):

```
In [554]: a = np.random.randn(100, 100)

In [555]: %timeit np.dot(a, a)
10000 loops, best of 3: 69.1 us per loop
```

Magic commands can be viewed as command line programs to be run within the IPython system. Many of them have additional "command line" options, which can all be viewed (as you might expect) using ?:

```
In [1]: %reset?
Resets the namespace by removing all names defined by the user.

Parameters
----------
  -f : force reset without asking for confirmation.

  -s : 'Soft' reset: Only clears your namespace, leaving history intact.
  References to objects may be kept. By default (without this option),
  we do a 'hard' reset, giving you a new session and removing all
  references to objects from the current session.

Examples
--------
In [6]: a = 1

In [7]: a
Out[7]: 1

In [8]: %reset -f

In [10]: a
---------------------------------------------------------------------
NameError                                 Traceback (most recent call last)
<ipython-input-10-60b725f10c9c> in <module>()
----> 1 a
```

```
NameError: name 'a' is not defined
```

Magic functions can be used by default without the percent sign, as long as no variable is defined with the same name as the magic function in question. This feature is called *automagic* and can be enabled or disabled using %automagic.

Since IPython's documentation is easily accessible from within the system, I encourage you to explore all of the special commands available by typing %quickref or %magic. I will highlight a few more of the most critical ones for being productive in interactive computing and Python development in IPython.

Table 3-2. Frequently-used IPython Magic Commands

Command	Description
%quickref	Display the IPython Quick Reference Card
%magic	Display detailed documentation for all of the available magic commands
%debug	Enter the interactive debugger at the bottom of the last exception traceback
%hist	Print command input (and optionally output) history
%pdb	Automatically enter debugger after any exception
%paste	Execute pre-formatted Python code from clipboard
%cpaste	Open a special prompt for manually pasting Python code to be executed
%reset	Delete all variables / names defined in interactive namespace
%page *OBJECT*	Pretty print the object and display it through a pager
%run *script.py*	Run a Python script inside IPython
%prun *statement*	Execute *statement* with cProfile and report the profiler output
%time *statement*	Report the execution time of single statement
%timeit *statement*	Run a statement multiple times to compute an emsemble average execution time. Useful for timing code with very short execution time
%who, %who_ls, %whos	Display variables defined in interactive namespace, with varying levels of information / verbosity
%xdel *variable*	Delete a variable and attempt to clear any references to the object in the IPython internals

Qt-based Rich GUI Console

The IPython team has developed a Qt framework-based GUI console, designed to wed the features of the terminal-only applications with the features provided by a rich text widget, like embedded images, multiline editing, and syntax highlighting. If you have either PyQt or PySide installed, the application can be launched with inline plotting by running this on the command line:

```
ipython qtconsole --pylab=inline
```

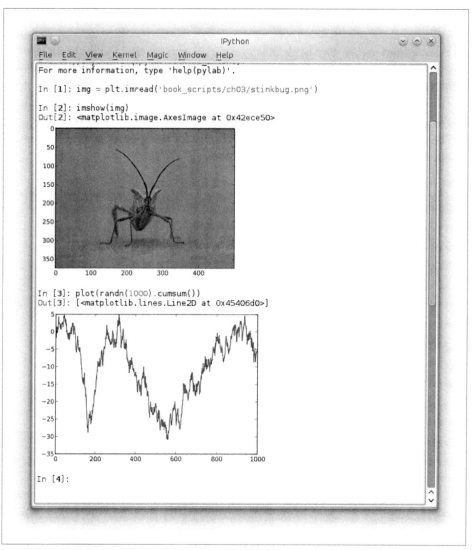

Figure 3-2. IPython Qt Console

The Qt console can launch multiple IPython processes in tabs, enabling you to switch between tasks. It can also share a process with the IPython HTML Notebook application, which I'll highlight later.

Matplotlib Integration and Pylab Mode

Part of why IPython is so widely used in scientific computing is that it is designed as a companion to libraries like matplotlib and other GUI toolkits. Don't worry if you have never used matplotlib before; it will be discussed in much more detail later in this book. If you create a matplotlib plot window in the regular Python shell, you'll be sad to find that the GUI event loop "takes control" of the Python session until the plot window is closed. That won't work for interactive data analysis and visualization, so IPython has implemented special handling for each GUI framework so that it will work seamlessly with the shell.

The typical way to launch IPython with matplotlib integration is by adding the `--pylab` flag (two dashes).

```
$ ipython --pylab
```

This will cause several things to happen. First IPython will launch with the default GUI backend integration enabled so that matplotlib plot windows can be created with no issues. Secondly, most of NumPy and matplotlib will be imported into the top level interactive namespace to produce an interactive computing environment reminiscent of MATLAB and other domain-specific scientific computing environments. It's possible to do this setup by hand by using `%gui`, too (try running `%gui?` to find out how).

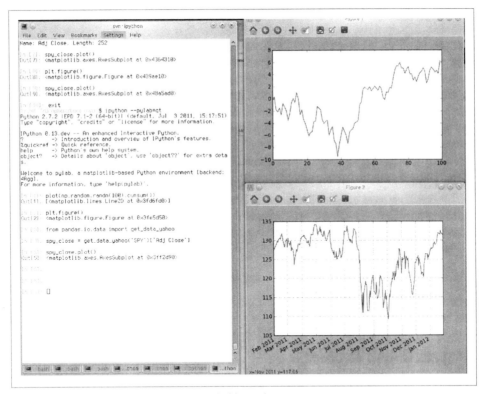

Figure 3-3. Pylab mode: IPython with matplotlib windows

Using the Command History

IPython maintains a small on-disk database containing the text of each command that you execute. This serves various purposes:

- Searching, completing, and executing previously-executed commands with minimal typing
- Persisting the command history between sessions.
- Logging the input/output history to a file

Searching and Reusing the Command History

Being able to search and execute previous commands is, for many people, the most useful feature. Since IPython encourages an iterative, interactive code development workflow, you may often find yourself repeating the same commands, such as a %run command or some other code snippet. Suppose you had run:

```
In[7]: %run first/second/third/data_script.py
```

and then explored the results of the script (assuming it ran successfully), only to find that you made an incorrect calculation. After figuring out the problem and modifying data_script.py, you can start typing a few letters of the %run command then press either the <Ctrl-P> key combination or the <up arrow> key. This will search the command history for the first prior command matching the letters you typed. Pressing either <Ctrl-P> or <up arrow> multiple times will continue to search through the history. If you pass over the command you wish to execute, fear not. You can move *forward* through the command history by pressing either <Ctrl-N> or <down arrow>. After doing this a few times you may start pressing these keys without thinking!

Using <Ctrl-R> gives you the same partial incremental searching capability provided by the readline used in UNIX-style shells, such as the bash shell. On Windows, read line functionality is emulated by IPython. To use this, press <Ctrl-R> then type a few characters contained in the input line you want to search for:

```
In [1]: a_command = foo(x, y, z)

(reverse-i-search)`com': a_command = foo(x, y, z)
```

Pressing <Ctrl-R> will cycle through the history for each line matching the characters you've typed.

Input and Output Variables

Forgetting to assign the result of a function call to a variable can be very annoying. Fortunately, IPython stores references to *both* the input (the text that you type) and output (the object that is returned) in special variables. The previous two outputs are stored in the _ (one underscore) and __ (two underscores) variables, respectively:

```
In [556]: 2 ** 27
Out[556]: 134217728

In [557]: _
Out[557]: 134217728
```

Input variables are stored in variables named like _iX, where X is the input line number. For each such input variables there is a corresponding output variable _X. So after input line 27, say, there will be two new variables _27 (for the output) and _i27 for the input.

```
In [26]: foo = 'bar'

In [27]: foo
Out[27]: 'bar'

In [28]: _i27
Out[28]: u'foo'

In [29]: _27
Out[29]: 'bar'
```

Since the input variables are strings, that can be executed again using the Python exec keyword:

```
In [30]: exec _i27
```

Several magic functions allow you to work with the input and output history. %hist is capable of printing all or part of the input history, with or without line numbers. %reset is for clearing the interactive namespace and optionally the input and output caches. The %xdel magic function is intended for removing all references to a *particular* object from the IPython machinery. See the documentation for both of these magics for more details.

 When working with very large data sets, keep in mind that IPython's input and output history causes any object referenced there to not be garbage collected (freeing up the memory), even if you delete the variables from the interactive namespace using the del keyword. In such cases, careful usage of %xdel and %reset can help you avoid running into memory problems.

Logging the Input and Output

IPython is capable of logging the entire console session including input and output. Logging is turned on by typing %logstart:

```
In [3]: %logstart
Activating auto-logging. Current session state plus future input saved.
Filename       : ipython_log.py
Mode           : rotate
Output logging : False
Raw input log  : False
```

```
Timestamping  : False
State         : active
```

IPython logging can be enabled at any time and it will record your entire session (including previous commands). Thus, if you are working on something and you decide you want to save everything you did, you can simply enable logging. See the docstring of %logstart for more options (including changing the output file path), as well as the companion functions %logoff, %logon, %logstate, and %logstop.

Interacting with the Operating System

Another important feature of IPython is that it provides very strong integration with the operating system shell. This means, among other things, that you can perform most standard command line actions as you would in the Windows or UNIX (Linux, OS X) shell without having to exit IPython. This includes executing shell commands, changing directories, and storing the results of a command in a Python object (list or string). There are also simple shell command aliasing and directory bookmarking features.

See Table 3-3 for a summary of magic functions and syntax for calling shell commands. I'll briefly visit these features in the next few sections.

Table 3-3. IPython system-related commands

Command	Description
!cmd	Execute cmd in the system shell
output = !cmd args	Run cmd and store the stdout in output
%alias *alias_name cmd*	Define an alias for a system (shell) command
%bookmark	Utilize IPython's directory bookmarking system
%cd *directory*	Change system working directory to passed directory
%pwd	Return the current system working directory
%pushd *directory*	Place current directory on stack and change to target directory
%popd	Change to directory popped off the top of the stack
%dirs	Return a list containing the current directory stack
%dhist	Print the history of visited directories
%env	Return the system environment variables as a dict

Shell Commands and Aliases

Starting a line in IPython with an exclamation point !, or bang, tells IPython to execute everything after the bang in the system shell. This means that you can delete files (using rm or del, depending on your OS), change directories, or execute any other process. It's even possible to start processes that take control away from IPython, even another Python interpreter:

```
In [2]: !python
Python 2.7.2 |EPD 7.1-2 (64-bit)| (default, Jul  3 2011, 15:17:51)
[GCC 4.1.2 20080704 (Red Hat 4.1.2-44)] on linux2
Type "packages", "demo" or "enthought" for more information.
>>>
```

The console output of a shell command can be stored in a variable by assigning the !-escaped expression to a variable. For example, on my Linux-based machine connected to the Internet via ethernet, I can get my IP address as a Python variable:

```
In [1]: ip_info = !ifconfig eth0 | grep "inet "

In [2]: ip_info[0].strip()
Out[2]: 'inet addr:192.168.1.137  Bcast:192.168.1.255  Mask:255.255.255.0'
```

The returned Python object `ip_info` is actually a custom list type containing various versions of the console output.

IPython can also substitute in Python values defined in the current environment when using !. To do this, preface the variable name by the dollar sign $:

```
In [3]: foo = 'test*'

In [4]: !ls $foo
test4.py  test.py  test.xml
```

The `%alias` magic function can define custom shortcuts for shell commands. As a simple example:

```
In [1]: %alias ll ls -l

In [2]: ll /usr
total 332
drwxr-xr-x   2 root root   69632 2012-01-29 20:36 bin/
drwxr-xr-x   2 root root    4096 2010-08-23 12:05 games/
drwxr-xr-x 123 root root   20480 2011-12-26 18:08 include/
drwxr-xr-x 265 root root  126976 2012-01-29 20:36 lib/
drwxr-xr-x  44 root root   69632 2011-12-26 18:08 lib32/
lrwxrwxrwx   1 root root       3 2010-08-23 16:02 lib64 -> lib/
drwxr-xr-x  15 root root    4096 2011-10-13 19:03 local/
drwxr-xr-x   2 root root   12288 2012-01-12 09:32 sbin/
drwxr-xr-x 387 root root   12288 2011-11-04 22:53 share/
drwxrwsr-x  24 root src     4096 2011-07-17 18:38 src/
```

Multiple commands can be executed just as on the command line by separating them with semicolons:

```
In [558]: %alias test_alias (cd ch08; ls; cd ..)

In [559]: test_alias
macrodata.csv  spx.csv    tips.csv
```

You'll notice that IPython "forgets" any aliases you define interactively as soon as the session is closed. To create permanent aliases, you will need to use the configuration system. See later in the chapter.

Directory Bookmark System

IPython has a simple directory bookmarking system to enable you to save aliases for common directories so that you can jump around very easily. For example, I'm an avid user of Dropbox, so I can define a bookmark to make it easy to change directories to my Dropbox:

```
In [6]: %bookmark db /home/wesm/Dropbox/
```

Once I've done this, when I use the %cd magic, I can use any bookmarks I've defined

```
In [7]: cd db
(bookmark:db) -> /home/wesm/Dropbox/
/home/wesm/Dropbox
```

If a bookmark name conflicts with a directory name in your current working directory, you can use the -b flag to override and use the bookmark location. Using the -l option with %bookmark lists all of your bookmarks:

```
In [8]: %bookmark -l
Current bookmarks:
db -> /home/wesm/Dropbox/
```

Bookmarks, unlike aliases, are automatically persisted between IPython sessions.

Software Development Tools

In addition to being a comfortable environment for interactive computing and data exploration, IPython is well suited as a software development environment. In data analysis applications, it's important first to have *correct* code. Fortunately, IPython has closely integrated and enhanced the built-in Python pdb debugger. Secondly you want your code to be *fast*. For this IPython has easy-to-use code timing and profiling tools. I will give an overview of these tools in detail here.

Interactive Debugger

IPython's debugger enhances pdb with tab completion, syntax highlighting, and context for each line in exception tracebacks. One of the best times to debug code is right after an error has occurred. The %debug command, when entered immediately after an exception, invokes the "post-mortem" debugger and drops you into the stack frame where the exception was raised:

```
In [2]: run ch03/ipython_bug.py
---------------------------------------------------------------------------
AssertionError                            Traceback (most recent call last)
/home/wesm/book_scripts/ch03/ipython_bug.py in <module>()
     13        throws_an_exception()
     14
---> 15 calling_things()

/home/wesm/book_scripts/ch03/ipython_bug.py in calling_things()
```

```
 11 def calling_things():
 12     works_fine()
---> 13     throws_an_exception()
 14
 15 calling_things()

/home/wesm/book_scripts/ch03/ipython_bug.py in throws_an_exception()
  7     a = 5
  8     b = 6
----> 9     assert(a + b == 10)
 10
 11 def calling_things():

AssertionError:

In [3]: %debug
> /home/wesm/book_scripts/ch03/ipython_bug.py(9)throws_an_exception()
  8     b = 6
----> 9     assert(a + b == 10)
 10


ipdb>
```

Once inside the debugger, you can execute arbitrary Python code and explore all of the objects and data (which have been "kept alive" by the interpreter) inside each stack frame. By default you start in the lowest level, where the error occurred. By pressing u (up) and d (down), you can switch between the levels of the stack trace:

```
ipdb> u
> /home/wesm/book_scripts/ch03/ipython_bug.py(13)calling_things()
 12     works_fine()
---> 13     throws_an_exception()
 14
```

Executing the %pdb command makes it so that IPython automatically invokes the debugger after any exception, a mode that many users will find especially useful.

It's also easy to use the debugger to help develop code, especially when you wish to set breakpoints or step through the execution of a function or script to examine the state at each stage. There are several ways to accomplish this. The first is by using %run with the -d flag, which invokes the debugger before executing any code in the passed script. You must immediately press s (step) to enter the script:

```
In [5]: run -d ch03/ipython_bug.py
Breakpoint 1 at /home/wesm/book_scripts/ch03/ipython_bug.py:1
NOTE: Enter 'c' at the ipdb>  prompt to start your script.
> <string>(1)<module>()

ipdb> s
--Call--
> /home/wesm/book_scripts/ch03/ipython_bug.py(1)<module>()
1---> 1 def works_fine():
 2     a = 5
 3     b = 6
```

After this point, it's up to you how you want to work your way through the file. For example, in the above exception, we could set a breakpoint right before calling the works_fine method and run the script until we reach the breakpoint by pressing c (continue):

```
ipdb> b 12
ipdb> c
> /home/wesm/book_scripts/ch03/ipython_bug.py(12)calling_things()
     11 def calling_things():
2--> 12     works_fine()
     13     throws_an_exception()
```

At this point, you can step into works_fine() or execute works_fine() by pressing n (next) to advance to the next line:

```
ipdb> n
> /home/wesm/book_scripts/ch03/ipython_bug.py(13)calling_things()
2    12     works_fine()
---> 13     throws_an_exception()
     14
```

Then, we could step into throws_an_exception and advance to the line where the error occurs and look at the variables in the scope. Note that debugger commands take precedence over variable names; in such cases preface the variables with ! to examine their contents.

```
ipdb> s
--Call--
> /home/wesm/book_scripts/ch03/ipython_bug.py(6)throws_an_exception()
      5
----> 6 def throws_an_exception():
      7     a = 5

ipdb> n
> /home/wesm/book_scripts/ch03/ipython_bug.py(7)throws_an_exception()
      6 def throws_an_exception():
----> 7     a = 5
      8     b = 6

ipdb> n
> /home/wesm/book_scripts/ch03/ipython_bug.py(8)throws_an_exception()
      7     a = 5
----> 8     b = 6
      9     assert(a + b == 10)

ipdb> n
> /home/wesm/book_scripts/ch03/ipython_bug.py(9)throws_an_exception()
      8     b = 6
----> 9     assert(a + b == 10)
     10

ipdb> !a
5
ipdb> !b
6
```

Becoming proficient in the interactive debugger is largely a matter of practice and experience. See Table 3-4 for a full catalogue of the debugger commands. If you are used to an IDE, you might find the terminal-driven debugger to be a bit bewildering at first, but that will improve in time. Most of the Python IDEs have excellent GUI debuggers, but it is usually a significant productivity gain to remain in IPython for your debugging.

Table 3-4. (I)Python debugger commands

Command	Action
h(elp)	Display command list
help *command*	Show documentation for *command*
c(ontinue)	Resume program execution
q(uit)	Exit debugger without executing any more code
b(reak) *number*	Set breakpoint at *number* in current file
b *path/to/file.py:number*	Set breakpoint at line *number* in specified file
s(tep)	Step *into* function call
n(ext)	Execute current line and advance to next line at current level
u(p) / d(own)	Move up/down in function call stack
a(rgs)	Show arguments for current function
debug *statement*	Invoke statement *statement* in new (recursive) debugger
l(ist) *statement*	Show current position and context at current level of stack
w(here)	Print full stack trace with context at current position

Other ways to make use of the debugger

There are a couple of other useful ways to invoke the debugger. The first is by using a special **set_trace** function (named after **pdb.set_trace**), which is basically a "poor man's breakpoint". Here are two small recipes you might want to put somewhere for your general use (potentially adding them to your IPython profile as I do):

```
def set_trace():
    from IPython.core.debugger import Pdb
    Pdb(color_scheme='Linux').set_trace(sys._getframe().f_back)

def debug(f, *args, **kwargs):
    from IPython.core.debugger import Pdb
    pdb = Pdb(color_scheme='Linux')
    return pdb.runcall(f, *args, **kwargs)
```

The first function, **set_trace**, is very simple. Put **set_trace()** anywhere in your code that you want to stop and take a look around (for example, right before an exception occurs):

```
In [7]: run ch03/ipython_bug.py
> /home/wesm/book_scripts/ch03/ipython_bug.py(16)calling_things()
     15     set_trace()
```

```
---> 16      throws_an_exception()
     17
```

Pressing c (continue) will cause the code to resume normally with no harm done.

The debug function above enables you to invoke the interactive debugger easily on an arbitrary function call. Suppose we had written a function like

```
def f(x, y, z=1):
    tmp = x + y
    return tmp / z
```

and we wished to step through its logic. Ordinarily using f would look like f(1, 2, z=3). To instead step into f, pass f as the first argument to debug followed by the positional and keyword arguments to be passed to f:

```
In [6]: debug(f, 1, 2, z=3)
> <ipython-input>(2)f()
      1 def f(x, y, z):
----> 2     tmp = x + y
      3     return tmp / z

ipdb>
```

I find that these two simple recipes save me a lot of time on a day-to-day basis.

Lastly, the debugger can be used in conjunction with %run. By running a script with %run -d, you will be dropped directly into the debugger, ready to set any breakpoints and start the script:

```
In [1]: %run -d ch03/ipython_bug.py
Breakpoint 1 at /home/wesm/book_scripts/ch03/ipython_bug.py:1
NOTE: Enter 'c' at the ipdb>  prompt to start your script.
> <string>(1)<module>()

ipdb>
```

Adding -b with a line number starts the debugger with a breakpoint set already:

```
In [2]: %run -d -b2 ch03/ipython_bug.py
Breakpoint 1 at /home/wesm/book_scripts/ch03/ipython_bug.py:2
NOTE: Enter 'c' at the ipdb>  prompt to start your script.
> <string>(1)<module>()

ipdb> c
> /home/wesm/book_scripts/ch03/ipython_bug.py(2)works_fine()
      1 def works_fine():
1---> 2     a = 5
      3     b = 6

ipdb>
```

Timing Code: %time and %timeit

For larger-scale or longer-running data analysis applications, you may wish to measure the execution time of various components or of individual statements or function calls. You may want a report of which functions are taking up the most time in a complex process. Fortunately, IPython enables you to get this information very easily while you are developing and testing your code.

Timing code by hand using the built-in `time` module and its functions `time.clock` and `time.time` is often tedious and repetitive, as you must write the same uninteresting boilerplate code:

```
import time
start = time.time()
for i in range(iterations):
    # some code to run here
elapsed_per = (time.time() - start) / iterations
```

Since this is such a common operation, IPython has two magic functions `%time` and `%timeit` to automate this process for you. `%time` runs a statement once, reporting the total execution time. Suppose we had a large list of strings and we wanted to compare different methods of selecting all strings starting with a particular prefix. Here is a simple list of 600,000 strings and two identical methods of selecting only the ones that start with `'foo'`:

```
# a very large list of strings
strings = ['foo', 'foobar', 'baz', 'qux',
           'python', 'Guido Van Rossum'] * 100000

method1 = [x for x in strings if x.startswith('foo')]

method2 = [x for x in strings if x[:3] == 'foo']
```

It looks like they should be about the same performance-wise, right? We can check for sure using `%time`:

```
In [561]: %time method1 = [x for x in strings if x.startswith('foo')]
CPU times: user 0.19 s, sys: 0.00 s, total: 0.19 s
Wall time: 0.19 s

In [562]: %time method2 = [x for x in strings if x[:3] == 'foo']
CPU times: user 0.09 s, sys: 0.00 s, total: 0.09 s
Wall time: 0.09 s
```

The `Wall time` is the main number of interest. So, it looks like the first method takes more than twice as long, but it's not a very precise measurement. If you try `%time`-ing those statements multiple times yourself, you'll find that the results are somewhat variable. To get a more precise measurement, use the `%timeit` magic function. Given an arbitrary statement, it has a heuristic to run a statement multiple times to produce a fairly accurate average runtime.

```
In [563]: %timeit [x for x in strings if x.startswith('foo')]
10 loops, best of 3: 159 ms per loop
```

```
In [564]: %timeit [x for x in strings if x[:3] == 'foo']
10 loops, best of 3: 59.3 ms per loop
```

This seemingly innocuous example illustrates that it is worth understanding the performance characteristics of the Python standard library, NumPy, pandas, and other libraries used in this book. In larger-scale data analysis applications, those milliseconds will start to add up!

%timeit is especially useful for analyzing statements and functions with very short execution times, even at the level of microseconds (1e-6 seconds) or nanoseconds (1e-9 seconds). These may seem like insignificant amounts of time, but of course a 20 microsecond function invoked 1 million times takes 15 seconds longer than a 5 microsecond function. In the above example, we could very directly compare the two string operations to understand their performance characteristics:

```
In [565]: x = 'foobar'

In [566]: y = 'foo'

In [567]: %timeit x.startswith(y)
1000000 loops, best of 3: 267 ns per loop

In [568]: %timeit x[:3] == y
10000000 loops, best of 3: 147 ns per loop
```

Basic Profiling: %prun and %run -p

Profiling code is closely related to timing code, except it is concerned with determining *where* time is spent. The main Python profiling tool is the cProfile module, which is not specific to IPython at all. cProfile executes a program or any arbitrary block of code while keeping track of how much time is spent in each function.

A common way to use cProfile is on the command line, running an entire program and outputting the aggregated time per function. Suppose we had a simple script which does some linear algebra in a loop (computing the maximum absolute eigenvalues of a series of 100 x 100 matrices):

```
import numpy as np
from numpy.linalg import eigvals

def run_experiment(niter=100):
    K = 100
    results = []
    for _ in xrange(niter):
        mat = np.random.randn(K, K)
        max_eigenvalue = np.abs(eigvals(mat)).max()
        results.append(max_eigenvalue)
    return results
some_results = run_experiment()
print 'Largest one we saw: %s' % np.max(some_results)
```

Don't worry if you are not familiar with NumPy. You can run this script through cProfile by running the following in the command line:

```
python -m cProfile cprof_example.py
```

If you try that, you'll find that the results are outputted sorted by function name. This makes it a bit hard to get an idea of where the most time is spent, so it's very common to specify a *sort order* using the -s flag:

```
$ python -m cProfile -s cumulative cprof_example.py
Largest one we saw: 11.923204422
        15116 function calls (14927 primitive calls) in 0.720 seconds

Ordered by: cumulative time

  ncalls  tottime  percall  cumtime  percall filename:lineno(function)
       1    0.001    0.001    0.721    0.721 cprof_example.py:1(<module>)
     100    0.003    0.000    0.586    0.006 linalg.py:702(eigvals)
     200    0.572    0.003    0.572    0.003 {numpy.linalg.lapack_lite.dgeev}
       1    0.002    0.002    0.075    0.075 __init__.py:106(<module>)
     100    0.059    0.001    0.059    0.001 {method 'randn'}
       1    0.000    0.000    0.044    0.044 add_newdocs.py:9(<module>)
       2    0.001    0.001    0.037    0.019 __init__.py:1(<module>)
       2    0.003    0.002    0.030    0.015 __init__.py:2(<module>)
       1    0.000    0.000    0.030    0.030 type_check.py:3(<module>)
       1    0.001    0.001    0.021    0.021 __init__.py:15(<module>)
       1    0.013    0.013    0.013    0.013 numeric.py:1(<module>)
       1    0.000    0.000    0.009    0.009 __init__.py:6(<module>)
       1    0.001    0.001    0.008    0.008 __init__.py:45(<module>)
     262    0.005    0.000    0.007    0.000 function_base.py:3178(add_newdoc)
     100    0.003    0.000    0.005    0.000 linalg.py:162(_assertFinite)
  ...
```

Only the first 15 rows of the output are shown. It's easiest to read by scanning down the cumtime column to see how much total time was spent *inside* each function. Note that if a function calls some other function, *the clock does not stop running*. cProfile records the start and end time of each function call and uses that to produce the timing.

In addition to the above command-line usage, cProfile can also be used programmatically to profile arbitrary blocks of code without having to run a new process. IPython has a convenient interface to this capability using the %prun command and the -p option to %run. %prun takes the same "command line options" as cProfile but will profile an arbitrary Python statement instead of a whole .py file:

```
In [4]: %prun -l 7 -s cumulative run_experiment()
        4203 function calls in 0.643 seconds

Ordered by: cumulative time
List reduced from 32 to 7 due to restriction <7>

  ncalls  tottime  percall  cumtime  percall filename:lineno(function)
       1    0.000    0.000    0.643    0.643 <string>:1(<module>)
       1    0.001    0.001    0.643    0.643 cprof_example.py:4(run_experiment)
     100    0.003    0.000    0.583    0.006 linalg.py:702(eigvals)
```

```
200   0.569   0.003   0.569   0.003 {numpy.linalg.lapack_lite.dgeev}
100   0.058   0.001   0.058   0.001 {method 'randn'}
100   0.003   0.000   0.005   0.000 linalg.py:162(_assertFinite)
200   0.002   0.000   0.002   0.000 {method 'all' of 'numpy.ndarray' objects}
```

Similarly, calling %run -p -s cumulative cprof_example.py has the same effect as the command-line approach above, except you never have to leave IPython.

Profiling a Function Line-by-Line

In some cases the information you obtain from %prun (or another cProfile-based profile method) may not tell the whole story about a function's execution time, or it may be so complex that the results, aggregated by function name, are hard to interpret. For this case, there is a small library called line_profiler (obtainable via PyPI or one of the package management tools). It contains an IPython extension enabling a new magic function %lprun that computes a line-by-line-profiling of one or more functions. You can enable this extension by modifying your IPython configuration (see the IPython documentation or the section on configuration later in this chapter) to include the following line:

```
# A list of dotted module names of IPython extensions to load.
c.TerminalIPythonApp.extensions = ['line_profiler']
```

line_profiler can be used programmatically (see the full documentation), but it is perhaps most powerful when used interactively in IPython. Suppose you had a module prof_mod with the following code doing some NumPy array operations:

```
from numpy.random import randn

def add_and_sum(x, y):
    added = x + y
    summed = added.sum(axis=1)
    return summed

def call_function():
    x = randn(1000, 1000)
    y = randn(1000, 1000)
    return add_and_sum(x, y)
```

If we wanted to understand the performance of the add_and_sum function, %prun gives us the following:

```
In [569]: %run prof_mod

In [570]: x = randn(3000, 3000)

In [571]: y = randn(3000, 3000)

In [572]: %prun add_and_sum(x, y)
         4 function calls in 0.049 seconds
   Ordered by: internal time
   ncalls  tottime  percall  cumtime  percall filename:lineno(function)
        1    0.036    0.036    0.046    0.046 prof_mod.py:3(add_and_sum)
```

```
        1    0.009    0.009    0.009    0.009 {method 'sum' of 'numpy.ndarray' objects}
        1    0.003    0.003    0.049    0.049 <string>:1(<module>)
        1    0.000    0.000    0.000    0.000 {method 'disable' of '_lsprof.Profiler' objects}
```

This is not especially enlightening. With the `line_profiler` IPython extension activated, a new command `%lprun` is available. The only difference in usage is that we must instruct `%lprun` which function or functions we wish to profile. The general syntax is:

```
%lprun -f func1 -f func2 statement_to_profile
```

In this case, we want to profile `add_and_sum`, so we run:

```
In [573]: %lprun -f add_and_sum add_and_sum(x, y)
Timer unit: 1e-06 s
File: book_scripts/prof_mod.py
Function: add_and_sum at line 3
Total time: 0.045936 s
Line #      Hits        Time  Per Hit   % Time  Line Contents
==============================================================
     3                                           def add_and_sum(x, y):
     4         1       36510  36510.0     79.5       added = x + y
     5         1        9425   9425.0     20.5       summed = added.sum(axis=1)
     6         1           1      1.0      0.0       return summed
```

You'll probably agree this is much easier to interpret. In this case we profiled the same function we used in the statement. Looking at the module code above, we could call `call_function` and profile that as well as `add_and_sum`, thus getting a full picture of the performance of the code:

```
In [574]: %lprun -f add_and_sum -f call_function call_function()
Timer unit: 1e-06 s
File: book_scripts/prof_mod.py
Function: add_and_sum at line 3
Total time: 0.005526 s
Line #      Hits        Time  Per Hit   % Time  Line Contents
==============================================================
     3                                           def add_and_sum(x, y):
     4         1        4375   4375.0     79.2       added = x + y
     5         1        1149   1149.0     20.8       summed = added.sum(axis=1)
     6         1           2      2.0      0.0       return summed
File: book_scripts/prof_mod.py
Function: call_function at line 8
Total time: 0.121016 s
Line #      Hits        Time  Per Hit   % Time  Line Contents
==============================================================
     8                                           def call_function():
     9         1       57169  57169.0     47.2       x = randn(1000, 1000)
    10         1       58304  58304.0     48.2       y = randn(1000, 1000)
    11         1        5543   5543.0      4.6       return add_and_sum(x, y)
```

As a general rule of thumb, I tend to prefer `%prun` (cProfile) for "macro" profiling and `%lprun` (`line_profiler`) for "micro" profiling. It's worthwhile to have a good understanding of both tools.

The reason that you have to specify explicitly the names of the functions you want to profile with %lprun is that the overhead of "tracing" the execution time of each line is significant. Tracing functions that are not of interest would potentially significantly alter the profile results.

IPython HTML Notebook

Starting in 2011, the IPython team, led by Brian Granger, built a web technology–based interactive computational document format that is commonly known as the IPython Notebook. It has grown into a wonderful tool for interactive computing and an ideal medium for reproducible research and teaching. I've used it while writing most of the examples in the book; I encourage you to make use of it, too.

It has a JSON-based .ipynb document format that enables easy sharing of code, output, and figures. Recently in Python conferences, a popular approach for demonstrations has been to use the notebook and post the .ipynb files online afterward for everyone to play with.

The notebook application runs as a lightweight server process on the command line. It can be started by running:

```
$ ipython notebook --pylab=inline
[NotebookApp] Using existing profile dir: u'/home/wesm/.config/ipython/profile_default'
[NotebookApp] Serving notebooks from /home/wesm/book_scripts
[NotebookApp] The IPython Notebook is running at: http://127.0.0.1:8888/
[NotebookApp] Use Control-C to stop this server and shut down all kernels.
```

On most platforms, your primary web browser will automatically open up to the notebook dashboard. In some cases you may have to navigate to the listed URL. From there, you can create a new notebook and start exploring.

Since you use the notebook inside a web browser, the server process can run anywhere. You can even securely connect to notebooks running on cloud service providers like Amazon EC2. As of this writing, a new project NotebookCloud (*http://notebookcloud .appspot.com*) makes it easy to launch notebooks on EC2.

Tips for Productive Code Development Using IPython

Writing code in a way that makes it easy to develop, debug, and ultimately *use* interactively may be a paradigm shift for many users. There are procedural details like code reloading that may require some adjustment as well as coding style concerns.

As such, most of this section is more of an art than a science and will require some experimentation on your part to determine a way to write your Python code that is effective and productive for you. Ultimately you want to structure your code in a way that makes it easy to use iteratively and to be able to explore the results of running a program or function as effortlessly as possible. I have found software designed with

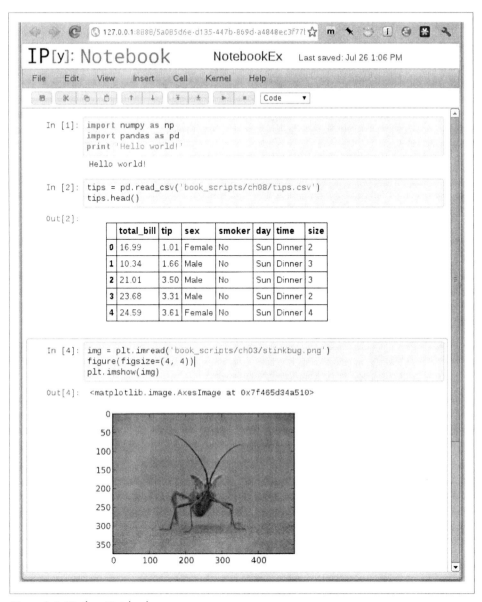

Figure 3-4. IPython Notebook

IPython in mind to be easier to work with than code intended only to be run as as standalone command-line application. This becomes especially important when something goes wrong and you have to diagnose an error in code that you or someone else might have written months or years beforehand.

Reloading Module Dependencies

In Python, when you type `import some_lib`, the code in `some_lib` is executed and all the variables, functions, and imports defined within are stored in the newly created `some_lib` module namespace. The next time you type `import some_lib`, you will get a reference to the existing module namespace. The potential difficulty in interactive code development in IPython comes when you, say, `%run` a script that depends on some other module where you may have made changes. Suppose I had the following code in `test_script.py`:

```
import some_lib

x = 5
y = [1, 2, 3, 4]
result = some_lib.get_answer(x, y)
```

If you were to execute `%run test_script.py` then modify `some_lib.py`, the next time you execute `%run test_script.py` you will still get the *old version* of `some_lib` because of Python's "load-once" module system. This behavior differs from some other data analysis environments, like MATLAB, which automatically propagate code changes.[1] To cope with this, you have a couple of options. The first way is to use Python's built-in `reload` function, altering `test_script.py` to look like the following:

```
import some_lib
reload(some_lib)

x = 5
y = [1, 2, 3, 4]
result = some_lib.get_answer(x, y)
```

This guarantees that you will get a fresh copy of `some_lib` every time you run `test_script.py`. Obviously, if the dependencies go deeper, it might be a bit tricky to be inserting usages of `reload` all over the place. For this problem, IPython has a special `dreload` function (*not* a magic function) for "deep" (recursive) reloading of modules. If I were to run `import some_lib` then type `dreload(some_lib)`, it will attempt to reload `some_lib` as well as all of its dependencies. This will not work in all cases, unfortunately, but when it does it beats having to restart IPython.

Code Design Tips

There's no simple recipe for this, but here are some high-level principles I have found effective in my own work.

---

1. Since a module or package may be imported in many different places in a particular program, Python caches a module's code the first time it is imported rather than executing the code in the module every time. Otherwise, modularity and good code organization could potentially cause inefficiency in an application.

Keep relevant objects and data alive

It's not unusual to see a program written for the command line with a structure somewhat like the following trivial example:

```
from my_functions import g

def f(x, y):
    return g(x + y)

def main():
    x = 6
    y = 7.5
    result = x + y

if __name__ == '__main__':
    main()
```

Do you see what might be wrong with this program if we were to run it in IPython?
After it's done, none of the results or objects defined in the main function will be accessible in the IPython shell. A better way is to have whatever code is in main execute
directly in the module's global namespace (or in the if __name__ == '__main__': block,
if you want the module to also be importable). That way, when you %run the code,
you'll be able to look at all of the variables defined in main. It's less meaningful in this
simple example, but in this book we'll be looking at some complex data analysis problems involving large data sets that you will want to be able to play with in IPython.

Flat is better than nested

Deeply nested code makes me think about the many layers of an onion. When testing
or debugging a function, how many layers of the onion must you peel back in order to
reach the code of interest? The idea that "flat is better than nested" is a part of the Zen
of Python, and it applies generally to developing code for interactive use as well. Making
functions and classes as decoupled and modular as possible makes them easier to test
(if you are writing unit tests), debug, and use interactively.

Overcome a fear of longer files

If you come from a Java (or another such language) background, you may have been
told to keep files short. In many languages, this is sound advice; long length is usually
a bad "code smell", indicating refactoring or reorganization may be necessary. However, while developing code using IPython, working with 10 small, but interconnected
files (under, say, 100 lines each) is likely to cause you more headache in general than a
single large file or two or three longer files. Fewer files means fewer modules to reload
and less jumping between files while editing, too. I have found maintaining larger
modules, each with high *internal* cohesion, to be much more useful and pythonic. After
iterating toward a solution, it sometimes will make sense to refactor larger files into
smaller ones.

Obviously, I don't support taking this argument to the extreme, which would to be to put all of your code in a single monstrous file. Finding a sensible and intuitive module and package structure for a large codebase often takes a bit of work, but it is especially important to get right in teams. Each module should be internally cohesive, and it should be as obvious as possible where to find functions and classes responsible for each area of functionality.

Advanced IPython Features

Making Your Own Classes IPython-friendly

IPython makes every effort to display a console-friendly string representation of any object that you inspect. For many objects, like dicts, lists, and tuples, the built-in pprint module is used to do the nice formatting. In user-defined classes, however, you have to generate the desired string output yourself. Suppose we had the following simple class:

```
class Message:
    def __init__(self, msg):
        self.msg = msg
```

If you wrote this, you would be disappointed to discover that the default output for your class isn't very nice:

```
In [576]: x = Message('I have a secret')

In [577]: x
Out[577]: <__main__.Message instance at 0x60ebbd8>
```

IPython takes the string returned by the __repr__ magic method (by doing output = repr(obj)) and prints that to the console. Thus, we can add a simple __repr__ method to the above class to get a more helpful output:

```
class Message:
    def __init__(self, msg):
        self.msg = msg

    def __repr__(self):
        return 'Message: %s' % self.msg

In [579]: x = Message('I have a secret')

In [580]: x
Out[580]: Message: I have a secret
```

Profiles and Configuration

Most aspects of the appearance (colors, prompt, spacing between lines, etc.) and be-havior of the IPython shell are configurable through an extensive configuration system. Here are some of the things you can do via configuration:

- Change the color scheme
- Change how the input and output prompts look, or remove the blank line after Out and before the next In prompt
- Execute an arbitrary list of Python statements. These could be imports that you use all the time or anything else you want to happen each time you launch IPython
- Enable IPython extensions, like the %lprun magic in line_profiler
- Define your own magics or system aliases

All of these configuration options are specified in a special ipython_config.py file which will be found in the ~/.config/ipython/ directory on UNIX-like systems and %HOME %/.ipython/ directory on Windows. Where your home directory is depends on your system. Configuration is performed based on a particular *profile*. When you start IPy-thon normally, you load up, by default, the *default profile*, stored in the pro file_default directory. Thus, on my Linux OS the full path to my default IPython configuration file is:

```
/home/wesm/.config/ipython/profile_default/ipython_config.py
```

I'll spare you the gory details of what's in this file. Fortunately it has comments de-scribing what each configuration option is for, so I will leave it to the reader to tinker and customize. One additional useful feature is that it's possible to have *multiple pro-files*. Suppose you wanted to have an alternate IPython configuration tailored for a particular application or project. Creating a new profile is as simple is typing something like

```
ipython profile create secret_project
```

Once you've done this, edit the config files in the newly-created pro file_secret_project directory then launch IPython like so

```
$ ipython --profile=secret_project
Python 2.7.2 |EPD 7.1-2 (64-bit)| (default, Jul  3 2011, 15:17:51)
Type "copyright", "credits" or "license" for more information.

IPython 0.13 -- An enhanced Interactive Python.
?         -> Introduction and overview of IPython's features.
%quickref -> Quick reference.
help      -> Python's own help system.
object?   -> Details about 'object', use 'object??' for extra details.

IPython profile: secret_project

In [1]:
```

As always, the online IPython documentation is an excellent resource for more on profiles and configuration.

Credits

Parts of this chapter were derived from the wonderful documentation put together by the IPython Development Team. I can't thank them enough for all of their work building this amazing set of tools.

## CHAPTER 4

NumPy Basics: Arrays and Vectorized Computation

NumPy, short for Numerical Python, is the fundamental package required for high performance scientific computing and data analysis. It is the foundation on which nearly all of the higher-level tools in this book are built. Here are some of the things it provides:

- ndarray, a fast and space-efficient multidimensional array providing vectorized arithmetic operations and sophisticated *broadcasting* capabilities
- Standard mathematical functions for fast operations on entire arrays of data without having to write loops
- Tools for reading / writing array data to disk and working with memory-mapped files
- Linear algebra, random number generation, and Fourier transform capabilities
- Tools for integrating code written in C, C++, and Fortran

The last bullet point is also one of the most important ones from an ecosystem point of view. Because NumPy provides an easy-to-use C API, it is very easy to pass data to external libraries written in a low-level language and also for external libraries to return data to Python as NumPy arrays. This feature has made Python a language of choice for wrapping legacy C/C++/Fortran codebases and giving them a dynamic and easy-to-use interface.

While NumPy by itself does not provide very much high-level data analytical functionality, having an understanding of NumPy arrays and array-oriented computing will help you use tools like pandas much more effectively. If you're new to Python and just looking to get your hands dirty working with data using pandas, feel free to give this chapter a skim. For more on advanced NumPy features like broadcasting, see Chapter 12.

For most data analysis applications, the main areas of functionality I'll focus on are:

- Fast vectorized array operations for data munging and cleaning, subsetting and filtering, transformation, and any other kinds of computations
- Common array algorithms like sorting, unique, and set operations
- Efficient descriptive statistics and aggregating/summarizing data
- Data alignment and relational data manipulations for merging and joining together heterogeneous data sets
- Expressing conditional logic as array expressions instead of loops with `if-elif-else` branches
- Group-wise data manipulations (aggregation, transformation, function application). Much more on this in Chapter 5

While NumPy provides the computational foundation for these operations, you will likely want to use pandas as your basis for most kinds of data analysis (especially for structured or tabular data) as it provides a rich, high-level interface making most common data tasks very concise and simple. pandas also provides some more domain-specific functionality like time series manipulation, which is not present in NumPy.

 In this chapter and throughout the book, I use the standard NumPy convention of always using `import numpy as np`. You are, of course, welcome to put `from numpy import *` in your code to avoid having to write `np.`, but I would caution you against making a habit of this.

The NumPy ndarray: A Multidimensional Array Object

One of the key features of NumPy is its N-dimensional array object, or ndarray, which is a fast, flexible container for large data sets in Python. Arrays enable you to perform mathematical operations on whole blocks of data using similar syntax to the equivalent operations between scalar elements:

```
In [8]: data
Out[8]:
array([[ 0.9526, -0.246 , -0.8856],
       [ 0.5639,  0.2379,  0.9104]])
```

```
In [9]: data * 10                          In [10]: data + data
Out[9]:                                     Out[10]:
array([[ 9.5256, -2.4601, -8.8565],        array([[ 1.9051, -0.492 , -1.7713],
       [ 5.6385,  2.3794,  9.104 ]])               [ 1.1277,  0.4759,  1.8208]])
```

An ndarray is a generic multidimensional container for homogeneous data; that is, all of the elements must be the same type. Every array has a `shape`, a tuple indicating the size of each dimension, and a `dtype`, an object describing the *data type* of the array:

```
In [11]: data.shape
Out[11]: (2, 3)
```

```
In [12]: data.dtype
Out[12]: dtype('float64')
```

This chapter will introduce you to the basics of using NumPy arrays, and should be sufficient for following along with the rest of the book. While it's not necessary to have a deep understanding of NumPy for many data analytical applications, becoming proficient in array-oriented programming and thinking is a key step along the way to becoming a scientific Python guru.

> Whenever you see "array", "NumPy array", or "ndarray" in the text, with few exceptions they all refer to the same thing: the ndarray object.

Creating ndarrays

The easiest way to create an array is to use the **array** function. This accepts any sequence-like object (including other arrays) and produces a new NumPy array containing the passed data. For example, a list is a good candidate for conversion:

```
In [13]: data1 = [6, 7.5, 8, 0, 1]

In [14]: arr1 = np.array(data1)

In [15]: arr1
Out[15]: array([ 6. ,  7.5,  8. ,  0. ,  1. ])
```

Nested sequences, like a list of equal-length lists, will be converted into a multidimensional array:

```
In [16]: data2 = [[1, 2, 3, 4], [5, 6, 7, 8]]

In [17]: arr2 = np.array(data2)

In [18]: arr2
Out[18]:
array([[1, 2, 3, 4],
       [5, 6, 7, 8]])

In [19]: arr2.ndim
Out[19]: 2

In [20]: arr2.shape
Out[20]: (2, 4)
```

Unless explicitly specified (more on this later), np.array tries to infer a good data type for the array that it creates. The data type is stored in a special dtype object; for example, in the above two examples we have:

```
In [21]: arr1.dtype
Out[21]: dtype('float64')
```

```
In [22]: arr2.dtype
Out[22]: dtype('int64')
```

In addition to np.array, there are a number of other functions for creating new arrays. As examples, zeros and ones create arrays of 0's or 1's, respectively, with a given length or shape. empty creates an array without initializing its values to any particular value. To create a higher dimensional array with these methods, pass a tuple for the shape:

```
In [23]: np.zeros(10)
Out[23]: array([ 0.,  0.,  0.,  0.,  0.,  0.,  0.,  0.,  0.,  0.])

In [24]: np.zeros((3, 6))
Out[24]:
array([[ 0.,  0.,  0.,  0.,  0.,  0.],
       [ 0.,  0.,  0.,  0.,  0.,  0.],
       [ 0.,  0.,  0.,  0.,  0.,  0.]])

In [25]: np.empty((2, 3, 2))
Out[25]:
array([[[  4.94065646e-324,   4.94065646e-324],
        [  3.87491056e-297,   2.46845796e-130],
        [  4.94065646e-324,   4.94065646e-324]],

       [[  1.90723115e+083,   5.73293533e-053],
        [ -2.33568637e+124,  -6.70608105e-012],
        [  4.42786966e+160,   1.27100354e+025]]])
```

 It's not safe to assume that np.empty will return an array of all zeros. In many cases, as previously shown, it will return uninitialized garbage values.

arange is an array-valued version of the built-in Python range function:

```
In [26]: np.arange(15)
Out[26]: array([ 0,  1,  2,  3,  4,  5,  6,  7,  8,  9, 10, 11, 12, 13, 14])
```

See Table 4-1 for a short list of standard array creation functions. Since NumPy is focused on numerical computing, the data type, if not specified, will in many cases be float64 (floating point).

Table 4-1. Array creation functions

Function	Description
array	Convert input data (list, tuple, array, or other sequence type) to an ndarray either by inferring a dtype or explicitly specifying a dtype. Copies the input data by default.
asarray	Convert input to ndarray, but do not copy if the input is already an ndarray
arange	Like the built-in range but returns an ndarray instead of a list.
ones, ones_like	Produce an array of all 1's with the given shape and dtype. ones_like takes another array and produces a ones array of the same shape and dtype.
zeros, zeros_like	Like ones and ones_like but producing arrays of 0's instead

Function	Description
empty, empty_like	Create new arrays by allocating new memory, but do not populate with any values like ones and zeros
eye, identity	Create a square N x N identity matrix (1's on the diagonal and 0's elsewhere)

Data Types for ndarrays

The *data type* or dtype is a special object containing the information the ndarray needs to interpret a chunk of memory as a particular type of data:

```
In [27]: arr1 = np.array([1, 2, 3], dtype=np.float64)

In [28]: arr2 = np.array([1, 2, 3], dtype=np.int32)

In [29]: arr1.dtype          In [30]: arr2.dtype
Out[29]: dtype('float64')    Out[30]: dtype('int32')
```

Dtypes are part of what make NumPy so powerful and flexible. In most cases they map directly onto an underlying machine representation, which makes it easy to read and write binary streams of data to disk and also to connect to code written in a low-level language like C or Fortran. The numerical dtypes are named the same way: a type name, like float or int, followed by a number indicating the number of bits per element. A standard double-precision floating point value (what's used under the hood in Python's float object) takes up 8 bytes or 64 bits. Thus, this type is known in NumPy as float64. See Table 4-2 for a full listing of NumPy's supported data types.

> Don't worry about memorizing the NumPy dtypes, especially if you're a new user. It's often only necessary to care about the general *kind* of data you're dealing with, whether floating point, complex, integer, boolean, string, or general Python object. When you need more control over how data are stored in memory and on disk, especially large data sets, it is good to know that you have control over the storage type.

Table 4-2. NumPy data types

Type	Type Code	Description
int8, uint8	i1, u1	Signed and unsigned 8-bit (1 byte) integer types
int16, uint16	i2, u2	Signed and unsigned 16-bit integer types
int32, uint32	i4, u4	Signed and unsigned 32-bit integer types
int64, uint64	i8, u8	Signed and unsigned 32-bit integer types
float16	f2	Half-precision floating point
float32	f4 or f	Standard single-precision floating point. Compatible with C float
float64	f8 or d	Standard double-precision floating point. Compatible with C double and Python float object

Type	Type Code	Description
float128	f16 or g	Extended-precision floating point
complex64, complex128, complex256	c8, c16, c32	Complex numbers represented by two 32, 64, or 128 floats, respectively
bool	?	Boolean type storing True and False values
object	O	Python object type
string_	S	Fixed-length string type (1 byte per character). For example, to create a string dtype with length 10, use 'S10'.
unicode_	U	Fixed-length unicode type (number of bytes platform specific). Same specification semantics as string_ (e.g. 'U10').

You can explicitly convert or *cast* an array from one dtype to another using ndarray's astype method:

```
In [31]: arr = np.array([1, 2, 3, 4, 5])

In [32]: arr.dtype
Out[32]: dtype('int64')

In [33]: float_arr = arr.astype(np.float64)

In [34]: float_arr.dtype
Out[34]: dtype('float64')
```

In this example, integers were cast to floating point. If I cast some floating point numbers to be of integer dtype, the decimal part will be truncated:

```
In [35]: arr = np.array([3.7, -1.2, -2.6, 0.5, 12.9, 10.1])

In [36]: arr
Out[36]: array([ 3.7,  -1.2,  -2.6,   0.5,  12.9,  10.1])

In [37]: arr.astype(np.int32)
Out[37]: array([ 3, -1, -2,  0, 12, 10], dtype=int32)
```

Should you have an array of strings representing numbers, you can use astype to convert them to numeric form:

```
In [38]: numeric_strings = np.array(['1.25', '-9.6', '42'], dtype=np.string_)

In [39]: numeric_strings.astype(float)
Out[39]: array([ 1.25,  -9.6 ,  42.  ])
```

If casting were to fail for some reason (like a string that cannot be converted to float64), a TypeError will be raised. See that I was a bit lazy and wrote float instead of np.float64; NumPy is smart enough to alias the Python types to the equivalent dtypes.

You can also use another array's dtype attribute:

```
In [40]: int_array = np.arange(10)
```

```
In [41]: calibers = np.array([.22, .270, .357, .380, .44, .50], dtype=np.float64)

In [42]: int_array.astype(calibers.dtype)
Out[42]: array([ 0.,  1.,  2.,  3.,  4.,  5.,  6.,  7.,  8.,  9.])
```

There are shorthand type code strings you can also use to refer to a dtype:

```
In [43]: empty_uint32 = np.empty(8, dtype='u4')
```

```
In [44]: empty_uint32
Out[44]:
array([        0,        0, 65904672,        0, 64856792,        0,
       39438163,        0], dtype=uint32)
```

  Calling astype *always* creates a new array (a copy of the data), even if the new dtype is the same as the old dtype.

It's worth keeping in mind that floating point numbers, such as those in float64 and float32 arrays, are only capable of approximating fractional quantities. In complex computations, you may accrue some *floating point error*, making comparisons only valid up to a certain number of decimal places.

Operations between Arrays and Scalars

Arrays are important because they enable you to express batch operations on data without writing any for loops. This is usually called *vectorization*. Any arithmetic operations between equal-size arrays applies the operation elementwise:

```
In [45]: arr = np.array([[1., 2., 3.], [4., 5., 6.]])
```

```
In [46]: arr
Out[46]:
array([[ 1.,  2.,  3.],
       [ 4.,  5.,  6.]])
```

```
In [47]: arr * arr              In [48]: arr - arr
Out[47]:                        Out[48]:
array([[  1.,   4.,   9.],      array([[ 0.,  0.,  0.],
       [ 16.,  25.,  36.]])            [ 0.,  0.,  0.]])
```

Arithmetic operations with scalars are as you would expect, propagating the value to each element:

```
In [49]: 1 / arr                      In [50]: arr ** 0.5
Out[49]:                              Out[50]:
array([[ 1.   , 0.5   , 0.3333],      array([[ 1.   , 1.4142, 1.7321],
       [ 0.25 , 0.2   , 0.1667]])            [ 2.   , 2.2361, 2.4495]])
```

Operations between differently sized arrays is called *broadcasting* and will be discussed in more detail in Chapter 12. Having a deep understanding of broadcasting is not necessary for most of this book.

Basic Indexing and Slicing

NumPy array indexing is a rich topic, as there are many ways you may want to select a subset of your data or individual elements. One-dimensional arrays are simple; on the surface they act similarly to Python lists:

```
In [51]: arr = np.arange(10)

In [52]: arr
Out[52]: array([0, 1, 2, 3, 4, 5, 6, 7, 8, 9])

In [53]: arr[5]
Out[53]: 5

In [54]: arr[5:8]
Out[54]: array([5, 6, 7])

In [55]: arr[5:8] = 12

In [56]: arr
Out[56]: array([ 0,  1,  2,  3,  4, 12, 12, 12,  8,  9])
```

As you can see, if you assign a scalar value to a slice, as in `arr[5:8]` = 12, the value is propagated (or *broadcasted* henceforth) to the entire selection. An important first distinction from lists is that array slices are *views* on the original array. This means that the data is not copied, and any modifications to the view will be reflected in the source array:

```
In [57]: arr_slice = arr[5:8]

In [58]: arr_slice[1] = 12345

In [59]: arr
Out[59]: array([    0,     1,     2,     3,     4,    12, 12345,    12,     8,     9])

In [60]: arr_slice[:] = 64

In [61]: arr
Out[61]: array([ 0,  1,  2,  3,  4, 64, 64, 64,  8,  9])
```

If you are new to NumPy, you might be surprised by this, especially if you have used other array programming languages which copy data more zealously. As NumPy has been designed with large data use cases in mind, you could imagine performance and memory problems if NumPy insisted on copying data left and right.

If you want a copy of a slice of an ndarray instead of a view, you will need to explicitly copy the array; for example arr[5:8].copy().

With higher dimensional arrays, you have many more options. In a two-dimensional array, the elements at each index are no longer scalars but rather one-dimensional arrays:

```
In [62]: arr2d = np.array([[1, 2, 3], [4, 5, 6], [7, 8, 9]])
```

```
In [63]: arr2d[2]
Out[63]: array([7, 8, 9])
```

Thus, individual elements can be accessed recursively. But that is a bit too much work, so you can pass a comma-separated list of indices to select individual elements. So these are equivalent:

```
In [64]: arr2d[0][2]
Out[64]: 3
```

```
In [65]: arr2d[0, 2]
Out[65]: 3
```

See Figure 4-1 for an illustration of indexing on a 2D array.

Figure 4-1. Indexing elements in a NumPy array

In multidimensional arrays, if you omit later indices, the returned object will be a lower-dimensional ndarray consisting of all the data along the higher dimensions. So in the 2 × 2 × 3 array arr3d

```
In [66]: arr3d = np.array([[[1, 2, 3], [4, 5, 6]], [[7, 8, 9], [10, 11, 12]]])
```

```
In [67]: arr3d
Out[67]:
array([[[ 1,  2,  3],
```

```
            [ 4,  5,  6]],
            [[ 7,  8,  9],
             [10, 11, 12]]])
```

arr3d[0] is a 2 × 3 array:

```
In [68]: arr3d[0]
Out[68]:
array([[1, 2, 3],
       [4, 5, 6]])
```

Both scalar values and arrays can be assigned to arr3d[0]:

```
In [69]: old_values = arr3d[0].copy()

In [70]: arr3d[0] = 42

In [71]: arr3d
Out[71]:
array([[[42, 42, 42],
        [42, 42, 42]],
       [[ 7,  8,  9],
        [10, 11, 12]]])

In [72]: arr3d[0] = old_values

In [73]: arr3d
Out[73]:
array([[[ 1,  2,  3],
        [ 4,  5,  6]],
       [[ 7,  8,  9],
        [10, 11, 12]]])
```

Similarly, arr3d[1, 0] gives you all of the values whose indices start with (1, 0), forming a 1-dimensional array:

```
In [74]: arr3d[1, 0]
Out[74]: array([7, 8, 9])
```

Note that in all of these cases where subsections of the array have been selected, the returned arrays are views.

Indexing with slices

Like one-dimensional objects such as Python lists, ndarrays can be sliced using the familiar syntax:

```
In [75]: arr[1:6]
Out[75]: array([ 1,  2,  3,  4, 64])
```

Higher dimensional objects give you more options as you can slice one or more axes and also mix integers. Consider the 2D array above, arr2d. Slicing this array is a bit different:

```
In [76]: arr2d          In [77]: arr2d[:2]
Out[76]:                Out[77]:
```

```
array([[1, 2, 3],          array([[1, 2, 3],
       [4, 5, 6],                 [4, 5, 6]])
       [7, 8, 9]])
```

As you can see, it has sliced along axis 0, the first axis. A slice, therefore, selects a range of elements along an axis. You can pass multiple slices just like you can pass multiple indexes:

```
In [78]: arr2d[:2, 1:]
Out[78]:
array([[2, 3],
       [5, 6]])
```

When slicing like this, you always obtain array views of the same number of dimensions. By mixing integer indexes and slices, you get lower dimensional slices:

```
In [79]: arr2d[1, :2]          In [80]: arr2d[2, :1]
Out[79]: array([4, 5])         Out[80]: array([7])
```

See Figure 4-2 for an illustration. Note that a colon by itself means to take the entire axis, so you can slice only higher dimensional axes by doing:

```
In [81]: arr2d[:, :1]
Out[81]:
array([[1],
       [4],
       [7]])
```

Of course, assigning to a slice expression assigns to the whole selection:

```
In [82]: arr2d[:2, 1:] = 0
```

Boolean Indexing

Let's consider an example where we have some data in an array and an array of names with duplicates. I'm going to use here the randn function in numpy.random to generate some random normally distributed data:

```
In [83]: names = np.array(['Bob', 'Joe', 'Will', 'Bob', 'Will', 'Joe', 'Joe'])

In [84]: data = np.random.randn(7, 4)

In [85]: names
Out[85]:
array(['Bob', 'Joe', 'Will', 'Bob', 'Will', 'Joe', 'Joe'],
      dtype='|S4')

In [86]: data
Out[86]:
array([[-0.048 ,  0.5433, -0.2349,  1.2792],
       [-0.268 ,  0.5465,  0.0939, -2.0445],
       [-0.047 , -2.026 ,  0.7719,  0.3103],
       [ 2.1452,  0.8799, -0.0523,  0.0672],
       [-1.0023, -0.1698,  1.1503,  1.7289],
```

```
[ 0.1913,  0.4544,  0.4519,  0.5535],
[ 0.5994,  0.8174, -0.9297, -1.2564]])
```

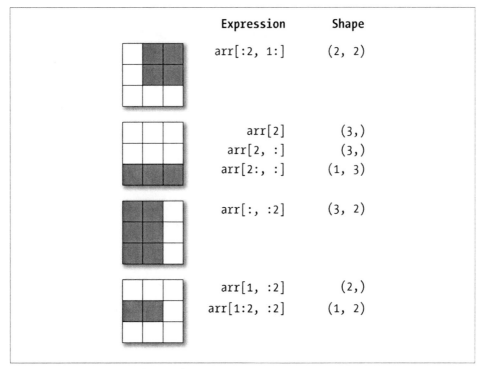

	Expression	Shape
	arr[:2, 1:]	(2, 2)
	arr[2] arr[2, :] arr[2:, :]	(3,) (3,) (1, 3)
	arr[:, :2]	(3, 2)
	arr[1, :2] arr[1:2, :2]	(2,) (1, 2)

Figure 4-2. Two-dimensional array slicing

Suppose each name corresponds to a row in the data array and we wanted to select all the rows with corresponding name 'Bob'. Like arithmetic operations, comparisons (such as ==) with arrays are also vectorized. Thus, comparing names with the string 'Bob' yields a boolean array:

```
In [87]: names == 'Bob'
Out[87]: array([ True, False, False, True, False, False, False], dtype=bool)
```

This boolean array can be passed when indexing the array:

```
In [88]: data[names == 'Bob']
Out[88]:
array([[-0.048 ,  0.5433, -0.2349,  1.2792],
       [ 2.1452,  0.8799, -0.0523,  0.0672]])
```

The boolean array must be of the same length as the axis it's indexing. You can even mix and match boolean arrays with slices or integers (or sequences of integers, more on this later):

```
In [89]: data[names == 'Bob', 2:]
Out[89]:
```

```
array([[-0.2349,  1.2792],
       [-0.0523,  0.0672]])

In [90]: data[names == 'Bob', 3]
Out[90]: array([ 1.2792,  0.0672])
```

To select everything but 'Bob', you can either use != or negate the condition using -:

```
In [91]: names != 'Bob'
Out[91]: array([False, True, True, False, True, True, True], dtype=bool)

In [92]: data[-(names == 'Bob')]
Out[92]:
array([[-0.268 ,  0.5465,  0.0939, -2.0445],
       [-0.047 , -2.026 ,  0.7719,  0.3103],
       [-1.0023, -0.1698,  1.1503,  1.7289],
       [ 0.1913,  0.4544,  0.4519,  0.5535],
       [ 0.5994,  0.8174, -0.9297, -1.2564]])
```

Selecting two of the three names to combine multiple boolean conditions, use boolean arithmetic operators like & (and) and | (or):

```
In [93]: mask = (names == 'Bob') | (names == 'Will')

In [94]: mask
Out[94]: array([True, False, True, True, True, False, False], dtype=bool)

In [95]: data[mask]
Out[95]:
array([[-0.048 ,  0.5433, -0.2349,  1.2792],
       [-0.047 , -2.026 ,  0.7719,  0.3103],
       [ 2.1452,  0.8799, -0.0523,  0.0672],
       [-1.0023, -0.1698,  1.1503,  1.7289]])
```

Selecting data from an array by boolean indexing *always* creates a copy of the data, even if the returned array is unchanged.

The Python keywords and and or do not work with boolean arrays.

Setting values with boolean arrays works in a common-sense way. To set all of the negative values in data to 0 we need only do:

```
In [96]: data[data < 0] = 0

In [97]: data
Out[97]:
array([[ 0.    ,  0.5433,  0.    ,  1.2792],
       [ 0.    ,  0.5465,  0.0939,  0.    ],
       [ 0.    ,  0.    ,  0.7719,  0.3103],
       [ 2.1452,  0.8799,  0.    ,  0.0672],
       [ 0.    ,  0.    ,  1.1503,  1.7289],
       [ 0.1913,  0.4544,  0.4519,  0.5535],
       [ 0.5994,  0.8174,  0.    ,  0.    ]])
```

Setting whole rows or columns using a 1D boolean array is also easy:

```
In [98]: data[names != 'Joe'] = 7
```

```
In [99]: data
Out[99]:
array([[ 7.    , 7.    , 7.    , 7.    ],
       [ 0.    , 0.5465, 0.0939, 0.    ],
       [ 7.    , 7.    , 7.    , 7.    ],
       [ 7.    , 7.    , 7.    , 7.    ],
       [ 7.    , 7.    , 7.    , 7.    ],
       [ 0.1913, 0.4544, 0.4519, 0.5535],
       [ 0.5994, 0.8174, 0.    , 0.    ]])
```

Fancy Indexing

Fancy indexing is a term adopted by NumPy to describe indexing using integer arrays. Suppose we had a 8 × 4 array:

```
In [100]: arr = np.empty((8, 4))
```

```
In [101]: for i in range(8):
    .....:     arr[i] = i
```

```
In [102]: arr
Out[102]:
array([[ 0., 0., 0., 0.],
       [ 1., 1., 1., 1.],
       [ 2., 2., 2., 2.],
       [ 3., 3., 3., 3.],
       [ 4., 4., 4., 4.],
       [ 5., 5., 5., 5.],
       [ 6., 6., 6., 6.],
       [ 7., 7., 7., 7.]])
```

To select out a subset of the rows in a particular order, you can simply pass a list or ndarray of integers specifying the desired order:

```
In [103]: arr[[4, 3, 0, 6]]
Out[103]:
array([[ 4., 4., 4., 4.],
       [ 3., 3., 3., 3.],
       [ 0., 0., 0., 0.],
       [ 6., 6., 6., 6.]])
```

Hopefully this code did what you expected! Using negative indices select rows from the end:

```
In [104]: arr[[-3, -5, -7]]
Out[104]:
array([[ 5., 5., 5., 5.],
       [ 3., 3., 3., 3.],
       [ 1., 1., 1., 1.]])
```

Passing multiple index arrays does something slightly different; it selects a 1D array of elements corresponding to each tuple of indices:

```
# more on reshape in Chapter 12
In [105]: arr = np.arange(32).reshape((8, 4))

In [106]: arr
Out[106]:
array([[ 0,  1,  2,  3],
       [ 4,  5,  6,  7],
       [ 8,  9, 10, 11],
       [12, 13, 14, 15],
       [16, 17, 18, 19],
       [20, 21, 22, 23],
       [24, 25, 26, 27],
       [28, 29, 30, 31]])

In [107]: arr[[1, 5, 7, 2], [0, 3, 1, 2]]
Out[107]: array([ 4, 23, 29, 10])
```

Take a moment to understand what just happened: the elements (1, 0), (5, 3), (7, 1), and (2, 2) were selected. The behavior of fancy indexing in this case is a bit different from what some users might have expected (myself included), which is the rectangular region formed by selecting a subset of the matrix's rows and columns. Here is one way to get that:

```
In [108]: arr[[1, 5, 7, 2]][:, [0, 3, 1, 2]]
Out[108]:
array([[ 4,  7,  5,  6],
       [20, 23, 21, 22],
       [28, 31, 29, 30],
       [ 8, 11,  9, 10]])
```

Another way is to use the np.ix_ function, which converts two 1D integer arrays to an indexer that selects the square region:

```
In [109]: arr[np.ix_([1, 5, 7, 2], [0, 3, 1, 2])]
Out[109]:
array([[ 4,  7,  5,  6],
       [20, 23, 21, 22],
       [28, 31, 29, 30],
       [ 8, 11,  9, 10]])
```

Keep in mind that fancy indexing, unlike slicing, always copies the data into a new array.

Transposing Arrays and Swapping Axes

Transposing is a special form of reshaping which similarly returns a view on the underlying data without copying anything. Arrays have the transpose method and also the special T attribute:

```
In [110]: arr = np.arange(15).reshape((3, 5))
```

```
In [111]: arr                          In [112]: arr.T
```

```
Out[111]:                          Out[112]:
array([[ 0,  1,  2,  3,  4],       array([[ 0,  5, 10],
       [ 5,  6,  7,  8,  9],              [ 1,  6, 11],
       [10, 11, 12, 13, 14]])            [ 2,  7, 12],
                                         [ 3,  8, 13],
                                         [ 4,  9, 14]])
```

When doing matrix computations, you will do this very often, like for example computing the inner matrix product $X^T X$ using np.dot:

```
In [113]: arr = np.random.randn(6, 3)
```

```
In [114]: np.dot(arr.T, arr)
Out[114]:
array([[ 2.584 ,  1.8753,  0.8888],
       [ 1.8753,  6.6636,  0.3884],
       [ 0.8888,  0.3884,  3.9781]])
```

For higher dimensional arrays, transpose will accept a tuple of axis numbers to permute the axes (for extra mind bending):

```
In [115]: arr = np.arange(16).reshape((2, 2, 4))
```

```
In [116]: arr
Out[116]:
array([[[ 0,  1,  2,  3],
        [ 4,  5,  6,  7]],
       [[ 8,  9, 10, 11],
        [12, 13, 14, 15]]])
```

```
In [117]: arr.transpose((1, 0, 2))
Out[117]:
array([[[ 0,  1,  2,  3],
        [ 8,  9, 10, 11]],
       [[ 4,  5,  6,  7],
        [12, 13, 14, 15]]])
```

Simple transposing with .T is just a special case of swapping axes. ndarray has the method swapaxes which takes a pair of axis numbers:

```
In [118]: arr                      In [119]: arr.swapaxes(1, 2)
Out[118]:                          Out[119]:
array([[[ 0,  1,  2,  3],          array([[[ 0,  4],
        [ 4,  5,  6,  7]],                 [ 1,  5],
                                           [ 2,  6],
       [[ 8,  9, 10, 11],                  [ 3,  7]],
        [12, 13, 14, 15]]])
                                          [[ 8, 12],
                                           [ 9, 13],
                                           [10, 14],
                                           [11, 15]]])
```

swapaxes similarly returns a view on the data without making a copy.

Universal Functions: Fast Element-wise Array Functions

A universal function, or *ufunc*, is a function that performs elementwise operations on data in ndarrays. You can think of them as fast vectorized wrappers for simple functions that take one or more scalar values and produce one or more scalar results.

Many ufuncs are simple elementwise transformations, like `sqrt` or `exp`:

```
In [120]: arr = np.arange(10)

In [121]: np.sqrt(arr)
Out[121]:
array([ 0.    , 1.    , 1.4142, 1.7321, 2.    , 2.2361, 2.4495,
        2.6458, 2.8284, 3.    ])

In [122]: np.exp(arr)
Out[122]:
array([    1.    ,    2.7183,    7.3891,   20.0855,   54.5982,
         148.4132,  403.4288, 1096.6332, 2980.958 , 8103.0839])
```

These are referred to as *unary* ufuncs. Others, such as `add` or `maximum`, take 2 arrays (thus, *binary* ufuncs) and return a single array as the result:

```
In [123]: x = np.random.randn(8)

In [124]: y = np.random.randn(8)

In [125]: x
Out[125]:
array([ 0.0749,  0.0974,  0.2002, -0.2551,  0.4655,  0.9222,  0.446 ,
       -0.9337])

In [126]: y
Out[126]:
array([ 0.267 , -1.1131, -0.3361,  0.6117, -1.2323,  0.4788,  0.4315,
       -0.7147])

In [127]: np.maximum(x, y) # element-wise maximum
Out[127]:
array([ 0.267 ,  0.0974,  0.2002,  0.6117,  0.4655,  0.9222,  0.446 ,
       -0.7147])
```

While not common, a ufunc can return multiple arrays. `modf` is one example, a vectorized version of the built-in Python `divmod`: it returns the fractional and integral parts of a floating point array:

```
In [128]: arr = randn(7) * 5

In [129]: np.modf(arr)
Out[129]:
(array([-0.6808,  0.0636, -0.386 ,  0.1393, -0.8806,  0.9363, -0.883 ]),
 array([-2.,  4., -3.,  5., -3.,  3., -6.]))
```

See Table 4-3 and Table 4-4 for a listing of available ufuncs.

Table 4-3. Unary ufuncs

Function	Description
abs, fabs	Compute the absolute value element-wise for integer, floating point, or complex values. Use fabs as a faster alternative for non-complex-valued data
sqrt	Compute the square root of each element. Equivalent to arr ** 0.5
square	Compute the square of each element. Equivalent to arr ** 2
exp	Compute the exponent e^x of each element
log, log10, log2, log1p	Natural logarithm (base e), log base 10, log base 2, and log(1 + x), respectively
sign	Compute the sign of each element: 1 (positive), 0 (zero), or -1 (negative)
ceil	Compute the ceiling of each element, i.e. the smallest integer greater than or equal to each element
floor	Compute the floor of each element, i.e. the largest integer less than or equal to each element
rint	Round elements to the nearest integer, preserving the dtype
modf	Return fractional and integral parts of array as separate array
isnan	Return boolean array indicating whether each value is NaN (Not a Number)
isfinite, isinf	Return boolean array indicating whether each element is finite (non-inf, non-NaN) or infinite, respectively
cos, cosh, sin, sinh, tan, tanh	Regular and hyperbolic trigonometric functions
arccos, arccosh, arcsin, arcsinh, arctan, arctanh	Inverse trigonometric functions
logical_not	Compute truth value of not x element-wise. Equivalent to -arr.

Table 4-4. Binary universal functions

Function	Description
add	Add corresponding elements in arrays
subtract	Subtract elements in second array from first array
multiply	Multiply array elements
divide, floor_divide	Divide or floor divide (truncating the remainder)
power	Raise elements in first array to powers indicated in second array
maximum, fmax	Element-wise maximum. fmax ignores NaN
minimum, fmin	Element-wise minimum. fmin ignores NaN
mod	Element-wise modulus (remainder of division)
copysign	Copy sign of values in second argument to values in first argument

Function	Description
greater, greater_equal, less, less_equal, equal, not_equal	Perform element-wise comparison, yielding boolean array. Equivalent to infix operators >, >=, <, <=, ==, !=
logical_and, logical_or, logical_xor	Compute element-wise truth value of logical operation. Equivalent to infix operators & |, ^

Data Processing Using Arrays

Using NumPy arrays enables you to express many kinds of data processing tasks as concise array expressions that might otherwise require writing loops. This practice of replacing explicit loops with array expressions is commonly referred to as *vectorization*. In general, vectorized array operations will often be one or two (or more) orders of magnitude faster than their pure Python equivalents, with the biggest impact in any kind of numerical computations. Later, in Chapter 12, I will explain *broadcasting*, a powerful method for vectorizing computations.

As a simple example, suppose we wished to evaluate the function sqrt(x^2 + y^2) across a regular grid of values. The np.meshgrid function takes two 1D arrays and produces two 2D matrices corresponding to all pairs of (x, y) in the two arrays:

```
In [130]: points = np.arange(-5, 5, 0.01) # 1000 equally spaced points

In [131]: xs, ys = np.meshgrid(points, points)

In [132]: ys
Out[132]:
array([[-5.  , -5.  , -5.  , ..., -5.  , -5.  , -5.  ],
       [-4.99, -4.99, -4.99, ..., -4.99, -4.99, -4.99],
       [-4.98, -4.98, -4.98, ..., -4.98, -4.98, -4.98],
       ...,
       [ 4.97,  4.97,  4.97, ...,  4.97,  4.97,  4.97],
       [ 4.98,  4.98,  4.98, ...,  4.98,  4.98,  4.98],
       [ 4.99,  4.99,  4.99, ...,  4.99,  4.99,  4.99]])
```

Now, evaluating the function is a simple matter of writing the same expression you would write with two points:

```
In [134]: import matplotlib.pyplot as plt

In [135]: z = np.sqrt(xs ** 2 + ys ** 2)

In [136]: z
Out[136]:
array([[ 7.0711,  7.064 ,  7.0569, ...,  7.0499,  7.0569,  7.064 ],
       [ 7.064 ,  7.0569,  7.0499, ...,  7.0428,  7.0499,  7.0569],
       [ 7.0569,  7.0499,  7.0428, ...,  7.0357,  7.0428,  7.0499],
       ...,
       [ 7.0499,  7.0428,  7.0357, ...,  7.0286,  7.0357,  7.0428],
       [ 7.0569,  7.0499,  7.0428, ...,  7.0357,  7.0428,  7.0499],
       [ 7.064 ,  7.0569,  7.0499, ...,  7.0428,  7.0499,  7.0569]])
```

```
In [137]: plt.imshow(z, cmap=plt.cm.gray); plt.colorbar()
Out[137]: <matplotlib.colorbar.Colorbar instance at 0x4e46d40>

In [138]: plt.title("Image plot of $\sqrt{x^2 + y^2}$ for a grid of values")
Out[138]: <matplotlib.text.Text at 0x4565790>
```

See Figure 4-3. Here I used the matplotlib function imshow to create an image plot from a 2D array of function values.

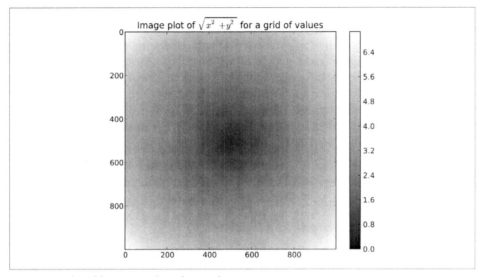

Figure 4-3. Plot of function evaluated on grid

Expressing Conditional Logic as Array Operations

The numpy.where function is a vectorized version of the ternary expression x if condi tion else y. Suppose we had a boolean array and two arrays of values:

```
In [140]: xarr = np.array([1.1, 1.2, 1.3, 1.4, 1.5])

In [141]: yarr = np.array([2.1, 2.2, 2.3, 2.4, 2.5])

In [142]: cond = np.array([True, False, True, True, False])
```

Suppose we wanted to take a value from xarr whenever the corresponding value in cond is True otherwise take the value from yarr. A list comprehension doing this might look like:

```
In [143]: result = [(x if c else y)
   .....:           for x, y, c in zip(xarr, yarr, cond)]

In [144]: result
Out[144]: [1.1000000000000001, 2.2000000000000002, 1.3, 1.3999999999999999, 2.5]
```

This has multiple problems. First, it will not be very fast for large arrays (because all the work is being done in pure Python). Secondly, it will not work with multidimensional arrays. With np.where you can write this very concisely:

```
In [145]: result = np.where(cond, xarr, yarr)

In [146]: result
Out[146]: array([ 1.1,  2.2,  1.3,  1.4,  2.5])
```

The second and third arguments to np.where don't need to be arrays; one or both of them can be scalars. A typical use of where in data analysis is to produce a new array of values based on another array. Suppose you had a matrix of randomly generated data and you wanted to replace all positive values with 2 and all negative values with -2. This is very easy to do with np.where:

```
In [147]: arr = randn(4, 4)

In [148]: arr
Out[148]:
array([[ 0.6372,  2.2043,  1.7904,  0.0752],
       [-1.5926, -1.1536,  0.4413,  0.3483],
       [-0.1798,  0.3299,  0.7827, -0.7585],
       [ 0.5857,  0.1619,  1.3583, -1.3865]])

In [149]: np.where(arr > 0, 2, -2)
Out[149]:
array([[ 2,  2,  2,  2],
       [-2, -2,  2,  2],
       [-2,  2,  2, -2],
       [ 2,  2,  2, -2]])

In [150]: np.where(arr > 0, 2, arr) # set only positive values to 2
Out[150]:
array([[ 2.    ,  2.    ,  2.    ,  2.    ],
       [-1.5926, -1.1536,  2.    ,  2.    ],
       [-0.1798,  2.    ,  2.    , -0.7585],
       [ 2.    ,  2.    ,  2.    , -1.3865]])
```

The arrays passed to where can be more than just equal sizes array or scalars.

With some cleverness you can use where to express more complicated logic; consider this example where I have two boolean arrays, cond1 and cond2, and wish to assign a different value for each of the 4 possible pairs of boolean values:

```
result = []
for i in range(n):
    if cond1[i] and cond2[i]:
        result.append(0)
    elif cond1[i]:
        result.append(1)
    elif cond2[i]:
        result.append(2)
    else:
        result.append(3)
```

While perhaps not immediately obvious, this for loop can be converted into a nested where expression:

```
np.where(cond1 & cond2, 0,
        np.where(cond1, 1,
                 np.where(cond2, 2, 3)))
```

In this particular example, we can also take advantage of the fact that boolean values are treated as 0 or 1 in calculations, so this could alternatively be expressed (though a bit more cryptically) as an arithmetic operation:

```
result = 1 * (cond1 & -cond2) + 2 * (cond2 & -cond1) + 3 * -(cond1 | cond2)
```

Mathematical and Statistical Methods

A set of mathematical functions which compute statistics about an entire array or about the data along an axis are accessible as array methods. Aggregations (often called *reductions*) like sum, mean, and standard deviation std can either be used by calling the array instance method or using the top level NumPy function:

```
In [151]: arr = np.random.randn(5, 4) # normally-distributed data

In [152]: arr.mean()
Out[152]: 0.062814911084854597

In [153]: np.mean(arr)
Out[153]: 0.062814911084854597

In [154]: arr.sum()
Out[154]: 1.2562982216970919
```

Functions like mean and sum take an optional axis argument which computes the statistic over the given axis, resulting in an array with one fewer dimension:

```
In [155]: arr.mean(axis=1)
Out[155]: array([-1.2833,  0.2844,  0.6574,  0.6743, -0.0187])

In [156]: arr.sum(0)
Out[156]: array([-3.1003, -1.6189,  1.4044,  4.5712])
```

Other methods like cumsum and cumprod do not aggregate, instead producing an array of the intermediate results:

```
In [157]: arr = np.array([[0, 1, 2], [3, 4, 5], [6, 7, 8]])
```

```
In [158]: arr.cumsum(0)          In [159]: arr.cumprod(1)
Out[158]:                         Out[159]:
array([[ 0,  1,  2],              array([[  0,   0,   0],
       [ 3,  5,  7],                     [  3,  12,  60],
       [ 9, 12, 15]])                    [  6,  42, 336]])
```

See Table 4-5 for a full listing. We'll see many examples of these methods in action in later chapters.

Table 4-5. Basic array statistical methods

Method	Description
sum	Sum of all the elements in the array or along an axis. Zero-length arrays have sum 0.
mean	Arithmetic mean. Zero-length arrays have NaN mean.
std, var	Standard deviation and variance, respectively, with optional degrees of freedom adjustment (default denominator n).
min, max	Minimum and maximum.
argmin, argmax	Indices of minimum and maximum elements, respectively.
cumsum	Cumulative sum of elements starting from 0
cumprod	Cumulative product of elements starting from 1

Methods for Boolean Arrays

Boolean values are coerced to 1 (True) and 0 (False) in the above methods. Thus, sum is often used as a means of counting True values in a boolean array:

```
In [160]: arr = randn(100)

In [161]: (arr > 0).sum() # Number of positive values
Out[161]: 44
```

There are two additional methods, any and all, useful especially for boolean arrays. any tests whether one or more values in an array is True, while all checks if every value is True:

```
In [162]: bools = np.array([False, False, True, False])

In [163]: bools.any()
Out[163]: True

In [164]: bools.all()
Out[164]: False
```

These methods also work with non-boolean arrays, where non-zero elements evaluate to True.

Sorting

Like Python's built-in list type, NumPy arrays can be sorted in-place using the sort method:

```
In [165]: arr = randn(8)

In [166]: arr
Out[166]:
array([ 0.6903,  0.4678,  0.0968, -0.1349,  0.9879,  0.0185, -1.3147,
       -0.5425])

In [167]: arr.sort()
```

```
In [168]: arr
Out[168]:
array([-1.3147, -0.5425, -0.1349,  0.0185,  0.0968,  0.4678,  0.6903,
        0.9879])
```

Multidimensional arrays can have each 1D section of values sorted in-place along an axis by passing the axis number to sort:

```
In [169]: arr = randn(5, 3)

In [170]: arr
Out[170]:
array([[-0.7139, -1.6331, -0.4959],
       [ 0.8236, -1.3132, -0.1935],
       [-1.6748,  3.0336, -0.863 ],
       [-0.3161,  0.5362, -2.468 ],
       [ 0.9058,  1.1184, -1.0516]])

In [171]: arr.sort(1)

In [172]: arr
Out[172]:
array([[-1.6331, -0.7139, -0.4959],
       [-1.3132, -0.1935,  0.8236],
       [-1.6748, -0.863 ,  3.0336],
       [-2.468 , -0.3161,  0.5362],
       [-1.0516,  0.9058,  1.1184]])
```

The top level method np.sort returns a sorted copy of an array instead of modifying the array in place. A quick-and-dirty way to compute the quantiles of an array is to sort it and select the value at a particular rank:

```
In [173]: large_arr = randn(1000)

In [174]: large_arr.sort()

In [175]: large_arr[int(0.05 * len(large_arr))] # 5% quantile
Out[175]: -1.5791023260896004
```

For more details on using NumPy's sorting methods, and more advanced techniques like indirect sorts, see Chapter 12. Several other kinds of data manipulations related to sorting (for example, sorting a table of data by one or more columns) are also to be found in pandas.

Unique and Other Set Logic

NumPy has some basic set operations for one-dimensional ndarrays. Probably the most commonly used one is np.unique, which returns the sorted unique values in an array:

```
In [176]: names = np.array(['Bob', 'Joe', 'Will', 'Bob', 'Will', 'Joe', 'Joe'])

In [177]: np.unique(names)
Out[177]:
```

```
array(['Bob', 'Joe', 'Will'],
      dtype='|S4')

In [178]: ints = np.array([3, 3, 3, 2, 2, 1, 1, 4, 4])

In [179]: np.unique(ints)
Out[179]: array([1, 2, 3, 4])
```

Contrast np.unique with the pure Python alternative:

```
In [180]: sorted(set(names))
Out[180]: ['Bob', 'Joe', 'Will']
```

Another function, np.in1d, tests membership of the values in one array in another, returning a boolean array:

```
In [181]: values = np.array([6, 0, 0, 3, 2, 5, 6])

In [182]: np.in1d(values, [2, 3, 6])
Out[182]: array([ True, False, False,  True,  True, False,  True], dtype=bool)
```

See Table 4-6 for a listing of set functions in NumPy.

Table 4-6. Array set operations

Method	Description
unique(x)	Compute the sorted, unique elements in x
intersect1d(x, y)	Compute the sorted, common elements in x and y
union1d(x, y)	Compute the sorted union of elements
in1d(x, y)	Compute a boolean array indicating whether each element of x is contained in y
setdiff1d(x, y)	Set difference, elements in x that are not in y
setxor1d(x, y)	Set symmetric differences; elements that are in either of the arrays, but not both

File Input and Output with Arrays

NumPy is able to save and load data to and from disk either in text or binary format. In later chapters you will learn about tools in pandas for reading tabular data into memory.

Storing Arrays on Disk in Binary Format

np.save and np.load are the two workhorse functions for efficiently saving and loading array data on disk. Arrays are saved by default in an uncompressed raw binary format with file extension .npy.

```
In [183]: arr = np.arange(10)

In [184]: np.save('some_array', arr)
```

If the file path does not already end in .npy, the extension will be appended. The array on disk can then be loaded using np.load:

```
In [185]: np.load('some_array.npy')
Out[185]: array([0, 1, 2, 3, 4, 5, 6, 7, 8, 9])
```

You save multiple arrays in a zip archive using np.savez and passing the arrays as keyword arguments:

```
In [186]: np.savez('array_archive.npz', a=arr, b=arr)
```

When loading an .npz file, you get back a dict-like object which loads the individual arrays lazily:

```
In [187]: arch = np.load('array_archive.npz')
```

```
In [188]: arch['b']
Out[188]: array([0, 1, 2, 3, 4, 5, 6, 7, 8, 9])
```

Saving and Loading Text Files

Loading text from files is a fairly standard task. The landscape of file reading and writing functions in Python can be a bit confusing for a newcomer, so I will focus mainly on the read_csv and read_table functions in pandas. It will at times be useful to load data into vanilla NumPy arrays using np.loadtxt or the more specialized np.genfromtxt.

These functions have many options allowing you to specify different delimiters, converter functions for certain columns, skipping rows, and other things. Take a simple case of a comma-separated file (CSV) like this:

```
In [191]: !cat array_ex.txt
0.580052,0.186730,1.040717,1.134411
0.194163,-0.636917,-0.938659,0.124094
-0.126410,0.268607,-0.695724,0.047428
-1.484413,0.004176,-0.744203,0.005487
2.302869,0.200131,1.670238,-1.881090
-0.193230,1.047233,0.482803,0.960334
```

This can be loaded into a 2D array like so:

```
In [192]: arr = np.loadtxt('array_ex.txt', delimiter=',')
```

```
In [193]: arr
Out[193]:
array([[ 0.5801,  0.1867,  1.0407,  1.1344],
       [ 0.1942, -0.6369, -0.9387,  0.1241],
       [-0.1264,  0.2686, -0.6957,  0.0474],
       [-1.4844,  0.0042, -0.7442,  0.0055],
       [ 2.3029,  0.2001,  1.6702, -1.8811],
       [-0.1932,  1.0472,  0.4828,  0.9603]])
```

np.savetxt performs the inverse operation: writing an array to a delimited text file. genfromtxt is similar to loadtxt but is geared for structured arrays and missing data handling; see Chapter 12 for more on structured arrays.

For more on file reading and writing, especially tabular or spreadsheet-like data, see the later chapters involving pandas and DataFrame objects.

Linear Algebra

Linear algebra, like matrix multiplication, decompositions, determinants, and other square matrix math, is an important part of any array library. Unlike some languages like MATLAB, multiplying two two-dimensional arrays with * is an element-wise product instead of a matrix dot product. As such, there is a function dot, both an array method, and a function in the numpy namespace, for matrix multiplication:

```
In [194]: x = np.array([[1., 2., 3.], [4., 5., 6.]])

In [195]: y = np.array([[6., 23.], [-1, 7], [8, 9]])

In [196]: x                    In [197]: y
Out[196]:                      Out[197]:
array([[ 1.,   2.,   3.],      array([[  6.,   23.],
       [ 4.,   5.,   6.]])            [ -1.,    7.],
                                      [  8.,    9.]])

In [198]: x.dot(y)  # equivalently np.dot(x, y)
Out[198]:
array([[  28.,    64.],
       [  67.,   181.]])
```

A matrix product between a 2D array and a suitably sized 1D array results in a 1D array:

```
In [199]: np.dot(x, np.ones(3))
Out[199]: array([ 6.,  15.])
```

numpy.linalg has a standard set of matrix decompositions and things like inverse and determinant. These are implemented under the hood using the same industry-standard Fortran libraries used in other languages like MATLAB and R, such as like BLAS, LA-PACK, or possibly (depending on your NumPy build) the Intel MKL:

```
In [201]: from numpy.linalg import inv, qr

In [202]: X = randn(5, 5)

In [203]: mat = X.T.dot(X)

In [204]: inv(mat)
Out[204]:
array([[ 3.0361, -0.1808, -0.6878, -2.8285, -1.1911],
       [-0.1808,  0.5035,  0.1215,  0.6702,  0.0956],
       [-0.6878,  0.1215,  0.2904,  0.8081,  0.3049],
       [-2.8285,  0.6702,  0.8081,  3.4152,  1.1557],
       [-1.1911,  0.0956,  0.3049,  1.1557,  0.6051]])

In [205]: mat.dot(inv(mat))
```

```
Out[205]:
array([[ 1.,  0.,  0.,  0., -0.],
       [ 0.,  1., -0.,  0.,  0.],
       [ 0., -0.,  1.,  0.,  0.],
       [ 0., -0., -0.,  1., -0.],
       [ 0.,  0.,  0.,  0.,  1.]])

In [206]: q, r = qr(mat)

In [207]: r
Out[207]:
array([[ -6.9271,   7.389 ,   6.1227,  -7.1163,  -4.9215],
       [  0.    ,  -3.9735,  -0.8671,   2.9747,  -5.7402],
       [  0.    ,   0.    , -10.2681,   1.8909,   1.6079],
       [  0.    ,   0.    ,   0.    ,  -1.2996,   3.3577],
       [  0.    ,   0.    ,   0.    ,   0.    ,   0.5571]])
```

See Table 4-7 for a list of some of the most commonly-used linear algebra functions.

> The scientific Python community is hopeful that there may be a matrix multiplication infix operator implemented someday, providing syntactically nicer alternative to using `np.dot`. But for now this is the way.

Table 4-7. Commonly-used numpy.linalg functions

Function	Description
diag	Return the diagonal (or off-diagonal) elements of a square matrix as a 1D array, or convert a 1D array into a square matrix with zeros on the off-diagonal
dot	Matrix multiplication
trace	Compute the sum of the diagonal elements
det	Compute the matrix determinant
eig	Compute the eigenvalues and eigenvectors of a square matrix
inv	Compute the inverse of a square matrix
pinv	Compute the Moore-Penrose pseudo-inverse inverse of a matrix
qr	Compute the QR decomposition
svd	Compute the singular value decomposition (SVD)
solve	Solve the linear system Ax = b for x, where A is a square matrix
lstsq	Compute the least-squares solution to Ax = b

Random Number Generation

The `numpy.random` module supplements the built-in Python `random` with functions for efficiently generating whole arrays of sample values from many kinds of probability distributions. For example, you can get a 4 by 4 array of samples from the standard normal distribution using `normal`:

```
In [208]: samples = np.random.normal(size=(4, 4))

In [209]: samples
Out[209]:
array([[ 0.1241,  0.3026,  0.5238,  0.0009],
       [ 1.3438, -0.7135, -0.8312, -2.3702],
       [-1.8608, -0.8608,  0.5601, -1.2659],
       [ 0.1198, -1.0635,  0.3329, -2.3594]])
```

Python's built-in `random` module, by contrast, only samples one value at a time. As you can see from this benchmark, `numpy.random` is well over an order of magnitude faster for generating very large samples:

```
In [210]: from random import normalvariate

In [211]: N = 1000000

In [212]: %timeit samples = [normalvariate(0, 1) for _ in xrange(N)]
1 loops, best of 3: 1.33 s per loop

In [213]: %timeit np.random.normal(size=N)
10 loops, best of 3: 57.7 ms per loop
```

See Table 4-8 for a partial list of functions available in `numpy.random`. I'll give some examples of leveraging these functions' ability to generate large arrays of samples all at once in the next section.

Table 4-8. Partial list of numpy.random functions

Function	Description
seed	Seed the random number generator
permutation	Return a random permutation of a sequence, or return a permuted range
shuffle	Randomly permute a sequence in place
rand	Draw samples from a uniform distribution
randint	Draw random integers from a given low-to-high range
randn	Draw samples from a normal distribution with mean 0 and standard deviation 1 (MATLAB-like interface)
binomial	Draw samples from a binomial distribution
normal	Draw samples from a normal (Gaussian) distribution
beta	Draw samples from a beta distribution
chisquare	Draw samples from a chi-square distribution
gamma	Draw samples from a gamma distribution
uniform	Draw samples from a uniform [0, 1) distribution

Example: Random Walks

An illustrative application of utilizing array operations is in the simulation of random walks. Let's first consider a simple random walk starting at 0 with steps of 1 and -1 occurring with equal probability. A pure Python way to implement a single random walk with 1,000 steps using the built-in random module:

```
import random
position = 0
walk = [position]
steps = 1000
for i in xrange(steps):
    step = 1 if random.randint(0, 1) else -1
    position += step
    walk.append(position)
```

See Figure 4-4 for an example plot of the first 100 values on one of these random walks.

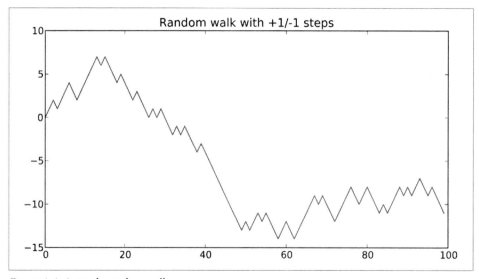

Figure 4-4. A simple random walk

You might make the observation that walk is simply the cumulative sum of the random steps and could be evaluated as an array expression. Thus, I use the np.random module to draw 1,000 coin flips at once, set these to 1 and -1, and compute the cumulative sum:

```
In [215]: nsteps = 1000

In [216]: draws = np.random.randint(0, 2, size=nsteps)

In [217]: steps = np.where(draws > 0, 1, -1)

In [218]: walk = steps.cumsum()
```

From this we can begin to extract statistics like the minimum and maximum value along the walk's trajectory:

```
In [219]: walk.min()        In [220]: walk.max()
Out[219]: -3                Out[220]: 31
```

A more complicated statistic is the *first crossing time*, the step at which the random walk reaches a particular value. Here we might want to know how long it took the random walk to get at least 10 steps away from the origin 0 in either direction. np.abs(walk) >= 10 gives us a boolean array indicating where the walk has reached or exceeded 10, but we want the index of the *first* 10 or -10. Turns out this can be computed using argmax, which returns the first index of the maximum value in the boolean array (True is the maximum value):

```
In [221]: (np.abs(walk) >= 10).argmax()
Out[221]: 37
```

Note that using argmax here is not always efficient because it always makes a full scan of the array. In this special case once a True is observed we know it to be the maximum value.

Simulating Many Random Walks at Once

If your goal was to simulate many random walks, say 5,000 of them, you can generate all of the random walks with minor modifications to the above code. The numpy.ran dom functions if passed a 2-tuple will generate a 2D array of draws, and we can compute the cumulative sum across the rows to compute all 5,000 random walks in one shot:

```
In [222]: nwalks = 5000

In [223]: nsteps = 1000

In [224]: draws = np.random.randint(0, 2, size=(nwalks, nsteps)) # 0 or 1

In [225]: steps = np.where(draws > 0, 1, -1)

In [226]: walks = steps.cumsum(1)

In [227]: walks
Out[227]:
array([[  1,   0,   1, ...,   8,   7,   8],
       [  1,   0,  -1, ...,  34,  33,  32],
       [  1,   0,  -1, ...,   4,   5,   4],
       ...,
       [  1,   2,   1, ...,  24,  25,  26],
       [  1,   2,   3, ...,  14,  13,  14],
       [ -1,  -2,  -3, ..., -24, -23, -22]])
```

Now, we can compute the maximum and minimum values obtained over all of the walks:

```
In [228]: walks.max()        In [229]: walks.min()
Out[228]: 138                Out[229]: -133
```

Out of these walks, let's compute the minimum crossing time to 30 or -30. This is slightly tricky because not all 5,000 of them reach 30. We can check this using the any method:

```
In [230]: hits30 = (np.abs(walks) >= 30).any(1)
```

```
In [231]: hits30
Out[231]: array([False, True, False, ..., False, True, False], dtype=bool)
```

```
In [232]: hits30.sum() # Number that hit 30 or -30
Out[232]: 3410
```

We can use this boolean array to select out the rows of walks that actually cross the absolute 30 level and call argmax across axis 1 to get the crossing times:

```
In [233]: crossing_times = (np.abs(walks[hits30]) >= 30).argmax(1)
```

```
In [234]: crossing_times.mean()
Out[234]: 498.88973607038122
```

Feel free to experiment with other distributions for the steps other than equal sized coin flips. You need only use a different random number generation function, like normal to generate normally distributed steps with some mean and standard deviation:

```
In [235]: steps = np.random.normal(loc=0, scale=0.25,
   .....:                          size=(nwalks, nsteps))
```

CHAPTER 5

Getting Started with pandas

pandas will be the primary library of interest throughout much of the rest of the book. It contains high-level data structures and manipulation tools designed to make data analysis fast and easy in Python. pandas is built on top of NumPy and makes it easy to use in NumPy-centric applications.

As a bit of background, I started building pandas in early 2008 during my tenure at AQR, a quantitative investment management firm. At the time, I had a distinct set of requirements that were not well-addressed by any single tool at my disposal:

- Data structures with labeled axes supporting automatic or explicit data alignment. This prevents common errors resulting from misaligned data and working with differently-indexed data coming from different sources.
- Integrated time series functionality.
- The same data structures handle both time series data and non-time series data.
- Arithmetic operations and reductions (like summing across an axis) would pass on the metadata (axis labels).
- Flexible handling of missing data.
- Merge and other relational operations found in popular database databases (SQL-based, for example).

I wanted to be able to do all of these things in one place, preferably in a language well-suited to general purpose software development. Python was a good candidate language for this, but at that time there was not an integrated set of data structures and tools providing this functionality.

Over the last four years, pandas has matured into a quite large library capable of solving a much broader set of data handling problems than I ever anticipated, but it has expanded in its scope without compromising the simplicity and ease-of-use that I desired from the very beginning. I hope that after reading this book, you will find it to be just as much of an indispensable tool as I do.

Throughout the rest of the book, I use the following import conventions for pandas:

```
In [1]: from pandas import Series, DataFrame

In [2]: import pandas as pd
```

Thus, whenever you see pd. in code, it's referring to pandas. Series and DataFrame are used so much that I find it easier to import them into the local namespace.

Introduction to pandas Data Structures

To get started with pandas, you will need to get comfortable with its two workhorse data structures: *Series* and *DataFrame*. While they are not a universal solution for every problem, they provide a solid, easy-to-use basis for most applications.

Series

A Series is a one-dimensional array-like object containing an array of data (of any NumPy data type) and an associated array of data labels, called its *index*. The simplest Series is formed from only an array of data:

```
In [4]: obj = Series([4, 7, -5, 3])

In [5]: obj
Out[5]:
0    4
1    7
2   -5
3    3
dtype: int64
```

The string representation of a Series displayed interactively shows the index on the left and the values on the right. Since we did not specify an index for the data, a default one consisting of the integers 0 through N - 1 (where N is the length of the data) is created. You can get the array representation and index object of the Series via its values and index attributes, respectively:

```
In [6]: obj.values
Out[6]: array([ 4,  7, -5,  3])

In [7]: obj.index
Out[7]: Int64Index([0, 1, 2, 3], dtype='int64')
```

Often it will be desirable to create a Series with an index identifying each data point:

```
In [8]: obj2 = Series([4, 7, -5, 3], index=['d', 'b', 'a', 'c'])

In [9]: obj2
Out[9]:
d    4
b    7
a   -5
c    3
dtype: int64
```

```
In [10]: obj2.index
Out[10]: Index([u'd', u'b', u'a', u'c'], dtype='object')
```

Compared with a regular NumPy array, you can use values in the index when selecting single values or a set of values:

```
In [11]: obj2['a']
Out[11]: -5

In [12]: obj2['d'] = 6

In [13]: obj2[['c', 'a', 'd']]
Out[13]:
c    3
a   -5
d    6
dtype: int64
```

NumPy array operations, such as filtering with a boolean array, scalar multiplication, or applying math functions, will preserve the index-value link:

```
In [14]: obj2[obj2 > 0]    In [15]: obj2 * 2    In [16]: np.exp(obj2)
Out[14]:                   Out[15]:             Out[16]:
d    6                     d    12              d     403.428793
b    7                     b    14              b    1096.633158
c    3                     a   -10              a       0.006738
dtype: int64               c     6              c      20.085537
                           dtype: int64         dtype: float64
```

Another way to think about a Series is as a fixed-length, ordered dict, as it is a mapping of index values to data values. It can be substituted into many functions that expect a dict:

```
In [17]: 'b' in obj2
Out[17]: True

In [18]: 'e' in obj2
Out[18]: False
```

Should you have data contained in a Python dict, you can create a Series from it by passing the dict:

```
In [19]: sdata = {'Ohio': 35000, 'Texas': 71000, 'Oregon': 16000, 'Utah': 5000}

In [20]: obj3 = Series(sdata)

In [21]: obj3
Out[21]:
Ohio      35000
Oregon    16000
Texas     71000
Utah       5000
dtype: int64
```

When only passing a dict, the index in the resulting Series will have the dict's keys in sorted order.

```
In [22]: states = ['California', 'Ohio', 'Oregon', 'Texas']

In [23]: obj4 = Series(sdata, index=states)

In [24]: obj4
Out[24]:
California      NaN
Ohio         35000
Oregon       16000
Texas        71000
dtype: float64
```

In this case, 3 values found in sdata were placed in the appropriate locations, but since no value for 'California' was found, it appears as NaN (not a number) which is considered in pandas to mark missing or *NA* values. I will use the terms "missing" or "NA" to refer to missing data. The isnull and notnull functions in pandas should be used to detect missing data:

```
In [25]: pd.isnull(obj4)        In [26]: pd.notnull(obj4)
Out[25]:                        Out[26]:
California      True            California     False
Ohio          False            Ohio            True
Oregon        False            Oregon          True
Texas         False            Texas           True
dtype: bool                     dtype: bool
```

Series also has these as instance methods:

```
In [27]: obj4.isnull()
Out[27]:
California      True
Ohio          False
Oregon        False
Texas         False
dtype: bool
```

I discuss working with missing data in more detail later in this chapter.

A critical Series feature for many applications is that it automatically aligns differently-indexed data in arithmetic operations:

```
In [28]: obj3            In [29]: obj4
Out[28]:                 Out[29]:
Ohio     35000          California      NaN
Oregon   16000          Ohio         35000
Texas    71000          Oregon       16000
Utah      5000          Texas        71000
dtype: int64            dtype: float64

In [30]: obj3 + obj4
Out[30]:
California      NaN
Ohio         70000
```

```
Oregon        32000
Texas        142000
Utah            NaN
dtype: float64
```

Data alignment features are addressed as a separate topic.

Both the Series object itself and its index have a name attribute, which integrates with other key areas of pandas functionality:

```
In [31]: obj4.name = 'population'

In [32]: obj4.index.name = 'state'

In [33]: obj4
Out[33]:
state
California      NaN
Ohio          35000
Oregon        16000
Texas         71000
Name: population, dtype: float64
```

A Series's index can be altered in place by assignment:

```
In [34]: obj.index = ['Bob', 'Steve', 'Jeff', 'Ryan']

In [35]: obj
Out[35]:
Bob      4
Steve    7
Jeff    -5
Ryan     3
dtype: int64
```

DataFrame

A DataFrame represents a tabular, spreadsheet-like data structure containing an or-dered collection of columns, each of which can be a different value type (numeric, string, boolean, etc.). The DataFrame has both a row and column index; it can be thought of as a dict of Series (one for all sharing the same index). Compared with other such DataFrame-like structures you may have used before (like R's data.frame), row-oriented and column-oriented operations in DataFrame are treated roughly symmet-rically. Under the hood, the data is stored as one or more two-dimensional blocks rather than a list, dict, or some other collection of one-dimensional arrays. The exact details of DataFrame's internals are far outside the scope of this book.

> While DataFrame stores the data internally in a two-dimensional for-mat, you can easily represent much higher-dimensional data in a tabular format using hierarchical indexing, a subject of a later section and a key ingredient in many of the more advanced data-handling features in pan-das.

There are numerous ways to construct a DataFrame, though one of the most common is from a dict of equal-length lists or NumPy arrays

```
data = {'state': ['Ohio', 'Ohio', 'Ohio', 'Nevada', 'Nevada'],
        'year': [2000, 2001, 2002, 2001, 2002],
        'pop': [1.5, 1.7, 3.6, 2.4, 2.9]}
frame = DataFrame(data)
```

The resulting DataFrame will have its index assigned automatically as with Series, and the columns are placed in sorted order:

```
In [37]: frame
Out[37]:
   pop   state  year
0  1.5    Ohio  2000
1  1.7    Ohio  2001
2  3.6    Ohio  2002
3  2.4  Nevada  2001
4  2.9  Nevada  2002
```

If you specify a sequence of columns, the DataFrame's columns will be exactly what you pass:

```
In [38]: DataFrame(data, columns=['year', 'state', 'pop'])
Out[38]:
   year   state  pop
0  2000    Ohio  1.5
1  2001    Ohio  1.7
2  2002    Ohio  3.6
3  2001  Nevada  2.4
4  2002  Nevada  2.9
```

As with Series, if you pass a column that isn't contained in data, it will appear with NA values in the result:

```
In [39]: frame2 = DataFrame(data, columns=['year', 'state', 'pop', 'debt'],
   ....:                    index=['one', 'two', 'three', 'four', 'five'])

In [40]: frame2
Out[40]:
       year   state  pop debt
one    2000    Ohio  1.5  NaN
two    2001    Ohio  1.7  NaN
three  2002    Ohio  3.6  NaN
four   2001  Nevada  2.4  NaN
five   2002  Nevada  2.9  NaN

In [41]: frame2.columns
Out[41]: Index([u'year', u'state', u'pop', u'debt'], dtype='object')
```

A column in a DataFrame can be retrieved as a Series either by dict-like notation or by attribute:

```
In [42]: frame2['state']        In [43]: frame2.year
Out[42]:                        Out[43]:
one        Ohio                 one        2000
```

```
two        Ohio              two      2001
three      Ohio              three    2002
four      Nevada             four     2001
five      Nevada             five     2002
Name: state, dtype: object   Name: year, dtype: int64
```

Note that the returned Series have the same index as the DataFrame, and their name attribute has been appropriately set.

Rows can also be retrieved by position or name by a couple of methods, such as the ix indexing field (much more on this later):

```
In [44]: frame2.ix['three']
Out[44]:
year     2002
state    Ohio
pop      3.6
debt     NaN
Name: three, dtype: object
```

Columns can be modified by assignment. For example, the empty 'debt' column could be assigned a scalar value or an array of values:

```
In [45]: frame2['debt'] = 16.5

In [46]: frame2
Out[46]:
       year   state   pop  debt
one    2000    Ohio   1.5  16.5
two    2001    Ohio   1.7  16.5
three  2002    Ohio   3.6  16.5
four   2001  Nevada   2.4  16.5
five   2002  Nevada   2.9  16.5

In [47]: frame2['debt'] = np.arange(5.)

In [48]: frame2
Out[48]:
       year   state   pop  debt
one    2000    Ohio   1.5     0
two    2001    Ohio   1.7     1
three  2002    Ohio   3.6     2
four   2001  Nevada   2.4     3
five   2002  Nevada   2.9     4
```

When assigning lists or arrays to a column, the value's length must match the length of the DataFrame. If you assign a Series, it will be instead conformed exactly to the DataFrame's index, inserting missing values in any holes:

```
In [49]: val = Series([-1.2, -1.5, -1.7], index=['two', 'four', 'five'])

In [50]: frame2['debt'] = val

In [51]: frame2
Out[51]:
       year   state   pop  debt
```

```
one    2000    Ohio    1.5    NaN
two    2001    Ohio    1.7   -1.2
three  2002    Ohio    3.6    NaN
four   2001  Nevada    2.4   -1.5
five   2002  Nevada    2.9   -1.7
```

Assigning a column that doesn't exist will create a new column. The del keyword will delete columns as with a dict:

```
In [52]: frame2['eastern'] = frame2.state == 'Ohio'
```

```
In [53]: frame2
Out[53]:
       year   state  pop  debt eastern
one    2000    Ohio  1.5   NaN    True
two    2001    Ohio  1.7  -1.2    True
three  2002    Ohio  3.6   NaN    True
four   2001  Nevada  2.4  -1.5   False
five   2002  Nevada  2.9  -1.7   False
```

```
In [54]: del frame2['eastern']
```

```
In [55]: frame2.columns
Out[55]: Index([u'year', u'state', u'pop', u'debt'], dtype='object')
```

 The column returned when indexing a DataFrame is a *view* on the underlying data, not a copy. Thus, any in-place modifications to the Series will be reflected in the DataFrame. The column can be explicitly copied using the Series's copy method.

Another common form of data is a nested dict of dicts format:

```
In [56]: pop = {'Nevada': {2001: 2.4, 2002: 2.9},
   ....:        'Ohio': {2000: 1.5, 2001: 1.7, 2002: 3.6}}
```

If passed to DataFrame, it will interpret the outer dict keys as the columns and the inner keys as the row indices:

```
In [57]: frame3 = DataFrame(pop)
```

```
In [58]: frame3
Out[58]:
      Nevada  Ohio
2000     NaN   1.5
2001     2.4   1.7
2002     2.9   3.6
```

Of course you can always transpose the result:

```
In [59]: frame3.T
Out[59]:
        2000  2001  2002
Nevada   NaN   2.4   2.9
Ohio     1.5   1.7   3.6
```

The keys in the inner dicts are unioned and sorted to form the index in the result. This isn't true if an explicit index is specified:

```
In [60]: DataFrame(pop, index=[2001, 2002, 2003])
Out[60]:
      Nevada  Ohio
2001     2.4   1.7
2002     2.9   3.6
2003     NaN   NaN
```

Dicts of Series are treated much in the same way:

```
In [61]: pdata = {'Ohio': frame3['Ohio'][:-1],
   ....:          'Nevada': frame3['Nevada'][:2]}

In [62]: DataFrame(pdata)
Out[62]:
      Nevada  Ohio
2000     NaN   1.5
2001     2.4   1.7
```

For a complete list of things you can pass the DataFrame constructor, see Table 5-1.

If a DataFrame's index and columns have their name attributes set, these will also be displayed:

```
In [63]: frame3.index.name = 'year'; frame3.columns.name = 'state'

In [64]: frame3
Out[64]:
state  Nevada  Ohio
year
2000      NaN   1.5
2001      2.4   1.7
2002      2.9   3.6
```

Like Series, the values attribute returns the data contained in the DataFrame as a 2D ndarray:

```
In [65]: frame3.values
Out[65]:
array([[ nan,  1.5],
       [ 2.4,  1.7],
       [ 2.9,  3.6]])
```

If the DataFrame's columns are different dtypes, the dtype of the values array will be chosen to accomodate all of the columns:

```
In [66]: frame2.values
Out[66]:
array([[2000, 'Ohio', 1.5, nan],
       [2001, 'Ohio', 1.7, -1.2],
       [2002, 'Ohio', 3.6, nan],
       [2001, 'Nevada', 2.4, -1.5],
       [2002, 'Nevada', 2.9, -1.7]], dtype=object)
```

Table 5-1. Possible data inputs to DataFrame constructor

Type	Notes
2D ndarray	A matrix of data, passing optional row and column labels
dict of arrays, lists, or tuples	Each sequence becomes a column in the DataFrame. All sequences must be the same length.
NumPy structured/record array	Treated as the "dict of arrays" case
dict of Series	Each value becomes a column. Indexes from each Series are unioned together to form the result's row index if no explicit index is passed.
dict of dicts	Each inner dict becomes a column. Keys are unioned to form the row index as in the "dict of Series" case.
list of dicts or Series	Each item becomes a row in the DataFrame. Union of dict keys or Series indexes become the DataFrame's column labels
List of lists or tuples	Treated as the "2D ndarray" case
Another DataFrame	The DataFrame's indexes are used unless different ones are passed
NumPy MaskedArray	Like the "2D ndarray" case except masked values become NA/missing in the DataFrame result

Index Objects

pandas's Index objects are responsible for holding the axis labels and other metadata (like the axis name or names). Any array or other sequence of labels used when constructing a Series or DataFrame is internally converted to an Index:

```
In [67]: obj = Series(range(3), index=['a', 'b', 'c'])

In [68]: index = obj.index

In [69]: index
Out[69]: Index([u'a', u'b', u'c'], dtype='object')

In [70]: index[1:]
Out[70]: Index([u'b', u'c'], dtype='object')
```

Index objects are immutable and thus can't be modified by the user:

```
In [71]: index[1] = 'd'
---------------------------------------------------------------------------
TypeError                                 Traceback (most recent call last)
<ipython-input-71-676fdeb26a68> in <module>()
----> 1 index[1] = 'd'
/home/phillip/miniconda3/envs/conda2/lib/python2.7/site-packages/pandas/core/
base.pyc in _disabled(self, *args, **kwargs)
    177         """This method will not function because object is immutable."""
    178         raise TypeError("'%s' does not support mutable operations." %
--> 179                         self.__class__)
    180
    181     __setitem__ = __setslice__ = __delitem__ = __delslice__ = _disabled
TypeError: '<class 'pandas.core.index.Index'>' does not support mutable operations.
```

Immutability is important so that Index objects can be safely shared among data structures:

```
In [72]: index = pd.Index(np.arange(3))

In [73]: obj2 = Series([1.5, -2.5, 0], index=index)

In [74]: obj2.index is index
Out[74]: True
```

Table 5-2 has a list of built-in Index classes in the library. With some development effort, Index can even be subclassed to implement specialized axis indexing functionality.

 Many users will not need to know much about Index objects, but they're nonetheless an important part of pandas's data model.

Table 5-2. Main Index objects in pandas

Class	Description
Index	The most general Index object, representing axis labels in a NumPy array of Python objects.
Int64Index	Specialized Index for integer values.
MultiIndex	"Hierarchical" index object representing multiple levels of indexing on a single axis. Can be thought of as similar to an array of tuples.
DatetimeIndex	Stores nanosecond timestamps (represented using NumPy's datetime64 dtype).
PeriodIndex	Specialized Index for Period data (timespans).

In addition to being array-like, an Index also functions as a fixed-size set:

```
In [75]: frame3
Out[75]:
state  Nevada  Ohio
year
2000      NaN   1.5
2001      2.4   1.7
2002      2.9   3.6

In [76]: 'Ohio' in frame3.columns
Out[76]: True

In [77]: 2003 in frame3.index
Out[77]: False
```

Each Index has a number of methods and properties for set logic and answering other common questions about the data it contains. These are summarized in Table 5-3.

Table 5-3. Index methods and properties

Method	Description
append	Concatenate with additional Index objects, producing a new Index
diff	Compute set difference as an Index
intersection	Compute set intersection
union	Compute set union
isin	Compute boolean array indicating whether each value is contained in the passed collection
delete	Compute new Index with element at index i deleted
drop	Compute new index by deleting passed values
insert	Compute new Index by inserting element at index i
is_monotonic	Returns True if each element is greater than or equal to the previous element
is_unique	Returns True if the Index has no duplicate values
unique	Compute the array of unique values in the Index

Essential Functionality

In this section, I'll walk you through the fundamental mechanics of interacting with the data contained in a Series or DataFrame. Upcoming chapters will delve more deeply into data analysis and manipulation topics using pandas. This book is not intended to serve as exhaustive documentation for the pandas library; I instead focus on the most important features, leaving the less common (that is, more esoteric) things for you to explore on your own.

Reindexing

A critical method on pandas objects is `reindex`, which means to create a new object with the data *conformed* to a new index. Consider a simple example from above:

```
In [78]: obj = Series([4.5, 7.2, -5.3, 3.6], index=['d', 'b', 'a', 'c'])
```

```
In [79]: obj
Out[79]:
d    4.5
b    7.2
a   -5.3
c    3.6
dtype: float64
```

Calling `reindex` on this Series rearranges the data according to the new index, introducing missing values if any index values were not already present:

```
In [80]: obj2 = obj.reindex(['a', 'b', 'c', 'd', 'e'])
```

```
In [81]: obj2
Out[81]:
```

```
a    -5.3
b     7.2
c     3.6
d     4.5
e     NaN
dtype: float64

In [82]: obj.reindex(['a', 'b', 'c', 'd', 'e'], fill_value=0)
Out[82]:
a    -5.3
b     7.2
c     3.6
d     4.5
e     0.0
dtype: float64
```

For ordered data like time series, it may be desirable to do some interpolation or filling of values when reindexing. The method option allows us to do this, using a method such as ffill which forward fills the values:

```
In [83]: obj3 = Series(['blue', 'purple', 'yellow'], index=[0, 2, 4])

In [84]: obj3.reindex(range(6), method='ffill')
Out[84]:
0       blue
1       blue
2     purple
3     purple
4     yellow
5     yellow
dtype: object
```

Table 5-4 lists available method options. At this time, interpolation more sophisticated than forward- and backfilling would need to be applied after the fact.

Table 5-4. reindex method (interpolation) options

Argument	Description
ffill or pad	Fill (or carry) values forward
bfill or backfill	Fill (or carry) values backward

With DataFrame, reindex can alter either the (row) index, columns, or both. When passed just a sequence, the rows are reindexed in the result:

```
In [85]: frame = DataFrame(np.arange(9).reshape((3, 3)), index=['a', 'c', 'd'],
   ....:                    columns=['Ohio', 'Texas', 'California'])

In [86]: frame
Out[86]:
   Ohio  Texas  California
a     0      1           2
c     3      4           5
d     6      7           8
```

```
In [87]: frame2 = frame.reindex(['a', 'b', 'c', 'd'])

In [88]: frame2
Out[88]:
   Ohio  Texas  California
a     0      1           2
b   NaN    NaN         NaN
c     3      4           5
d     6      7           8
```

The columns can be reindexed using the columns keyword:

```
In [89]: states = ['Texas', 'Utah', 'California']

In [90]: frame.reindex(columns=states)
Out[90]:
   Texas  Utah  California
a      1   NaN           2
c      4   NaN           5
d      7   NaN           8
```

Both can be reindexed in one shot, though interpolation will only apply row-wise (axis 0):

```
In [91]: frame.reindex(index=['a', 'b', 'c', 'd'], method='ffill',
   ....:               columns=states)
Out[91]:
   Texas  Utah  California
a      1   NaN           2
b      1   NaN           2
c      4   NaN           5
d      7   NaN           8
```

As you'll see soon, reindexing can be done more succinctly by label-indexing with ix:

```
In [92]: frame.ix[['a', 'b', 'c', 'd'], states]
Out[92]:
   Texas  Utah  California
a      1   NaN           2
b    NaN   NaN         NaN
c      4   NaN           5
d      7   NaN           8
```

Table 5-5. reindex function arguments

Argument	Description
index	New sequence to use as index. Can be Index instance or any other sequence-like Python data structure. An Index will be used exactly as is without any copying
method	Interpolation (fill) method, see Table 5-4 for options.
fill_value	Substitute value to use when introducing missing data by reindexing
limit	When forward- or backfilling, maximum size gap to fill
level	Match simple Index on level of MultiIndex, otherwise select subset of

Argument	Description
copy	If True, always copy underlying data even if new index is equivalent to old index. If False, do not copy the data when the indexes are equivalent.

Dropping entries from an axis

Dropping one or more entries from an axis is easy if you have an index array or list without those entries. As that can require a bit of munging and set logic, the drop method will return a new object with the indicated value or values deleted from an axis:

```
In [93]: obj = Series(np.arange(5.), index=['a', 'b', 'c', 'd', 'e'])

In [94]: new_obj = obj.drop('c')

In [95]: new_obj
Out[95]:
a    0
b    1
d    3
e    4
dtype: float64

In [96]: obj.drop(['d', 'c'])
Out[96]:
a    0
b    1
e    4
dtype: float64
```

With DataFrame, index values can be deleted from either axis:

```
In [97]: data = DataFrame(np.arange(16).reshape((4, 4)),
   ....:                  index=['Ohio', 'Colorado', 'Utah', 'New York'],
   ....:                  columns=['one', 'two', 'three', 'four'])

In [98]: data.drop(['Colorado', 'Ohio'])
Out[98]:
          one  two  three  four
Utah        8    9     10    11
New York   12   13     14    15
```

```
In [99]: data.drop('two', axis=1)
Out[99]:
          one  three  four
Ohio        0      2     3
Colorado    4      6     7
Utah        8     10    11
New York   12     14    15
```

```
In [100]: data.drop(['two', 'four'], axis=1)
Out[100]:
          one  three
Ohio        0      2
Colorado    4      6
Utah        8     10
New York   12     14
```

Indexing, selection, and filtering

Series indexing (obj[...]) works analogously to NumPy array indexing, except you can use the Series's index values instead of only integers. Here are some examples of this:

```
In [101]: obj = Series(np.arange(4.), index=['a', 'b', 'c', 'd'])

In [102]: obj['b']          In [103]: obj[1]
Out[102]: 1.0               Out[103]: 1.0

In [104]: obj[2:4]          In [105]: obj[['b', 'a', 'd']]
Out[104]:                   Out[105]:
c    2                      b    1
d    3                      a    0
dtype: float64              d    3
                            dtype: float64

In [106]: obj[[1, 3]]       In [107]: obj[obj < 2]
Out[106]:                   Out[107]:
b    1                      a    0
d    3                      b    1
dtype: float64              dtype: float64
```

Slicing with labels behaves differently than normal Python slicing in that the endpoint is inclusive:

```
In [108]: obj['b':'c']
Out[108]:
b    1
c    2
dtype: float64
```

Setting using these methods works just as you would expect:

```
In [109]: obj['b':'c'] = 5

In [110]: obj
Out[110]:
a    0
b    5
c    5
d    3
dtype: float64
```

As you've seen above, indexing into a DataFrame is for retrieving one or more columns either with a single value or sequence:

```
In [111]: data = DataFrame(np.arange(16).reshape((4, 4)),
   .....:                  index=['Ohio', 'Colorado', 'Utah', 'New York'],
   .....:                  columns=['one', 'two', 'three', 'four'])

In [112]: data
Out[112]:
          one  two  three  four
Ohio        0    1      2     3
Colorado    4    5      6     7
```

```
Utah          8    9    10   11
New York      12   13   14   15

In [113]: data['two']          In [114]: data[['three', 'one']]
Out[113]:                      Out[114]:
Ohio          1                          three  one
Colorado      5                Ohio        2     0
Utah          9                Colorado    6     4
New York      13               Utah       10     8
Name: two, dtype: int64        New York   14    12
```

Indexing like this has a few special cases. First selecting rows by slicing or a boolean array:

```
In [115]: data[:2]             In [116]: data[data['three'] > 5]
Out[115]:                      Out[116]:
          one  two  three  four            one  two  three  four
Ohio       0    1     2     3   Colorado    4    5     6     7
Colorado   4    5     6     7   Utah        8    9    10    11
                                New York   12   13    14    15
```

This might seem inconsistent to some readers, but this syntax arose out of practicality and nothing more. Another use case is in indexing with a boolean DataFrame, such as one produced by a scalar comparison:

```
In [117]: data < 5
Out[117]:
            one     two   three   four
Ohio       True    True   True   True
Colorado   True   False  False  False
Utah      False   False  False  False
New York  False   False  False  False

In [118]: data[data < 5] = 0

In [119]: data
Out[119]:
          one  two  three  four
Ohio       0    0     0     0
Colorado   0    5     6     7
Utah       8    9    10    11
New York  12   13    14    15
```

This is intended to make DataFrame syntactically more like an ndarray in this case.

For DataFrame label-indexing on the rows, I introduce the special indexing field ix. It enables you to select a subset of the rows and columns from a DataFrame with NumPy-like notation plus axis labels. As I mentioned earlier, this is also a less verbose way to do reindexing:

```
In [120]: data.ix['Colorado', ['two', 'three']]
Out[120]:
two      5
three    6
Name: Colorado, dtype: int64
```

```
In [121]: data.ix[['Colorado', 'Utah'], [3, 0, 1]]
Out[121]:
          four  one  two
Colorado     7    0    5
Utah        11    8    9

In [122]: data.ix[2]          In [123]: data.ix[:'Utah', 'two']
Out[122]:                     Out[123]:
one       8                   Ohio         0
two       9                   Colorado     5
three    10                   Utah         9
four     11                   Name: two, dtype: int64
Name: Utah, dtype: int64

In [124]: data.ix[data.three > 5, :3]
Out[124]:
          one  two  three
Colorado    0    5      6
Utah        8    9     10
New York   12   13     14
```

So there are many ways to select and rearrange the data contained in a pandas object. For DataFrame, there is a short summary of many of them in Table 5-6. You have a number of additional options when working with hierarchical indexes as you'll later see.

 When designing pandas, I felt that having to type `frame[:, col]` to select a column was too verbose (and error-prone), since column selection is one of the most common operations. Thus I made the design trade-off to push all of the rich label-indexing into `ix`.

Table 5-6. Indexing options with DataFrame

Type	Notes
obj[val]	Select single column or sequence of columns from the DataFrame. Special case conveniences: boolean array (filter rows), slice (slice rows), or boolean DataFrame (set values based on some criterion).
obj.ix[val]	Selects single row or subset of rows from the DataFrame.
obj.ix[:, val]	Selects single column of subset of columns.
obj.ix[val1, val2]	Select both rows and columns.
reindex method	Conform one or more axes to new indexes.
xs method	Select single row or column as a Series by label.
icol, irow methods	Select single column or row, respectively, as a Series by integer location.
get_value, set_value methods	Select single value by row and column label.

Arithmetic and data alignment

One of the most important pandas features is the behavior of arithmetic between objects with different indexes. When adding together objects, if any index pairs are not the same, the respective index in the result will be the union of the index pairs. Let's look at a simple example:

```
In [125]: s1 = Series([7.3, -2.5, 3.4, 1.5], index=['a', 'c', 'd', 'e'])

In [126]: s2 = Series([-2.1, 3.6, -1.5, 4, 3.1], index=['a', 'c', 'e', 'f', 'g'])

In [127]: s1            In [128]: s2
Out[127]:               Out[128]:
a    7.3                a   -2.1
c   -2.5                c    3.6
d    3.4                e   -1.5
e    1.5                f    4.0
dtype: float64          g    3.1
                        dtype: float64
```

Adding these together yields:

```
In [129]: s1 + s2
Out[129]:
a    5.2
c    1.1
d    NaN
e    0.0
f    NaN
g    NaN
dtype: float64
```

The internal data alignment introduces NA values in the indices that don't overlap. Missing values propagate in arithmetic computations.

In the case of DataFrame, alignment is performed on both the rows and the columns:

```
In [130]: df1 = DataFrame(np.arange(9.).reshape((3, 3)), columns=list('bcd'),
   .....:                 index=['Ohio', 'Texas', 'Colorado'])

In [131]: df2 = DataFrame(np.arange(12.).reshape((4, 3)), columns=list('bde'),
   .....:                 index=['Utah', 'Ohio', 'Texas', 'Oregon'])

In [132]: df1             In [133]: df2
Out[132]:                 Out[133]:
          b  c  d                   b  d   e
Ohio      0  1  2         Utah      0  1   2
Texas     3  4  5         Ohio      3  4   5
Colorado  6  7  8         Texas     6  7   8
                          Oregon    9  10  11
```

Adding these together returns a DataFrame whose index and columns are the unions of the ones in each DataFrame:

```
In [134]: df1 + df2
Out[134]:
           b   c    d    e
Colorado NaN NaN  NaN  NaN
Ohio       3 NaN    6  NaN
Oregon   NaN NaN  NaN  NaN
Texas      9 NaN   12  NaN
Utah     NaN NaN  NaN  NaN
```

Arithmetic methods with fill values

In arithmetic operations between differently-indexed objects, you might want to fill with a special value, like 0, when an axis label is found in one object but not the other:

```
In [135]: df1 = DataFrame(np.arange(12.).reshape((3, 4)), columns=list('abcd'))

In [136]: df2 = DataFrame(np.arange(20.).reshape((4, 5)), columns=list('abcde'))

In [137]: df1             In [138]: df2
Out[137]:                 Out[138]:
   a  b   c   d              a   b   c   d   e
0  0  1   2   3           0  0   1   2   3   4
1  4  5   6   7           1  5   6   7   8   9
2  8  9  10  11           2  10  11  12  13  14
                          3  15  16  17  18  19
```

Adding these together results in NA values in the locations that don't overlap:

```
In [139]: df1 + df2
Out[139]:
     a   b   c   d   e
0    0   2   4   6 NaN
1    9  11  13  15 NaN
2   18  20  22  24 NaN
3  NaN NaN NaN NaN NaN
```

Using the add method on df1, I pass df2 and an argument to fill_value:

```
In [140]: df1.add(df2, fill_value=0)
Out[140]:
    a   b   c   d   e
0   0   2   4   6   4
1   9  11  13  15   9
2  18  20  22  24  14
3  15  16  17  18  19
```

Relatedly, when reindexing a Series or DataFrame, you can also specify a different fill value:

```
In [141]: df1.reindex(columns=df2.columns, fill_value=0)
Out[141]:
   a  b   c   d  e
0  0  1   2   3  0
1  4  5   6   7  0
2  8  9  10  11  0
```

Table 5-7. Flexible arithmetic methods

Method	Description
add	Method for addition (+)
sub	Method for subtraction (-)
div	Method for division (/)
mul	Method for multiplication (*)

Operations between DataFrame and Series

As with NumPy arrays, arithmetic between DataFrame and Series is well-defined. First, as a motivating example, consider the difference between a 2D array and one of its rows:

```
In [142]: arr = np.arange(12.).reshape((3, 4))

In [143]: arr
Out[143]:
array([[  0.,   1.,   2.,   3.],
       [  4.,   5.,   6.,   7.],
       [  8.,   9.,  10.,  11.]])

In [144]: arr[0]
Out[144]: array([ 0.,  1.,  2.,  3.])

In [145]: arr - arr[0]
Out[145]:
array([[ 0.,  0.,  0.,  0.],
       [ 4.,  4.,  4.,  4.],
       [ 8.,  8.,  8.,  8.]])
```

This is referred to as *broadcasting* and is explained in more detail in Chapter 12. Operations between a DataFrame and a Series are similar:

```
In [146]: frame = DataFrame(np.arange(12.).reshape((4, 3)), columns=list('bde'),
   .....:                   index=['Utah', 'Ohio', 'Texas', 'Oregon'])

In [147]: series = frame.ix[0]

In [148]: frame            In [149]: series
Out[148]:                  Out[149]:
        b   d   e          b    0
Utah    0   1   2          d    1
Ohio    3   4   5          e    2
Texas   6   7   8          Name: Utah, dtype: float64
Oregon  9  10  11
```

By default, arithmetic between DataFrame and Series matches the index of the Series on the DataFrame's columns, broadcasting down the rows:

```
In [150]: frame - series
Out[150]:
        b  d  e
Utah    0  0  0
```

```
Ohio     3   3   3
Texas    6   6   6
Oregon   9   9   9
```

If an index value is not found in either the DataFrame's columns or the Series's index, the objects will be reindexed to form the union:

```
In [151]: series2 = Series(range(3), index=['b', 'e', 'f'])

In [152]: frame + series2
Out[152]:
          b   d   e   f
Utah      0  NaN   3  NaN
Ohio      3  NaN   6  NaN
Texas     6  NaN   9  NaN
Oregon    9  NaN  12  NaN
```

If you want to instead broadcast over the columns, matching on the rows, you have to use one of the arithmetic methods. For example:

```
In [153]: series3 = frame['d']

In [154]: frame          In [155]: series3
Out[154]:                Out[155]:
          b   d   e       Utah        1
Utah      0   1   2       Ohio        4
Ohio      3   4   5       Texas       7
Texas     6   7   8       Oregon     10
Oregon    9  10  11       Name: d, dtype: float64

In [156]: frame.sub(series3, axis=0)
Out[156]:
          b   d   e
Utah     -1   0   1
Ohio     -1   0   1
Texas    -1   0   1
Oregon   -1   0   1
```

The axis number that you pass is the *axis to match on*. In this case we mean to match on the DataFrame's row index and broadcast across.

Function application and mapping

NumPy ufuncs (element-wise array methods) work fine with pandas objects:

```
In [157]: frame = DataFrame(np.random.randn(4, 3), columns=list('bde'),
   .....:                   index=['Utah', 'Ohio', 'Texas', 'Oregon'])

In [158]: frame                          In [159]: np.abs(frame)
Out[158]:                                Out[159]:
               b         d         e              b         d         e
Utah   -0.204708  0.478943 -0.519439     Utah   0.204708  0.478943  0.519439
Ohio   -0.555730  1.965781  1.393406     Ohio   0.555730  1.965781  1.393406
Texas   0.092908  0.281746  0.769023     Texas  0.092908  0.281746  0.769023
Oregon  1.246435  1.007189 -1.296221     Oregon 1.246435  1.007189  1.296221
```

Another frequent operation is applying a function on 1D arrays to each column or row. DataFrame's apply method does exactly this:

```
In [160]: f = lambda x: x.max() - x.min()
```

```
In [161]: frame.apply(f)        In [162]: frame.apply(f, axis=1)
Out[161]:                       Out[162]:
b    1.802165                   Utah      0.998382
d    1.684034                   Ohio      2.521511
e    2.689627                   Texas     0.676115
dtype: float64                  Oregon    2.542656
                                dtype: float64
```

Many of the most common array statistics (like sum and mean) are DataFrame methods, so using apply is not necessary.

The function passed to apply need not return a scalar value, it can also return a Series with multiple values:

```
In [163]: def f(x):
   .....:     return Series([x.min(), x.max()], index=['min', 'max'])
```

```
In [164]: frame.apply(f)
Out[164]:
            b         d         e
min -0.555730  0.281746 -1.296221
max  1.246435  1.965781  1.393406
```

Element-wise Python functions can be used, too. Suppose you wanted to compute a formatted string from each floating point value in frame. You can do this with applymap:

```
In [165]: format = lambda x: '%.2f' % x
```

```
In [166]: frame.applymap(format)
Out[166]:
            b     d     e
Utah    -0.20  0.48 -0.52
Ohio    -0.56  1.97  1.39
Texas    0.09  0.28  0.77
Oregon   1.25  1.01 -1.30
```

The reason for the name applymap is that Series has a map method for applying an element-wise function:

```
In [167]: frame['e'].map(format)
Out[167]:
Utah     -0.52
Ohio      1.39
Texas     0.77
Oregon   -1.30
Name: e, dtype: object
```

Sorting and ranking

Sorting a data set by some criterion is another important built-in operation. To sort lexicographically by row or column index, use the `sort_index` method, which returns a new, sorted object:

```
In [168]: obj = Series(range(4), index=['d', 'a', 'b', 'c'])

In [169]: obj.sort_index()
Out[169]:
a    1
b    2
c    3
d    0
dtype: int64
```

With a DataFrame, you can sort by index on either axis:

```
In [170]: frame = DataFrame(np.arange(8).reshape((2, 4)), index=['three', 'one'],
   .....:                   columns=['d', 'a', 'b', 'c'])

In [171]: frame.sort_index()        In [172]: frame.sort_index(axis=1)
Out[171]:                           Out[172]:
       d  a  b  c                          a  b  c  d
one    4  5  6  7                   three  1  2  3  0
three  0  1  2  3                   one    5  6  7  4
```

The data is sorted in ascending order by default, but can be sorted in descending order, too:

```
In [173]: frame.sort_index(axis=1, ascending=False)
Out[173]:
       d  c  b  a
three  0  3  2  1
one    4  7  6  5
```

To sort a Series by its values, use its `order` method:

```
In [174]: obj = Series([4, 7, -3, 2])

In [175]: obj.order()
Out[175]:
2   -3
3    2
0    4
1    7
dtype: int64
```

Any missing values are sorted to the end of the Series by default:

```
In [176]: obj = Series([4, np.nan, 7, np.nan, -3, 2])

In [177]: obj.order()
Out[177]:
4   -3
5    2
0    4
```

```
2     7
1    NaN
3    NaN
dtype: float64
```

On DataFrame, you may want to sort by the values in one or more columns. To do so, pass one or more column names to the by option:

```
In [178]: frame = DataFrame({'b': [4, 7, -3, 2], 'a': [0, 1, 0, 1]})
```

```
In [179]: frame          In [180]: frame.sort_index(by='b')
Out[179]:                 Out[180]:
   a  b                       a  b
0  0  4                    2  0 -3
1  1  7                    3  1  2
2  0 -3                    0  0  4
3  1  2                    1  1  7
```

To sort by multiple columns, pass a list of names:

```
In [181]: frame.sort_index(by=['a', 'b'])
Out[181]:
   a  b
2  0 -3
0  0  4
3  1  2
1  1  7
```

Ranking is closely related to sorting, assigning ranks from one through the number of valid data points in an array. It is similar to the indirect sort indices produced by numpy.argsort, except that ties are broken according to a rule. The rank methods for Series and DataFrame are the place to look; by default rank breaks ties by assigning each group the mean rank:

```
In [182]: obj = Series([7, -5, 7, 4, 2, 0, 4])
```

```
In [183]: obj.rank()
Out[183]:
0    6.5
1    1.0
2    6.5
3    4.5
4    3.0
5    2.0
6    4.5
dtype: float64
```

Ranks can also be assigned according to the order they're observed in the data:

```
In [184]: obj.rank(method='first')
Out[184]:
0    6
1    1
2    7
3    4
4    3
```

```
5    2
6    5
dtype: float64
```

Naturally, you can rank in descending order, too:

```
In [185]: obj.rank(ascending=False, method='max')
Out[185]:
0    2
1    7
2    2
3    4
4    5
5    6
6    4
dtype: float64
```

See Table 5-8 for a list of tie-breaking methods available. DataFrame can compute ranks over the rows or the columns:

```
In [186]: frame = DataFrame({'b': [4.3, 7, -3, 2], 'a': [0, 1, 0, 1],
   .....:                    'c': [-2, 5, 8, -2.5]})
```

```
In [187]: frame            In [188]: frame.rank(axis=1)
Out[187]:                  Out[188]:
   a    b    c                a  b  c
0  0  4.3 -2.0             0  2  3  1
1  1  7.0  5.0             1  1  3  2
2  0 -3.0  8.0             2  2  1  3
3  1  2.0 -2.5             3  2  3  1
```

Table 5-8. Tie-breaking methods with rank

Method	Description
'average'	Default: assign the average rank to each entry in the equal group.
'min'	Use the minimum rank for the whole group.
'max'	Use the maximum rank for the whole group.
'first'	Assign ranks in the order the values appear in the data.

Axis indexes with duplicate values

Up until now all of the examples I've showed you have had unique axis labels (index values). While many pandas functions (like reindex) require that the labels be unique, it's not mandatory. Let's consider a small Series with duplicate indices:

```
In [189]: obj = Series(range(5), index=['a', 'a', 'b', 'b', 'c'])
```

```
In [190]: obj
Out[190]:
a    0
a    1
b    2
b    3
```

```
c    4
dtype: int64
```

The index's `is_unique` property can tell you whether its values are unique or not:

```
In [191]: obj.index.is_unique
Out[191]: False
```

Data selection is one of the main things that behaves differently with duplicates. In-dexing a value with multiple entries returns a Series while single entries return a scalar value:

```
In [192]: obj['a']    In [193]: obj['c']
Out[192]:             Out[193]: 4
a    0
a    1
dtype: int64
```

The same logic extends to indexing rows in a DataFrame:

```
In [194]: df = DataFrame(np.random.randn(4, 3), index=['a', 'a', 'b', 'b'])

In [195]: df
Out[195]:
          0         1         2
a  0.274992  0.228913  1.352917
a  0.886429 -2.001637 -0.371843
b  1.669025 -0.438570 -0.539741
b  0.476985  3.248944 -1.021228

In [196]: df.ix['b']
Out[196]:
          0         1         2
b  1.669025 -0.438570 -0.539741
b  0.476985  3.248944 -1.021228
```

Summarizing and Computing Descriptive Statistics

pandas objects are equipped with a set of common mathematical and statistical meth-ods. Most of these fall into the category of *reductions* or *summary statistics*, methods that extract a single value (like the sum or mean) from a Series or a Series of values from the rows or columns of a DataFrame. Compared with the equivalent methods of vanilla NumPy arrays, they are all built from the ground up to exclude missing data. Consider a small DataFrame:

```
In [197]: df = DataFrame([[1.4, np.nan], [7.1, -4.5],
   .....:                 [np.nan, np.nan], [0.75, -1.3]],
   .....:                index=['a', 'b', 'c', 'd'],
   .....:                columns=['one', 'two'])

In [198]: df
Out[198]:
    one   two
a  1.40   NaN
```

```
b   7.10 -4.5
c    NaN  NaN
d   0.75 -1.3
```

Calling DataFrame's sum method returns a Series containing column sums:

```
In [199]: df.sum()
Out[199]:
one    9.25
two   -5.80
dtype: float64
```

Passing axis=1 sums over the rows instead:

```
In [200]: df.sum(axis=1)
Out[200]:
a    1.40
b    2.60
c     NaN
d   -0.55
dtype: float64
```

NA values are excluded unless the entire slice (row or column in this case) is NA. This can be disabled using the skipna option:

```
In [201]: df.mean(axis=1, skipna=False)
Out[201]:
a      NaN
b    1.300
c      NaN
d   -0.275
dtype: float64
```

See Table 5-9 for a list of common options for each reduction method options.

Table 5-9. Options for reduction methods

Method	Description
axis	Axis to reduce over. 0 for DataFrame's rows and 1 for columns.
skipna	Exclude missing values, True by default.
level	Reduce grouped by level if the axis is hierarchically-indexed (MultiIndex).

Some methods, like idxmin and idxmax, return indirect statistics like the index value where the minimum or maximum values are attained:

```
In [202]: df.idxmax()
Out[202]:
one    b
two    d
dtype: object
```

Other methods are *accumulations*:

```
In [203]: df.cumsum()
Out[203]:
```

```
        one   two
a      1.40   NaN
b      8.50  -4.5
c       NaN   NaN
d      9.25  -5.8
```

Another type of method is neither a reduction nor an accumulation. describe is one such example, producing multiple summary statistics in one shot:

```
In [204]: df.describe()
Out[204]:
              one       two
count    3.000000  2.000000
mean     3.083333 -2.900000
std      3.493685  2.262742
min      0.750000 -4.500000
25%      1.075000 -3.700000
50%      1.400000 -2.900000
75%      4.250000 -2.100000
max      7.100000 -1.300000
```

On non-numeric data, describe produces alternate summary statistics:

```
In [205]: obj = Series(['a', 'a', 'b', 'c'] * 4)
```

```
In [206]: obj.describe()
Out[206]:
count     16
unique     3
top        a
freq       8
dtype: object
```

See Table 5-10 for a full list of summary statistics and related methods.

Table 5-10. Descriptive and summary statistics

Method	Description
count	Number of non-NA values
describe	Compute set of summary statistics for Series or each DataFrame column
min, max	Compute minimum and maximum values
argmin, argmax	Compute index locations (integers) at which minimum or maximum value obtained, respectively
idxmin, idxmax	Compute index values at which minimum or maximum value obtained, respectively
quantile	Compute sample quantile ranging from 0 to 1
sum	Sum of values
mean	Mean of values
median	Arithmetic median (50% quantile) of values
mad	Mean absolute deviation from mean value
var	Sample variance of values
std	Sample standard deviation of values

Method	Description
skew	Sample skewness (3rd moment) of values
kurt	Sample kurtosis (4th moment) of values
cumsum	Cumulative sum of values
cummin, cummax	Cumulative minimum or maximum of values, respectively
cumprod	Cumulative product of values
diff	Compute 1st arithmetic difference (useful for time series)
pct_change	Compute percent changes

Correlation and Covariance

Some summary statistics, like correlation and covariance, are computed from pairs of arguments. Let's consider some DataFrames of stock prices and volumes obtained from Yahoo! Finance:

```
import pandas.io.data as web

all_data = {}
for ticker in ['AAPL', 'IBM', 'MSFT', 'GOOG']:
    all_data[ticker] = web.get_data_yahoo(ticker)

price = DataFrame({tic: data['Adj Close']
                   for tic, data in all_data.iteritems()})
volume = DataFrame({tic: data['Volume']
                    for tic, data in all_data.iteritems()})
```

I now compute percent changes of the prices:

```
In [208]: returns = price.pct_change()

In [209]: returns.tail()
Out[209]:
                 AAPL      GOOG       IBM      MSFT
Date
2014-07-07   0.020632 -0.004241 -0.002599  0.004545
2014-07-08  -0.006460 -0.019167 -0.004361 -0.005001
2014-07-09   0.000420  0.008738  0.006410 -0.002633
2014-07-10  -0.003669 -0.008645 -0.003821  0.000480
2014-07-11   0.001894  0.014148  0.001598  0.009595
```

The corr method of Series computes the correlation of the overlapping, non-NA, aligned-by-index values in two Series. Relatedly, cov computes the covariance:

```
In [210]: returns.MSFT.corr(returns.IBM)
Out[210]: 0.51360438136345077

In [211]: returns.MSFT.cov(returns.IBM)
Out[211]: 8.4825099973219876e-05
```

DataFrame's corr and cov methods, on the other hand, return a full correlation or covariance matrix as a DataFrame, respectively:

```
In [212]: returns.corr()
Out[212]:
          AAPL      GOOG       IBM      MSFT
AAPL  1.000000  0.180425  0.384439  0.346196
GOOG  0.180425  1.000000  0.368115  0.534293
IBM   0.384439  0.368115  1.000000  0.513604
MSFT  0.346196  0.534293  0.513604  1.000000

In [213]: returns.cov()
Out[213]:
          AAPL      GOOG       IBM      MSFT
AAPL  0.000294  0.000037  0.000077  0.000084
GOOG  0.000037  0.000233  0.000051  0.000085
IBM   0.000077  0.000051  0.000137  0.000085
MSFT  0.000084  0.000085  0.000085  0.000200
```

Using DataFrame's corrwith method, you can compute pairwise correlations between a DataFrame's columns or rows with another Series or DataFrame. Passing a Series returns a Series with the correlation value computed for each column:

```
In [214]: returns.corrwith(returns.IBM)
Out[214]:
AAPL    0.384439
GOOG    0.368115
IBM     1.000000
MSFT    0.513604
dtype: float64
```

Passing a DataFrame computes the correlations of matching column names. Here I compute correlations of percent changes with volume:

```
In [215]: returns.corrwith(volume)
Out[215]:
AAPL   -0.108623
GOOG   -0.255828
IBM    -0.158163
MSFT   -0.117687
dtype: float64
```

Passing axis=1 does things row-wise instead. In all cases, the data points are aligned by label before computing the correlation.

Unique Values, Value Counts, and Membership

Another class of related methods extracts information about the values contained in a one-dimensional Series. To illustrate these, consider this example:

```
In [216]: obj = Series(['c', 'a', 'd', 'a', 'a', 'b', 'b', 'c', 'c'])
```

The first function is unique, which gives you an array of the unique values in a Series:

```
In [217]: uniques = obj.unique()

In [218]: uniques
Out[218]: array(['c', 'a', 'd', 'b'], dtype=object)
```

The unique values are not necessarily returned in sorted order, but could be sorted after the fact if needed (`uniques.sort()`). Relatedly, `value_counts` computes a Series containing value frequencies:

```
In [219]: obj.value_counts()
Out[219]:
c    3
a    3
b    2
d    1
dtype: int64
```

The Series is sorted by value in descending order as a convenience. `value_counts` is also available as a top-level pandas method that can be used with any array or sequence:

```
In [220]: pd.value_counts(obj.values, sort=False)
Out[220]:
a    3
c    3
b    2
d    1
dtype: int64
```

Lastly, `isin` is responsible for vectorized set membership and can be very useful in filtering a data set down to a subset of values in a Series or column in a DataFrame:

```
In [221]: mask = obj.isin(['b', 'c'])
```

```
In [222]: mask          In [223]: obj[mask]
Out[222]:               Out[223]:
0    True               0    c
1    False              5    b
2    False              6    b
3    False              7    c
4    False              8    c
5    True               dtype: object
6    True
7    True
8    True
dtype: bool
```

See Table 5-11 for a reference on these methods.

Table 5-11. Unique, value counts, and binning methods

Method	Description
isin	Compute boolean array indicating whether each Series value is contained in the passed sequence of values.
unique	Compute array of unique values in a Series, returned in the order observed.
value_counts	Return a Series containing unique values as its index and frequencies as its values, ordered count in descending order.

In some cases, you may want to compute a histogram on multiple related columns in a DataFrame. Here's an example:

```
In [224]: data = DataFrame({'Qu1': [1, 3, 4, 3, 4],
   .....:                    'Qu2': [2, 3, 1, 2, 3],
   .....:                    'Qu3': [1, 5, 2, 4, 4]})

In [225]: data
Out[225]:
   Qu1  Qu2  Qu3
0    1    2    1
1    3    3    5
2    4    1    2
3    3    2    4
4    4    3    4
```

Passing `pandas.value_counts` to this DataFrame's `apply` function gives:

```
In [226]: result = data.apply(pd.value_counts).fillna(0)

In [227]: result
Out[227]:
   Qu1  Qu2  Qu3
1    1    1    1
2    0    2    1
3    2    2    0
4    2    0    2
5    0    0    1
```

Handling Missing Data

Missing data is common in most data analysis applications. One of the goals in designing pandas was to make working with missing data as painless as possible. For example, all of the descriptive statistics on pandas objects exclude missing data as you've seen earlier in the chapter.

pandas uses the floating point value NaN (Not a Number) to represent missing data in both floating as well as in non-floating point arrays. It is just used as a *sentinel* that can be easily detected:

```
In [228]: string_data = Series(['aardvark', 'artichoke', np.nan, 'avocado'])
```

```
In [229]: string_data          In [230]: string_data.isnull()
Out[229]:                       Out[230]:
0      aardvark                 0    False
1     artichoke                 1    False
2           NaN                 2     True
3       avocado                 3    False
dtype: object                  dtype: bool
```

The built-in Python None value is also treated as NA in object arrays:

```
In [231]: string_data[0] = None

In [232]: string_data.isnull()
Out[232]:
0    True
```

```
1    False
2    True
3    False
dtype: bool
```

I do not claim that pandas's NA representation is optimal, but it is simple and reasonably consistent. It's the best solution, with good all-around performance characteristics and a simple API, that I could concoct in the absence of a true NA data type or bit pattern in NumPy's data types. Ongoing development work in NumPy may change this in the future.

Table 5-12. NA handling methods

Argument	Description
dropna	Filter axis labels based on whether values for each label have missing data, with varying thresholds for how much missing data to tolerate.
fillna	Fill in missing data with some value or using an interpolation method such as 'ffill' or 'bfill'.
isnull	Return like-type object containing boolean values indicating which values are missing / NA.
notnull	Negation of isnull.

Filtering Out Missing Data

You have a number of options for filtering out missing data. While doing it by hand is always an option, dropna can be very helpful. On a Series, it returns the Series with only the non-null data and index values:

```
In [233]: from numpy import nan as NA

In [234]: data = Series([1, NA, 3.5, NA, 7])

In [235]: data.dropna()
Out[235]:
0    1.0
2    3.5
4    7.0
dtype: float64
```

Naturally, you could have computed this yourself by boolean indexing:

```
In [236]: data[data.notnull()]
Out[236]:
0    1.0
2    3.5
4    7.0
dtype: float64
```

With DataFrame objects, these are a bit more complex. You may want to drop rows or columns which are all NA or just those containing any NAs. dropna by default drops any row containing a missing value:

```
In [237]: data = DataFrame([[1., 6.5, 3.], [1., NA, NA],
   .....:                    [NA, NA, NA], [NA, 6.5, 3.]])

In [238]: cleaned = data.dropna()

In [239]: data          In [240]: cleaned
Out[239]:               Out[240]:
     0    1    2             0    1  2
0    1  6.5    3        0    1  6.5  3
1    1  NaN  NaN
2  NaN  NaN  NaN
3  NaN  6.5    3
```

Passing how='all' will only drop rows that are all NA:

```
In [241]: data.dropna(how='all')
Out[241]:
     0    1    2
0    1  6.5    3
1    1  NaN  NaN
3  NaN  6.5    3
```

Dropping columns in the same way is only a matter of passing axis=1:

```
In [242]: data[4] = NA
```

```
In [243]: data              In [244]: data.dropna(axis=1, how='all')
Out[243]:                   Out[244]:
     0    1    2    4             0    1    2
0    1  6.5    3  NaN        0    1  6.5    3
1    1  NaN  NaN  NaN        1    1  NaN  NaN
2  NaN  NaN  NaN  NaN        2  NaN  NaN  NaN
3  NaN  6.5    3  NaN        3  NaN  6.5    3
```

A related way to filter out DataFrame rows tends to concern time series data. Suppose you want to keep only rows containing a certain number of observations. You can indicate this with the thresh argument:

```
In [245]: df = DataFrame(np.random.randn(7, 3))

In [246]: df.ix[:4, 1] = NA; df.ix[:2, 2] = NA

In [247]: df                              In [248]: df.dropna(thresh=3)
Out[247]:                                 Out[248]:
          0         1         2                   0         1         2
0 -0.577087       NaN       NaN           5  0.332883 -2.359419 -0.199543
1  0.523772       NaN       NaN           6 -1.541996 -0.970736 -1.307030
2 -0.713544       NaN       NaN
3 -1.860761       NaN  0.560145
4 -1.265934       NaN -1.063512
5  0.332883 -2.359419 -0.199543
6 -1.541996 -0.970736 -1.307030
```

Filling in Missing Data

Rather than filtering out missing data (and potentially discarding other data along with it), you may want to fill in the "holes" in any number of ways. For most purposes, the `fillna` method is the workhorse function to use. Calling `fillna` with a constant replaces missing values with that value:

```
In [249]: df.fillna(0)
Out[249]:
          0         1         2
0 -0.577087  0.000000  0.000000
1  0.523772  0.000000  0.000000
2 -0.713544  0.000000  0.000000
3 -1.860761  0.000000  0.560145
4 -1.265934  0.000000 -1.063512
5  0.332883 -2.359419 -0.199543
6 -1.541996 -0.970736 -1.307030
```

Calling `fillna` with a dict you can use a different fill value for each column:

```
In [250]: df.fillna({1: 0.5, 3: -1})
Out[250]:
          0         1         2
0 -0.577087  0.500000       NaN
1  0.523772  0.500000       NaN
2 -0.713544  0.500000       NaN
3 -1.860761  0.500000  0.560145
4 -1.265934  0.500000 -1.063512
5  0.332883 -2.359419 -0.199543
6 -1.541996 -0.970736 -1.307030
```

`fillna` returns a new object, but you can modify the existing object in place:

```
# always returns a reference to the filled object
In [251]: _ = df.fillna(0, inplace=True)

In [252]: df
Out[252]:
          0         1         2
0 -0.577087  0.000000  0.000000
1  0.523772  0.000000  0.000000
2 -0.713544  0.000000  0.000000
3 -1.860761  0.000000  0.560145
4 -1.265934  0.000000 -1.063512
5  0.332883 -2.359419 -0.199543
6 -1.541996 -0.970736 -1.307030
```

The same interpolation methods available for reindexing can be used with `fillna`:

```
In [253]: df = DataFrame(np.random.randn(6, 3))

In [254]: df.ix[2:, 1] = NA; df.ix[4:, 2] = NA

In [255]: df
Out[255]:
          0         1         2
```

```
0  0.286350  0.377984 -0.753887
1  0.331286  1.349742  0.069877
2  0.246674       NaN  1.004812
3  1.327195       NaN -1.549106
4  0.022185       NaN       NaN
5  0.862580       NaN       NaN

In [256]: df.fillna(method='ffill')        In [257]: df.fillna(method='ffill', limit=2)
Out[256]:                                   Out[257]:
          0         1         2                       0         1         2
0  0.286350  0.377984 -0.753887             0  0.286350  0.377984 -0.753887
1  0.331286  1.349742  0.069877             1  0.331286  1.349742  0.069877
2  0.246674  1.349742  1.004812             2  0.246674  1.349742  1.004812
3  1.327195  1.349742 -1.549106             3  1.327195  1.349742 -1.549106
4  0.022185  1.349742 -1.549106             4  0.022185       NaN -1.549106
5  0.862580  1.349742 -1.549106             5  0.862580       NaN -1.549106
```

With `fillna` you can do lots of other things with a little creativity. For example, you might pass the mean or median value of a Series:

```
In [258]: data = Series([1., NA, 3.5, NA, 7])

In [259]: data.fillna(data.mean())
Out[259]:
0    1.000000
1    3.833333
2    3.500000
3    3.833333
4    7.000000
dtype: float64
```

See Table 5-13 for a reference on `fillna`.

Table 5-13. fillna function arguments

Argument	Description
value	Scalar value or dict-like object to use to fill missing values
method	Interpolation, by default `'ffill'` if function called with no other arguments
axis	Axis to fill on, default `axis=0`
inplace	Modify the calling object without producing a copy
limit	For forward and backward filling, maximum number of consecutive periods to fill

Hierarchical Indexing

Hierarchical indexing is an important feature of pandas enabling you to have multiple (two or more) index *levels* on an axis. Somewhat abstractly, it provides a way for you to work with higher dimensional data in a lower dimensional form. Let's start with a simple example; create a Series with a list of lists or arrays as the index:

```
In [260]: data = Series(np.random.randn(10),
   .....:               index=[['a', 'a', 'a', 'b', 'b', 'b', 'c', 'c', 'd', 'd'],
```

```
    .....:                    [1, 2, 3, 1, 2, 3, 1, 2, 2, 3]])

In [261]: data
Out[261]:
a  1    0.670216
   2    0.852965
   3   -0.955869
b  1   -0.023493
   2   -2.304234
   3   -0.652469
c  1   -1.218302
   2   -1.332610
d  2    1.074623
   3    0.723642
dtype: float64
```

What you're seeing is a prettified view of a Series with a `MultiIndex` as its index. The "gaps" in the index display mean "use the label directly above":

```
In [262]: data.index
Out[262]:
MultiIndex(levels=[[u'a', u'b', u'c', u'd'], [1, 2, 3]],
           labels=[[0, 0, 0, 1, 1, 1, 2, 2, 3, 3],
           [0, 1, 2, 0, 1, 2, 0, 1, 1, 2]])
```

With a hierarchically-indexed object, so-called *partial* indexing is possible, enabling you to concisely select subsets of the data:

```
In [263]: data['b']
Out[263]:
1   -0.023493
2   -2.304234
3   -0.652469
dtype: float64
```

```
In [264]: data['b':'c']        In [265]: data.ix[['b', 'd']]
Out[264]:                      Out[265]:
b  1   -0.023493               b  1   -0.023493
   2   -2.304234                  2   -2.304234
   3   -0.652469                  3   -0.652469
c  1   -1.218302               d  2    1.074623
   2   -1.332610                  3    0.723642
dtype: float64                 dtype: float64
```

Selection is even possible in some cases from an "inner" level:

```
In [266]: data[:, 2]
Out[266]:
a    0.852965
b   -2.304234
c   -1.332610
d    1.074623
dtype: float64
```

Hierarchical indexing plays a critical role in reshaping data and group-based operations like forming a pivot table. For example, this data could be rearranged into a DataFrame using its unstack method:

```
In [267]: data.unstack()
Out[267]:
          1         2         3
a  0.670216  0.852965 -0.955869
b -0.023493 -2.304234 -0.652469
c -1.218302 -1.332610       NaN
d       NaN  1.074623  0.723642
```

The inverse operation of unstack is stack:

```
In [268]: data.unstack().stack()
Out[268]:
a  1     0.670216
   2     0.852965
   3    -0.955869
b  1    -0.023493
   2    -2.304234
   3    -0.652469
c  1    -1.218302
   2    -1.332610
d  2     1.074623
   3     0.723642
dtype: float64
```

stack and unstack will be explored in more detail in Chapter 7.

With a DataFrame, either axis can have a hierarchical index:

```
In [269]: frame = DataFrame(np.arange(12).reshape((4, 3)),
   .....:                   index=[['a', 'a', 'b', 'b'], [1, 2, 1, 2]],
   .....:                   columns=[['Ohio', 'Ohio', 'Colorado'],
   .....:                            ['Green', 'Red', 'Green']])

In [270]: frame
Out[270]:
      Ohio       Colorado
     Green  Red     Green
a 1      0    1         2
  2      3    4         5
b 1      6    7         8
  2      9   10        11
```

The hierarchical levels can have names (as strings or any Python objects). If so, these will show up in the console output (don't confuse the index names with the axis labels!):

```
In [271]: frame.index.names = ['key1', 'key2']

In [272]: frame.columns.names = ['state', 'color']

In [273]: frame
Out[273]:
state       Ohio       Colorado
color      Green  Red     Green
```

```
       key1 key2
       a    1        0   1        2
            2        3   4        5
       b    1        6   7        8
            2        9  10       11
```

With partial column indexing you can similarly select groups of columns:

```
In [274]: frame['Ohio']
Out[274]:
color        Green  Red
key1 key2
a    1           0    1
     2           3    4
b    1           6    7
     2           9   10
```

A `MultiIndex` can be created by itself and then reused; the columns in the above Data-Frame with level names could be created like this:

```
MultiIndex.from_arrays([['Ohio', 'Ohio', 'Colorado'], ['Green', 'Red', 'Green']],
                        names=['state', 'color'])
```

Reordering and Sorting Levels

At times you will need to rearrange the order of the levels on an axis or sort the data by the values in one specific level. The `swaplevel` takes two level numbers or names and returns a new object with the levels interchanged (but the data is otherwise unaltered):

```
In [275]: frame.swaplevel('key1', 'key2')
Out[275]:
state        Ohio       Colorado
color        Green  Red   Green
key2 key1
1    a           0    1       2
2    a           3    4       5
1    b           6    7       8
2    b           9   10      11
```

`sortlevel`, on the other hand, sorts the data (stably) using only the values in a single level. When swapping levels, it's not uncommon to also use `sortlevel` so that the result is lexicographically sorted:

```
In [276]: frame.sortlevel(1)        In [277]: frame.swaplevel(0, 1).sortlevel(0)
Out[276]:                            Out[277]:
state        Ohio       Colorado    state        Ohio       Colorado
color        Green  Red   Green      color        Green  Red   Green
key1 key2                            key2 key1
a    1           0    1       2      1    a           0    1       2
b    1           6    7       8           b           6    7       8
a    2           3    4       5      2    a           3    4       5
b    2           9   10      11           b           9   10      11
```

Data selection performance is much better on hierarchically indexed objects if the index is lexicographically sorted starting with the outermost level, that is, the result of calling sortlevel(0) or sort_index().

Summary Statistics by Level

Many descriptive and summary statistics on DataFrame and Series have a `level` option in which you can specify the level you want to sum by on a particular axis. Consider the above DataFrame; we can sum by level on either the rows or columns like so:

```
In [278]: frame.sum(level='key2')
Out[278]:
state  Ohio       Colorado
color  Green  Red  Green
key2
1         6    8       10
2        12   14       16

In [279]: frame.sum(level='color', axis=1)
Out[279]:
color       Green  Red
key1 key2
a    1          2    1
     2          8    4
b    1         14    7
     2         20   10
```

Under the hood, this utilizes pandas's `groupby` machinery which will be discussed in more detail later in the book.

Using a DataFrame's Columns

It's not unusual to want to use one or more columns from a DataFrame as the row index; alternatively, you may wish to move the row index into the DataFrame's columns. Here's an example DataFrame:

```
In [280]: frame = DataFrame({'a': range(7), 'b': range(7, 0, -1),
   .....:                    'c': ['one', 'one', 'one', 'two', 'two', 'two', 'two'],
   .....:                    'd': [0, 1, 2, 0, 1, 2, 3]})

In [281]: frame
Out[281]:
   a  b    c  d
0  0  7  one  0
1  1  6  one  1
2  2  5  one  2
3  3  4  two  0
4  4  3  two  1
5  5  2  two  2
6  6  1  two  3
```

DataFrame's `set_index` function will create a new DataFrame using one or more of its columns as the index:

```
In [282]: frame2 = frame.set_index(['c', 'd'])

In [283]: frame2
Out[283]:
       a  b
c   d
one 0  0  7
    1  1  6
    2  2  5
two 0  3  4
    1  4  3
    2  5  2
    3  6  1
```

By default the columns are removed from the DataFrame, though you can leave them in:

```
In [284]: frame.set_index(['c', 'd'], drop=False)
Out[284]:
       a  b    c  d
c   d
one 0  0  7  one  0
    1  1  6  one  1
    2  2  5  one  2
two 0  3  4  two  0
    1  4  3  two  1
    2  5  2  two  2
    3  6  1  two  3
```

`reset_index`, on the other hand, does the opposite of `set_index`; the hierarchical index levels are are moved into the columns:

```
In [285]: frame2.reset_index()
Out[285]:
     c  d  a  b
0  one  0  0  7
1  one  1  1  6
2  one  2  2  5
3  two  0  3  4
4  two  1  4  3
5  two  2  5  2
6  two  3  6  1
```

Other pandas Topics

Here are some additional topics that may be of use to you in your data travels.

Integer Indexing

Working with pandas objects indexed by integers is something that often trips up new users due to some differences with indexing semantics on built-in Python data structures like lists and tuples. For example, you would not expect the following code to generate an error:

```
ser = Series(np.arange(3.))
ser[-1]
```

In this case, pandas could "fall back" on integer indexing, but there's not a safe and general way (that I know of) to do this without introducing subtle bugs. Here we have an index containing 0, 1, 2, but inferring what the user wants (label-based indexing or position-based) is difficult:

```
In [287]: ser
Out[287]:
0    0
1    1
2    2
dtype: float64
```

On the other hand, with a non-integer index, there is no potential for ambiguity:

```
In [288]: ser2 = Series(np.arange(3.), index=['a', 'b', 'c'])

In [289]: ser2[-1]
Out[289]: 2.0
```

To keep things consistent, if you have an axis index containing indexers, data selection with integers will always be label-oriented. This includes slicing with ix, too:

```
In [290]: ser.ix[:1]
Out[290]:
0    0
1    1
dtype: float64
```

In cases where you need reliable position-based indexing regardless of the index type, you can use the iget_value method from Series and irow and icol methods from DataFrame:

```
In [291]: ser3 = Series(range(3), index=[-5, 1, 3])

In [292]: ser3.iget_value(2)
Out[292]: 2

In [293]: frame = DataFrame(np.arange(6).reshape(3, 2), index=[2, 0, 1])

In [294]: frame.irow(0)
Out[294]:
0    0
1    1
Name: 2, dtype: int64
```

Panel Data

While not a major topic of this book, pandas has a Panel data structure, which you can think of as a three-dimensional analogue of DataFrame. Much of the development focus of pandas has been in tabular data manipulations as these are easier to reason about, and hierarchical indexing makes using truly N-dimensional arrays unnecessary in a lot of cases.

To create a Panel, you can use a dict of DataFrame objects or a three-dimensional ndarray:

```
import pandas.io.data as web

pdata = pd.Panel(dict((stk, web.get_data_yahoo(stk))
                        for stk in ['AAPL', 'GOOG', 'MSFT', 'DELL']))
```

Each item (the analogue of columns in a DataFrame) in the Panel is a DataFrame:

```
In [298]: pdata
Out[298]:
<class 'pandas.core.panel.Panel'>
Dimensions: 4 (items) x 1158 (major_axis) x 6 (minor_axis)
Items axis: AAPL to MSFT
Major_axis axis: 2010-01-04 00:00:00 to 2014-07-11 00:00:00
Minor_axis axis: Open to Adj Close

In [299]: pdata = pdata.swapaxes('items', 'minor')

In [300]: pdata['Adj Close']
Out[300]:
              AAPL   DELL    GOOG   MSFT
Date
2010-01-04   29.22  14.07    NaN   27.48
2010-01-05   29.27  14.38    NaN   27.49
2010-01-06   28.81  14.10    NaN   27.32
2010-01-07   28.75  14.24    NaN   27.03
2010-01-08   28.94  14.37    NaN   27.22
...           ...    ...     ...    ...
2014-07-07   95.97   NaN   582.25  41.99
2014-07-08   95.35   NaN   571.09  41.78
2014-07-09   95.39   NaN   576.08  41.67
2014-07-10   95.04   NaN   571.10  41.69
2014-07-11   95.22   NaN   579.18  42.09
[1158 rows x 4 columns]
```

ix-based label indexing generalizes to three dimensions, so we can select all data at a particular date or a range of dates like so:

```
In [301]: pdata.ix[:, '6/1/2012', :]
Out[301]:
        Open     High    Low    Close   Volume    Adj Close
AAPL  569.16   572.65  560.52  560.99  130246900    76.60
DELL   12.15    12.30   12.05   12.07   19397600     11.68
GOOG    NaN      NaN     NaN     NaN       NaN        NaN
MSFT   28.76    28.96   28.44   28.45   56634300     26.82

In [302]: pdata.ix['Adj Close', '5/22/2012':, :]
Out[302]:
              AAPL   DELL    GOOG   MSFT
Date
```

```
2012-05-22  76.05  14.59     NaN  28.05
2012-05-23  77.91  12.08     NaN  27.44
2012-05-24  77.19  12.04     NaN  27.40
2012-05-25  76.78  12.05     NaN  27.39
2012-05-28    NaN  12.05     NaN    NaN
...           ...    ...     ...    ...
2014-07-07  95.97    NaN  582.25  41.99
2014-07-08  95.35    NaN  571.09  41.78
2014-07-09  95.39    NaN  576.08  41.67
2014-07-10  95.04    NaN  571.10  41.69
2014-07-11  95.22    NaN  579.18  42.09
[551 rows x 4 columns]
```

An alternate way to represent panel data, especially for fitting statistical models, is in
"stacked" DataFrame form:

```
In [303]: stacked = pdata.ix[:, '5/30/2012':, :].to_frame()

In [304]: stacked
Out[304]:
                   Open    High     Low   Close      Volume  Adj Close
Date       minor
2012-05-30 AAPL  569.20  579.99  566.56  579.17  132357400      79.08
           DELL   12.59   12.70   12.46   12.56   19787800      12.15
           MSFT   29.35   29.48   29.12   29.34   41585500      27.66
2012-05-31 AAPL  580.74  581.50  571.46  577.73  122918600      78.89
           DELL   12.53   12.54   12.33   12.33   19955600      11.93
...                 ...     ...     ...     ...        ...        ...
2014-07-10 GOOG  565.91  576.59  565.01  571.10    1353000     571.10
           MSFT   41.37   42.00   41.05   41.69   21854700      41.69
2014-07-11 AAPL   95.36   95.89   94.86   95.22   33988800      95.22
           GOOG  571.91  580.85  571.42  579.18    1617300     579.18
           MSFT   41.70   42.09   41.48   42.09   24083000      42.09
[1508 rows x 6 columns]
```

DataFrame has a related to_panel method, the inverse of to_frame:

```
In [305]: stacked.to_panel()
Out[305]:
<class 'pandas.core.panel.Panel'>
Dimensions: 6 (items) x 545 (major_axis) x 4 (minor_axis)
Items axis: Open to Adj Close
Major_axis axis: 2012-05-30 00:00:00 to 2014-07-11 00:00:00
Minor_axis axis: AAPL to MSFT
```

Data Loading, Storage, and File Formats

The tools in this book are of little use if you can't easily import and export data in Python. I'm going to be focused on input and output with pandas objects, though there are of course numerous tools in other libraries to aid in this process. NumPy, for example, features low-level but extremely fast binary data loading and storage, including support for memory-mapped array. See Chapter 12 for more on those.

Input and output typically falls into a few main categories: reading text files and other more efficient on-disk formats, loading data from databases, and interacting with network sources like web APIs.

Reading and Writing Data in Text Format

Python has become a beloved language for text and file munging due to its simple syntax for interacting with files, intuitive data structures, and convenient features like tuple packing and unpacking.

pandas features a number of functions for reading tabular data as a DataFrame object. Table 6-1 has a summary of all of them, though `read_csv` and `read_table` are likely the ones you'll use the most.

Table 6-1. Parsing functions in pandas

Function	Description
read_csv	Load delimited data from a file, URL, or file-like object. Use comma as default delimiter
read_table	Load delimited data from a file, URL, or file-like object. Use tab ('\t') as default delimiter
read_fwf	Read data in fixed-width column format (that is, no delimiters)
read_clipboard	Version of read_table that reads data from the clipboard. Useful for converting tables from web pages

I'll give an overview of the mechanics of these functions, which are meant to convert text data into a DataFrame. The options for these functions fall into a few categories:

- Indexing: can treat one or more columns as the returned DataFrame, and whether to get column names from the file, the user, or not at all.
- Type inference and data conversion: this includes the user-defined value conversions and custom list of missing value markers.
- Datetime parsing: includes combining capability, including combining date and time information spread over multiple columns into a single column in the result.
- Iterating: support for iterating over chunks of very large files.
- Unclean data issues: skipping rows or a footer, comments, or other minor things like numeric data with thousands separated by commas.

Type inference is one of the more important features of these functions; that means you don't have to specify which columns are numeric, integer, boolean, or string. Handling dates and other custom types requires a bit more effort, though. Let's start with a small comma-separated (CSV) text file:

```
In [469]: !cat ch06/ex1.csv
a,b,c,d,message
1,2,3,4,hello
5,6,7,8,world
9,10,11,12,foo
```

Since this is comma-delimited, we can use `read_csv` to read it into a DataFrame:

```
In [470]: df = pd.read_csv('ch06/ex1.csv')

In [471]: df
Out[471]:
   a   b   c   d message
0  1   2   3   4   hello
1  5   6   7   8   world
2  9  10  11  12     foo
```

We could also have used `read_table` and specifying the delimiter:

```
In [472]: pd.read_table('ch06/ex1.csv', sep=',')
Out[472]:
   a   b   c   d message
0  1   2   3   4   hello
1  5   6   7   8   world
2  9  10  11  12     foo
```

 Here I used the Unix `cat` shell command to print the raw contents of the file to the screen. If you're on Windows, you can use `type` instead of `cat` to achieve the same effect.

A file will not always have a header row. Consider this file:

```
In [473]: !cat ch06/ex2.csv
1,2,3,4,hello
5,6,7,8,world
9,10,11,12,foo
```

To read this in, you have a couple of options. You can allow pandas to assign default column names, or you can specify names yourself:

```
In [474]: pd.read_csv('ch06/ex2.csv', header=None)
Out[474]:
   0   1   2   3      4
0  1   2   3   4  hello
1  5   6   7   8  world
2  9  10  11  12    foo

In [475]: pd.read_csv('ch06/ex2.csv', names=['a', 'b', 'c', 'd', 'message'])
Out[475]:
   a   b   c   d message
0  1   2   3   4   hello
1  5   6   7   8   world
2  9  10  11  12     foo
```

Suppose you wanted the message column to be the index of the returned DataFrame. You can either indicate you want the column at index 4 or named 'message' using the index_col argument:

```
In [476]: names = ['a', 'b', 'c', 'd', 'message']

In [477]: pd.read_csv('ch06/ex2.csv', names=names, index_col='message')
Out[477]:
         a   b   c   d
message
hello    1   2   3   4
world    5   6   7   8
foo      9  10  11  12
```

In the event that you want to form a hierarchical index from multiple columns, just pass a list of column numbers or names:

```
In [478]: !cat ch06/csv_mindex.csv
key1,key2,value1,value2
one,a,1,2
one,b,3,4
one,c,5,6
one,d,7,8
two,a,9,10
two,b,11,12
two,c,13,14
two,d,15,16

In [479]: parsed = pd.read_csv('ch06/csv_mindex.csv', index_col=['key1', 'key2'])

In [480]: parsed
Out[480]:
```

```
            value1  value2
key1 key2
one  a          1       2
     b          3       4
     c          5       6
     d          7       8
two  a          9      10
     b         11      12
     c         13      14
     d         15      16
```

In some cases, a table might not have a fixed delimiter, using whitespace or some other pattern to separate fields. In these cases, you can pass a regular expression as a delimiter for read_table. Consider a text file that looks like this:

```
In [481]: list(open('ch06/ex3.txt'))
Out[481]:
['            A         B         C\n',
 'aaa -0.264438 -1.026059 -0.619500\n',
 'bbb  0.927272  0.302904 -0.032399\n',
 'ccc -0.264273 -0.386314 -0.217601\n',
 'ddd -0.871858 -0.348382  1.100491\n']
```

While you could do some munging by hand, in this case fields are separated by a variable amount of whitespace. This can be expressed by the regular expression \s+, so we have then:

```
In [482]: result = pd.read_table('ch06/ex3.txt', sep='\s+')

In [483]: result
Out[483]:
            A         B         C
aaa -0.264438 -1.026059 -0.619500
bbb  0.927272  0.302904 -0.032399
ccc -0.264273 -0.386314 -0.217601
ddd -0.871858 -0.348382  1.100491
```

Because there was one fewer column name than the number of data rows, read_table infers that the first column should be the DataFrame's index in this special case.

The parser functions have many additional arguments to help you handle the wide variety of exception file formats that occur (see Table 6-2). For example, you can skip the first, third, and fourth rows of a file with skiprows:

```
In [484]: !cat ch06/ex4.csv
# hey!
a,b,c,d,message
# just wanted to make things more difficult for you
# who reads CSV files with computers, anyway?
1,2,3,4,hello
5,6,7,8,world
9,10,11,12,foo
In [485]: pd.read_csv('ch06/ex4.csv', skiprows=[0, 2, 3])
Out[485]:
   a   b   c   d message
```

```
0  1   2   3   4  hello
1  5   6   7   8  world
2  9  10  11  12    foo
```

Handling missing values is an important and frequently nuanced part of the file parsing process. Missing data is usually either not present (empty string) or marked by some *sentinel* value. By default, pandas uses a set of commonly occurring sentinels, such as NA, -1.#IND, and NULL:

```
In [486]: !cat ch06/ex5.csv
something,a,b,c,d,message
one,1,2,3,4,NA
two,5,6,,8,world
three,9,10,11,12,foo
In [487]: result = pd.read_csv('ch06/ex5.csv')

In [488]: result
Out[488]:
  something  a   b    c   d message
0       one  1   2    3   4     NaN
1       two  5   6  NaN   8   world
2     three  9  10   11  12     foo

In [489]: pd.isnull(result)
Out[489]:
  something      a      b      c      d message
0     False  False  False  False  False    True
1     False  False  False   True  False   False
2     False  False  False  False  False   False
```

The na_values option can take either a list or set of strings to consider missing values:

```
In [490]: result = pd.read_csv('ch06/ex5.csv', na_values=['NULL'])

In [491]: result
Out[491]:
  something  a   b    c   d message
0       one  1   2    3   4     NaN
1       two  5   6  NaN   8   world
2     three  9  10   11  12     foo
```

Different NA sentinels can be specified for each column in a dict:

```
In [492]: sentinels = {'message': ['foo', 'NA'], 'something': ['two']}

In [493]: pd.read_csv('ch06/ex5.csv', na_values=sentinels)
Out[493]:
  something  a   b    c   d message
0       one  1   2    3   4     NaN
1       NaN  5   6  NaN   8   world
2     three  9  10   11  12     NaN
```

Table 6-2. read_csv /read_table function arguments

Argument	Description
path	String indicating filesystem location, URL, or file-like object
sep or delimiter	Character sequence or regular expression to use to split fields in each row
header	Row number to use as column names. Defaults to 0 (first row), but should be None if there is no header row
index_col	Column numbers or names to use as the row index in the result. Can be a single name/number or a list of them for a hierarchical index
names	List of column names for result, combine with header=None
skiprows	Number of rows at beginning of file to ignore or list of row numbers (starting from 0) to skip
na_values	Sequence of values to replace with NA
comment	Character or characters to split comments off the end of lines
parse_dates	Attempt to parse data to datetime; False by default. If True, will attempt to parse all columns. Otherwise can specify a list of column numbers or name to parse. If element of list is tuple or list, will combine multiple columns together and parse to date (for example if date/time split across two columns)
keep_date_col	If joining columns to parse date, keep the joined columns. Default False
converters	Dict containing column number of name mapping to functions. For example {'foo': f} would apply the function f to all values in the 'foo' column
dayfirst	When parsing potentially ambiguous dates, treat as international format (e.g. 7/6/2012 -> June 7, 2012). Default False
date_parser	Function to use to parse dates
nrows	Number of rows to read from beginning of file
iterator	Return a TextParser object for reading file piecemeal
chunksize	For iteration, size of file chunks
skip_footer	Number of lines to ignore at end of file
verbose	Print various parser output information, like the number of missing values placed in non-numeric columns
encoding	Text encoding for unicode. For example 'utf-8' for UTF-8 encoded text
squeeze	If the parsed data only contains one column return a Series
thousands	Separator for thousands, e.g. ',' or '.'

Reading Text Files in Pieces

When processing very large files or figuring out the right set of arguments to correctly process a large file, you may only want to read in a small piece of a file or iterate through smaller chunks of the file.

```
In [494]: result = pd.read_csv('ch06/ex6.csv')

In [495]: result
Out[495]:
```

```
          one       two     three      four key
0    0.467976 -0.038649 -0.295344 -1.824726   L
1   -0.358893  1.404453  0.704965 -0.200638   B
2   -0.501840  0.659254 -0.421691 -0.057688   G
3    0.204886  1.074134  1.388361 -0.982404   R
4    0.354628 -0.133116  0.283763 -0.837063   Q
...       ...       ...       ...       ...  ..
9995 2.311896 -0.417070 -1.409599 -0.515821   L
9996 -0.479893 -0.650419  0.745152 -0.646038   E
9997 0.523331  0.787112  0.486066  1.093156   K
9998 -0.362559  0.598894 -1.843201  0.887292   G
9999 -0.096376 -1.012999 -0.657431 -0.573315   0
[10000 rows x 5 columns]
```

If you want to only read out a small number of rows (avoiding reading the entire file),
specify that with nrows:

```
In [496]: pd.read_csv('ch06/ex6.csv', nrows=5)
Out[496]:
        one       two     three      four key
0  0.467976 -0.038649 -0.295344 -1.824726   L
1 -0.358893  1.404453  0.704965 -0.200638   B
2 -0.501840  0.659254 -0.421691 -0.057688   G
3  0.204886  1.074134  1.388361 -0.982404   R
4  0.354628 -0.133116  0.283763 -0.837063   Q
```

To read out a file in pieces, specify a chunksize as a number of rows:

```
In [497]: chunker = pd.read_csv('ch06/ex6.csv', chunksize=1000)

In [498]: chunker
Out[498]: <pandas.io.parsers.TextFileReader at 0x7ff58b678590>
```

The TextParser object returned by read_csv allows you to iterate over the parts of the
file according to the chunksize. For example, we can iterate over ex6.csv, aggregating
the value counts in the 'key' column like so:

```
chunker = pd.read_csv('ch06/ex6.csv', chunksize=1000)

tot = Series([])
for piece in chunker:
    tot = tot.add(piece['key'].value_counts(), fill_value=0)

tot = tot.order(ascending=False)
```

We have then:

```
In [500]: tot[:10]
Out[500]:
E    368
X    364
L    346
O    343
Q    340
M    338
J    337
F    335
```

```
K    334
H    330
dtype: float64
```

TextParser is also equipped with a get_chunk method which enables you to read pieces of an arbitrary size.

Writing Data Out to Text Format

Data can also be exported to delimited format. Let's consider one of the CSV files read above:

```
In [501]: data = pd.read_csv('ch06/ex5.csv')
```

```
In [502]: data
Out[502]:
  something  a   b    c   d message
0      one  1   2    3   4     NaN
1      two  5   6  NaN   8   world
2    three  9  10   11  12     foo
```

Using DataFrame's to_csv method, we can write the data out to a comma-separated file:

```
In [503]: data.to_csv('ch06/out.csv')
```

```
In [504]: !cat ch06/out.csv
,something,a,b,c,d,message
0,one,1,2,3.0,4,
1,two,5,6,,8,world
2,three,9,10,11.0,12,foo
```

Other delimiters can be used, of course (writing to sys.stdout so it just prints the text result; make sure to import sys):

```
In [505]: data.to_csv(sys.stdout, sep='|')
|something|a|b|c|d|message
0|one|1|2|3.0|4|
1|two|5|6||8|world
2|three|9|10|11.0|12|foo
```

Missing values appear as empty strings in the output. You might want to denote them by some other sentinel value:

```
In [506]: data.to_csv(sys.stdout, na_rep='NULL')
,something,a,b,c,d,message
0,one,1,2,3.0,4,NULL
1,two,5,6,NULL,8,world
2,three,9,10,11.0,12,foo
```

With no other options specified, both the row and column labels are written. Both of these can be disabled:

```
In [507]: data.to_csv(sys.stdout, index=False, header=False)
one,1,2,3.0,4,
two,5,6,,8,world
three,9,10,11.0,12,foo
```

You can also write only a subset of the columns, and in an order of your choosing:

```
In [508]: data.to_csv(sys.stdout, index=False, cols=['a', 'b', 'c'])
a,b,c
1,2,3.0
5,6,
9,10,11.0
```

Series also has a to_csv method:

```
In [509]: dates = pd.date_range('1/1/2000', periods=7)

In [510]: ts = Series(np.arange(7), index=dates)

In [511]: ts.to_csv('ch06/tseries.csv')

In [512]: !cat ch06/tseries.csv
2000-01-01,0
2000-01-02,1
2000-01-03,2
2000-01-04,3
2000-01-05,4
2000-01-06,5
2000-01-07,6
```

With a bit of wrangling (no header, first column as index), you can read a CSV version of a Series with read_csv, but there is also a from_csv convenience method that makes it a bit simpler:

```
In [513]: Series.from_csv('ch06/tseries.csv', parse_dates=True)
Out[513]:
2000-01-01    0
2000-01-02    1
2000-01-03    2
2000-01-04    3
2000-01-05    4
2000-01-06    5
2000-01-07    6
dtype: int64
```

See the docstrings for to_csv and from_csv in IPython for more information.

Manually Working with Delimited Formats

Most forms of tabular data can be loaded from disk using functions like pan das.read_table. In some cases, however, some manual processing may be necessary. It's not uncommon to receive a file with one or more malformed lines that trip up read_table. To illustrate the basic tools, consider a small CSV file:

```
In [514]: !cat ch06/ex7.csv
"a","b","c"
"1","2","3"
"1","2","3","4"
```

For any file with a single-character delimiter, you can use Python's built-in `csv` module. To use it, pass any open file or file-like object to `csv.reader`:

```
import csv
f = open('ch06/ex7.csv')

reader = csv.reader(f)
```

Iterating through the reader like a file yields tuples of values in each like with any quote characters removed:

```
In [516]: for line in reader:
   .....:     print line
['a', 'b', 'c']
['1', '2', '3']
['1', '2', '3', '4']
```

From there, it's up to you to do the wrangling necessary to put the data in the form that you need it. For example:

```
In [517]: lines = list(csv.reader(open('ch06/ex7.csv')))

In [518]: header, values = lines[0], lines[1:]

In [519]: data_dict = {h: v for h, v in zip(header, zip(*values))}

In [520]: data_dict
Out[520]: {'a': ('1', '1'), 'b': ('2', '2'), 'c': ('3', '3')}
```

CSV files come in many different flavors. Defining a new format with a different delimiter, string quoting convention, or line terminator is done by defining a simple subclass of `csv.Dialect`:

```
class my_dialect(csv.Dialect):
    lineterminator = '\n'
    delimiter = ';'
    quotechar = '"'
    quoting = csv.QUOTE_MINIMAL

reader = csv.reader(f, dialect=my_dialect)
```

Individual CSV dialect parameters can also be given as keywords to `csv.reader` without having to define a subclass:

```
reader = csv.reader(f, delimiter='|')
```

The possible options (attributes of `csv.Dialect`) and what they do can be found in Table 6-3.

Table 6-3. CSV dialect options

Argument	Description
delimiter	One-character string to separate fields. Defaults to ','.
lineterminator	Line terminator for writing, defaults to '\r\n'. Reader ignores this and recognizes cross-platform line terminators.

Argument	Description
quotechar	Quote character for fields with special characters (like a delimiter). Default is ' " '.
quoting	Quoting convention. Options include csv.QUOTE_ALL (quote all fields), csv.QUOTE_MINIMAL (only fields with special characters like the delimiter), csv.QUOTE_NONNUMERIC, and csv.QUOTE_NON (no quoting). See Python's documentation for full details. Defaults to QUOTE_MINIMAL.
skipinitialspace	Ignore whitespace after each delimiter. Default False.
doublequote	How to handle quoting character inside a field. If True, it is doubled. See online documentation for full detail and behavior.
escapechar	String to escape the delimiter if quoting is set to csv.QUOTE_NONE. Disabled by default

 For files with more complicated or fixed multicharacter delimiters, you will not be able to use the csv module. In those cases, you'll have to do the line splitting and other cleanup using string's split method or the regular expression method re.split.

To *write* delimited files manually, you can use csv.writer. It accepts an open, writable file object and the same dialect and format options as csv.reader:

```
with open('mydata.csv', 'w') as f:
    writer = csv.writer(f, dialect=my_dialect)
    writer.writerow(('one', 'two', 'three'))
    writer.writerow(('1', '2', '3'))
    writer.writerow(('4', '5', '6'))
    writer.writerow(('7', '8', '9'))
```

JSON Data

JSON (short for JavaScript Object Notation) has become one of the standard formats for sending data by HTTP request between web browsers and other applications. It is a much more flexible data format than a tabular text form like CSV. Here is an example:

```
obj = """
{"name": "Wes",
 "places_lived": ["United States", "Spain", "Germany"],
 "pet": null,
 "siblings": [{"name": "Scott", "age": 25, "pet": "Zuko"},
             {"name": "Katie", "age": 33, "pet": "Cisco"}]
}
"""
```

JSON is very nearly valid Python code with the exception of its null value null and some other nuances (such as disallowing trailing commas at the end of lists). The basic types are objects (dicts), arrays (lists), strings, numbers, booleans, and nulls. All of the keys in an object must be strings. There are several Python libraries for reading and writing JSON data. I'll use `json` here as it is built into the Python standard library. To convert a JSON string to Python form, use `json.loads`:

```
In [522]: import json

In [523]: result = json.loads(obj)

In [524]: result
Out[524]:
{u'name': u'Wes',
 u'pet': None,
 u'places_lived': [u'United States', u'Spain', u'Germany'],
 u'siblings': [{u'age': 25, u'name': u'Scott', u'pet': u'Zuko'},
 {u'age': 33, u'name': u'Katie', u'pet': u'Cisco'}]}
```

`json.dumps` on the other hand converts a Python object back to JSON:

```
In [525]: asjson = json.dumps(result)
```

How you convert a JSON object or list of objects to a DataFrame or some other data structure for analysis will be up to you. Conveniently, you can pass a list of JSON objects to the DataFrame constructor and select a subset of the data fields:

```
In [526]: siblings = DataFrame(result['siblings'], columns=['name', 'age'])

In [527]: siblings
Out[527]:
    name  age
0  Scott   25
1  Katie   33
```

For an extended example of reading and manipulating JSON data (including nested records), see the USDA Food Database example in the next chapter.

Starting from pandas 0.12, fast native JSON export (`to_json`) and decoding (`read_json`) is available.

XML and HTML: Web Scraping

Python has many libraries for reading and writing data in the ubiquitous HTML and XML formats. lxml (*http://lxml.de*) is one that has consistently strong performance in parsing very large files. lxml has multiple programmer interfaces; first I'll show using `lxml.html` for HTML, then parse some XML using `lxml.objectify`.

Many websites make data available in HTML tables for viewing in a browser, but not downloadable as an easily machine-readable format like JSON, HTML, or XML. I noticed that this was the case with Yahoo! Finance's stock options data. If you aren't familiar with this data; options are derivative contracts giving you the right to buy (*call* option) or sell (*put* option) a company's stock at some particular price (the *strike*) between now and some fixed point in the future (the *expiry*). People trade both call and put options across many strikes and expiries; this data can all be found together in tables on Yahoo! Finance.

To get started, find the URL you want to extract data from, open it with `urllib2` and parse the stream with lxml like so:

```
from lxml.html import parse
from urllib2 import urlopen

parsed = parse(urlopen('http://finance.yahoo.com/q/op?s=AAPL+Options'))

doc = parsed.getroot()
```

Using this object, you can extract all HTML tags of a particular type, such as `table` tags containing the data of interest. As a simple motivating example, suppose you wanted to get a list of every URL linked to in the document; links are a tags in HTML. Using the document root's `findall` method along with an XPath (a means of expressing "queries" on the document):

```
In [529]: links = doc.findall('.//a')

In [530]: links[15:20]
Out[530]:
[<Element a at 0x7ff58b64e158>,
 <Element a at 0x7ff58b64e1b0>,
 <Element a at 0x7ff58b64e208>,
 <Element a at 0x7ff58b64e260>,
 <Element a at 0x7ff58b64e2b8>]
```

But these are objects representing HTML elements; to get the URL and link text you have to use each element's `get` method (for the URL) and `text_content` method (for the display text):

```
In [531]: lnk = links[28]

In [532]: lnk
Out[532]: <Element a at 0x7ff58b64e5d0>

In [533]: lnk.get('href')
Out[533]: 'https://login.yahoo.com/config/login?.src=
quote&.intl=us&.lang=en-US&.done=
http://finance.yahoo.com/q/op%3fs=AAPL%2bOptions'

In [534]: lnk.text_content()
Out[534]: ' Sign In '
```

Thus, getting a list of all URLs in the document is a matter of writing this list comprehension:

```
In [535]: urls = [lnk.get('href') for lnk in doc.findall('.//a')]

In [536]: urls[-10:]
Out[536]:
['/q?s=AAPL140725P00104000',
 '/q/op?s=AAPL&k=105.000000',
```

```
 '/q?s=AAPL140725P00105000',
 '/q/op?s=AAPL&k=110.000000',
 '/q?s=AAPL140725P00110000',
 '/q/os?s=AAPL&m=2014-07-25',
 'http://help.yahoo.com/l/us/yahoo/finance/quotes/fitadelay.html',
 'http://www.capitaliq.com',
 'http://www.csidata.com',
 'http://www.morningstar.com/']
```

Now, finding the right tables in the document can be a matter of trial and error; some websites make it easier by giving a table of interest an id attribute. I determined that these were the two tables containing the call data and put data, respectively:

```
tables = doc.findall('.//table')
calls = tables[9]
puts = tables[13]
```

Each table has a header row followed by each of the data rows:

```
In [538]: rows = calls.findall('.//tr')
```

For the header as well as the data rows, we want to extract the text from each cell; in the case of the header these are th cells and td cells for the data:

```
def _unpack(row, kind='td'):
    elts = row.findall('.//%s' % kind)
    return [val.text_content() for val in elts]
```

Thus, we obtain:

```
In [540]: _unpack(rows[0], kind='th')
Out[540]: ['Strike', 'Symbol', 'Last', 'Chg', 'Bid', 'Ask', 'Vol', 'Open Int']

In [541]: _unpack(rows[1], kind='td')
Out[541]: ['75.00', 'AAPL140725C00075000', '18.85', ' 0.00', '18.45', '20.00', '7', '35']
```

Now, it's a matter of combining all of these steps together to convert this data into a DataFrame. Since the numerical data is still in string format, we want to convert some, but perhaps not all of the columns to floating point format. You could do this by hand, but, luckily, pandas has a class TextParser that is used internally in the read_csv and other parsing functions to do the appropriate automatic type conversion:

```
from pandas.io.parsers import TextParser
```

```
def parse_options_data(table):
    rows = table.findall('.//tr')
    header = _unpack(rows[0], kind='th')
    data = [_unpack(r) for r in rows[1:]]
    return TextParser(data, names=header).get_chunk()
```

Finally, we invoke this parsing function on the lxml table objects and get DataFrame results:

```
In [543]: call_data = parse_options_data(calls)
```

```
In [544]: put_data = parse_options_data(puts)
```

```
In [545]: call_data[:10]
Out[545]:
   Strike             Symbol   Last   Chg    Bid    Ask  Vol Open Int
0   75.00  AAPL140725C00075000  18.85  0.00  18.45  20.00    7       35
1   78.57  AAPL140725C00078570  16.00  0.00  15.05  16.25  196      287
2   80.00  AAPL140725C00080000  14.20  0.10  13.85  14.40  205      800
3   81.43  AAPL140725C00081430  13.17  0.00  12.30  13.30    2       72
4   82.00  AAPL140725C00082000  12.15  0.00  11.90  12.10   51       51
5   82.14  AAPL140725C00082140   8.40  0.00  11.75  12.00   63       98
6   82.86  AAPL140725C00082860  11.27  0.25  11.05  11.30    7      659
7   83.00  AAPL140725C00083000  11.35  0.10  10.90  11.15   50       10
8   83.57  AAPL140725C00083570  10.60  2.23  10.35  10.60    7       45
9   84.00  AAPL140725C00084000  10.57  0.26   9.95  10.15   10       37
```

Parsing XML with lxml.objectify

XML (extensible markup language) is another common structured data format supporting hierarchical, nested data with metadata. The files that generate the book you are reading actually form a series of large XML documents.

Above, I showed the lxml library and its `lxml.html` interface. Here I show an alternate interface that's convenient for XML data, `lxml.objectify`.

The New York Metropolitan Transportation Authority (MTA) publishes a number of data series about its bus and train services (*http://www.mta.info/developers/download .html*). Here we'll look at the performance data which is contained in a set of XML files. Each train or bus service has a different file (like `Performance_MNR.xml` for the Metro-North Railroad) containing monthly data as a series of XML records that look like this:

```
INDICATOR>
  <INDICATOR_SEQ>373889</INDICATOR_SEQ>
  <PARENT_SEQ></PARENT_SEQ>
  <AGENCY_NAME>Metro-North Railroad</AGENCY_NAME>
  <INDICATOR_NAME>Escalator Availability</INDICATOR_NAME>
  <DESCRIPTION>Percent of the time that escalators are operational
  systemwide. The availability rate is based on physical observations performed
  the morning of regular business days only. This is a new indicator the agency
  began reporting in 2009.</DESCRIPTION>
  <PERIOD_YEAR>2011</PERIOD_YEAR>
  <PERIOD_MONTH>12</PERIOD_MONTH>
  <CATEGORY>Service Indicators</CATEGORY>
  <FREQUENCY>M</FREQUENCY>
  <DESIRED_CHANGE>U</DESIRED_CHANGE>
  <INDICATOR_UNIT>%</INDICATOR_UNIT>
  <DECIMAL_PLACES>1</DECIMAL_PLACES>
  <YTD_TARGET>97.00</YTD_TARGET>
  <YTD_ACTUAL></YTD_ACTUAL>
  <MONTHLY_TARGET>97.00</MONTHLY_TARGET>
  <MONTHLY_ACTUAL></MONTHLY_ACTUAL>
</INDICATOR>
```

Using `lxml.objectify`, we parse the file and get a reference to the root node of the XML file with `getroot`:

```
from lxml import objectify

path = 'Performance_MNR.xml'
parsed = objectify.parse(open(path))
root = parsed.getroot()
```

`root.INDICATOR` return a generator yielding each `<INDICATOR>` XML element. For each record, we can populate a dict of tag names (like `YTD_ACTUAL`) to data values (excluding a few tags):

```
data = []

skip_fields = ['PARENT_SEQ', 'INDICATOR_SEQ',
               'DESIRED_CHANGE', 'DECIMAL_PLACES']

for elt in root.INDICATOR:
    el_data = {}
    for child in elt.getchildren():
        if child.tag in skip_fields:
            continue
        el_data[child.tag] = child.pyval
    data.append(el_data)
```

Lastly, convert this list of dicts into a DataFrame:

```
In [550]: perf = DataFrame(data)

In [551]: perf
Out[551]:
Empty DataFrame
Columns: []
Index: []
```

XML data can get much more complicated than this example. Each tag can have metadata, too. Consider an HTML link tag which is also valid XML:

```
from StringIO import StringIO
tag = '<a href="http://www.google.com">Google</a>'

root = objectify.parse(StringIO(tag)).getroot()
```

You can now access any of the fields (like `href`) in the tag or the link text:

```
In [553]: root
Out[553]: <Element a at 0x7ff58ade3dd0>

In [554]: root.get('href')
Out[554]: 'http://www.google.com'

In [555]: root.text
Out[555]: 'Google'
```

Binary Data Formats

One of the easiest ways to store data efficiently in binary format is using Python's built-in `pickle` serialization. Conveniently, pandas objects all have a **save** method which writes the data to disk as a pickle:

```
In [556]: frame = pd.read_csv('ch06/ex1.csv')

In [557]: frame
Out[557]:
   a   b   c   d message
0  1   2   3   4   hello
1  5   6   7   8   world
2  9  10  11  12     foo

In [558]: frame.save('ch06/frame_pickle')
```

You read the data back into Python with `pandas.load`, another pickle convenience function:

```
In [559]: pd.load('ch06/frame_pickle')
Out[559]:
   a   b   c   d message
0  1   2   3   4   hello
1  5   6   7   8   world
2  9  10  11  12     foo
```

 pickle is only recommended as a short-term storage format. The problem is that it is hard to guarantee that the format will be stable over time; an object pickled today may not unpickle with a later version of a library. I have made every effort to ensure that this does not occur with pandas, but at some point in the future it may be necessary to "break" the pickle format.

Using HDF5 Format

There are a number of tools that facilitate efficiently reading and writing large amounts of scientific data in binary format on disk. A popular industry-grade library for this is HDF5, which is a C library with interfaces in many other languages like Java, Python, and MATLAB. The "HDF" in HDF5 stands for *hierarchical data format*. Each HDF5 file contains an internal file system-like node structure enabling you to store multiple datasets and supporting metadata. Compared with simpler formats, HDF5 supports on-the-fly compression with a variety of compressors, enabling data with repeated patterns to be stored more efficiently. For very large datasets that don't fit into memory, HDF5 is a good choice as you can efficiently read and write small sections of much larger arrays.

There are not one but two interfaces to the HDF5 library in Python, PyTables and h5py, each of which takes a different approach to the problem. h5py provides a direct, but high-level interface to the HDF5 API, while PyTables abstracts many of the details of

HDF5 to provide multiple flexible data containers, table indexing, querying capability, and some support for out-of-core computations.

pandas has a minimal dict-like HDFStore class, which uses PyTables to store pandas objects:

```
In [560]: store = pd.HDFStore('mydata.h5')

In [561]: store['obj1'] = frame

In [562]: store['obj1_col'] = frame['a']

In [563]: store
Out[563]:
<class 'pandas.io.pytables.HDFStore'>
File path: mydata.h5
/obj1                 frame        (shape->[3,5])
/obj1_col             series       (shape->[3])
```

Objects contained in the HDF5 file can be retrieved in a dict-like fashion:

```
In [564]: store['obj1']
Out[564]:
   a   b   c   d message
0  1   2   3   4   hello
1  5   6   7   8   world
2  9  10  11  12     foo
```

If you work with huge quantities of data, I would encourage you to explore PyTables and h5py to see how they can suit your needs. Since many data analysis problems are IO-bound (rather than CPU-bound), using a tool like HDF5 can massively accelerate your applications.

 HDF5 is *not* a database. It is best suited for write-once, read-many datasets. While data can be added to a file at any time, if multiple writers do so simultaneously, the file can become corrupted.

Reading Microsoft Excel Files

pandas also supports reading tabular data stored in Excel 2003 (and higher) files using the ExcelFile class. Internally ExcelFile uses the xlrd and openpyxl packages, so you may have to install them first. To use ExcelFile, create an instance by passing a path to an xls or xlsx file:

```
xls_file = pd.ExcelFile('data.xls')
```

Data stored in a sheet can then be read into DataFrame using parse:

```
table = xls_file.parse('Sheet1')
```

Interacting with HTML and Web APIs

Many websites have public APIs providing data feeds via JSON or some other format. There are a number of ways to access these APIs from Python; one easy-to-use method that I recommend is the requests package (*http://docs.python-requests.org*). To find the first 30 GitHub issue labels associated with the next pandas release (v0.15.0 as of this writing), we can make a GET HTTP request like so:

```
In [567]: import requests

In [568]: url = 'https://api.github.com/repos/pydata/pandas/milestones/28/labels'

In [569]: resp = requests.get(url)

In [570]: resp
Out[570]: <Response [200]>
```

The Response object's `json` method will return a dictionary containing JSON parsed into native Python objects.

```
data = resp.json()
data[:5]
```

Each element in `data` is a dictionary containing the color, URL, and name of the issue label. We can pass `data` directly to DataFrame:

```
In [573]: issue_labels = DataFrame(data)

In [574]: issue_labels
Out[574]:
      color         name                                              url
0     e10c02         Bug  https://api.github.com/repos/pydata/pandas/lab...
1     4E9A06  Enhancement  https://api.github.com/repos/pydata/pandas/lab...
2     FCE94F     Refactor  https://api.github.com/repos/pydata/pandas/lab...
3     75507B  Build problem  https://api.github.com/repos/pydata/pandas/lab...
4     3465A4         Docs  https://api.github.com/repos/pydata/pandas/lab...
..       ...          ...                                              ...
25    eb6420       Period  https://api.github.com/repos/pydata/pandas/lab...
26    207de5    MultiIndex  https://api.github.com/repos/pydata/pandas/lab...
27    0052cc    Low-Memory  https://api.github.com/repos/pydata/pandas/lab...
28    e11d21   Categorical  https://api.github.com/repos/pydata/pandas/lab...
29    5319e7        Stata  https://api.github.com/repos/pydata/pandas/lab...
[30 rows x 3 columns]
```

Each row in the DataFrame now has the extracted data from each issue label:

```
issue_labels.ix[7]
```

With a bit of elbow grease, you can create some higher-level interfaces to common web APIs that return DataFrame objects for easy analysis.

Interacting with Databases

In many applications data rarely comes from text files, that being a fairly inefficient way to store large amounts of data. SQL-based relational databases (such as SQL Server, PostgreSQL, and MySQL) are in wide use, and many alternative non-SQL (so-called *NoSQL*) databases have become quite popular. The choice of database is usually dependent on the performance, data integrity, and scalability needs of an application.

Loading data from SQL into a DataFrame is fairly straightforward, and pandas has some functions to simplify the process. As an example, I'll use an in-memory SQLite database using Python's built-in `sqlite3` driver:

```
import sqlite3

query = """
CREATE TABLE test
(a VARCHAR(20), b VARCHAR(20),
 c REAL,        d INTEGER
);"""

con = sqlite3.connect(':memory:')
con.execute(query)
con.commit()
```

Then, insert a few rows of data:

```
data = [('Atlanta', 'Georgia', 1.25, 6),
        ('Tallahassee', 'Florida', 2.6, 3),
        ('Sacramento', 'California', 1.7, 5)]
stmt = "INSERT INTO test VALUES(?, ?, ?, ?)"

con.executemany(stmt, data)
con.commit()
```

Most Python SQL drivers (PyODBC, psycopg2, MySQLdb, pymssql, etc.) return a list of tuples when selecting data from a table:

```
In [578]: cursor = con.execute('select * from test')

In [579]: rows = cursor.fetchall()

In [580]: rows
Out[580]:
[(u'Atlanta', u'Georgia', 1.25, 6),
 (u'Tallahassee', u'Florida', 2.6, 3),
 (u'Sacramento', u'California', 1.7, 5)]
```

You can pass the list of tuples to the DataFrame constructor, but you also need the column names, contained in the cursor's `description` attribute:

```
In [581]: cursor.description
Out[581]:
(('a', None, None, None, None, None, None),
 ('b', None, None, None, None, None, None),
```

```
('c', None, None, None, None, None, None),
('d', None, None, None, None, None, None))
In [582]: DataFrame(rows, columns=zip(*cursor.description)[0])
Out[582]:
            a           b     c  d
0      Atlanta     Georgia  1.25  6
1   Tallahassee    Florida  2.60  3
2   Sacramento  California  1.70  5
```

This is quite a bit of munging that you'd rather not repeat each time you query the database. pandas has a `read_sql` function that simplifies the process. Just pass the select statement and the connection object:

```
In [584]: pd.read_sql('select * from test', con)
Out[584]:
            a           b     c  d
0      Atlanta     Georgia  1.25  6
1   Tallahassee    Florida  2.60  3
2   Sacramento  California  1.70  5
```

Storing and Loading Data in MongoDB

NoSQL databases take many different forms. Some are simple dict-like key-value stores like BerkeleyDB or Tokyo Cabinet, while others are document-based, with a dict-like object being the basic unit of storage. I've chosen MongoDB (*http://mongodb.org*) for my example. I started a MongoDB instance locally on my machine, and connect to it on the default port using pymongo, the official driver for MongoDB:

```
import pymongo
con = pymongo.Connection('localhost', port=27017)
```

Documents stored in MongoDB are found in collections inside databases. Each running instance of the MongoDB server can have multiple databases, and each database can have multiple collections. Suppose I wanted to store the Twitter API data from earlier in the chapter. First, I can access the (currently empty) tweets collection:

```
tweets = con.db.tweets
```

Then, I load the list of tweets and write each of them to the collection using `tweets.save` (which writes the Python dict to MongoDB):

```
import requests, json
url = 'http://search.twitter.com/search.json?q=python%20pandas'
data = json.loads(requests.get(url).text)

for tweet in data['results']:
    tweets.save(tweet)
```

Now, if I wanted to get all of my tweets (if any) from the collection, I can query the collection with the following syntax:

```
cursor = tweets.find({'from_user': 'wesmckinn'})
```

The cursor returned is an iterator that yields each document as a dict. As above I can convert this into a DataFrame, optionally extracting a subset of the data fields in each tweet:

```
tweet_fields = ['created_at', 'from_user', 'id', 'text']
result = DataFrame(list(cursor), columns=tweet_fields)
```

## CHAPTER 7

Data Wrangling: Clean, Transform, Merge, Reshape

Much of the programming work in data analysis and modeling is spent on data prep-aration: loading, cleaning, transforming, and rearranging. Sometimes the way that data is stored in files or databases is not the way you need it for a data processing application. Many people choose to do ad hoc processing of data from one form to another using a general purpose programming, like Python, Perl, R, or Java, or UNIX text processing tools like sed or awk. Fortunately, pandas along with the Python standard library pro-vide you with a high-level, flexible, and high-performance set of core manipulations and algorithms to enable you to wrangle data into the right form without much trouble.

If you identify a type of data manipulation that isn't anywhere in this book or elsewhere in the pandas library, feel free to suggest it on the mailing list or GitHub site. Indeed, much of the design and implementation of pandas has been driven by the needs of real world applications.

Combining and Merging Data Sets

Data contained in pandas objects can be combined together in a number of built-in ways:

- `pandas.merge` connects rows in DataFrames based on one or more keys. This will be familiar to users of SQL or other relational databases, as it implements database *join* operations.
- `pandas.concat` glues or stacks together objects along an axis.
- `combine_first` instance method enables splicing together overlapping data to fill in missing values in one object with values from another.

I will address each of these and give a number of examples. They'll be utilized in ex-amples throughout the rest of the book.

Database-style DataFrame Merges

Merge or *join* operations combine data sets by linking rows using one or more *keys*. These operations are central to relational databases. The `merge` function in pandas is the main entry point for using these algorithms on your data.

Let's start with a simple example:

```
In [15]: df1 = DataFrame({'key': ['b', 'b', 'a', 'c', 'a', 'a', 'b'],
   ....:                  'data1': range(7)})

In [16]: df2 = DataFrame({'key': ['a', 'b', 'd'],
   ....:                  'data2': range(3)})

In [17]: df1            In [18]: df2
Out[17]:                Out[18]:
   data1 key               data2 key
0      0   b            0       0   a
1      1   b            1       1   b
2      2   a            2       2   d
3      3   c
4      4   a
5      5   a
6      6   b
```

This is an example of a *many-to-one* merge situation; the data in `df1` has multiple rows labeled a and b, whereas `df2` has only one row for each value in the key column. Calling `merge` with these objects we obtain:

```
In [19]: pd.merge(df1, df2)
Out[19]:
   data1 key  data2
0      0   b      1
1      1   b      1
2      6   b      1
3      2   a      0
4      4   a      0
5      5   a      0
```

Note that I didn't specify which column to join on. If not specified, `merge` uses the overlapping column names as the keys. It's a good practice to specify explicitly, though:

```
In [20]: pd.merge(df1, df2, on='key')
Out[20]:
   data1 key  data2
0      0   b      1
1      1   b      1
2      6   b      1
3      2   a      0
4      4   a      0
5      5   a      0
```

If the column names are different in each object, you can specify them separately:

```
In [21]: df3 = DataFrame({'lkey': ['b', 'b', 'a', 'c', 'a', 'a', 'b'],
   ....:                  'data1': range(7)})
```

```
In [22]: df4 = DataFrame({'rkey': ['a', 'b', 'd'],
   ....:                   'data2': range(3)})

In [23]: pd.merge(df3, df4, left_on='lkey', right_on='rkey')
Out[23]:
   data1 lkey  data2 rkey
0      0    b      1    b
1      1    b      1    b
2      6    b      1    b
3      2    a      0    a
4      4    a      0    a
5      5    a      0    a
```

You probably noticed that the 'c' and 'd' values and associated data are missing from the result. By default merge does an 'inner' join; the keys in the result are the intersection. Other possible options are 'left', 'right', and 'outer'. The outer join takes the union of the keys, combining the effect of applying both left and right joins:

```
In [24]: pd.merge(df1, df2, how='outer')
Out[24]:
   data1 key  data2
0      0   b      1
1      1   b      1
2      6   b      1
3      2   a      0
4      4   a      0
5      5   a      0
6      3   c    NaN
7    NaN   d      2
```

Many-to-many merges have well-defined though not necessarily intuitive behavior. Here's an example:

```
In [25]: df1 = DataFrame({'key': ['b', 'b', 'a', 'c', 'a', 'b'],
   ....:                   'data1': range(6)})

In [26]: df2 = DataFrame({'key': ['a', 'b', 'a', 'b', 'd'],
   ....:                   'data2': range(5)})

In [27]: df1         In [28]: df2
Out[27]:             Out[28]:
   data1 key            data2 key
0      0   b         0      0   a
1      1   b         1      1   b
2      2   a         2      2   a
3      3   c         3      3   b
4      4   a         4      4   d
5      5   b

In [29]: pd.merge(df1, df2, on='key', how='left')
Out[29]:
   data1 key  data2
0      0   b      1
1      0   b      3
```

```
2     1   b     1
3     1   b     3
4     5   b     1
..   ...  ..   ...
6     2   a     0
7     2   a     2
8     4   a     0
9     4   a     2
10    3   c   NaN
[11 rows x 3 columns]
```

Many-to-many joins form the Cartesian product of the rows. Since there were 3 'b' rows in the left DataFrame and 2 in the right one, there are 6 'b' rows in the result. The join method only affects the distinct key values appearing in the result:

```
In [30]: pd.merge(df1, df2, how='inner')
Out[30]:
   data1 key  data2
0      0   b      1
1      0   b      3
2      1   b      1
3      1   b      3
4      5   b      1
5      5   b      3
6      2   a      0
7      2   a      2
8      4   a      0
9      4   a      2
```

To merge with multiple keys, pass a list of column names:

```
In [31]: left = DataFrame({'key1': ['foo', 'foo', 'bar'],
   ....:                   'key2': ['one', 'two', 'one'],
   ....:                   'lval': [1, 2, 3]})

In [32]: right = DataFrame({'key1': ['foo', 'foo', 'bar', 'bar'],
   ....:                    'key2': ['one', 'one', 'one', 'two'],
   ....:                    'rval': [4, 5, 6, 7]})

In [33]: pd.merge(left, right, on=['key1', 'key2'], how='outer')
Out[33]:
  key1 key2  lval  rval
0  foo  one     1     4
1  foo  one     1     5
2  foo  two     2   NaN
3  bar  one     3     6
4  bar  two   NaN     7
```

To determine which key combinations will appear in the result depending on the choice of merge method, think of the multiple keys as forming an array of tuples to be used as a single join key (even though it's not actually implemented that way).

When joining columns-on-columns, the indexes on the passed Data-Frame objects are discarded.

A last issue to consider in merge operations is the treatment of overlapping column names. While you can address the overlap manually (see the later section on renaming axis labels), merge has a suffixes option for specifying strings to append to overlapping names in the left and right DataFrame objects:

```
In [34]: pd.merge(left, right, on='key1')
Out[34]:
  key1 key2_x  lval key2_y  rval
0  foo    one     1    one     4
1  foo    one     1    one     5
2  foo    two     2    one     4
3  foo    two     2    one     5
4  bar    one     3    one     6
5  bar    one     3    two     7

In [35]: pd.merge(left, right, on='key1', suffixes=('_left', '_right'))
Out[35]:
  key1 key2_left  lval key2_right  rval
0  foo       one     1        one     4
1  foo       one     1        one     5
2  foo       two     2        one     4
3  foo       two     2        one     5
4  bar       one     3        one     6
5  bar       one     3        two     7
```

See Table 7-1 for an argument reference on merge. Joining on index is the subject of the next section.

Table 7-1. merge function arguments

Argument	Description
left	DataFrame to be merged on the left side
right	DataFrame to be merged on the right side
how	One of 'inner', 'outer', 'left' or 'right'. 'inner' by default
on	Column names to join on. Must be found in both DataFrame objects. If not specified and no other join keys given, will use the intersection of the column names in left and right as the join keys
left_on	Columns in left DataFrame to use as join keys
right_on	Analogous to left_on for left DataFrame
left_index	Use row index in left as its join key (or keys, if a MultiIndex)
right_index	Analogous to left_index
sort	Sort merged data lexicographically by join keys; True by default. Disable to get better performance in some cases on large datasets
suffixes	Tuple of string values to append to column names in case of overlap; defaults to ('_x', '_y'). For example, if 'data' in both DataFrame objects, would appear as 'data_x' and 'data_y' in result
copy	If False, avoid copying data into resulting data structure in some exceptional cases. By default always copies

Merging on Index

In some cases, the merge key or keys in a DataFrame will be found in its index. In this case, you can pass `left_index=True` or `right_index=True` (or both) to indicate that the index should be used as the merge key:

```
In [36]: left1 = DataFrame({'key': ['a', 'b', 'a', 'a', 'b', 'c'],
   ....:                    'value': range(6)})

In [37]: right1 = DataFrame({'group_val': [3.5, 7]}, index=['a', 'b'])

In [38]: left1          In [39]: right1
Out[38]:                Out[39]:
   key  value              group_val
0  a      0            a        3.5
1  b      1            b        7.0
2  a      2
3  a      3
4  b      4
5  c      5

In [40]: pd.merge(left1, right1, left_on='key', right_index=True)
Out[40]:
   key  value  group_val
0  a      0        3.5
2  a      2        3.5
3  a      3        3.5
1  b      1        7.0
4  b      4        7.0
```

Since the default merge method is to intersect the join keys, you can instead form the union of them with an outer join:

```
In [41]: pd.merge(left1, right1, left_on='key', right_index=True, how='outer')
Out[41]:
   key  value  group_val
0  a      0        3.5
2  a      2        3.5
3  a      3        3.5
1  b      1        7.0
4  b      4        7.0
5  c      5        NaN
```

With hierarchically-indexed data, things are a bit more complicated:

```
In [42]: lefth = DataFrame({'key1': ['Ohio', 'Ohio', 'Ohio', 'Nevada', 'Nevada'],
   ....:                    'key2': [2000, 2001, 2002, 2001, 2002],
   ....:                    'data': np.arange(5.)})

In [43]: righth = DataFrame(np.arange(12).reshape((6, 2)),
   ....:                    index=[['Nevada', 'Nevada', 'Ohio', 'Ohio', 'Ohio', 'Ohio'],
   ....:                           [2001, 2000, 2000, 2000, 2001, 2002]],
   ....:                    columns=['event1', 'event2'])

In [44]: lefth              In [45]: righth
Out[44]:                    Out[45]:
```

```
    data   key1 key2                    event1 event2
0    0    Ohio  2000    Nevada  2001       0      1
1    1    Ohio  2001            2000       2      3
2    2    Ohio  2002    Ohio    2000       4      5
3    3  Nevada  2001            2000       6      7
4    4  Nevada  2002            2001       8      9
                                 2002      10     11
```

In this case, you have to indicate multiple columns to merge on as a list (pay attention to the handling of duplicate index values):

```
In [46]: pd.merge(lefth, righth, left_on=['key1', 'key2'], right_index=True)
Out[46]:
    data   key1 key2 event1 event2
0    0    Ohio  2000     4      5
0    0    Ohio  2000     6      7
1    1    Ohio  2001     8      9
2    2    Ohio  2002    10     11
3    3  Nevada  2001     0      1

In [47]: pd.merge(lefth, righth, left_on=['key1', 'key2'],
   ....:          right_index=True, how='outer')
Out[47]:
    data   key1 key2 event1 event2
0    0    Ohio  2000     4      5
0    0    Ohio  2000     6      7
1    1    Ohio  2001     8      9
2    2    Ohio  2002    10     11
3    3  Nevada  2001     0      1
4    4  Nevada  2002   NaN    NaN
4  NaN  Nevada  2000     2      3
```

Using the indexes of both sides of the merge is also not an issue:

```
In [48]: left2 = DataFrame([[1., 2.], [3., 4.], [5., 6.]], index=['a', 'c', 'e'],
   ....:                    columns=['Ohio', 'Nevada'])

In [49]: right2 = DataFrame([[7., 8.], [9., 10.], [11., 12.], [13, 14]],
   ....:                     index=['b', 'c', 'd', 'e'], columns=['Missouri', 'Alabama'])

In [50]: left2        In [51]: right2
Out[50]:             Out[51]:
   Ohio  Nevada        Missouri  Alabama
a    1      2       b       7        8
c    3      4       c       9       10
e    5      6       d      11       12
                    e      13       14

In [52]: pd.merge(left2, right2, how='outer', left_index=True, right_index=True)
Out[52]:
   Ohio  Nevada  Missouri  Alabama
a    1      2      NaN      NaN
b  NaN    NaN       7        8
c    3      4       9       10
d  NaN    NaN      11       12
e    5      6      13       14
```

DataFrame has a more convenient `join` instance for merging by index. It can also be used to combine together many DataFrame objects having the same or similar indexes but non-overlapping columns. In the prior example, we could have written:

```
In [53]: left2.join(right2, how='outer')
Out[53]:
   Ohio  Nevada  Missouri  Alabama
a     1       2       NaN      NaN
b   NaN     NaN         7        8
c     3       4         9       10
d   NaN     NaN        11       12
e     5       6        13       14
```

In part for legacy reasons (much earlier versions of pandas), DataFrame's `join` method performs a left join on the join keys. It also supports joining the index of the passed DataFrame on one of the columns of the calling DataFrame:

```
In [54]: left1.join(right1, on='key')
Out[54]:
  key  value  group_val
0   a      0        3.5
1   b      1        7.0
2   a      2        3.5
3   a      3        3.5
4   b      4        7.0
5   c      5        NaN
```

Lastly, for simple index-on-index merges, you can pass a list of DataFrames to `join` as an alternative to using the more general `concat` function described below:

```
In [55]: another = DataFrame([[7., 8.], [9., 10.], [11., 12.], [16., 17.]],
   ....:                      index=['a', 'c', 'e', 'f'], columns=['New York', 'Oregon'])
```

```
In [56]: left2.join([right2, another])
Out[56]:
   Ohio  Nevada  Missouri  Alabama  New York  Oregon
a     1       2       NaN      NaN         7       8
c     3       4         9       10         9      10
e     5       6        13       14        11      12
```

```
In [57]: left2.join([right2, another], how='outer')
Out[57]:
   Ohio  Nevada  Missouri  Alabama  New York  Oregon
a     1       2       NaN      NaN         7       8
b   NaN     NaN         7        8       NaN     NaN
c     3       4         9       10         9      10
d   NaN     NaN        11       12       NaN     NaN
e     5       6        13       14        11      12
f   NaN     NaN       NaN      NaN        16      17
```

Concatenating Along an Axis

Another kind of data combination operation is alternatively referred to as concatenation, binding, or stacking. NumPy has a `concatenate` function for doing this with raw NumPy arrays:

```
In [58]: arr = np.arange(12).reshape((3, 4))

In [59]: arr
Out[59]:
array([[ 0,  1,  2,  3],
       [ 4,  5,  6,  7],
       [ 8,  9, 10, 11]])

In [60]: np.concatenate([arr, arr], axis=1)
Out[60]:
array([[ 0,  1,  2,  3,  0,  1,  2,  3],
       [ 4,  5,  6,  7,  4,  5,  6,  7],
       [ 8,  9, 10, 11,  8,  9, 10, 11]])
```

In the context of pandas objects such as Series and DataFrame, having labeled axes enable you to further generalize array concatenation. In particular, you have a number of additional things to think about:

- If the objects are indexed differently on the other axes, should the collection of axes be unioned or intersected?
- Do the groups need to be identifiable in the resulting object?
- Does the concatenation axis matter at all?

The `concat` function in pandas provides a consistent way to address each of these concerns. I'll give a number of examples to illustrate how it works. Suppose we have three Series with no index overlap:

```
In [61]: s1 = Series([0, 1], index=['a', 'b'])

In [62]: s2 = Series([2, 3, 4], index=['c', 'd', 'e'])

In [63]: s3 = Series([5, 6], index=['f', 'g'])
```

Calling `concat` with these object in a list glues together the values and indexes:

```
In [64]: pd.concat([s1, s2, s3])
Out[64]:
a    0
b    1
c    2
d    3
e    4
f    5
g    6
dtype: int64
```

By default `concat` works along `axis=0`, producing another Series. If you pass `axis=1`, the result will instead be a DataFrame (`axis=1` is the columns):

```
In [65]: pd.concat([s1, s2, s3], axis=1)
Out[65]:
     0    1    2
a    0  NaN  NaN
b    1  NaN  NaN
c  NaN    2  NaN
d  NaN    3  NaN
e  NaN    4  NaN
f  NaN  NaN    5
g  NaN  NaN    6
```

In this case there is no overlap on the other axis, which as you can see is the sorted union (the `'outer'` join) of the indexes. You can instead intersect them by passing `join='inner'`:

```
In [66]: s4 = pd.concat([s1 * 5, s3])
```

```
In [67]: pd.concat([s1, s4], axis=1)        In [68]: pd.concat([s1, s4], axis=1, join='inner')
Out[67]:                                     Out[68]:
     0  1                                         0  1
a    0  0                                    a    0  0
b    1  5                                    b    1  5
f  NaN  5
g  NaN  6
```

You can even specify the axes to be used on the other axes with `join_axes`:

```
In [69]: pd.concat([s1, s4], axis=1, join_axes=[['a', 'c', 'b', 'e']])
Out[69]:
     0    1
a    0    0
c  NaN  NaN
b    1    5
e  NaN  NaN
```

One issue is that the concatenated pieces are not identifiable in the result. Suppose instead you wanted to create a hierarchical index on the concatenation axis. To do this, use the `keys` argument:

```
In [70]: result = pd.concat([s1, s1, s3], keys=['one', 'two', 'three'])
```

```
In [71]: result
Out[71]:
one    a    0
       b    1
two    a    0
       b    1
three  f    5
       g    6
dtype: int64
```

```
# Much more on the unstack function later
In [72]: result.unstack()
```

```
Out[72]:
        a    b    f   g
one     0    1   NaN NaN
two     0    1   NaN NaN
three  NaN  NaN   5   6
```

In the case of combining Series along `axis=1`, the `keys` become the DataFrame column headers:

```
In [73]: pd.concat([s1, s2, s3], axis=1, keys=['one', 'two', 'three'])
Out[73]:
    one  two  three
a    0   NaN   NaN
b    1   NaN   NaN
c   NaN   2    NaN
d   NaN   3    NaN
e   NaN   4    NaN
f   NaN  NaN    5
g   NaN  NaN    6
```

The same logic extends to DataFrame objects:

```
In [74]: df1 = DataFrame(np.arange(6).reshape(3, 2), index=['a', 'b', 'c'],
   ....:                  columns=['one', 'two'])

In [75]: df2 = DataFrame(5 + np.arange(4).reshape(2, 2), index=['a', 'c'],
   ....:                  columns=['three', 'four'])

In [76]: pd.concat([df1, df2], axis=1, keys=['level1', 'level2'])
Out[76]:
    level1       level2
    one  two    three  four
a    0    1       5     6
b    2    3      NaN   NaN
c    4    5       7     8
```

If you pass a dict of objects instead of a list, the dict's keys will be used for the `keys` option:

```
In [77]: pd.concat({'level1': df1, 'level2': df2}, axis=1)
Out[77]:
    level1       level2
    one  two    three  four
a    0    1       5     6
b    2    3      NaN   NaN
c    4    5       7     8
```

There are a couple of additional arguments governing how the hierarchical index is created (see Table 7-2):

```
In [78]: pd.concat([df1, df2], axis=1, keys=['level1', 'level2'],
   ....:           names=['upper', 'lower'])
Out[78]:
upper  level1       level2
lower   one  two    three  four
a        0    1       5     6
```

```
b        2    3    NaN   NaN
c        4    5     7     8
```

A last consideration concerns DataFrames in which the row index is not meaningful in the context of the analysis:

```
In [79]: df1 = DataFrame(np.random.randn(3, 4), columns=['a', 'b', 'c', 'd'])

In [80]: df2 = DataFrame(np.random.randn(2, 3), columns=['b', 'd', 'a'])

In [81]: df1                                    In [82]: df2
Out[81]:                                        Out[82]:
          a         b         c         d                 b         d         a
0 -0.204708  0.478943 -0.519439 -0.555730       0  0.274992  0.228913  1.352917
1  1.965781  1.393406  0.092908  0.281746       1  0.886429 -2.001637 -0.371843
2  0.769023  1.246435  1.007189 -1.296221
```

In this case, you can pass ignore_index=True:

```
In [83]: pd.concat([df1, df2], ignore_index=True)
Out[83]:
          a         b         c         d
0 -0.204708  0.478943 -0.519439 -0.555730
1  1.965781  1.393406  0.092908  0.281746
2  0.769023  1.246435  1.007189 -1.296221
3  1.352917  0.274992       NaN  0.228913
4 -0.371843  0.886429       NaN -2.001637
```

Table 7-2. concat function arguments

Argument	Description
objs	List or dict of pandas objects to be concatenated. The only required argument
axis	Axis to concatenate along; defaults to 0
join	One of 'inner', 'outer', defaulting to 'outer'; whether to intersection (inner) or union (outer) together indexes along the other axes
join_axes	Specific indexes to use for the other n-1 axes instead of performing union/intersection logic
keys	Values to associate with objects being concatenated, forming a hierarchical index along the concatenation axis. Can either be a list or array of arbitrary values, an array of tuples, or a list of arrays (if multiple level arrays passed in levels)
levels	Specific indexes to use as hierarchical index level or levels if keys passed
names	Names for created hierarchical levels if keys and / or levels passed
verify_integrity	Check new axis in concatenated object for duplicates and raise exception if so. By default (False) allows duplicates
ignore_index	Do not preserve indexes along concatenation axis, instead producing a new range(total_length) index

Combining Data with Overlap

Another data combination situation can't be expressed as either a merge or concatenation operation. You may have two datasets whose indexes overlap in full or part. As a motivating example, consider NumPy's where function, which expressed a vectorized if-else:

```
In [84]: a = Series([np.nan, 2.5, np.nan, 3.5, 4.5, np.nan],
   ....:            index=['f', 'e', 'd', 'c', 'b', 'a'])

In [85]: b = Series(np.arange(len(a), dtype=np.float64),
   ....:            index=['f', 'e', 'd', 'c', 'b', 'a'])

In [86]: b[-1] = np.nan
```

```
In [87]: a            In [88]: b            In [89]: np.where(pd.isnull(a), b, a)
Out[87]:              Out[88]:              Out[89]: array([ 0. ,  2.5,  2. ,
                                                            3.5,  4.5,  nan])
f    NaN              f     0
e    2.5              e     1
d    NaN              d     2
c    3.5              c     3
b    4.5              b     4
a    NaN              a    NaN
dtype: float64        dtype: float64
```

Series has a combine_first method, which performs the equivalent of this operation plus data alignment:

```
In [90]: b[:-2].combine_first(a[2:])
Out[90]:
a    NaN
b    4.5
c    3.0
d    2.0
e    1.0
f    0.0
dtype: float64
```

With DataFrames, combine_first naturally does the same thing column by column, so you can think of it as "patching" missing data in the calling object with data from the object you pass:

```
In [91]: df1 = DataFrame({'a': [1., np.nan, 5., np.nan],
   ....:                  'b': [np.nan, 2., np.nan, 6.],
   ....:                  'c': range(2, 18, 4)})

In [92]: df2 = DataFrame({'a': [5., 4., np.nan, 3., 7.],
   ....:                  'b': [np.nan, 3., 4., 6., 8.]})

In [93]: df1.combine_first(df2)
Out[93]:
   a    b   c
0  1  NaN   2
1  4    2   6
```

```
2  5  4  10
3  3  6  14
4  7  8  NaN
```

Reshaping and Pivoting

There are a number of fundamental operations for rearranging tabular data. These are alternatingly referred to as *reshape* or *pivot* operations.

Reshaping with Hierarchical Indexing

Hierarchical indexing provides a consistent way to rearrange data in a DataFrame. There are two primary actions:

- stack: this "rotates" or pivots from the columns in the data to the rows
- unstack: this pivots from the rows into the columns

I'll illustrate these operations through a series of examples. Consider a small DataFrame with string arrays as row and column indexes:

```
In [94]: data = DataFrame(np.arange(6).reshape((2, 3)),
   ....:                  index=pd.Index(['Ohio', 'Colorado'], name='state'),
   ....:                  columns=pd.Index(['one', 'two', 'three'], name='number'))

In [95]: data
Out[95]:
number    one  two  three
state
Ohio        0    1      2
Colorado    3    4      5
```

Using the stack method on this data pivots the columns into the rows, producing a Series:

```
In [96]: result = data.stack()

In [97]: result
Out[97]:
state     number
Ohio      one       0
          two       1
          three     2
Colorado  one       3
          two       4
          three     5
dtype: int64
```

From a hierarchically-indexed Series, you can rearrange the data back into a DataFrame with unstack:

```
In [98]: result.unstack()
Out[98]:
number    one  two  three
```

```
state
Ohio        0   1   2
Colorado    3   4   5
```

By default the innermost level is unstacked (same with **stack**). You can unstack a different level by passing a level number or name:

```
In [99]: result.unstack(0)          In [100]: result.unstack('state')
Out[99]:                            Out[100]:
state    Ohio   Colorado            state    Ohio   Colorado
number                              number
one       0        3                one       0        3
two       1        4                two       1        4
three     2        5                three     2        5
```

Unstacking might introduce missing data if all of the values in the level aren't found in each of the subgroups:

```
In [101]: s1 = Series([0, 1, 2, 3], index=['a', 'b', 'c', 'd'])

In [102]: s2 = Series([4, 5, 6], index=['c', 'd', 'e'])

In [103]: data2 = pd.concat([s1, s2], keys=['one', 'two'])

In [104]: data2.unstack()
Out[104]:
       a    b   c   d   e
one    0    1   2   3  NaN
two  NaN  NaN   4   5   6
```

Stacking filters out missing data by default, so the operation is easily invertible:

```
In [105]: data2.unstack().stack()    In [106]: data2.unstack().stack(dropna=False)
Out[105]:                            Out[106]:
one  a    0                          one  a      0
     b    1                               b      1
     c    2                               c      2
     d    3                               d      3
two  c    4                               e    NaN
     d    5                          two  a    NaN
     e    6                               b    NaN
dtype: float64                            c      4
                                          d      5
                                          e      6
                                     dtype: float64
```

When unstacking in a DataFrame, the level unstacked becomes the lowest level in the result:

```
In [107]: df = DataFrame({'left': result, 'right': result + 5},
   .....:                 columns=pd.Index(['left', 'right'], name='side'))

In [108]: df
Out[108]:
side              left  right
state    number
Ohio     one         0      5
```

```
                two          1    6
                three        2    7
Colorado    one          3    8
                two          4    9
                three        5   10
```

```
In [109]: df.unstack('state')
Out[109]:
side     left            right
state    Ohio  Colorado  Ohio  Colorado
number
one       0       3        5      8
two       1       4        6      9
three     2       5        7     10
```

```
In [110]: df.unstack('state').stack('side')
Out[110]:
state           Ohio  Colorado
number  side
one     left      0       3
        right     5       8
two     left      1       4
        right     6       9
three   left      2       5
        right     7      10
```

Pivoting "long" to "wide" Format

A common way to store multiple time series in databases and CSV is in so-called *long* or *stacked* format:

```
data = pd.read_csv('ch07/macrodata.csv')
periods = pd.PeriodIndex(year=data.year, quarter=data.quarter, name='date')
data = DataFrame(data.to_records(),
                 columns=pd.Index(['realgdp', 'infl', 'unemp'], name='item'),
                 index=periods.to_timestamp('D', 'end'))

ldata = data.stack().reset_index().rename(columns={0: 'value'})
```

```
In [116]: ldata[:10]
Out[116]:
        date      item     value
0  1959-03-31  realgdp  2710.349
1  1959-03-31     infl     0.000
2  1959-03-31    unemp     5.800
3  1959-06-30  realgdp  2778.801
4  1959-06-30     infl     2.340
5  1959-06-30    unemp     5.100
6  1959-09-30  realgdp  2775.488
7  1959-09-30     infl     2.740
8  1959-09-30    unemp     5.300
9  1959-12-31  realgdp  2785.204
```

Data is frequently stored this way in relational databases like MySQL as a fixed schema (column names and data types) allows the number of distinct values in the `item` column to increase or decrease as data is added or deleted in the table. In the above example `date` and `item` would usually be the primary keys (in relational database parlance), offering both relational integrity and easier joins and programmatic queries in many cases. The downside, of course, is that the data may not be easy to work with in long format; you might prefer to have a DataFrame containing one column per distinct `item` value indexed by timestamps in the `date` column. DataFrame's `pivot` method performs exactly this transformation:

```
In [117]: pivoted = ldata.pivot('date', 'item', 'value')

In [118]: pivoted.head()
Out[118]:
item        infl   realgdp  unemp
date
1959-03-31  0.00  2710.349    5.8
1959-06-30  2.34  2778.801    5.1
1959-09-30  2.74  2775.488    5.3
1959-12-31  0.27  2785.204    5.6
1960-03-31  2.31  2847.699    5.2
```

The first two values passed are the columns to be used as the row and column index, and finally an optional value column to fill the DataFrame. Suppose you had two value columns that you wanted to reshape simultaneously:

```
In [119]: ldata['value2'] = np.random.randn(len(ldata))

In [120]: ldata[:10]
Out[120]:
         date     item     value     value2
0  1959-03-31  realgdp  2710.349   1.669025
1  1959-03-31     infl     0.000  -0.438570
2  1959-03-31    unemp     5.800  -0.539741
3  1959-06-30  realgdp  2778.801   0.476985
4  1959-06-30     infl     2.340   3.248944
5  1959-06-30    unemp     5.100  -1.021228
6  1959-09-30  realgdp  2775.488  -0.577087
7  1959-09-30     infl     2.740   0.124121
8  1959-09-30    unemp     5.300   0.302614
9  1959-12-31  realgdp  2785.204   0.523772
```

By omitting the last argument, you obtain a DataFrame with hierarchical columns:

```
In [121]: pivoted = ldata.pivot('date', 'item')

In [122]: pivoted[:5]
Out[122]:
           value                      value2
item        infl   realgdp  unemp      infl   realgdp      unemp
date
1959-03-31  0.00  2710.349    5.8  -0.438570  1.669025  -0.539741
1959-06-30  2.34  2778.801    5.1   3.248944  0.476985  -1.021228
1959-09-30  2.74  2775.488    5.3   0.124121 -0.577087   0.302614
1959-12-31  0.27  2785.204    5.6   0.000940  0.523772   1.343810
1960-03-31  2.31  2847.699    5.2  -0.831154 -0.713544  -2.370232

In [123]: pivoted['value'][:5]
Out[123]:
item        infl   realgdp  unemp
date
1959-03-31  0.00  2710.349    5.8
1959-06-30  2.34  2778.801    5.1
```

```
1959-09-30  2.74  2775.488   5.3
1959-12-31  0.27  2785.204   5.6
1960-03-31  2.31  2847.699   5.2
```

Note that pivot is just a shortcut for creating a hierarchical index using set_index and reshaping with unstack:

```
In [124]: unstacked = ldata.set_index(['date', 'item']).unstack('item')

In [125]: unstacked[:7]
Out[125]:
            value                    value2
item         infl   realgdp  unemp     infl   realgdp     unemp
date
1959-03-31   0.00  2710.349    5.8 -0.438570  1.669025 -0.539741
1959-06-30   2.34  2778.801    5.1  3.248944  0.476985 -1.021228
1959-09-30   2.74  2775.488    5.3  0.124121 -0.577087  0.302614
1959-12-31   0.27  2785.204    5.6  0.000940  0.523772  1.343810
1960-03-31   2.31  2847.699    5.2 -0.831154 -0.713544 -2.370232
1960-06-30   0.14  2834.390    5.2 -0.860757 -1.860761  0.560145
1960-09-30   2.70  2839.022    5.6  0.119827 -1.265934 -1.063512
```

Data Transformation

So far in this chapter we've been concerned with rearranging data. Filtering, cleaning, and other tranformations are another class of important operations.

Removing Duplicates

Duplicate rows may be found in a DataFrame for any number of reasons. Here is an example:

```
In [126]: data = DataFrame({'k1': ['one'] * 3 + ['two'] * 4,
   .....:                    'k2': [1, 1, 2, 3, 3, 4, 4]})

In [127]: data
Out[127]:
    k1  k2
0  one   1
1  one   1
2  one   2
3  two   3
4  two   3
5  two   4
6  two   4
```

The DataFrame method duplicated returns a boolean Series indicating whether each row is a duplicate or not:

```
In [128]: data.duplicated()
Out[128]:
0    False
1     True
```

```
2     False
3     False
4      True
5     False
6      True
dtype: bool
```

Relatedly, `drop_duplicates` returns a DataFrame where the `duplicated` array is `False`:

```
In [129]: data.drop_duplicates()
Out[129]:
     k1  k2
0   one   1
2   one   2
3   two   3
5   two   4
```

Both of these methods by default consider all of the columns; alternatively you can specify any subset of them to detect duplicates. Suppose we had an additional column of values and wanted to filter duplicates only based on the `'k1'` column:

```
In [130]: data['v1'] = range(7)

In [131]: data.drop_duplicates(['k1'])
Out[131]:
     k1  k2  v1
0   one   1   0
3   two   3   3
```

`duplicated` and `drop_duplicates` by default keep the first observed value combination. Passing `take_last=True` will return the last one:

```
In [132]: data.drop_duplicates(['k1', 'k2'], take_last=True)
Out[132]:
     k1  k2  v1
1   one   1   1
2   one   2   2
4   two   3   4
6   two   4   6
```

Transforming Data Using a Function or Mapping

For many data sets, you may wish to perform some transformation based on the values in an array, Series, or column in a DataFrame. Consider the following hypothetical data collected about some kinds of meat:

```
In [133]: data = DataFrame({'food': ['bacon', 'pulled pork', 'bacon', 'Pastrami',
   .....:                            'corned beef', 'Bacon', 'pastrami', 'honey ham',
   .....:                            'nova lox'],
   .....:                   'ounces': [4, 3, 12, 6, 7.5, 8, 3, 5, 6]})

In [134]: data
Out[134]:
          food  ounces
0        bacon     4.0
```

```
1   pulled pork      3.0
2        bacon      12.0
3     Pastrami       6.0
4  corned beef       7.5
5        Bacon       8.0
6     pastrami       3.0
7    honey ham       5.0
8     nova lox       6.0
```

Suppose you wanted to add a column indicating the type of animal that each food came from. Let's write down a mapping of each distinct meat type to the kind of animal:

```
meat_to_animal = {
  'bacon': 'pig',
  'pulled pork': 'pig',
  'pastrami': 'cow',
  'corned beef': 'cow',
  'honey ham': 'pig',
  'nova lox': 'salmon'
}
```

The map method on a Series accepts a function or dict-like object containing a mapping, but here we have a small problem in that some of the meats above are capitalized and others are not. Thus, we also need to convert each value to lower case:

```
In [136]: data['animal'] = data['food'].map(str.lower).map(meat_to_animal)

In [137]: data
Out[137]:
          food  ounces  animal
0        bacon     4.0     pig
1  pulled pork     3.0     pig
2        bacon    12.0     pig
3     Pastrami     6.0     cow
4  corned beef     7.5     cow
5        Bacon     8.0     pig
6     pastrami     3.0     cow
7    honey ham     5.0     pig
8     nova lox     6.0  salmon
```

We could also have passed a function that does all the work:

```
In [138]: data['food'].map(lambda x: meat_to_animal[x.lower()])
Out[138]:
0       pig
1       pig
2       pig
3       cow
4       cow
5       pig
6       cow
7       pig
8    salmon
Name: food, dtype: object
```

Using map is a convenient way to perform element-wise transformations and other data cleaning-related operations.

Replacing Values

Filling in missing data with the `fillna` method can be thought of as a special case of more general value replacement. While map, as you've seen above, can be used to modify a subset of values in an object, `replace` provides a simpler and more flexible way to do so. Let's consider this Series:

```
In [139]: data = Series([1., -999., 2., -999., -1000., 3.])

In [140]: data
Out[140]:
0        1
1     -999
2        2
3     -999
4    -1000
5        3
dtype: float64
```

The -999 values might be sentinel values for missing data. To replace these with NA values that pandas understands, we can use `replace`, producing a new Series:

```
In [141]: data.replace(-999, np.nan)
Out[141]:
0        1
1      NaN
2        2
3      NaN
4    -1000
5        3
dtype: float64
```

If you want to replace multiple values at once, you instead pass a list then the substitute value:

```
In [142]: data.replace([-999, -1000], np.nan)
Out[142]:
0      1
1    NaN
2      2
3    NaN
4    NaN
5      3
dtype: float64
```

To use a different replacement for each value, pass a list of substitutes:

```
In [143]: data.replace([-999, -1000], [np.nan, 0])
Out[143]:
0      1
1    NaN
2      2
```

```
3   NaN
4    0
5    3
dtype: float64
```

The argument passed can also be a dict:

```
In [144]: data.replace({-999: np.nan, -1000: 0})
Out[144]:
0    1
1   NaN
2    2
3   NaN
4    0
5    3
dtype: float64
```

Renaming Axis Indexes

Like values in a Series, axis labels can be similarly transformed by a function or mapping of some form to produce new, differently labeled objects. The axes can also be modified in place without creating a new data structure. Here's a simple example:

```
In [145]: data = DataFrame(np.arange(12).reshape((3, 4)),
   .....:                  index=['Ohio', 'Colorado', 'New York'],
   .....:                  columns=['one', 'two', 'three', 'four'])
```

Like a Series, the axis indexes have a `map` method:

```
In [146]: data.index.map(str.upper)
Out[146]: array(['OHIO', 'COLORADO', 'NEW YORK'], dtype=object)
```

You can assign to `index`, modifying the DataFrame in place:

```
In [147]: data.index = data.index.map(str.upper)

In [148]: data
Out[148]:
          one  two  three  four
OHIO        0    1      2     3
COLORADO    4    5      6     7
NEW YORK    8    9     10    11
```

If you want to create a transformed version of a data set without modifying the original, a useful method is `rename`:

```
In [149]: data.rename(index=str.title, columns=str.upper)
Out[149]:
          ONE  TWO  THREE  FOUR
Ohio        0    1      2     3
Colorado    4    5      6     7
New York    8    9     10    11
```

Notably, `rename` can be used in conjunction with a dict-like object providing new values for a subset of the axis labels:

```
In [150]: data.rename(index={'OHIO': 'INDIANA'},
   .....:               columns={'three': 'peekaboo'})
Out[150]:
          one  two  peekaboo  four
INDIANA    0    1         2     3
COLORADO   4    5         6     7
NEW YORK   8    9        10    11
```

rename saves having to copy the DataFrame manually and assign to its index and col
umns attributes. Should you wish to modify a data set in place, pass inplace=True:

```
# Always returns a reference to a DataFrame
In [151]: _ = data.rename(index={'OHIO': 'INDIANA'}, inplace=True)

In [152]: data
Out[152]:
          one  two  three  four
INDIANA    0    1      2     3
COLORADO   4    5      6     7
NEW YORK   8    9     10    11
```

Discretization and Binning

Continuous data is often discretized or otherwised separated into "bins" for analysis.
Suppose you have data about a group of people in a study, and you want to group them
into discrete age buckets:

```
In [153]: ages = [20, 22, 25, 27, 21, 23, 37, 31, 61, 45, 41, 32]
```

Let's divide these into bins of 18 to 25, 26 to 35, 36 to 60, and finally 61 and older. To
do so, you have to use cut, a function in pandas:

```
In [154]: bins = [18, 25, 35, 60, 100]

In [155]: cats = pd.cut(ages, bins)

In [156]: cats
Out[156]:
 (18, 25]
 (18, 25]
 (18, 25]
 ...
 (35, 60]
 (35, 60]
 (25, 35]
Levels (4): Index(['(18, 25]', '(25, 35]', '(35, 60]', '(60, 100]'], dtype=object)
Length: 12
```

The object pandas returns is a special Categorical object. You can treat it like an array
of strings indicating the bin name; internally it contains a levels array indicating the
distinct category names along with a labeling for the ages data in the labels attribute:

```
In [157]: cats.labels
Out[157]: array([0, 0, 0, 1, 0, 0, 2, 1, 3, 2, 2, 1])

In [158]: cats.levels
```

```
Out[158]: Index([u'(18, 25]', u'(25, 35]', u'(35, 60]', u'(60, 100]'], dtype='object')

In [159]: pd.value_counts(cats)
Out[159]:
(18, 25]     5
(35, 60]     3
(25, 35]     3
(60, 100]    1
dtype: int64
```

Consistent with mathematical notation for intervals, a parenthesis means that the side is *open* while the square bracket means it is *closed* (inclusive). Which side is closed can be changed by passing right=False:

```
In [160]: pd.cut(ages, [18, 26, 36, 61, 100], right=False)
Out[160]:
[18, 26)
[18, 26)
[18, 26)
...
[36, 61)
[36, 61)
[26, 36)
Levels (4): Index(['[18, 26)', '[26, 36)', '[36, 61)', '[61, 100)'], dtype=object)
Length: 12
```

You can also pass your own bin names by passing a list or array to the labels option:

```
In [161]: group_names = ['Youth', 'YoungAdult', 'MiddleAged', 'Senior']

In [162]: pd.cut(ages, bins, labels=group_names)
Out[162]:
Youth
Youth
Youth
...
MiddleAged
MiddleAged
YoungAdult
Levels (4): Index(['Youth', 'YoungAdult', 'MiddleAged', 'Senior'], dtype=object)
Length: 12
```

If you pass cut a integer number of bins instead of explicit bin edges, it will compute equal-length bins based on the minimum and maximum values in the data. Consider the case of some uniformly distributed data chopped into fourths:

```
In [163]: data = np.random.rand(20)

In [164]: pd.cut(data, 4, precision=2)
Out[164]:
(0.45, 0.67]
(0.23, 0.45]
(0.0037, 0.23]
...
(0.0037, 0.23]
(0.23, 0.45]
```

```
      (0.23, 0.45]
Levels (4): Index(['(0.0037, 0.23]', '(0.23, 0.45]', '(0.45, 0.67]',
                   '(0.67, 0.9]'], dtype=object)
Length: 20
```

A closely related function, qcut, bins the data based on sample quantiles. Depending on the distribution of the data, using cut will not usually result in each bin having the same number of data points. Since qcut uses sample quantiles instead, by definition you will obtain roughly equal-size bins:

```
In [165]: data = np.random.randn(1000) # Normally distributed

In [166]: cats = pd.qcut(data, 4) # Cut into quartiles

In [167]: cats
Out[167]:
  (-0.022, 0.641]
 [-3.745, -0.635]
   (0.641, 3.26]
...
 (-0.635, -0.022]
   (0.641, 3.26]
 (-0.635, -0.022]
Levels (4): Index(['[-3.745, -0.635]', '(-0.635, -0.022]',
                   '(-0.022, 0.641]', '(0.641, 3.26]'], dtype=object)
Length: 1000

In [168]: pd.value_counts(cats)
Out[168]:
(0.641, 3.26]      250
[-3.745, -0.635]   250
(-0.635, -0.022]   250
(-0.022, 0.641]    250
dtype: int64
```

Similar to cut you can pass your own quantiles (numbers between 0 and 1, inclusive):

```
In [169]: pd.qcut(data, [0, 0.1, 0.5, 0.9, 1.])
Out[169]:
  (-0.022, 1.302]
  (-1.266, -0.022]
  (-0.022, 1.302]
...
  (-1.266, -0.022]
  (-0.022, 1.302]
  (-1.266, -0.022]
Levels (4): Index(['[-3.745, -1.266]', '(-1.266, -0.022]',
                   '(-0.022, 1.302]', '(1.302, 3.26]'], dtype=object)
Length: 1000
```

We'll return to cut and qcut later in the chapter on aggregation and group operations, as these discretization functions are especially useful for quantile and group analysis.

Detecting and Filtering Outliers

Filtering or transforming outliers is largely a matter of applying array operations. Consider a DataFrame with some normally distributed data:

```
In [170]: np.random.seed(12345)

In [171]: data = DataFrame(np.random.randn(1000, 4))

In [172]: data.describe()
Out[172]:
                 0            1            2            3
count  1000.000000  1000.000000  1000.000000  1000.000000
mean     -0.067684     0.067924     0.025598    -0.002298
std       0.998035     0.992106     1.006835     0.996794
min      -3.428254    -3.548824    -3.184377    -3.745356
25%      -0.774890    -0.591841    -0.641675    -0.644144
50%      -0.116401     0.101143     0.002073    -0.013611
75%       0.616366     0.780282     0.680391     0.654328
max       3.366626     2.653656     3.260383     3.927528
```

Suppose you wanted to find values in one of the columns exceeding three in magnitude:

```
In [173]: col = data[3]

In [174]: col[np.abs(col) > 3]
Out[174]:
97     3.927528
305   -3.399312
400   -3.745356
Name: 3, dtype: float64
```

To select all rows having a value exceeding 3 or -3, you can use the any method on a boolean DataFrame:

```
In [175]: data[(np.abs(data) > 3).any(1)]
Out[175]:
            0         1         2         3
5   -0.539741  0.476985  3.248944 -1.021228
97  -0.774363  0.552936  0.106061  3.927528
102 -0.655054 -0.565230  3.176873  0.959533
305 -2.315555  0.457246 -0.025907 -3.399312
324  0.050188  1.951312  3.260383  0.963301
..        ...       ...       ...       ...
499 -0.293333 -0.242459 -3.056990  1.918403
523 -3.428254 -0.296336 -0.439938 -0.867165
586  0.275144  1.179227 -3.184377  1.369891
808 -0.362528 -3.548824  1.553205 -2.186301
900  3.366626 -2.372214  0.851010  1.332846
[11 rows x 4 columns]
```

Values can just as easily be set based on these criteria. Here is code to cap values outside the interval -3 to 3:

```
In [176]: data[np.abs(data) > 3] = np.sign(data) * 3
```

```
In [177]: data.describe()
Out[177]:
                 0            1            2            3
count  1000.000000  1000.000000  1000.000000  1000.000000
mean     -0.067623     0.068473     0.025153    -0.002081
std       0.995485     0.990253     1.003977     0.989736
min      -3.000000    -3.000000    -3.000000    -3.000000
25%      -0.774890    -0.591841    -0.641675    -0.644144
50%      -0.116401     0.101143     0.002073    -0.013611
75%       0.616366     0.780282     0.680391     0.654328
max       3.000000     2.653656     3.000000     3.000000
```

The ufunc `np.sign` returns an array of 1 and -1 depending on the sign of the values.

Permutation and Random Sampling

Permuting (randomly reordering) a Series or the rows in a DataFrame is easy to do using the `numpy.random.permutation` function. Calling `permutation` with the length of the axis you want to permute produces an array of integers indicating the new ordering:

```
In [178]: df = DataFrame(np.arange(5 * 4).reshape((5, 4)))

In [179]: sampler = np.random.permutation(5)

In [180]: sampler
Out[180]: array([1, 0, 2, 3, 4])
```

That array can then be used in `ix`-based indexing or the `take` function:

```
In [181]: df                    In [182]: df.take(sampler)
Out[181]:                        Out[182]:
    0   1   2   3                    0   1   2   3
0   0   1   2   3                1   4   5   6   7
1   4   5   6   7                0   0   1   2   3
2   8   9  10  11                2   8   9  10  11
3  12  13  14  15                3  12  13  14  15
4  16  17  18  19                4  16  17  18  19
```

To select a random subset without replacement, one way is to slice off the first k elements of the array returned by `permutation`, where k is the desired subset size. There are much more efficient sampling-without-replacement algorithms, but this is an easy strategy that uses readily available tools:

```
In [183]: df.take(np.random.permutation(len(df))[:3])
Out[183]:
    0   1   2   3
1   4   5   6   7
3  12  13  14  15
4  16  17  18  19
```

To generate a sample *with* replacement, the fastest way is to use `np.random.randint` to draw random integers:

```
In [184]: bag = np.array([5, 7, -1, 6, 4])
```

```
In [185]: sampler = np.random.randint(0, len(bag), size=10)

In [186]: sampler
Out[186]: array([4, 4, 2, 2, 2, 0, 3, 0, 4, 1])

In [187]: draws = bag.take(sampler)

In [188]: draws
Out[188]: array([ 4,  4, -1, -1, -1,  5,  6,  5,  4,  7])
```

Computing Indicator/Dummy Variables

Another type of transformation for statistical modeling or machine learning applications is converting a categorical variable into a "dummy" or "indicator" matrix. If a column in a DataFrame has k distinct values, you would derive a matrix or DataFrame containing k columns containing all 1's and 0's. pandas has a get_dummies function for doing this, though devising one yourself is not difficult. Let's return to an earlier example DataFrame:

```
In [189]: df = DataFrame({'key': ['b', 'b', 'a', 'c', 'a', 'b'],
   .....:                 'data1': range(6)})

In [190]: pd.get_dummies(df['key'])
Out[190]:
   a  b  c
0  0  1  0
1  0  1  0
2  1  0  0
3  0  0  1
4  1  0  0
5  0  1  0
```

In some cases, you may want to add a prefix to the columns in the indicator DataFrame, which can then be merged with the other data. get_dummies has a prefix argument for doing just this:

```
In [191]: dummies = pd.get_dummies(df['key'], prefix='key')

In [192]: df_with_dummy = df[['data1']].join(dummies)

In [193]: df_with_dummy
Out[193]:
   data1  key_a  key_b  key_c
0      0      0      1      0
1      1      0      1      0
2      2      1      0      0
3      3      0      0      1
4      4      1      0      0
5      5      0      1      0
```

If a row in a DataFrame belongs to multiple categories, things are a bit more complicated. Let's return to the MovieLens 1M dataset from earlier in the book:

```
In [194]: mnames = ['movie_id', 'title', 'genres']

In [195]: movies = pd.read_table('ch07/movies.dat', sep='::', header=None,
   .....:                        names=mnames)

In [196]: movies[:10]
Out[196]:
   movie_id                               title                        genres
0         1                    Toy Story (1995)   Animation|Children's|Comedy
1         2                      Jumanji (1995)  Adventure|Children's|Fantasy
2         3             Grumpier Old Men (1995)                Comedy|Romance
3         4            Waiting to Exhale (1995)                  Comedy|Drama
4         5  Father of the Bride Part II (1995)                        Comedy
5         6                         Heat (1995)         Action|Crime|Thriller
6         7                      Sabrina (1995)                Comedy|Romance
7         8                 Tom and Huck (1995)            Adventure|Children's
8         9                 Sudden Death (1995)                        Action
9        10                    GoldenEye (1995)     Action|Adventure|Thriller
```

Adding indicator variables for each genre requires a little bit of wrangling. First, we extract the list of unique genres in the dataset (using a nice set.union trick):

```
In [197]: genre_iter = (set(x.split('|')) for x in movies.genres)
```

```
In [198]: genres = sorted(set.union(*genre_iter))
```

Now, one way to construct the indicator DataFrame is to start with a DataFrame of all zeros:

```
In [199]: dummies = DataFrame(np.zeros((len(movies), len(genres))), columns=genres)
```

Now, iterate through each movie and set entries in each row of dummies to 1:

```
In [200]: for i, gen in enumerate(movies.genres):
   .....:     dummies.ix[i, gen.split('|')] = 1
```

Then, as above, you can combine this with movies:

```
In [201]: movies_windic = movies.join(dummies.add_prefix('Genre_'))
```

```
In [202]: movies_windic.ix[0]
Out[202]:
movie_id                                  1
title                      Toy Story (1995)
genres          Animation|Children's|Comedy
...
Genre_Thriller         0
Genre_War              0
Genre_Western          0
Name: 0, Length: 21, dtype: object
```

 For much larger data, this method of constructing indicator variables with multiple membership is not especially speedy. A lower-level function leveraging the internals of the DataFrame could certainly be written.

A useful recipe for statistical applications is to combine get_dummies with a discretization function like cut:

```
In [204]: values = np.random.rand(10)

In [205]: values
Out[205]:
array([ 0.9296,  0.3164,  0.1839,  0.2046,  0.5677,  0.5955,  0.9645,
        0.6532,  0.7489,  0.6536])

In [206]: bins = [0, 0.2, 0.4, 0.6, 0.8, 1]

In [207]: pd.get_dummies(pd.cut(values, bins))
Out[207]:
   (0, 0.2]  (0.2, 0.4]  (0.4, 0.6]  (0.6, 0.8]  (0.8, 1]
0         0           0           0           0         1
1         0           1           0           0         0
2         1           0           0           0         0
3         0           1           0           0         0
4         0           0           1           0         0
5         0           0           1           0         0
6         0           0           0           0         1
7         0           0           0           1         0
8         0           0           0           1         0
9         0           0           0           1         0
```

String Manipulation

Python has long been a popular data munging language in part due to its ease-of-use for string and text processing. Most text operations are made simple with the string object's built-in methods. For more complex pattern matching and text manipulations, regular expressions may be needed. pandas adds to the mix by enabling you to apply string and regular expressions concisely on whole arrays of data, additionally handling the annoyance of missing data.

String Object Methods

In many string munging and scripting applications, built-in string methods are sufficient. As an example, a comma-separated string can be broken into pieces with split:

```
In [208]: val = 'a,b,  guido'

In [209]: val.split(',')
Out[209]: ['a', 'b', '  guido']
```

split is often combined with strip to trim whitespace (including newlines):

```
In [210]: pieces = [x.strip() for x in val.split(',')]

In [211]: pieces
Out[211]: ['a', 'b', 'guido']
```

These substrings could be concatenated together with a two-colon delimiter using addition:

```
In [212]: first, second, third = pieces

In [213]: first + '::' + second + '::' + third
Out[213]: 'a::b::guido
```

But, this isn't a practical generic method. A faster and more Pythonic way is to pass a list or tuple to the join method on the string '::':

```
In [214]: '::'.join(pieces)
Out[214]: 'a::b::guido'
```

Other methods are concerned with locating substrings. Using Python's in keyword is the best way to detect a substring, though index and find can also be used:

```
In [215]: 'guido' in val
Out[215]: True

In [216]: val.index(',')          In [217]: val.find(':')
Out[216]: 1                        Out[217]: -1
```

Note the difference between find and index is that index raises an exception if the string isn't found (versus returning -1):

```
In [218]: val.index(':')
---------------------------------------------------------------------------
ValueError                                Traceback (most recent call last)
<ipython-input-218-280f8b2856ce> in <module>()
----> 1 val.index(':')
ValueError: substring not found
```

Relatedly, count returns the number of occurrences of a particular substring:

```
In [219]: val.count(',')
Out[219]: 2
```

replace will substitute occurrences of one pattern for another. This is commonly used to delete patterns, too, by passing an empty string:

```
In [220]: val.replace(',', '::')        In [221]: val.replace(',', '')
Out[220]: 'a::b::  guido'               Out[221]: 'ab  guido'
```

Regular expressions can also be used with many of these operations as you'll see below.

Table 7-3. Python built-in string methods

Argument	Description
count	Return the number of non-overlapping occurrences of substring in the string.
endswith, startswith	Returns True if string ends with suffix (starts with prefix).
join	Use string as delimiter for concatenating a sequence of other strings.
index	Return position of first character in substring if found in the string. Raises ValueError if not found.

Argument	Description
find	Return position of first character of *first* occurrence of substring in the string. Like index, but returns -1 if not found.
rfind	Return position of first character of *last* occurrence of substring in the string. Returns -1 if not found.
replace	Replace occurrences of string with another string.
strip, rstrip, lstrip	Trim whitespace, including newlines; equivalent to x.strip() (and rstrip, lstrip, respectively) for each element.
split	Break string into list of substrings using passed delimiter.
lower, upper	Convert alphabet characters to lowercase or uppercase, respectively.
ljust, rjust	Left justify or right justify, respectively. Pad opposite side of string with spaces (or some other fill character) to return a string with a minimum width.

Regular expressions

Regular expressions provide a flexible way to search or match string patterns in text. A single expression, commonly called a *regex*, is a string formed according to the regular expression language. Python's built-in re module is responsible for applying regular expressions to strings; I'll give a number of examples of its use here.

 The art of writing regular expressions could be a chapter of its own and thus is outside the book's scope. There are many excellent tutorials and references on the internet, such as Zed Shaw's *Learn Regex The Hard Way* (*http://regex.learncodethehardway.org/book/*).

The re module functions fall into three categories: pattern matching, substitution, and splitting. Naturally these are all related; a regex describes a pattern to locate in the text, which can then be used for many purposes. Let's look at a simple example: suppose I wanted to split a string with a variable number of whitespace characters (tabs, spaces, and newlines). The regex describing one or more whitespace characters is \s+:

```
In [222]: import re

In [223]: text = "foo    bar\t baz  \tqux"

In [224]: re.split('\s+', text)
Out[224]: ['foo', 'bar', 'baz', 'qux']
```

When you call re.split('\s+', text), the regular expression is first *compiled*, then its split method is called on the passed text. You can compile the regex yourself with re.compile, forming a reusable regex object:

```
In [225]: regex = re.compile('\s+')

In [226]: regex.split(text)
Out[226]: ['foo', 'bar', 'baz', 'qux']
```

If, instead, you wanted to get a list of all patterns matching the regex, you can use the `findall` method:

```
In [227]: regex.findall(text)
Out[227]: ['    ', '\t ', '  \t']
```

 To avoid unwanted escaping with \ in a regular expression, use *raw* string literals like `r'C:\x'` instead of the equivalent `'C:\\x'`.

Creating a regex object with `re.compile` is highly recommended if you intend to apply the same expression to many strings; doing so will save CPU cycles.

`match` and `search` are closely related to `findall`. While `findall` returns all matches in a string, `search` returns only the first match. More rigidly, `match` *only* matches at the beginning of the string. As a less trivial example, let's consider a block of text and a regular expression capable of identifying most email addresses:

```
text = """Dave dave@google.com
Steve steve@gmail.com
Rob rob@gmail.com
Ryan ryan@yahoo.com
"""
pattern = r'[A-Z0-9._%+-]+@[A-Z0-9.-]+\.[A-Z]{2,4}'

# re.IGNORECASE makes the regex case-insensitive
regex = re.compile(pattern, flags=re.IGNORECASE)
```

Using `findall` on the text produces a list of the e-mail addresses:

```
In [229]: regex.findall(text)
Out[229]: ['dave@google.com', 'steve@gmail.com', 'rob@gmail.com', 'ryan@yahoo.com']
```

`search` returns a special match object for the first email address in the text. For the above regex, the match object can only tell us the start and end position of the pattern in the string:

```
In [230]: m = regex.search(text)

In [231]: m
Out[231]: <_sre.SRE_Match at 0x7fb006dfbf38>

In [232]: text[m.start():m.end()]
Out[232]: 'dave@google.com'
```

`regex.match` returns `None`, as it only will match if the pattern occurs at the start of the string:

```
In [233]: print regex.match(text)
None
```

Relatedly, `sub` will return a new string with occurrences of the pattern replaced by the a new string:

```
In [234]: print regex.sub('REDACTED', text)
Dave REDACTED
Steve REDACTED
Rob REDACTED
Ryan REDACTED
```

Suppose you wanted to find email addresses and simultaneously segment each address into its 3 components: username, domain name, and domain suffix. To do this, put parentheses around the parts of the pattern to segment:

```
In [235]: pattern = r'([A-Z0-9._%+-]+)@([A-Z0-9.-]+)\.([A-Z]{2,4})'

In [236]: regex = re.compile(pattern, flags=re.IGNORECASE)
```

A match object produced by this modified regex returns a tuple of the pattern components with its **groups** method:

```
In [237]: m = regex.match('wesm@bright.net')

In [238]: m.groups()
Out[238]: ('wesm', 'bright', 'net')
```

findall returns a list of tuples when the pattern has groups:

```
In [239]: regex.findall(text)
Out[239]:
[('dave', 'google', 'com'),
 ('steve', 'gmail', 'com'),
 ('rob', 'gmail', 'com'),
 ('ryan', 'yahoo', 'com')]
```

sub also has access to groups in each match using special symbols like \1, \2, etc.:

```
In [240]: print regex.sub(r'Username: \1, Domain: \2, Suffix: \3', text)
Dave Username: dave, Domain: google, Suffix: com
Steve Username: steve, Domain: gmail, Suffix: com
Rob Username: rob, Domain: gmail, Suffix: com
Ryan Username: ryan, Domain: yahoo, Suffix: com
```

There is much more to regular expressions in Python, most of which is outside the book's scope. To give you a flavor, one variation on the above email regex gives names to the match groups:

```
regex = re.compile(r"""
    (?P<username>[A-Z0-9._%+-]+)
    @
    (?P<domain>[A-Z0-9.-]+)
    \.
    (?P<suffix>[A-Z]{2,4})""", flags=re.IGNORECASE|re.VERBOSE)
```

The match object produced by such a regex can produce a handy dict with the specified group names:

```
In [242]: m = regex.match('wesm@bright.net')

In [243]: m.groupdict()
Out[243]: {'domain': 'bright', 'suffix': 'net', 'username': 'wesm'}
```

Table 7-4. Regular expression methods

Argument	Description
findall, finditer	Return all non-overlapping matching patterns in a string. findall returns a list of all patterns while finditer returns them one by one from an iterator.
match	Match pattern at start of string and optionally segment pattern components into groups. If the pattern matches, returns a match object, otherwise None.
search	Scan string for match to pattern; returning a match object if so. Unlike match, the match can be anywhere in the string as opposed to only at the beginning.
split	Break string into pieces at each occurrence of pattern.
sub, subn	Replace all (sub) or first n occurrences (subn) of pattern in string with replacement expression. Use symbols \1, \2, ... to refer to match group elements in the replacement string.

Vectorized string functions in pandas

Cleaning up a messy data set for analysis often requires a lot of string munging and regularization. To complicate matters, a column containing strings will sometimes have missing data:

```
In [244]: data = {'Dave': 'dave@google.com', 'Steve': 'steve@gmail.com',
   .....:          'Rob': 'rob@gmail.com', 'Wes': np.nan}

In [245]: data = Series(data)

In [246]: data                        In [247]: data.isnull()
Out[246]:                             Out[247]:
Dave     dave@google.com              Dave     False
Rob        rob@gmail.com              Rob      False
Steve    steve@gmail.com              Steve    False
Wes                  NaN              Wes       True
dtype: object                        dtype: bool
```

String and regular expression methods can be applied (passing a lambda or other function) to each value using data.map, but it will fail on the NA. To cope with this, Series has concise methods for string operations that skip NA values. These are accessed through Series's str attribute; for example, we could check whether each email address has 'gmail' in it with str.contains:

```
In [248]: data.str.contains('gmail')
Out[248]:
Dave     False
Rob       True
Steve     True
Wes        NaN
dtype: object
```

Regular expressions can be used, too, along with any re options like IGNORECASE:

```
In [249]: pattern
Out[249]: '([A-Z0-9._%+-]+)@([A-Z0-9.-]+)\\.([A-Z]{2,4})'
```

```
In [250]: data.str.findall(pattern, flags=re.IGNORECASE)
Out[250]:
Dave       [(dave, google, com)]
Rob         [(rob, gmail, com)]
Steve     [(steve, gmail, com)]
Wes                        NaN
dtype: object
```

There are a couple of ways to do vectorized element retrieval. Either use str.get or index into the str attribute:

```
In [251]: matches = data.str.match(pattern, flags=re.IGNORECASE)

In [252]: matches
Out[252]:
Dave       (dave, google, com)
Rob         (rob, gmail, com)
Steve     (steve, gmail, com)
Wes                       NaN
dtype: object
```

```
In [253]: matches.str.get(1)        In [254]: matches.str[0]
Out[253]:                           Out[254]:
Dave      google                    Dave      dave
Rob        gmail                    Rob        rob
Steve      gmail                    Steve     steve
Wes          NaN                    Wes         NaN
dtype: object                       dtype: object
```

You can similarly slice strings using this syntax:

```
In [255]: data.str[:5]
Out[255]:
Dave      dave@
Rob       rob@g
Steve     steve
Wes         NaN
dtype: object
```

Table 7-5. Vectorized string methods

Method	Description
cat	Concatenate strings element-wise with optional delimiter
contains	Return boolean array if each string contains pattern/regex
count	Count occurrences of pattern
endswith, startswith	Equivalent to x.endswith(pattern) or x.startswith(pattern) for each element.
findall	Compute list of all occurrences of pattern/regex for each string
get	Index into each element (retrieve i-th element)
join	Join strings in each element of the Series with passed separator
len	Compute length of each string

Method	Description
lower, upper	Convert cases; equivalent to x.lower() or x.upper() for each element.
match	Use re.match with the passed regular expression on each element, returning matched groups as list.
pad	Add whitespace to left, right, or both sides of strings
center	Equivalent to pad(side='both')
repeat	Duplicate values; for example s.str.repeat(3) equivalent to x * 3 for each string.
replace	Replace occurrences of pattern/regex with some other string
slice	Slice each string in the Series.
split	Split strings on delimiter or regular expression
strip, rstrip, lstrip	Trim whitespace, including newlines; equivalent to x.strip() (and rstrip, lstrip, respectively) for each element.

Example: USDA Food Database

The US Department of Agriculture makes available a database of food nutrient information. Ashley Williams, an English hacker, has made available a version of this database in JSON format (*http://ashleyw.co.uk/project/food-nutrient-database*). The records look like this:

```
{
  "id": 21441,
  "description": "KENTUCKY FRIED CHICKEN, Fried Chicken, EXTRA CRISPY,
Wing, meat and skin with breading",
  "tags": ["KFC"],
  "manufacturer": "Kentucky Fried Chicken",
  "group": "Fast Foods",
  "portions": [
    {
      "amount": 1,
      "unit": "wing, with skin",
      "grams": 68.0
    },

    ...
  ],
  "nutrients": [
    {
      "value": 20.8,
      "units": "g",
      "description": "Protein",
      "group": "Composition"
    },

    ...
  ]
}
```

Each food has a number of identifying attributes along with two lists of nutrients and portion sizes. Having the data in this form is not particularly amenable for analysis, so we need to do some work to wrangle the data into a better form.

After downloading and extracting the data from the link above, you can load it into Python with any JSON library of your choosing. I'll use the built-in Python json module:

```
In [256]: import json

In [257]: db = json.load(open('ch07/foods-2011-10-03.json'))

In [258]: len(db)
Out[258]: 6636
```

Each entry in db is a dict containing all the data for a single food. The 'nutrients' field is a list of dicts, one for each nutrient:

```
In [259]: db[0].keys()          In [260]: db[0]['nutrients'][0]
Out[259]:                       Out[260]:
[u'portions',                   {u'description': u'Protein',
 u'description',                 u'group': u'Composition',
 u'tags',                        u'units': u'g',
 u'nutrients',                   u'value': 25.18}
 u'group',
 u'id',
 u'manufacturer']

In [261]: nutrients = DataFrame(db[0]['nutrients'])

In [262]: nutrients[:7]
Out[262]:
                     description        group units    value
0                        Protein  Composition     g    25.18
1               Total lipid (fat)  Composition     g    29.20
2   Carbohydrate, by difference  Composition     g     3.06
3                            Ash        Other     g     3.28
4                         Energy       Energy  kcal   376.00
5                          Water  Composition     g    39.28
6                         Energy       Energy    kJ  1573.00
```

When converting a list of dicts to a DataFrame, we can specify a list of fields to extract. We'll take the food names, group, id, and manufacturer:

```
In [263]: info_keys = ['description', 'group', 'id', 'manufacturer']

In [264]: info = DataFrame(db, columns=info_keys)

In [265]: info[:5]
Out[265]:
                 description                    group    id  \
0            Cheese, caraway  Dairy and Egg Products  1008
1            Cheese, cheddar  Dairy and Egg Products  1009
2              Cheese, edam  Dairy and Egg Products  1018
3              Cheese, feta  Dairy and Egg Products  1019
```

```
4  Cheese, mozzarella, part skim milk  Dairy and Egg Products  1028
   manufacturer
0
1
2
3
4

In [266]: info.info()
<class 'pandas.core.frame.DataFrame'>
Int64Index: 6636 entries, 0 to 6635
Data columns (total 4 columns):
description    6636 non-null object
group          6636 non-null object
id             6636 non-null int64
manufacturer   5195 non-null object
dtypes: int64(1), object(3)
```

You can see the distribution of food groups with value_counts:

```
In [267]: pd.value_counts(info.group)[:10]
Out[267]:
Vegetables and Vegetable Products    812
Beef Products                        618
Baked Products                       496
Breakfast Cereals                    403
Legumes and Legume Products          365
Fast Foods                           365
Lamb, Veal, and Game Products        345
Sweets                               341
Fruits and Fruit Juices              328
Pork Products                        328
dtype: int64
```

Now, to do some analysis on all of the nutrient data, it's easiest to assemble the nutrients for each food into a single large table. To do so, we need to take several steps. First, I'll convert each list of food nutrients to a DataFrame, add a column for the food id, and append the DataFrame to a list. Then, these can be concatenated together with concat:

```
nutrients = []

for rec in db:
    fnuts = DataFrame(rec['nutrients'])
    fnuts['id'] = rec['id']
    nutrients.append(fnuts)

nutrients = pd.concat(nutrients, ignore_index=True)
```

If all goes well, nutrients should look like this:

```
In [269]: nutrients
Out[269]:
                            description        group units    value    id
0                               Protein  Composition     g   25.180  1008
1                     Total lipid (fat)  Composition     g   29.200  1008
2         Carbohydrate, by difference  Composition     g    3.060  1008
```

```
3                               Ash    Other     g    3.280  1008
4                            Energy   Energy   kcal  376.000  1008
...                             ...      ...   ...      ...   ...
389350            Vitamin B-12, added  Vitamins  mcg    0.000  43546
389351                   Cholesterol    Other    mg    0.000  43546
389352       Fatty acids, total saturated   Other     g    0.072  43546
389353 Fatty acids, total monounsaturated   Other     g    0.028  43546
389354 Fatty acids, total polyunsaturated   Other     g    0.041  43546
[389355 rows x 5 columns]
```

I noticed that, for whatever reason, there are duplicates in this DataFrame, so it makes things easier to drop them:

```
In [270]: nutrients.duplicated().sum()
Out[270]: 14179

In [271]: nutrients = nutrients.drop_duplicates()
```

Since 'group' and 'description' is in both DataFrame objects, we can rename them to make it clear what is what:

```
In [272]: col_mapping = {'description' : 'food',
   .....:                'group'       : 'fgroup'}

In [273]: info = info.rename(columns=col_mapping, copy=False)

In [274]: info.info()
<class 'pandas.core.frame.DataFrame'>
Int64Index: 6636 entries, 0 to 6635
Data columns (total 4 columns):
food          6636 non-null object
fgroup        6636 non-null object
id            6636 non-null int64
manufacturer  5195 non-null object
dtypes: int64(1), object(3)
In [275]: col_mapping = {'description' : 'nutrient',
   .....:                'group' : 'nutgroup'}

In [276]: nutrients = nutrients.rename(columns=col_mapping, copy=False)

In [277]: nutrients
Out[277]:
                             nutrient     nutgroup units    value     id
0                             Protein  Composition     g   25.180   1008
1                   Total lipid (fat)  Composition     g   29.200   1008
2         Carbohydrate, by difference  Composition     g    3.060   1008
3                                 Ash        Other     g    3.280   1008
4                              Energy       Energy  kcal  376.000   1008
...                               ...          ...   ...      ...    ...
389350            Vitamin B-12, added     Vitamins   mcg    0.000  43546
389351                    Cholesterol        Other    mg    0.000  43546
389352       Fatty acids, total saturated     Other     g    0.072  43546
389353 Fatty acids, total monounsaturated     Other     g    0.028  43546
389354 Fatty acids, total polyunsaturated     Other     g    0.041  43546
[375176 rows x 5 columns]
```

With all of this done, we're ready to merge info with nutrients:

```
In [278]: ndata = pd.merge(nutrients, info, on='id', how='outer')
```

```
In [279]: ndata.info()
<class 'pandas.core.frame.DataFrame'>
Int64Index: 375176 entries, 0 to 375175
Data columns (total 8 columns):
nutrient        375176 non-null object
nutgroup        375176 non-null object
units           375176 non-null object
value           375176 non-null float64
id              375176 non-null int64
food            375176 non-null object
fgroup          375176 non-null object
manufacturer    293054 non-null object
dtypes: float64(1), int64(1), object(6)
In [280]: ndata.ix[30000]
Out[280]:
nutrient                                    Glycine
nutgroup                                Amino Acids
units                                             g
value                                          0.04
id                                             6158
food           Soup, tomato bisque, canned, condensed
fgroup                    Soups, Sauces, and Gravies
manufacturer
Name: 30000, dtype: object
```

The tools that you need to slice and dice, aggregate, and visualize this dataset will be explored in detail in the next two chapters, so after you get a handle on those methods you might return to this dataset. For example, we could a plot of median values by food group and nutrient type (see Figure 7-1):

```
In [281]: result = ndata.groupby(['nutrient', 'fgroup'])['value'].quantile(0.5)
```

```
In [282]: result['Zinc, Zn'].order().plot(kind='barh')
```

With a little cleverness, you can find which food is most dense in each nutrient:

```
by_nutrient = ndata.groupby(['nutgroup', 'nutrient'])

get_maximum = lambda x: x.xs(x.value.idxmax())
get_minimum = lambda x: x.xs(x.value.idxmin())

max_foods = by_nutrient.apply(get_maximum)[['value', 'food']]

# make the food a little smaller
max_foods.food = max_foods.food.str[:50]
```

The resulting DataFrame is a bit too large to display in the book; here is just the 'Amino Acids' nutrient group:

```
In [284]: max_foods.ix['Amino Acids']['food']
Out[284]:
nutrient
```

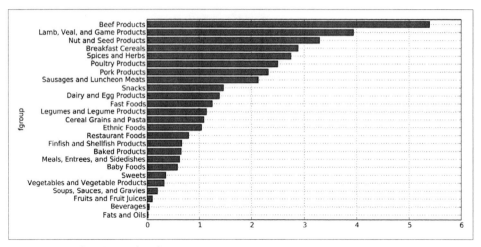

Figure 7-1. Median Zinc values by nutrient group

```
Alanine              Gelatins, dry powder, unsweetened
Arginine                Seeds, sesame flour, low-fat
Aspartic acid                  Soy protein isolate
...
Tryptophan       Sea lion, Steller, meat with fat (Alaska Native)
Tyrosine         Soy protein isolate, PROTEIN TECHNOLOGIES INTE...
Valine           Soy protein isolate, PROTEIN TECHNOLOGIES INTE...
Name: food, Length: 19, dtype: object
```

## CHAPTER 8

Plotting and Visualization

Making plots and static or interactive visualizations is one of the most important tasks in data analysis. It may be a part of the exploratory process; for example, helping identify outliers, needed data transformations, or coming up with ideas for models. For others, building an interactive visualization for the web using a toolkit like d3.js (*http://d3js.org/*) may be the end goal. Python has many visualization tools (see the end of this chapter), but I'll be mainly focused on matplotlib (*http://matplotlib.sourceforge.net*).

matplotlib is a (primarily 2D) desktop plotting package designed for creating publication-quality plots. The project was started by John Hunter in 2002 to enable a MATLAB-like plotting interface in Python. He, Fernando Pérez (of IPython), and others have collaborated for many years since then to make IPython combined with matplotlib a very functional and productive environment for scientific computing. When used in tandem with a GUI toolkit (for example, within IPython), matplotlib has interactive features like zooming and panning. It supports many different GUI backends on all operating systems and additionally can export graphics to all of the common vector and raster graphics formats: PDF, SVG, JPG, PNG, BMP, GIF, etc. I have used it to produce almost all of the graphics outside of diagrams in this book.

matplotlib has a number of add-on toolkits, such as `mplot3d` for 3D plots and `basemap` for mapping and projections. I will give an example using `basemap` to plot data on a map and to read *shapefiles* at the end of the chapter.

To follow along with the code examples in the chapter, make sure you have started IPython in Pylab mode (`ipython --pylab`) or enabled GUI event loop integration with the `%gui` magic.

A Brief matplotlib API Primer

There are several ways to interact with matplotlib. The most common is through *pylab mode* in IPython by running `ipython --pylab`. This launches IPython configured to be able to support the matplotlib GUI backend of your choice (Tk, wxPython, PyQt, Mac

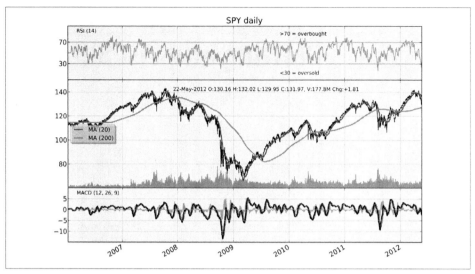

Figure 8-1. A more complex matplotlib financial plot

OS X native, GTK). For most users, the default backend will be sufficient. Pylab mode also imports a large set of modules and functions into IPython to provide a more MAT-LAB-like interface. You can test that everything is working by making a simple plot:

```
plot(np.arange(10))
```

If everything is set up right, a new window should pop up with a line plot. You can close it by using the mouse or entering `close()`. Matplotlib API functions like `plot` and `close` are all in the `matplotlib.pyplot` module, which is typically imported by convention as:

```
import matplotlib.pyplot as plt
```

While the pandas plotting functions described later deal with many of the mundane details of making plots, should you wish to customize them beyond the function options provided you will need to learn a bit about the matplotlib API.

 There is not enough room in the book to give a comprehensive treatment to the breadth and depth of functionality in matplotlib. It should be enough to teach you the ropes to get up and running. The matplotlib gallery and documentation are the best resource for becoming a plotting guru and using advanced features.

Figures and Subplots

Plots in matplotlib reside within a `Figure` object. You can create a new figure with `plt.figure`:

```
In [590]: fig = plt.figure()
```

If you are in pylab mode in IPython, a new empty window should pop up. `plt.fig`
`ure` has a number of options, notably `figsize` will guarantee the figure has a certain size
and aspect ratio if saved to disk. Figures in matplotlib also support a numbering scheme
(for example, `plt.figure(2)`) that mimics MATLAB. You can get a reference to the
active figure using `plt.gcf()`.

You can't make a plot with a blank figure. You have to create one or more `subplots`
using `add_subplot`:

```
In [591]: ax1 = fig.add_subplot(2, 2, 1)
```

This means that the figure should be 2 × 2, and we're selecting the first of 4 subplots
(numbered from 1). If you create the next two subplots, you'll end up with a figure that
looks like Figure 8-2.

```
In [592]: ax2 = fig.add_subplot(2, 2, 2)
```

```
In [593]: ax3 = fig.add_subplot(2, 2, 3)
```

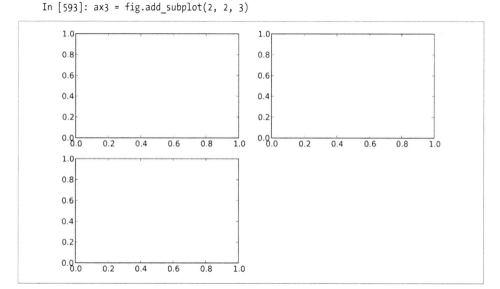

Figure 8-2. An empty matplotlib Figure with 3 subplots

When you issue a plotting command like `plt.plot([1.5, 3.5, -2, 1.6])`, matplotlib
draws on the last figure and subplot used (creating one if necessary), thus hiding the
figure and subplot creation. Thus, if we run the following command, you'll get something like Figure 8-3:

```
In [594]: from numpy.random import randn
```

```
In [595]: plt.plot(randn(50).cumsum(), 'k--')
```

The `'k--'` is a *style* option instructing matplotlib to plot a black dashed line. The objects
returned by `fig.add_subplot` above are `AxesSubplot` objects, on which you can directly
plot on the other empty subplots by calling each one's instance methods, see Figure 8-4:

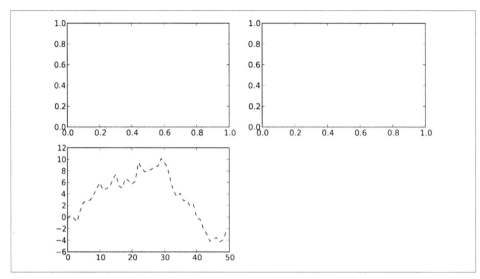

Figure 8-3. Figure after single plot

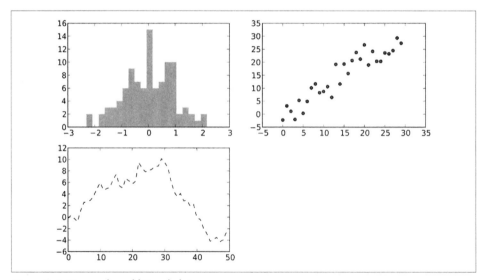

Figure 8-4. Figure after additional plots

```
In [596]: _ = ax1.hist(randn(100), bins=20, color='k', alpha=0.3)

In [597]: ax2.scatter(np.arange(30), np.arange(30) + 3 * randn(30))
```

You can find a comprehensive catalogue of plot types in the matplotlib documentation.

Since creating a figure with multiple subplots according to a particular layout is such a common task, there is a convenience method, plt.subplots, that creates a new figure and returns a NumPy array containing the created subplot objects:

```
In [599]: fig, axes = plt.subplots(2, 3)

In [600]: axes
Out[600]:
array([[<matplotlib.axes.AxesSubplot object at 0x7f5893019b50>,
        <matplotlib.axes.AxesSubplot object at 0x7f587fba4cd0>,
        <matplotlib.axes.AxesSubplot object at 0x7f587faba090>],
       [<matplotlib.axes.AxesSubplot object at 0x7f587fa9b290>,
        <matplotlib.axes.AxesSubplot object at 0x7f587fa1b050>,
        <matplotlib.axes.AxesSubplot object at 0x7f587f972d10>]], dtype=object)
```

This is very useful as the `axes` array can be easily indexed like a two-dimensional array; for example, `axes[0, 1]`. You can also indicate that subplots should have the same X or Y axis using `sharex` and `sharey`, respectively. This is especially useful when comparing data on the same scale; otherwise, matplotlib auto-scales plot limits independently. See Table 8-1 for more on this method.

Table 8-1. pyplot.subplots options

Argument	Description
nrows	Number of rows of subplots
ncols	Number of columns of subplots
sharex	All subplots should use the same X-axis ticks (adjusting the `xlim` will affect all subplots)
sharey	All subplots should use the same Y-axis ticks (adjusting the `ylim` will affect all subplots)
subplot_kw	Dict of keywords passed to `add_subplot` call used to create each subplot.
**fig_kw	Additional keywords to `subplots` are used when creating the figure, such as `plt.subplots(2, 2, figsize=(8, 6))`

Adjusting the spacing around subplots

By default matplotlib leaves a certain amount of padding around the outside of the subplots and spacing between subplots. This spacing is all specified relative to the height and width of the plot, so that if you resize the plot either programmatically or manually using the GUI window, the plot will dynamically adjust itself. The spacing can be most easily changed using the `subplots_adjust` Figure method, also available as a top-level function:

```
subplots_adjust(left=None, bottom=None, right=None, top=None,
                wspace=None, hspace=None)
```

`wspace` and `hspace` controls the percent of the figure width and figure height, respectively, to use as spacing between subplots. Here is a small example where I shrink the spacing all the way to zero (see Figure 8-5):

```
fig, axes = plt.subplots(2, 2, sharex=True, sharey=True)
for i in range(2):
    for j in range(2):
        axes[i, j].hist(randn(500), bins=50, color='k', alpha=0.5)
plt.subplots_adjust(wspace=0, hspace=0)
```

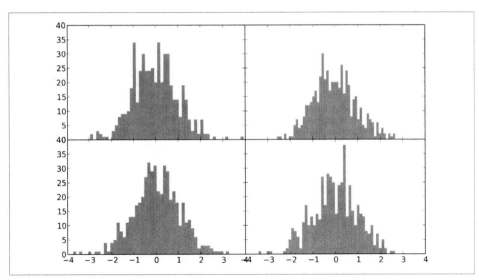

Figure 8-5. Figure with no inter-subplot spacing

You may notice that the axis labels overlap. matplotlib doesn't check whether the labels overlap, so in a case like this you would need to fix the labels yourself by specifying explicit tick locations and tick labels. More on this in the coming sections.

Colors, Markers, and Line Styles

Matplotlib's main `plot` function accepts arrays of X and Y coordinates and optionally a string abbreviation indicating color and line style. For example, to plot x versus y with green dashes, you would execute:

```
ax.plot(x, y, 'g--')
```

This way of specifying both color and linestyle in a string is provided as a convenience; in practice if you were creating plots programmatically you might prefer not to have to munge strings together to create plots with the desired style. The same plot could also have been expressed more explicitly as:

```
ax.plot(x, y, linestyle='--', color='g')
```

There are a number of color abbreviations provided for commonly-used colors, but any color on the spectrum can be used by specifying its RGB value (for example, '#CECE CE'). You can see the full set of linestyles by looking at the docstring for `plot`.

Line plots can additionally have *markers* to highlight the actual data points. Since matplotlib creates a continuous line plot, interpolating between points, it can occasionally be unclear where the points lie. The marker can be part of the style string, which must have color followed by marker type and line style (see Figure 8-6):

```
In [605]: plt.plot(randn(30).cumsum(), 'ko--')
```

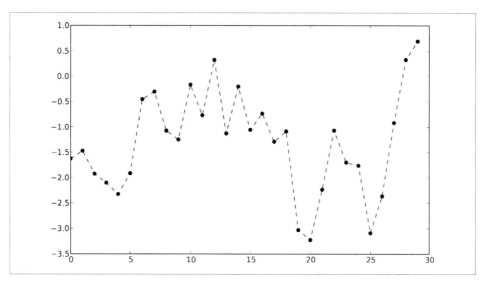

Figure 8-6. Line plot with markers example

This could also have been written more explicitly as:

```
plot(randn(30).cumsum(), color='k', linestyle='dashed', marker='o')
```

For line plots, you will notice that subsequent points are linearly interpolated by default. This can be altered with the **drawstyle** option:

```
In [607]: data = randn(30).cumsum()

In [608]: plt.plot(data, 'k--', label='Default')
Out[608]: [<matplotlib.lines.Line2D at 0x7f587f1220d0>]

In [609]: plt.plot(data, 'k-', drawstyle='steps-post', label='steps-post')
Out[609]: [<matplotlib.lines.Line2D at 0x7f587f122810>]

In [610]: plt.legend(loc='best')
```

Ticks, Labels, and Legends

For most kinds of plot decorations, there are two main ways to do things: using the procedural **pyplot** interface (which will be very familiar to MATLAB users) and the more object-oriented native matplotlib API.

The **pyplot** interface, designed for interactive use, consists of methods like **xlim**, **xticks**, and **xticklabels**. These control the plot range, tick locations, and tick labels, respectively. They can be used in two ways:

- Called with no arguments returns the current parameter value. For example **plt.xlim()** returns the current X axis plotting range

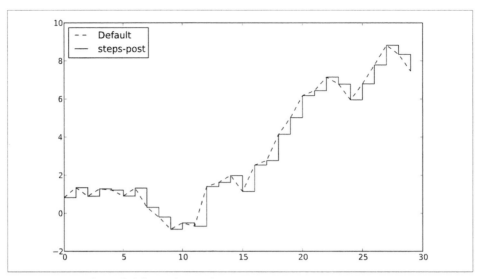

Figure 8-7. Line plot with different drawstyle options

- Called with parameters sets the parameter value. So `plt.xlim([0, 10])`, sets the X axis range to 0 to 10

All such methods act on the active or most recently-created `AxesSubplot`. Each of them corresponds to two methods on the subplot object itself; in the case of `xlim` these are `ax.get_xlim` and `ax.set_xlim`. I prefer to use the subplot instance methods myself in the interest of being explicit (and especially when working with multiple subplots), but you can certainly use whichever you find more convenient.

Setting the title, axis labels, ticks, and ticklabels

To illustrate customizing the axes, I'll create a simple figure and plot of a random walk (see Figure 8-8):

```
In [611]: fig = plt.figure(); ax = fig.add_subplot(1, 1, 1)

In [612]: ax.plot(randn(1000).cumsum())
```

To change the X axis ticks, it's easiest to use `set_xticks` and `set_xticklabels`. The former instructs matplotlib where to place the ticks along the data range; by default these locations will also be the labels. But we can set any other values as the labels using `set_xticklabels`:

```
In [613]: ticks = ax.set_xticks([0, 250, 500, 750, 1000])

In [614]: labels = ax.set_xticklabels(['one', 'two', 'three', 'four', 'five'],
   .....:                             rotation=30, fontsize='small')
```

Lastly, `set_xlabel` gives a name to the X axis and `set_title` the subplot title:

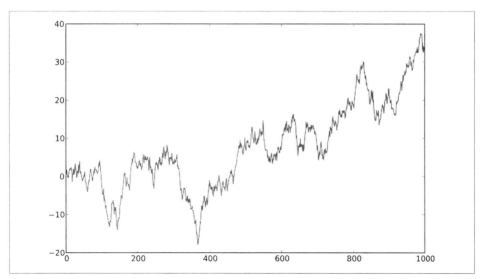

Figure 8-8. Simple plot for illustrating xticks

```
In [615]: ax.set_title('My first matplotlib plot')
Out[615]: <matplotlib.text.Text at 0x7f587f154750>

In [616]: ax.set_xlabel('Stages')
```

See Figure 8-9 for the resulting figure. Modifying the Y axis consists of the same process, substituting y for x in the above.

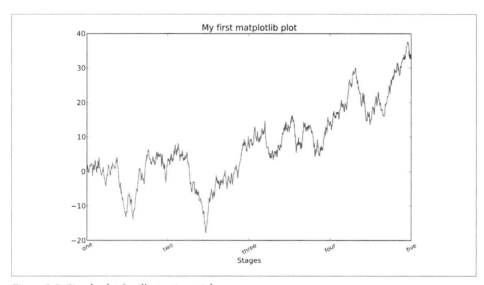

Figure 8-9. Simple plot for illustrating xticks

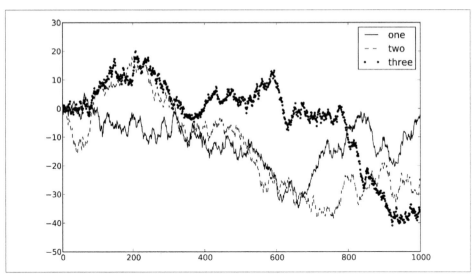

Figure 8-10. Simple plot with 3 lines and legend

Adding legends

Legends are another critical element for identifying plot elements. There are a couple of ways to add one. The easiest is to pass the label argument when adding each piece of the plot:

```
In [617]: fig = plt.figure(); ax = fig.add_subplot(1, 1, 1)

In [618]: ax.plot(randn(1000).cumsum(), 'k', label='one')
Out[618]: [<matplotlib.lines.Line2D at 0x7f587ef34350>]

In [619]: ax.plot(randn(1000).cumsum(), 'k--', label='two')
Out[619]: [<matplotlib.lines.Line2D at 0x7f587f20fdd0>]

In [620]: ax.plot(randn(1000).cumsum(), 'k.', label='three')
Out[620]: [<matplotlib.lines.Line2D at 0x7f587efc13d0>]
```

Once you've done this, you can either call ax.legend() or plt.legend() to automatically create a legend:

```
In [621]: ax.legend(loc='best')
```

See Figure 8-10. The loc tells matplotlib where to place the plot. If you aren't picky 'best' is a good option, as it will choose a location that is most out of the way. To exclude one or more elements from the legend, pass no label or label='_nolegend_'.

Annotations and Drawing on a Subplot

In addition to the standard plot types, you may wish to draw your own plot annotations, which could consist of text, arrows, or other shapes.

Annotations and text can be added using the `text`, `arrow`, and `annotate` functions. `text` draws text at given coordinates (x, y) on the plot with optional custom styling:

```
ax.text(x, y, 'Hello world!',
        family='monospace', fontsize=10)
```

Annotations can draw both text and arrows arranged appropriately. As an example, let's plot the closing S&P 500 index price since 2007 (obtained from Yahoo! Finance) and annotate it with some of the important dates from the 2008-2009 financial crisis. See Figure 8-11 for the result:

```
from datetime import datetime

fig = plt.figure()
ax = fig.add_subplot(1, 1, 1)

data = pd.read_csv('ch08/spx.csv', index_col=0, parse_dates=True)
spx = data['SPX']

spx.plot(ax=ax, style='k-')

crisis_data = [
    (datetime(2007, 10, 11), 'Peak of bull market'),
    (datetime(2008, 3, 12), 'Bear Stearns Fails'),
    (datetime(2008, 9, 15), 'Lehman Bankruptcy')
]

for date, label in crisis_data:
    ax.annotate(label, xy=(date, spx.asof(date) + 50),
                xytext=(date, spx.asof(date) + 200),
                arrowprops=dict(facecolor='black'),
                horizontalalignment='left', verticalalignment='top')

# Zoom in on 2007-2010
ax.set_xlim(['1/1/2007', '1/1/2011'])
ax.set_ylim([600, 1800])

ax.set_title('Important dates in 2008-2009 financial crisis')
```

See the online matplotlib gallery for many more annotation examples to learn from.

Drawing shapes requires some more care. matplotlib has objects that represent many common shapes, referred to as *patches*. Some of these, like `Rectangle` and `Circle` are found in `matplotlib.pyplot`, but the full set is located in `matplotlib.patches`.

To add a shape to a plot, you create the patch object `shp` and add it to a subplot by calling `ax.add_patch(shp)` (see Figure 8-12):

```
fig = plt.figure()
ax = fig.add_subplot(1, 1, 1)

rect = plt.Rectangle((0.2, 0.75), 0.4, 0.15, color='k', alpha=0.3)
circ = plt.Circle((0.7, 0.2), 0.15, color='b', alpha=0.3)
pgon = plt.Polygon([[0.15, 0.15], [0.35, 0.4], [0.2, 0.6]],
                   color='g', alpha=0.5)
```

```
ax.add_patch(rect)
ax.add_patch(circ)
ax.add_patch(pgon)
```

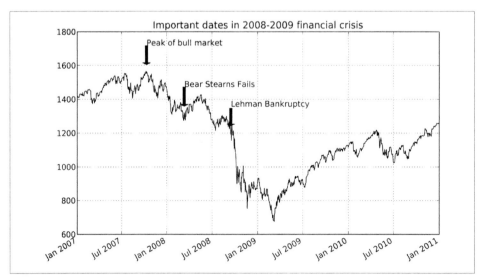

Figure 8-11. Important dates in 2008-2009 financial crisis

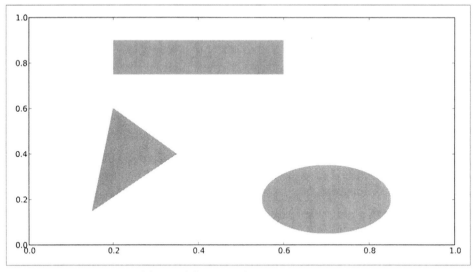

Figure 8-12. Figure composed from 3 different patches

If you look at the implementation of many familiar plot types, you will see that they are assembled from patches.

Saving Plots to File

The active figure can be saved to file using `plt.savefig`. This method is equivalent to the figure object's `savefig` instance method. For example, to save an SVG version of a figure, you need only type:

```
plt.savefig('figpath.svg')
```

The file type is inferred from the file extension. So if you used `.pdf` instead you would get a PDF. There are a couple of important options that I use frequently for publishing graphics: `dpi`, which controls the dots-per-inch resolution, and `bbox_inches`, which can trim the whitespace around the actual figure. To get the same plot as a PNG above with minimal whitespace around the plot and at 400 DPI, you would do:

```
plt.savefig('figpath.png', dpi=400, bbox_inches='tight')
```

`savefig` doesn't have to write to disk; it can also write to any file-like object, such as a `BytesIO`:

```
from io import BytesIO
buffer = BytesIO()
plt.savefig(buffer)
plot_data = buffer.getvalue()
```

For example, this is useful for serving dynamically-generated images over the web.

Table 8-2. Figure.savefig options

Argument	Description
fname	String containing a filepath or a Python file-like object. The figure format is inferred from the file extension, e.g. `.pdf` for PDF or `.png` for PNG.
dpi	The figure resolution in dots per inch; defaults to 100 out of the box but can be configured
facecolor, edge color	The color of the figure background outside of the subplots. `'w'` (white), by default
format	The explicit file format to use (`'png'`, `'pdf'`, `'svg'`, `'ps'`, `'eps'`, ...)
bbox_inches	The portion of the figure to save. If `'tight'` is passed, will attempt to trim the empty space around the figure

matplotlib Configuration

matplotlib comes configured with color schemes and defaults that are geared primarily toward preparing figures for publication. Fortunately, nearly all of the default behavior can be customized via an extensive set of global parameters governing figure size, subplot spacing, colors, font sizes, grid styles, and so on. There are two main ways to interact with the matplotlib configuration system. The first is programmatically from Python using the `rc` method. For example, to set the global default figure size to be 10 x 10, you could enter:

```
plt.rc('figure', figsize=(10, 10))
```

The first argument to rc is the component you wish to customize, such as 'figure', 'axes', 'xtick', 'ytick', 'grid', 'legend' or many others. After that can follow a sequence of keyword arguments indicating the new parameters. An easy way to write down the options in your program is as a dict:

```
font_options = {'family' : 'monospace',
                'weight' : 'bold',
                'size'   : 'small'}
plt.rc('font', **font_options)
```

For more extensive customization and to see a list of all the options, matplotlib comes with a configuration file matplotlibrc in the matplotlib/mpl-data directory. If you customize this file and place it in your home directory titled .matplotlibrc, it will be loaded each time you use matplotlib.

Plotting Functions in pandas

As you've seen, matplotlib is actually a fairly low-level tool. You assemble a plot from its base components: the data display (the type of plot: line, bar, box, scatter, contour, etc.), legend, title, tick labels, and other annotations. Part of the reason for this is that in many cases the data needed to make a complete plot is spread across many objects. In pandas we have row labels, column labels, and possibly grouping information. This means that many kinds of fully-formed plots that would ordinarily require a lot of matplotlib code can be expressed in one or two concise statements. Therefore, pandas has an increasing number of high-level plotting methods for creating standard visualizations that take advantage of how data is organized in DataFrame objects.

 As of this writing, the plotting functionality in pandas is undergoing quite a bit of work. As part of the 2012 Google Summer of Code program, a student is working full time to add features and to make the interface more consistent and usable. Thus, it's possible that this code may fall out-of-date faster than the other things in this book. The online pandas documentation will be the best resource in that event.

Line Plots

Series and DataFrame each have a plot method for making many different plot types. By default, they make line plots (see Figure 8-13):

```
In [632]: s = Series(np.random.randn(10).cumsum(), index=np.arange(0, 100, 10))

In [633]: s.plot()
```

The Series object's index is passed to matplotlib for plotting on the X axis, though this can be disabled by passing use_index=False. The X axis ticks and limits can be adjusted using the xticks and xlim options, and Y axis respectively using yticks and ylim. See

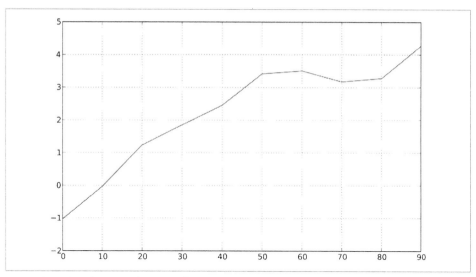

Figure 8-13. Simple Series plot example

Table 8-3 for a full listing of `plot` options. I'll comment on a few more of them throughout this section and leave the rest to you to explore.

Most of pandas's plotting methods accept an optional `ax` parameter, which can be a matplotlib subplot object. This gives you more flexible placement of subplots in a grid layout. There will be more on this in the later section on the matplotlib API.

DataFrame's `plot` method plots each of its columns as a different line on the same subplot, creating a legend automatically (see Figure 8-14):

```
In [634]: df = DataFrame(np.random.randn(10, 4).cumsum(0),
   .....:                 columns=['A', 'B', 'C', 'D'],
   .....:                 index=np.arange(0, 100, 10))

In [635]: df.plot()
```

 Additional keyword arguments to `plot` are passed through to the respective matplotlib plotting function, so you can further customize these plots by learning more about the matplotlib API.

Table 8-3. Series.plot method arguments

Argument	Description
label	Label for plot legend
ax	matplotlib subplot object to plot on. If nothing passed, uses active matplotlib subplot
style	Style string, like ' ko-- ', to be passed to matplotlib.
alpha	The plot fill opacity (from 0 to 1)

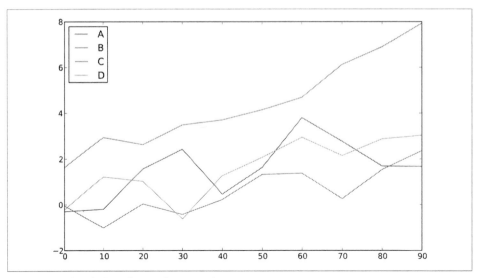

Figure 8-14. Simple DataFrame plot example

Argument	Description
kind	Can be 'line', 'bar', 'barh', 'kde'
logy	Use logarithmic scaling on the Y axis
use_index	Use the object index for tick labels
rot	Rotation of tick labels (0 through 360)
xticks	Values to use for X axis ticks
yticks	Values to use for Y axis ticks
xlim	X axis limits (e.g. [0, 10])
ylim	Y axis limits
grid	Display axis grid (on by default)

DataFrame has a number of options allowing some flexibility with how the columns are handled; for example, whether to plot them all on the same subplot or to create separate subplots. See Table 8-4 for more on these.

Table 8-4. DataFrame-specific plot arguments

Argument	Description
subplots	Plot each DataFrame column in a separate subplot
sharex	If subplots=True, share the same X axis, linking ticks and limits
sharey	If subplots=True, share the same Y axis
figsize	Size of figure to create as tuple

Argument	Description
title	Plot title as string
legend	Add a subplot legend (True by default)
sort_columns	Plot columns in alphabetical order; by default uses existing column order

 For time series plotting, see Chapter 10.

Bar Plots

Making bar plots instead of line plots is as simple as passing kind='bar' (for vertical bars) or kind='barh' (for horizontal bars). In this case, the Series or DataFrame index will be used as the X (bar) or Y (barh) ticks (see Figure 8-15):

```
In [636]: fig, axes = plt.subplots(2, 1)

In [637]: data = Series(np.random.rand(16), index=list('abcdefghijklmnop'))

In [638]: data.plot(kind='bar', ax=axes[0], color='k', alpha=0.7)
Out[638]: <matplotlib.axes.AxesSubplot at 0x7f587ebba190>

In [639]: data.plot(kind='barh', ax=axes[1], color='k', alpha=0.7)
```

 For more on the plt.subplots function and matplotlib axes and figures, see the later section in this chapter.

With a DataFrame, bar plots group the values in each row together in a group in bars, side by side, for each value. See Figure 8-16:

```
In [640]: df = DataFrame(np.random.rand(6, 4),
   .....:               index=['one', 'two', 'three', 'four', 'five', 'six'],
   .....:               columns=pd.Index(['A', 'B', 'C', 'D'], name='Genus'))

In [641]: df
Out[641]:
Genus         A         B         C         D
one    0.301686  0.156333  0.371943  0.270731
two    0.750589  0.525587  0.689429  0.358974
three  0.381504  0.667707  0.473772  0.632528
four   0.942408  0.180186  0.708284  0.641783
five   0.840278  0.909589  0.010041  0.653207
six    0.062854  0.589813  0.811318  0.060217

In [642]: df.plot(kind='bar')
```

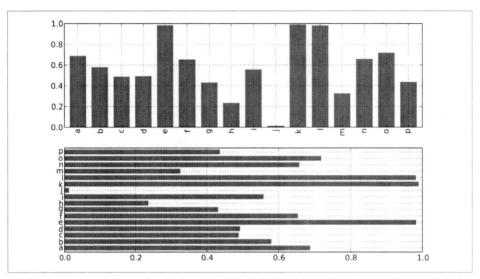

Figure 8-15. Horizontal and vertical bar plot example

Note that the name "Genus" on the DataFrame's columns is used to title the legend.

Stacked bar plots are created from a DataFrame by passing `stacked=True`, resulting in the value in each row being stacked together (see Figure 8-17):

```
In [644]: df.plot(kind='barh', stacked=True, alpha=0.5)
```

> A useful recipe for bar plots (as seen in an earlier chapter) is to visualize a Series's value frequency using `value_counts`: `s.value_counts ().plot(kind='bar')`

Returning to the tipping data set used earlier in the book, suppose we wanted to make a stacked bar plot showing the percentage of data points for each party size on each day. I load the data using `read_csv` and make a cross-tabulation by day and party size:

```
In [645]: tips = pd.read_csv('ch08/tips.csv')

In [646]: party_counts = pd.crosstab(tips.day, tips.size)

In [647]: party_counts
Out[647]:
size  1   2   3   4  5  6
day
Fri   1  16   1   1  0  0
Sat   2  53  18  13  1  0
Sun   0  39  15  18  3  1
Thur  1  48   4   5  1  3
```

```
# Not many 1- and 6-person parties
In [648]: party_counts = party_counts.ix[:, 2:5]
```

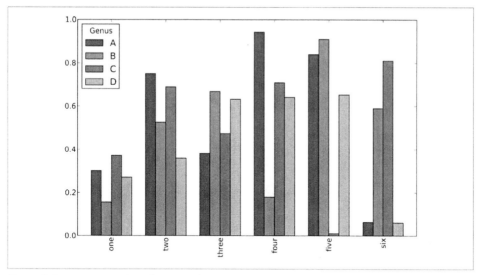

Figure 8-16. DataFrame bar plot example

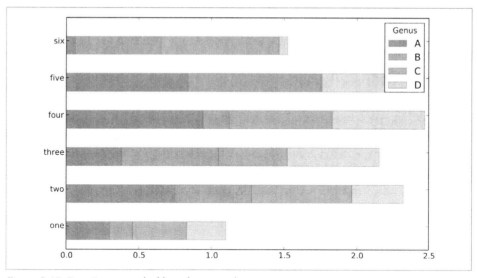

Figure 8-17. DataFrame stacked bar plot example

Then, normalize so that each row sums to 1 (I have to cast to float to avoid integer division issues on Python 2.7) and make the plot (see Figure 8-18):

```
# Normalize to sum to 1
party_pcts = party_counts.div(party_counts.sum(1).astype(float), axis=0)
```

```
party_pcts

#! figure,id=vis_tips_barplot,width=4in,title="Fraction of parties by size on each day"
party_pcts.plot(kind='bar', stacked=True)
```

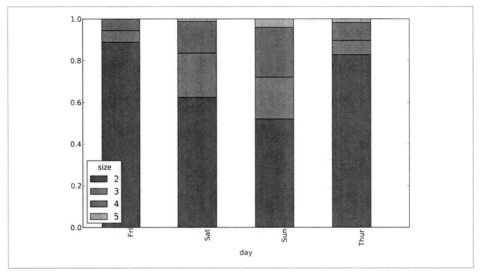

Figure 8-18. Fraction of parties by size on each day

So you can see that party sizes appear to increase on the weekend in this data set.

Histograms and Density Plots

A histogram, with which you may be well-acquainted, is a kind of bar plot that gives a discretized display of value frequency. The data points are split into discrete, evenly spaced bins, and the number of data points in each bin is plotted. Using the tipping data from before, we can make a histogram of tip percentages of the total bill using the hist method on the Series (see Figure 8-19):

```
In [652]: tips['tip_pct'] = tips['tip'] / tips['total_bill']

In [653]: tips['tip_pct'].hist(bins=50)
```

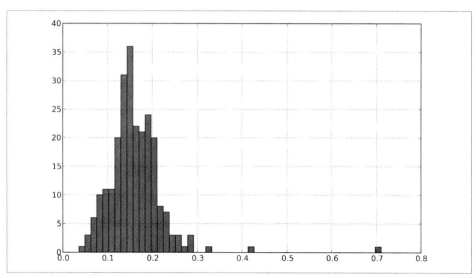

Figure 8-19. Histogram of tip percentages

A related plot type is a *density plot*, which is formed by computing an estimate of a continuous probability distribution that might have generated the observed data. A usual procedure is to approximate this distribution as a mixture of kernels, that is, simpler distributions like the normal (Gaussian) distribution. Thus, density plots are also known as KDE (kernel density estimate) plots. Using plot with kind='kde' makes a density plot using the standard mixture-of-normals KDE (see Figure 8-20):

```
In [655]: tips['tip_pct'].plot(kind='kde')
```

These two plot types are often plotted together; the histogram in normalized form (to give a binned density) with a kernel density estimate plotted on top. As an example, consider a bimodal distribution consisting of draws from two different standard normal distributions (see Figure 8-21):

```
In [657]: comp1 = np.random.normal(0, 1, size=200)  # N(0, 1)

In [658]: comp2 = np.random.normal(10, 2, size=200)  # N(10, 4)

In [659]: values = Series(np.concatenate([comp1, comp2]))

In [660]: values.hist(bins=100, alpha=0.3, color='k', normed=True)
Out[660]: <matplotlib.axes.AxesSubplot at 0x7f587e4a5cd0>

In [661]: values.plot(kind='kde', style='k--')
```

Scatter Plots

Scatter plots are a useful way of examining the relationship between two one-dimensional data series. matplotlib has a scatter plotting method that is the workhorse of

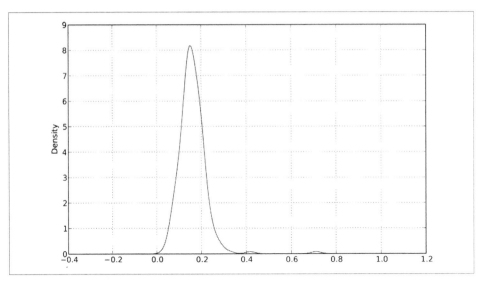

Figure 8-20. Density plot of tip percentages

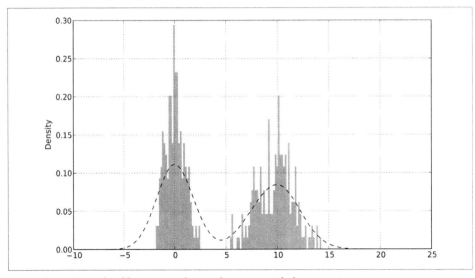

Figure 8-21. Normalized histogram of normal mixture with density estimate

making these kinds of plots. To give an example, I load the macrodata dataset from the
statsmodels project, select a few variables, then compute log differences:

```
In [662]: macro = pd.read_csv('ch08/macrodata.csv')

In [663]: data = macro[['cpi', 'm1', 'tbilrate', 'unemp']]

In [664]: trans_data = np.log(data).diff().dropna()
```

```
In [665]: trans_data[-5:]
Out[665]:
          cpi       m1   tbilrate      unemp
198  -0.007904  0.045361  -0.396881  0.105361
199  -0.021979  0.066753  -2.277267  0.139762
200   0.002340  0.010286   0.606136  0.160343
201   0.008419  0.037461  -0.200671  0.127339
202   0.008894  0.012202  -0.405465  0.042560
```

It's easy to plot a simple scatter plot using plt.scatter (see Figure 8-22):

```
In [667]: plt.scatter(trans_data['m1'], trans_data['unemp'])
Out[667]: <matplotlib.collections.PathCollection at 0x7f587f3b2d10>

In [668]: plt.title('Changes in log %s vs. log %s' % ('m1', 'unemp'))
```

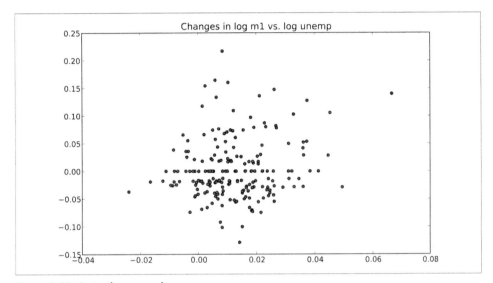

Figure 8-22. A simple scatter plot

In exploratory data analysis it's helpful to be able to look at all the scatter plots among a group of variables; this is known as a *pairs* plot or *scatter plot matrix*. Making such a plot from scratch is a bit of work, so pandas has a scatter_matrix function for creating one from a DataFrame. It also supports placing histograms or density plots of each variable along the diagonal. See Figure 8-23 for the resulting plot:

```
In [669]: pd.scatter_matrix(trans_data, diagonal='kde', color='k', alpha=0.3)
```

Plotting Maps: Visualizing Haiti Earthquake Crisis Data

Ushahidi is a non-profit software company that enables crowdsourcing of information related to natural disasters and geopolitical events via text message. Many of these data sets are then published on their website (*http://community.ushahidi.com/research/data*

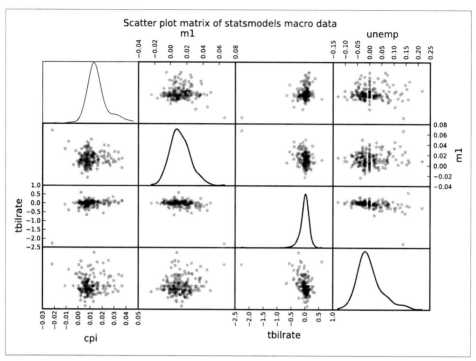

Figure 8-23. Scatter plot matrix of statsmodels macro data

sets/) for analysis and visualization. I downloaded the data collected during the 2010 Haiti earthquake crisis and aftermath, and I'll show you how I prepared the data for analysis and visualization using pandas and other tools we have looked at thus far. After downloading the CSV file from the above link, we can load it into a DataFrame using read_csv:

```
In [670]: data = pd.read_csv('ch08/Haiti.csv')

In [671]: data.info()
<class 'pandas.core.frame.DataFrame'>
Int64Index: 3593 entries, 0 to 3592
Data columns (total 10 columns):
Serial          3593 non-null int64
INCIDENT TITLE  3593 non-null object
INCIDENT DATE   3593 non-null object
LOCATION        3592 non-null object
DESCRIPTION     3593 non-null object
CATEGORY        3587 non-null object
LATITUDE        3593 non-null float64
LONGITUDE       3593 non-null float64
APPROVED        3593 non-null object
VERIFIED        3593 non-null object
dtypes: float64(2), int64(1), object(7)
```

It's easy now to tinker with this data set to see what kinds of things we might want to do with it. Each row represents a report sent from someone's mobile phone indicating an emergency or some other problem. Each has an associated timestamp and a location as latitude and longitude:

```
In [672]: data[['INCIDENT DATE', 'LATITUDE', 'LONGITUDE']][:10]
Out[672]:
       INCIDENT DATE    LATITUDE    LONGITUDE
0   05/07/2010 17:26   18.233333   -72.533333
1   28/06/2010 23:06   50.226029     5.729886
2   24/06/2010 16:21   22.278381   114.174287
3   20/06/2010 21:59   44.407062     8.933989
4   18/05/2010 16:26   18.571084   -72.334671
5   26/04/2010 13:14   18.593707   -72.310079
6   26/04/2010 14:19   18.482800   -73.638800
7   26/04/2010 14:27   18.415000   -73.195000
8   15/03/2010 10:58   18.517443   -72.236841
9   15/03/2010 11:00   18.547790   -72.410010
```

The CATEGORY field contains a comma-separated list of codes indicating the type of message:

```
In [673]: data['CATEGORY'][:6]
Out[673]:
0            1. Urgences | Emergency, 3. Public Health,
1      1. Urgences | Emergency, 2. Urgences logistiqu...
2      2. Urgences logistiques | Vital Lines, 8. Autr...
3                              1. Urgences | Emergency,
4                              1. Urgences | Emergency,
5                    5e. Communication lines down,
Name: CATEGORY, dtype: object
```

If you notice above in the data summary, some of the categories are missing, so we might want to drop these data points. Additionally, calling describe shows that there are some aberrant locations:

```
In [674]: data.describe()
Out[674]:
              Serial      LATITUDE     LONGITUDE
count    3593.000000   3593.000000   3593.000000
mean     2080.277484     18.611495    -72.322680
std      1171.100360      0.738572      3.650776
min         4.000000     18.041313    -74.452757
25%      1074.000000     18.524070    -72.417500
50%      2163.000000     18.539269    -72.335000
75%      3088.000000     18.561820    -72.293570
max      4052.000000     50.226029    114.174287
```

Cleaning the bad locations and removing the missing categories is now fairly simple:

```
In [675]: data = data[(data.LATITUDE > 18) & (data.LATITUDE < 20) &
    .....:            (data.LONGITUDE > -75) & (data.LONGITUDE < -70)
    .....:            & data.CATEGORY.notnull()]
```

Now we might want to do some analysis or visualization of this data by category, but each category field may have multiple categories. Additionally, each category is given as a code plus an English and possibly also a French code name. Thus, a little bit of wrangling is required to get the data into a more agreeable form. First, I wrote these two functions to get a list of all the categories and to split each category into a code and an English name:

```
def to_cat_list(catstr):
    stripped = (x.strip() for x in catstr.split(','))
    return [x for x in stripped if x]

def get_all_categories(cat_series):
    cat_sets = (set(to_cat_list(x)) for x in cat_series)
    return sorted(set.union(*cat_sets))

def get_english(cat):
    code, names = cat.split('.')
    if '|' in names:
        names = names.split(' | ')[1]
    return code, names.strip()
```

You can test out that the get_english function does what you expect:

```
In [677]: get_english('2. Urgences logistiques | Vital Lines')
Out[677]: ('2', 'Vital Lines')
```

Now, I make a dict mapping code to name because we'll use the codes for analysis. We'll use this later when adorning plots (note the use of a generator expression in lieu of a list comprehension):

```
In [678]: all_cats = get_all_categories(data.CATEGORY)

# Generator expression
In [679]: english_mapping = dict(get_english(x) for x in all_cats)

In [680]: english_mapping['2a']
Out[680]: 'Food Shortage'

In [681]: english_mapping['6c']
Out[681]: 'Earthquake and aftershocks'
```

There are many ways to go about augmenting the data set to be able to easily select records by category. One way is to add indicator (or dummy) columns, one for each category. To do that, first extract the unique category codes and construct a DataFrame of zeros having those as its columns and the same index as data:

```
def get_code(seq):
    return [x.split('.')[0] for x in seq if x]

all_codes = get_code(all_cats)
code_index = pd.Index(np.unique(all_codes))
dummy_frame = DataFrame(np.zeros((len(data), len(code_index))),
                        index=data.index, columns=code_index)
```

If all goes well, dummy_frame should look something like this:

```
In [683]: dummy_frame.ix[:, :6].info()
<class 'pandas.core.frame.DataFrame'>
Int64Index: 3569 entries, 0 to 3592
Data columns (total 6 columns):
1     3569 non-null float64
1a    3569 non-null float64
1b    3569 non-null float64
1c    3569 non-null float64
1d    3569 non-null float64
2     3569 non-null float64
dtypes: float64(6)
```

As you recall, the trick is then to set the appropriate entries of each row to 1, lastly joining this with data:

```
for row, cat in zip(data.index, data.CATEGORY):
    codes = get_code(to_cat_list(cat))
    dummy_frame.ix[row, codes] = 1

data = data.join(dummy_frame.add_prefix('category_'))
```

data finally now has new columns like:

```
In [685]: data.ix[:, 10:15].info()
<class 'pandas.core.frame.DataFrame'>
Int64Index: 3569 entries, 0 to 3592
Data columns (total 5 columns):
category_1     3569 non-null float64
category_1a    3569 non-null float64
category_1b    3569 non-null float64
category_1c    3569 non-null float64
category_1d    3569 non-null float64
dtypes: float64(5)
```

Let's make some plots! As this is spatial data, we'd like to plot the data by category on a map of Haiti. The basemap toolkit (*http://matplotlib.github.com/basemap*), an add-on to matplotlib, enables plotting 2D data on maps in Python. basemap provides many different globe projections and a means for transforming projecting latitude and longitude coordinates on the globe onto a two-dimensional matplotlib plot. After some trial and error and using the above data as a guideline, I wrote this function which draws a simple black and white map of Haiti:

```
from mpl_toolkits.basemap import Basemap
import matplotlib.pyplot as plt

def basic_haiti_map(ax=None, lllat=17.25, urlat=20.25,
                    lllon=-75, urlon=-71):
    # create polar stereographic Basemap instance.
    m = Basemap(ax=ax, projection='stere',
                lon_0=(urlon + lllon) / 2,
                lat_0=(urlat + lllat) / 2,
                llcrnrlat=lllat, urcrnrlat=urlat,
                llcrnrlon=lllon, urcrnrlon=urlon,
                resolution='f')
    # draw coastlines, state and country boundaries, edge of map.
```

```
m.drawcoastlines()
m.drawstates()
m.drawcountries()
return m
```

The idea, now, is that the returned `Basemap` object, knows how to transform coordinates onto the canvas. I wrote the following code to plot the data observations for a number of report categories. For each category, I filter down the data set to the coordinates labeled by that category, plot a `Basemap` on the appropriate subplot, transform the coordinates, then plot the points using the `Basemap`'s `plot` method:

```
fig, axes = plt.subplots(nrows=2, ncols=2, figsize=(12, 10))
fig.subplots_adjust(hspace=0.05, wspace=0.05)

to_plot = ['2a', '1', '3c', '7a']

lllat=17.25; urlat=20.25; lllon=-75; urlon=-71

for code, ax in zip(to_plot, axes.flat):
    m = basic_haiti_map(ax, lllat=lllat, urlat=urlat,
                        lllon=lllon, urlon=urlon)

    cat_data = data[data['category_%s' % code] == 1]

    # compute map proj coordinates.
    x, y = m(cat_data.LONGITUDE.values, cat_data.LATITUDE.values)

    m.plot(x, y, 'k.', alpha=0.5)
    ax.set_title('%s: %s' % (code, english_mapping[code]))

plt.show()
```

The resulting figure can be seen in Figure 8-24.

It seems from the plot that most of the data is concentrated around the most populous city, Port-au-Prince. basemap allows you to overlap additional map data which comes from what are called *shapefiles*. I first downloaded a shapefile with roads in Port-au-Prince (see *http://cegrp.cga.harvard.edu/haiti/?q=resources_data*). The `Basemap` object conveniently has a `readshapefile` method so that, after extracting the road data archive, I added just the following lines to my code:

```
shapefile_path = 'ch08/PortAuPrince_Roads/PortAuPrince_Roads'
m.readshapefile(shapefile_path, 'roads')
```

After a little more trial and error with the latitude and longitude boundaries, I was able to make Figure 8-25 for the "Food shortage" category.

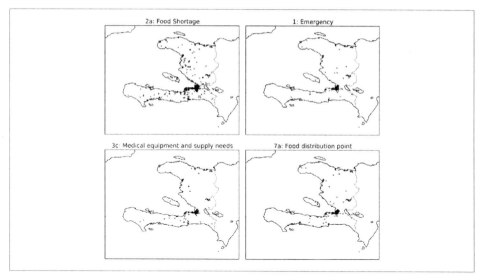

Figure 8-24. Haiti crisis data for 4 categories

Figure 8-25. Food shortage reports in Port-au-Prince during the Haiti earthquake crisis

Python Visualization Tool Ecosystem

As is common with open source, there are a plethora of options for creating graphics in Python (too many to list). In addition to open source, there are numerous commercial libraries with Python bindings.

In this chapter and throughout the book, I have been primarily concerned with matplotlib as it is the most widely used plotting tool in Python. While it's an important part of the scientific Python ecosystem, matplotlib has plenty of shortcomings when it comes to the creation and display of statistical graphics. MATLAB users will likely find matplotlib familiar, while R users (especially users of the excellent `ggplot2` and `trellis` packages) may be somewhat disappointed (at least as of this writing). It is possible to make beautiful plots for display on the web in matplotlib, but doing so often requires significant effort as the library is designed for the printed page. Aesthetics aside, it is sufficient for most needs. In pandas, I, along with the other developers, have sought to build a convenient user interface that makes it easier to make most kinds of plots commonplace in data analysis.

There are a number of other visualization tools in wide use. I list a few of them here and encourage you to explore the ecosystem.

Chaco

Chaco (*http://code.enthought.com/chaco/*), developed by Enthought, is a plotting toolkit suitable both for static plotting and interactive visualizations. It is especially well-suited for expressing complex visualizations with data interrelationships. Compared with matplotlib, Chaco has much better support for interacting with plot elements and rendering is very fast, making it a good choice for building interactive GUI applications.

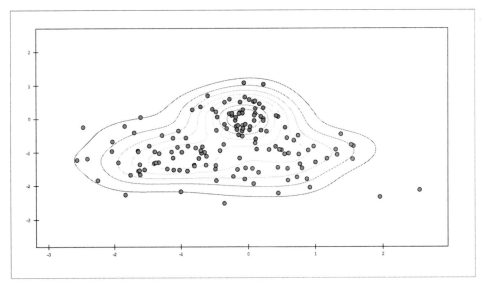

Figure 8-26. A Chaco example plot

mayavi

The mayavi project, developed by Prabhu Ramachandran, Gaël Varoquaux, and others, is a 3D graphics toolkit built on the open source C++ graphics library VTK. mayavi, like matplotlib, integrates with IPython so that it is easy to use interactively. The plots can be panned, rotated, and zoomed using the mouse and keyboard. I used mayavi to make one of the illustrations of broadcasting in Chapter 12. While I don't show any mayavi-using code here, there is plenty of documentation and examples available online. In many cases, I believe it is a good alternative to a technology like WebGL, though the graphics are harder to share in interactive form.

Other Packages

Of course, there are numerous other visualization libraries and applications available in Python: PyQwt, Veusz, gnuplot-py, biggles, and others. I have seen PyQwt put to good use in GUI applications built using the Qt application framework using PyQt. While many of these libraries continue to be under active development (some of them are part of much larger applications), I have noted in the last few years a general trend toward web-based technologies and away from desktop graphics. I'll say a few more words about this in the next section.

The Future of Visualization Tools?

Visualizations built on web technologies (that is, JavaScript-based) appear to be the inevitable future. Doubtlessly you have used many different kinds of static or interactive visualizations built in Flash or JavaScript over the years. New toolkits (such as d3.js and its numerous off-shoot projects) for building such displays are appearing all the time. In contrast, development in non web-based visualization has slowed significantly in recent years. This holds true of Python as well as other data analysis and statistical computing environments like R.

The development challenge, then, will be in building tighter integration between data analysis and preparation tools, such as pandas, and the web browser. I am hopeful that this will become a fruitful point of collaboration between Python and non-Python users as well.

CHAPTER 9

Data Aggregation and
Group Operations

Categorizing a data set and applying a function to each group, whether an aggregation or transformation, is often a critical component of a data analysis workflow. After loading, merging, and preparing a data set, a familiar task is to compute group statistics or possibly *pivot tables* for reporting or visualization purposes. pandas provides a flexible and high-performance groupby facility, enabling you to slice and dice, and summarize data sets in a natural way.

One reason for the popularity of relational databases and SQL (which stands for "structured query language") is the ease with which data can be joined, filtered, transformed, and aggregated. However, query languages like SQL are rather limited in the kinds of group operations that can be performed. As you will see, with the expressiveness and power of Python and pandas, we can perform much more complex grouped operations by utilizing any function that accepts a pandas object or NumPy array. In this chapter, you will learn how to:

- Split a pandas object into pieces using one or more keys (in the form of functions, arrays, or DataFrame column names)
- Computing group summary statistics, like count, mean, or standard deviation, or a user-defined function
- Apply a varying set of functions to each column of a DataFrame
- Apply within-group transformations or other manipulations, like normalization, linear regression, rank, or subset selection
- Compute pivot tables and cross-tabulations
- Perform quantile analysis and other data-derived group analyses

Aggregation of time series data, a special use case of groupby, is referred to as *resampling* in this book and will receive separate treatment in Chapter 10.

GroupBy Mechanics

Hadley Wickham, an author of many popular packages for the R programming language, coined the term *split-apply-combine* for talking about group operations, and I think that's a good description of the process. In the first stage of the process, data contained in a pandas object, whether a Series, DataFrame, or otherwise, is *split* into groups based on one or more *keys* that you provide. The splitting is performed on a particular axis of an object. For example, a DataFrame can be grouped on its rows (axis=0) or its columns (axis=1). Once this is done, a function is *applied* to each group, producing a new value. Finally, the results of all those function applications are *combined* into a result object. The form of the resulting object will usually depend on what's being done to the data. See Figure 9-1 for a mockup of a simple group aggregation.

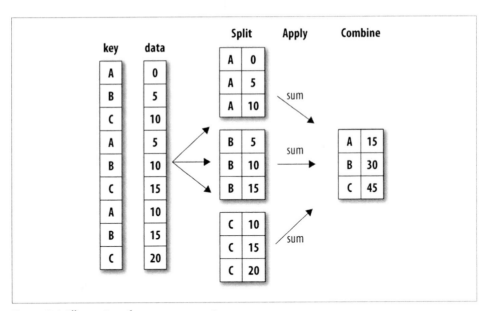

Figure 9-1. Illustration of a group aggregation

Each grouping key can take many forms, and the keys do not have to be all of the same type:

- A list or array of values that is the same length as the axis being grouped
- A value indicating a column name in a DataFrame

- A dict or Series giving a correspondence between the values on the axis being grouped and the group names
- A function to be invoked on the axis index or the individual labels in the index

Note that the latter three methods are all just shortcuts for producing an array of values to be used to split up the object. Don't worry if this all seems very abstract. Throughout this chapter, I will give many examples of all of these methods. To get started, here is a very simple small tabular dataset as a DataFrame:

```
In [160]: df = DataFrame({'key1' : ['a', 'a', 'b', 'b', 'a'],
   .....:                  'key2' : ['one', 'two', 'one', 'two', 'one'],
   .....:                  'data1' : np.random.randn(5),
   .....:                  'data2' : np.random.randn(5)})

In [161]: df
Out[161]:
      data1     data2 key1 key2
0 -0.204708  1.393406    a  one
1  0.478943  0.092908    a  two
2 -0.519439  0.281746    b  one
3 -0.555730  0.769023    b  two
4  1.965781  1.246435    a  one
```

Suppose you wanted to compute the mean of the data1 column using the groups labels from key1. There are a number of ways to do this. One is to access data1 and call groupby with the column (a Series) at key1:

```
In [162]: grouped = df['data1'].groupby(df['key1'])

In [163]: grouped
Out[163]: <pandas.core.groupby.SeriesGroupBy object at 0x7f5893ec7750>
```

This grouped variable is now a *GroupBy* object. It has not actually computed anything yet except for some intermediate data about the group key df['key1']. The idea is that this object has all of the information needed to then apply some operation to each of the groups. For example, to compute group means we can call the GroupBy's mean method:

```
In [164]: grouped.mean()
Out[164]:
key1
a       0.746672
b      -0.537585
Name: data1, dtype: float64
```

Later, I'll explain more about what's going on when you call .mean(). The important thing here is that the data (a Series) has been aggregated according to the group key, producing a new Series that is now indexed by the unique values in the key1 column. The result index has the name 'key1' because the DataFrame column df['key1'] did.

If instead we had passed multiple arrays as a list, we get something different:

```
In [165]: means = df['data1'].groupby([df['key1'], df['key2']]).mean()

In [166]: means
Out[166]:
key1  key2
a     one      0.880536
      two      0.478943
b     one     -0.519439
      two     -0.555730
Name: data1, dtype: float64
```

In this case, we grouped the data using two keys, and the resulting Series now has a hierarchical index consisting of the unique pairs of keys observed:

```
In [167]: means.unstack()
Out[167]:
key2         one       two
key1
a       0.880536  0.478943
b      -0.519439 -0.555730
```

In these examples, the group keys are all Series, though they could be any arrays of the right length:

```
In [168]: states = np.array(['Ohio', 'California', 'California', 'Ohio', 'Ohio'])

In [169]: years = np.array([2005, 2005, 2006, 2005, 2006])

In [170]: df['data1'].groupby([states, years]).mean()
Out[170]:
California  2005     0.478943
            2006    -0.519439
Ohio        2005    -0.380219
            2006     1.965781
Name: data1, dtype: float64
```

Frequently the grouping information to be found in the same DataFrame as the data you want to work on. In that case, you can pass column names (whether those are strings, numbers, or other Python objects) as the group keys:

```
In [171]: df.groupby('key1').mean()
Out[171]:
         data1     data2
key1
a     0.746672  0.910916
b    -0.537585  0.525384

In [172]: df.groupby(['key1', 'key2']).mean()
Out[172]:
               data1     data2
key1 key2
a    one    0.880536  1.319920
     two    0.478943  0.092908
b    one   -0.519439  0.281746
     two   -0.555730  0.769023
```

You may have noticed in the first case df.groupby('key1').mean() that there is no key2 column in the result. Because df['key2'] is not numeric data, it is said to be a *nuisance column*, which is therefore excluded from the result. By default, all of the numeric columns are aggregated, though it is possible to filter down to a subset as you'll see soon.

Regardless of the objective in using groupby, a generally useful GroupBy method is size which return a Series containing group sizes:

```
In [173]: df.groupby(['key1', 'key2']).size()
Out[173]:
key1  key2
a     one     2
      two     1
b     one     1
      two     1
dtype: int64
```

 As of this writing, any missing values in a group key will be excluded from the result. It's possible (and, in fact, quite likely), that by the time you are reading this there will be an option to include the NA group in the result.

Iterating Over Groups

The GroupBy object supports iteration, generating a sequence of 2-tuples containing the group name along with the chunk of data. Consider the following small example data set:

```
In [174]: for name, group in df.groupby('key1'):
   .....:     print(name)
   .....:     print(group)
   .....:
a
      data1     data2 key1 key2
0 -0.204708  1.393406    a  one
1  0.478943  0.092908    a  two
4  1.965781  1.246435    a  one
b
      data1     data2 key1 key2
2 -0.519439  0.281746    b  one
3 -0.555730  0.769023    b  two
```

In the case of multiple keys, the first element in the tuple will be a tuple of key values:

```
In [175]: for (k1, k2), group in df.groupby(['key1', 'key2']):
   .....:     print((k1, k2))
   .....:     print(group)
   .....:
a one
      data1     data2 key1 key2
0 -0.204708  1.393406    a  one
4  1.965781  1.246435    a  one
```

```
a two
      data1     data2 key1 key2
1  0.478943  0.092908    a  two
b one
      data1     data2 key1 key2
2 -0.519439  0.281746    b  one
b two
      data1     data2 key1 key2
3 -0.55573  0.769023    b  two
```

Of course, you can choose to do whatever you want with the pieces of data. A recipe you may find useful is computing a dict of the data pieces as a one-liner:

```
In [176]: pieces = dict(list(df.groupby('key1')))

In [177]: pieces['b']
Out[177]:
      data1     data2 key1 key2
2 -0.519439  0.281746    b  one
3 -0.555730  0.769023    b  two
```

By default groupby groups on axis=0, but you can group on any of the other axes. For example, we could group the columns of our example df here by dtype like so:

```
In [178]: df.dtypes
Out[178]:
data1    float64
data2    float64
key1      object
key2      object
dtype: object

In [179]: grouped = df.groupby(df.dtypes, axis=1)

In [180]: dict(list(grouped))
Out[180]:
{dtype('float64'):      data1     data2
0 -0.204708  1.393406
1  0.478943  0.092908
2 -0.519439  0.281746
3 -0.555730  0.769023
4  1.965781  1.246435, dtype('O'):   key1 key2
0    a  one
1    a  two
2    b  one
3    b  two
4    a  one}
```

Selecting a Column or Subset of Columns

Indexing a GroupBy object created from a DataFrame with a column name or array of column names has the effect of *selecting those columns* for aggregation. This means that:

```
df.groupby('key1')['data1']
df.groupby('key1')[['data2']]
```

are syntactic sugar for:

```
df['data1'].groupby(df['key1'])
df[['data2']].groupby(df['key1'])
```

Especially for large data sets, it may be desirable to aggregate only a few columns. For example, in the above data set, to compute means for just the data2 column and get the result as a DataFrame, we could write:

```
In [181]: df.groupby(['key1', 'key2'])[['data2']].mean()
Out[181]:
                data2
key1 key2
a    one     1.319920
     two     0.092908
b    one     0.281746
     two     0.769023
```

The object returned by this indexing operation is a grouped DataFrame if a list or array is passed and a grouped Series is just a single column name that is passed as a scalar:

```
In [182]: s_grouped = df.groupby(['key1', 'key2'])['data2']

In [183]: s_grouped
Out[183]: <pandas.core.groupby.SeriesGroupBy object at 0x7f5893e77890>

In [184]: s_grouped.mean()
Out[184]:
key1  key2
a     one     1.319920
      two     0.092908
b     one     0.281746
      two     0.769023
Name: data2, dtype: float64
```

Grouping with Dicts and Series

Grouping information may exist in a form other than an array. Let's consider another example DataFrame:

```
In [185]: people = DataFrame(np.random.randn(5, 5),
   .....:                    columns=['a', 'b', 'c', 'd', 'e'],
   .....:                    index=['Joe', 'Steve', 'Wes', 'Jim', 'Travis'])

In [186]: people.ix[2:3, ['b', 'c']] = np.nan # Add a few NA values

In [187]: people
Out[187]:
               a         b         c         d         e
Joe     1.007189 -1.296221  0.274992  0.228913  1.352917
Steve   0.886429 -2.001637 -0.371843  1.669025 -0.438570
Wes    -0.539741       NaN       NaN -1.021228 -0.577087
Jim     0.124121  0.302614  0.523772  0.000940  1.343810
Travis -0.713544 -0.831154 -2.370232 -1.860761 -0.860757
```

Now, suppose I have a group correspondence for the columns and want to sum together the columns by group:

```
In [188]: mapping = {'a': 'red', 'b': 'red', 'c': 'blue',
   .....:            'd': 'blue', 'e': 'red', 'f' : 'orange'}
```

Now, you could easily construct an array from this dict to pass to groupby, but instead we can just pass the dict:

```
In [189]: by_column = people.groupby(mapping, axis=1)
```

```
In [190]: by_column.sum()
Out[190]:
            blue       red
Joe     0.503905  1.063885
Steve   1.297183 -1.553778
Wes    -1.021228 -1.116829
Jim     0.524712  1.770545
Travis -4.230992 -2.405455
```

The same functionality holds for Series, which can be viewed as a fixed size mapping. When I used Series as group keys in the above examples, pandas does, in fact, inspect each Series to ensure that its index is aligned with the axis it's grouping:

```
In [191]: map_series = Series(mapping)
```

```
In [192]: map_series
Out[192]:
a       red
b       red
c       blue
d       blue
e       red
f       orange
dtype: object
```

```
In [193]: people.groupby(map_series, axis=1).count()
Out[193]:
        blue  red
Joe        2    3
Steve      2    3
Wes        1    2
Jim        2    3
Travis     2    3
```

Grouping with Functions

Using Python functions in what can be fairly creative ways is a more abstract way of defining a group mapping compared with a dict or Series. Any function passed as a group key will be called once per index value, with the return values being used as the group names. More concretely, consider the example DataFrame from the previous section, which has people's first names as index values. Suppose you wanted to group by the length of the names; you could compute an array of string lengths, but instead you can just pass the len function:

```
In [194]: people.groupby(len).sum()
Out[194]:
          a         b         c         d         e
3  0.591569 -0.993608  0.798764 -0.791374  2.119639
5  0.886429 -2.001637 -0.371843  1.669025 -0.438570
6 -0.713544 -0.831154 -2.370232 -1.860761 -0.860757
```

Mixing functions with arrays, dicts, or Series is not a problem as everything gets converted to arrays internally:

```
In [195]: key_list = ['one', 'one', 'one', 'two', 'two']

In [196]: people.groupby([len, key_list]).min()
Out[196]:
            a         b         c         d         e
3 one -0.539741 -1.296221  0.274992 -1.021228 -0.577087
  two  0.124121  0.302614  0.523772  0.000940  1.343810
5 one  0.886429 -2.001637 -0.371843  1.669025 -0.438570
6 two -0.713544 -0.831154 -2.370232 -1.860761 -0.860757
```

Grouping by Index Levels

A final convenience for hierarchically-indexed data sets is the ability to aggregate using one of the levels of an axis index. To do this, pass the level number or name using the level keyword:

```
In [197]: columns = pd.MultiIndex.from_arrays([['US', 'US', 'US', 'JP', 'JP'],
   .....:                                      [1, 3, 5, 1, 3]], names=['cty', 'tenor'])

In [198]: hier_df = DataFrame(np.random.randn(4, 5), columns=columns)

In [199]: hier_df
Out[199]:
cty          US                             JP
tenor         1         3         5          1         3
0      0.560145 -1.265934  0.119827 -1.063512  0.332883
1     -2.359419 -0.199543 -1.541996 -0.970736 -1.307030
2      0.286350  0.377984 -0.753887  0.331286  1.349742
3      0.069877  0.246674 -0.011862  1.004812  1.327195

In [200]: hier_df.groupby(level='cty', axis=1).count()
Out[200]:
cty  JP  US
0     2   3
1     2   3
2     2   3
3     2   3
```

Data Aggregation

By aggregation, I am generally referring to any data transformation that produces scalar values from arrays. In the examples above I have used several of them, such as mean, count, min and sum. You may wonder what is going on when you invoke mean() on a GroupBy object. Many common aggregations, such as those found in Table 9-1, have optimized implementations that compute the statistics on the dataset *in place*. However, you are not limited to only this set of methods. You can use aggregations of your own devising and additionally call any method that is also defined on the grouped object. For example, as you recall quantile computes sample quantiles of a Series or a DataFrame's columns [1]:

```
In [201]: df
Out[201]:
       data1     data2 key1 key2
0 -0.204708  1.393406    a  one
1  0.478943  0.092908    a  two
2 -0.519439  0.281746    b  one
3 -0.555730  0.769023    b  two
4  1.965781  1.246435    a  one

In [202]: grouped = df.groupby('key1')

In [203]: grouped['data1'].quantile(0.9)
Out[203]:
key1
a     1.668413
b    -0.523068
Name: data1, dtype: float64
```

While quantile is not explicitly implemented for GroupBy, it is a Series method and thus available for use. Internally, GroupBy efficiently slices up the Series, calls piece.quantile(0.9) for each piece, then assembles those results together into the result object.

To use your own aggregation functions, pass any function that aggregates an array to the aggregate or agg method:

```
In [204]: def peak_to_peak(arr):
   .....:     return arr.max() - arr.min()

In [205]: grouped.agg(peak_to_peak)
Out[205]:
         data1     data2
key1
a     2.170488  1.300498
b     0.036292  0.487276
```

---

1. Note that quantile performs linear interpolation if there is no value at exactly the passed percentile.

You'll notice that some methods like describe also work, even though they are not aggregations, strictly speaking:

```
In [206]: grouped.describe()
Out[206]:
                  data1       data2
key1
a     count   3.000000    3.000000
      mean    0.746672    0.910916
      std     1.109736    0.712217
      min    -0.204708    0.092908
      25%     0.137118    0.669671
...                ...         ...
b     min    -0.555730    0.281746
      25%    -0.546657    0.403565
      50%    -0.537585    0.525384
      75%    -0.528512    0.647203
      max    -0.519439    0.769023
[16 rows x 2 columns]
```

I will explain in more detail what has happened here in the next major section on group-wise operations and transformations.

> You may notice that custom aggregation functions are much slower than the optimized functions found in Table 9-1. This is because there is significant overhead (function calls, data rearrangement) in constructing the intermediate group data chunks.

Table 9-1. Optimized groupby methods

Function name	Description
count	Number of non-NA values in the group
sum	Sum of non-NA values
mean	Mean of non-NA values
median	Arithmetic median of non-NA values
std, var	Unbiased (n - 1 denominator) standard deviation and variance
min, max	Minimum and maximum of non-NA values
prod	Product of non-NA values
first, last	First and last non-NA values

To illustrate some more advanced aggregation features, I'll use a less trivial dataset, a dataset on restaurant tipping. I obtained it from the R reshape2 package; it was originally found in Bryant & Smith's 1995 text on business statistics (and found in the book's GitHub repository). After loading it with read_csv, I add a tipping percentage column tip_pct.

```
In [207]: tips = pd.read_csv('ch08/tips.csv')

# Add tip percentage of total bill
In [208]: tips['tip_pct'] = tips['tip'] / tips['total_bill']

In [209]: tips[:6]
Out[209]:
   total_bill   tip     sex smoker  day    time  size   tip_pct
0       16.99  1.01  Female     No  Sun  Dinner     2  0.059447
1       10.34  1.66    Male     No  Sun  Dinner     3  0.160542
2       21.01  3.50    Male     No  Sun  Dinner     3  0.166587
3       23.68  3.31    Male     No  Sun  Dinner     2  0.139780
4       24.59  3.61  Female     No  Sun  Dinner     4  0.146808
5       25.29  4.71    Male     No  Sun  Dinner     4  0.186240
```

Column-wise and Multiple Function Application

As you've seen above, aggregating a Series or all of the columns of a DataFrame is a matter of using aggregate with the desired function or calling a method like mean or std. However, you may want to aggregate using a different function depending on the column or multiple functions at once. Fortunately, this is straightforward to do, which I'll illustrate through a number of examples. First, I'll group the tips by sex and smoker:

```
In [210]: grouped = tips.groupby(['sex', 'smoker'])
```

Note that for descriptive statistics like those in Table 9-1, you can pass the name of the function as a string:

```
In [211]: grouped_pct = grouped['tip_pct']

In [212]: grouped_pct.agg('mean')
Out[212]:
sex     smoker
Female  No        0.156921
        Yes       0.182150
Male    No        0.160669
        Yes       0.152771
Name: tip_pct, dtype: float64
```

If you pass a list of functions or function names instead, you get back a DataFrame with column names taken from the functions:

```
In [213]: grouped_pct.agg(['mean', 'std', peak_to_peak])
Out[213]:
                   mean       std  peak_to_peak
sex     smoker
Female  No     0.156921  0.036421      0.195876
        Yes    0.182150  0.071595      0.360233
Male    No     0.160669  0.041849      0.220186
        Yes    0.152771  0.090588      0.674707
```

You don't need to accept the names that GroupBy gives to the columns; notably lambda functions have the name '<lambda>' which make them hard to identify (you can see for yourself by looking at a function's __name__ attribute). As such, if you pass a list of (name, function) tuples, the first element of each tuple will be used as the DataFrame column names (you can think of a list of 2-tuples as an ordered mapping):

```
In [214]: grouped_pct.agg([('foo', 'mean'), ('bar', np.std)])
Out[214]:
                     foo       bar
sex     smoker
Female  No      0.156921  0.036421
        Yes     0.182150  0.071595
Male    No      0.160669  0.041849
        Yes     0.152771  0.090588
```

With a DataFrame, you have more options as you can specify a list of functions to apply to all of the columns or different functions per column. To start, suppose we wanted to compute the same three statistics for the tip_pct and total_bill columns:

```
In [215]: functions = ['count', 'mean', 'max']

In [216]: result = grouped['tip_pct', 'total_bill'].agg(functions)

In [217]: result
Out[217]:
                tip_pct                        total_bill
                count     mean       max       count     mean       max
sex     smoker
Female  No         54  0.156921  0.252672         54  18.105185  35.83
        Yes        33  0.182150  0.416667         33  17.977879  44.30
Male    No         97  0.160669  0.291990         97  19.791237  48.33
        Yes        60  0.152771  0.710345         60  22.284500  50.81
```

As you can see, the resulting DataFrame has hierarchical columns, the same as you would get aggregating each column separately and using concat to glue the results together using the column names as the keys argument:

```
In [218]: result['tip_pct']
Out[218]:
                count     mean       max
sex     smoker
Female  No         54  0.156921  0.252672
        Yes        33  0.182150  0.416667
Male    No         97  0.160669  0.291990
        Yes        60  0.152771  0.710345
```

As above, a list of tuples with custom names can be passed:

```
In [219]: ftuples = [('Durchschnitt', 'mean'), ('Abweichung', np.var)]

In [220]: grouped['tip_pct', 'total_bill'].agg(ftuples)
Out[220]:
                    tip_pct                   total_bill
                Durchschnitt  Abweichung  Durchschnitt  Abweichung
sex     smoker
Female  No          0.156921    0.001327     18.105185   53.092422
        Yes         0.182150    0.005126     17.977879   84.451517
Male    No          0.160669    0.001751     19.791237   76.152961
        Yes         0.152771    0.008206     22.284500   98.244673
```

Now, suppose you wanted to apply potentially different functions to one or more of the columns. The trick is to pass a dict to agg that contains a mapping of column names to any of the function specifications listed so far:

```
In [221]: grouped.agg({'tip' : np.max, 'size' : 'sum'})
Out[221]:
               tip  size
sex    smoker
Female No      5.2   140
       Yes     6.5    74
Male   No      9.0   263
       Yes    10.0   150

In [222]: grouped.agg({'tip_pct' : ['min', 'max', 'mean', 'std'],
   .....:              'size' : 'sum'})
Out[222]:
               tip_pct                                size
                   min       max      mean       std   sum
sex    smoker
Female No     0.056797  0.252672  0.156921  0.036421   140
       Yes    0.056433  0.416667  0.182150  0.071595    74
Male   No     0.071804  0.291990  0.160669  0.041849   263
       Yes    0.035638  0.710345  0.152771  0.090588   150
```

A DataFrame will have hierarchical columns only if multiple functions are applied to at least one column.

Returning Aggregated Data in "unindexed" Form

In all of the examples up until now, the aggregated data comes back with an index, potentially hierarchical, composed from the unique group key combinations observed. Since this isn't always desirable, you can disable this behavior in most cases by passing as_index=False to groupby:

```
In [223]: tips.groupby(['sex', 'smoker'], as_index=False).mean()
Out[223]:
      sex smoker  total_bill       tip      size   tip_pct
0  Female     No   18.105185  2.773519  2.592593  0.156921
1  Female    Yes   17.977879  2.931515  2.242424  0.182150
2    Male     No   19.791237  3.113402  2.711340  0.160669
3    Male    Yes   22.284500  3.051167  2.500000  0.152771
```

Of course, it's always possible to obtain the result in this format by calling reset_index on the result.

> Using groupby in this way is generally less flexible; results with hierarchical columns, for example, are not currently implemented as the form of the result would have to be somewhat arbitrary.

Group-wise Operations and Transformations

Aggregation is only one kind of group operation. It is a special case in the more general class of data transformations; that is, it accepts functions that reduce a one-dimensional array to a scalar value. In this section, I will introduce you to the `transform` and `apply` methods, which will enable you to do many other kinds of group operations.

Suppose, instead, we wanted to add a column to a DataFrame containing group means for each index. One way to do this is to aggregate, then merge:

```
In [224]: df
Out[224]:
      data1     data2 key1 key2
0 -0.204708  1.393406    a  one
1  0.478943  0.092908    a  two
2 -0.519439  0.281746    b  one
3 -0.555730  0.769023    b  two
4  1.965781  1.246435    a  one

In [225]: k1_means = df.groupby('key1').mean().add_prefix('mean_')

In [226]: k1_means
Out[226]:
      mean_data1  mean_data2
key1
a       0.746672    0.910916
b      -0.537585    0.525384

In [227]: pd.merge(df, k1_means, left_on='key1', right_index=True)
Out[227]:
      data1     data2 key1 key2  mean_data1  mean_data2
0 -0.204708  1.393406    a  one    0.746672    0.910916
1  0.478943  0.092908    a  two    0.746672    0.910916
4  1.965781  1.246435    a  one    0.746672    0.910916
2 -0.519439  0.281746    b  one   -0.537585    0.525384
3 -0.555730  0.769023    b  two   -0.537585    0.525384
```

This works, but is somewhat inflexible. You can think of the operation as transforming the two data columns using the `np.mean` function. Let's look back at the `people` Data-Frame from earlier in the chapter and use the `transform` method on GroupBy:

```
In [228]: key = ['one', 'two', 'one', 'two', 'one']

In [229]: people.groupby(key).mean()
Out[229]:
            a         b         c         d         e
one -0.082032 -1.063687 -1.047620 -0.884358 -0.028309
two  0.505275 -0.849512  0.075965  0.834983  0.452620

In [230]: people.groupby(key).transform(np.mean)
Out[230]:
       a    b    c    d    e
Jim  NaN  NaN  NaN  NaN  NaN
Joe  NaN  NaN  NaN  NaN  NaN
```

```
Steve      NaN       NaN       NaN       NaN       NaN
Travis     NaN       NaN       NaN       NaN       NaN
Wes        NaN       NaN       NaN       NaN       NaN
one  -0.082032 -1.063687 -1.047620 -0.884358 -0.028309
two   0.505275 -0.849512  0.075965  0.834983  0.452620
```

As you may guess, `transform` applies a function to each group, then places the results in the appropriate locations. If each group produces a scalar value, it will be propagated (broadcasted). Suppose instead you wanted to subtract the mean value from each group. To do this, create a demeaning function and pass it to `transform`:

```
In [231]: def demean(arr):
   .....:     return arr - arr.mean()

In [232]: demeaned = people.groupby(key).transform(demean)

In [233]: demeaned
Out[233]:
               a         b         c         d         e
Jim    -0.381154  1.152125  0.447807 -0.834043  0.891190
Joe     1.089221 -0.232534  1.322612  1.113271  1.381226
Steve   0.381154 -1.152125 -0.447807  0.834043 -0.891190
Travis -0.631512  0.232534 -1.322612 -0.976402 -0.832448
Wes    -0.457709       NaN       NaN -0.136869 -0.548778
```

You can check that `demeaned` now has zero group means:

```
In [234]: demeaned.groupby(key).mean()
Out[234]:
            a             b  c         d         e
one -0.152570  0.000000e+00  0 -0.045623 -0.182926
two  0.228855 -1.110223e-16  0  0.068435  0.274389
```

As you'll see in the next section, group demeaning can be achieved using `apply` also.

Apply: General split-apply-combine

Like `aggregate`, `transform` is a more specialized function having rigid requirements: the passed function must either produce a scalar value to be broadcasted (like `np.mean`) or a transformed array of the same size. The most general purpose GroupBy method is `apply`, which is the subject of the rest of this section. As in Figure 9-1, `apply` splits the object being manipulated into pieces, invokes the passed function on each piece, then attempts to concatenate the pieces together.

Returning to the tipping data set above, suppose you wanted to select the top five `tip_pct` values by group. First, it's straightforward to write a function that selects the rows with the largest values in a particular column:

```
In [235]: def top(df, n=5, column='tip_pct'):
   .....:     return df.sort_index(by=column)[-n:]

In [236]: top(tips, n=6)
Out[236]:
      total_bill    tip      sex smoker   day      time  size   tip_pct
```

109	14.31	4.00	Female	Yes	Sat	Dinner	2	0.279525
183	23.17	6.50	Male	Yes	Sun	Dinner	4	0.280535
232	11.61	3.39	Male	No	Sat	Dinner	2	0.291990
67	3.07	1.00	Female	Yes	Sat	Dinner	1	0.325733
178	9.60	4.00	Female	Yes	Sun	Dinner	2	0.416667
172	7.25	5.15	Male	Yes	Sun	Dinner	2	0.710345

Now, if we group by smoker, say, and call apply with this function, we get the following:

```
In [237]: tips.groupby('smoker').apply(top)
Out[237]:
              total_bill   tip     sex smoker   day    time  size   tip_pct
smoker
No     88          24.71  5.85    Male     No  Thur   Lunch     2  0.236746
       185         20.69  5.00    Male     No   Sun  Dinner     5  0.241663
       51          10.29  2.60  Female     No   Sun  Dinner     2  0.252672
       149          7.51  2.00    Male     No  Thur   Lunch     2  0.266312
       232         11.61  3.39    Male     No   Sat  Dinner     2  0.291990
Yes    109         14.31  4.00  Female    Yes   Sat  Dinner     2  0.279525
       183         23.17  6.50    Male    Yes   Sun  Dinner     4  0.280535
       67           3.07  1.00  Female    Yes   Sat  Dinner     1  0.325733
       178          9.60  4.00  Female    Yes   Sun  Dinner     2  0.416667
       172          7.25  5.15    Male    Yes   Sun  Dinner     2  0.710345
```

What has happened here? The top function is called on each piece of the DataFrame, then the results are glued together using pandas.concat, labeling the pieces with the group names. The result therefore has a hierarchical index whose inner level contains index values from the original DataFrame.

If you pass a function to apply that takes other arguments or keywords, you can pass these after the function:

```
In [238]: tips.groupby(['smoker', 'day']).apply(top, n=1, column='total_bill')
Out[238]:
                 total_bill    tip     sex smoker   day    time  size  \
smoker day
No     Fri  94        22.75   3.25  Female     No   Fri  Dinner     2
       Sat  212       48.33   9.00    Male     No   Sat  Dinner     4
       Sun  156       48.17   5.00    Male     No   Sun  Dinner     6
       Thur 142       41.19   5.00    Male     No  Thur   Lunch     5
Yes    Fri  95        40.17   4.73    Male    Yes   Fri  Dinner     4
       Sat  170       50.81  10.00    Male    Yes   Sat  Dinner     3
       Sun  182       45.35   3.50    Male    Yes   Sun  Dinner     3
       Thur 197       43.11   5.00  Female    Yes  Thur   Lunch     4
                 tip_pct
smoker day
No     Fri  94   0.142857
       Sat  212  0.186220
       Sun  156  0.103799
       Thur 142  0.121389
Yes    Fri  95   0.117750
       Sat  170  0.196812
       Sun  182  0.077178
       Thur 197  0.115982
```

Beyond these basic usage mechanics, getting the most out of apply is largely a matter of creativity. What occurs inside the function passed is up to you; it only needs to return a pandas object or a scalar value. The rest of this chapter will mainly consist of examples showing you how to solve various problems using groupby.

You may recall above I called describe on a GroupBy object:

```
In [239]: result = tips.groupby('smoker')['tip_pct'].describe()

In [240]: result
Out[240]:
smoker
No      count    151.000000
        mean       0.159328
        std        0.039910
...
Yes     50%        0.153846
        75%        0.195059
        max        0.710345
Length: 16, dtype: float64

In [241]: result.unstack('smoker')
Out[241]:
smoker          No        Yes
count   151.000000  93.000000
mean      0.159328   0.163196
std       0.039910   0.085119
min       0.056797   0.035638
25%       0.136906   0.106771
50%       0.155625   0.153846
75%       0.185014   0.195059
max       0.291990   0.710345
```

Inside GroupBy, when you invoke a method like describe, it is actually just a shortcut for:

```
f = lambda x: x.describe()
grouped.apply(f)
```

Suppressing the group keys

In the examples above, you see that the resulting object has a hierarchical index formed from the group keys along with the indexes of each piece of the original object. This can be disabled by passing group_keys=False to groupby:

```
In [242]: tips.groupby('smoker', group_keys=False).apply(top)
Out[242]:
     total_bill   tip     sex smoker   day    time  size   tip_pct
88        24.71  5.85    Male     No  Thur   Lunch     2  0.236746
185       20.69  5.00    Male     No   Sun  Dinner     5  0.241663
51        10.29  2.60  Female     No   Sun  Dinner     2  0.252672
149        7.51  2.00    Male     No  Thur   Lunch     2  0.266312
```

```
232   11.61  3.39    Male    No   Sat  Dinner   2  0.291990
109   14.31  4.00  Female   Yes   Sat  Dinner   2  0.279525
183   23.17  6.50    Male   Yes   Sun  Dinner   4  0.280535
 67    3.07  1.00  Female   Yes   Sat  Dinner   1  0.325733
178    9.60  4.00  Female   Yes   Sun  Dinner   2  0.416667
172    7.25  5.15    Male   Yes   Sun  Dinner   2  0.710345
```

Quantile and Bucket Analysis

As you may recall from Chapter 7, pandas has some tools, in particular cut and qcut, for slicing data up into buckets with bins of your choosing or by sample quantiles. Combining these functions with groupby, it becomes very simple to perform bucket or quantile analysis on a data set. Consider a simple random data set and an equal-length bucket categorization using cut:

```
In [243]: frame = DataFrame({'data1': np.random.randn(1000),
    .....:                    'data2': np.random.randn(1000)})

In [244]: factor = pd.cut(frame.data1, 4)

In [245]: factor[:10]
Out[245]:
  (-1.23, 0.489]
 (-2.956, -1.23]
  (-1.23, 0.489]
  (0.489, 2.208]
  (-1.23, 0.489]
  (0.489, 2.208]
  (-1.23, 0.489]
  (-1.23, 0.489]
  (0.489, 2.208]
  (0.489, 2.208]
Levels (4): Index(['(-2.956, -1.23]', '(-1.23, 0.489]',
                    '(0.489, 2.208]', '(2.208, 3.928]'], dtype=object)
```

The Factor object returned by cut can be passed directly to groupby. So we could compute a set of statistics for the data2 column like so:

```
def get_stats(group):
    return {'min': group.min(), 'max': group.max(),
            'count': group.count(), 'mean': group.mean()}

grouped = frame.data2.groupby(factor)
grouped.apply(get_stats).unstack()
```

These were equal-length buckets; to compute equal-size buckets based on sample quantiles, use qcut. I'll pass labels=False to just get quantile numbers.

```
# Return quantile numbers
grouping = pd.qcut(frame.data1, 10, labels=False)

grouped = frame.data2.groupby(grouping)
grouped.apply(get_stats).unstack()
```

Example: Filling Missing Values with Group-specific Values

When cleaning up missing data, in some cases you will filter out data observations using dropna, but in others you may want to impute (fill in) the NA values using a fixed value or some value derived from the data. fillna is the right tool to use; for example here I fill in NA values with the mean:

```
In [248]: s = Series(np.random.randn(6))

In [249]: s[::2] = np.nan

In [250]: s
Out[250]:
0         NaN
1    -0.125921
2         NaN
3    -0.884475
4         NaN
5     0.227290
dtype: float64

In [251]: s.fillna(s.mean())
Out[251]:
0    -0.261035
1    -0.125921
2    -0.261035
3    -0.884475
4    -0.261035
5     0.227290
dtype: float64
```

Suppose you need the fill value to vary by group. As you may guess, you need only group the data and use apply with a function that calls fillna on each data chunk. Here is some sample data on some US states divided into eastern and western states:

```
In [252]: states = ['Ohio', 'New York', 'Vermont', 'Florida',
   .....:           'Oregon', 'Nevada', 'California', 'Idaho']

In [253]: group_key = ['East'] * 4 + ['West'] * 4

In [254]: data = Series(np.random.randn(8), index=states)

In [255]: data[['Vermont', 'Nevada', 'Idaho']] = np.nan

In [256]: data
Out[256]:
Ohio           0.922264
New York      -2.153545
Vermont            NaN
Florida       -0.375842
Oregon         0.329939
Nevada             NaN
California     1.105913
Idaho              NaN
dtype: float64
```

```
In [257]: data.groupby(group_key).mean()
Out[257]:
East    -0.535707
West     0.717926
dtype: float64
```

We can fill the NA values using the group means like so:

```
In [258]: fill_mean = lambda g: g.fillna(g.mean())

In [259]: data.groupby(group_key).apply(fill_mean)
Out[259]:
Ohio          0.922264
New York     -2.153545
Vermont      -0.535707
Florida      -0.375842
Oregon        0.329939
Nevada        0.717926
California    1.105913
Idaho         0.717926
dtype: float64
```

In another case, you might have pre-defined fill values in your code that vary by group. Since the groups have a name attribute set internally, we can use that:

```
fill_values = {'East': 0.5, 'West': -1}
fill_func = lambda g: g.fillna(fill_values[g.name])

data.groupby(group_key).apply(fill_func)
```

Example: Random Sampling and Permutation

Suppose you wanted to draw a random sample (with or without replacement) from a large dataset for Monte Carlo simulation purposes or some other application. There are a number of ways to perform the "draws"; some are much more efficient than others. One way is to select the first K elements of np.random.permutation(N), where N is the size of your complete dataset and K the desired sample size. As a more fun example, here's a way to construct a deck of English-style playing cards:

```
# Hearts, Spades, Clubs, Diamonds
suits = ['H', 'S', 'C', 'D']
card_val = (range(1, 11) + [10] * 3) * 4
base_names = ['A'] + range(2, 11) + ['J', 'K', 'Q']
cards = []
for suit in ['H', 'S', 'C', 'D']:
    cards.extend(str(num) + suit for num in base_names)

deck = Series(card_val, index=cards)
```

So now we have a Series of length 52 whose index contains card names and values are the ones used in blackjack and other games (to keep things simple, I just let the ace be 1):

```
In [263]: deck[:13]
Out[263]:
AH     1
2H     2
3H     3
...
JH    10
KH    10
QH    10
Length: 13, dtype: int64
```

Now, based on what I said above, drawing a hand of 5 cards from the desk could be written as:

```
In [264]: def draw(deck, n=5):
    .....:     return deck.take(np.random.permutation(len(deck))[:n])

In [265]: draw(deck)
Out[265]:
AD     1
8C     8
5H     5
KC    10
2C     2
dtype: int64
```

Suppose you wanted two random cards from each suit. Because the suit is the last character of each card name, we can group based on this and use apply:

```
In [266]: get_suit = lambda card: card[-1] # last letter is suit

In [267]: deck.groupby(get_suit).apply(draw, n=2)
Out[267]:
C  2C     2
   3C     3
D  KD    10
   8D     8
H  KH    10
   3H     3
S  2S     2
   4S     4
dtype: int64

# alternatively
In [268]: deck.groupby(get_suit, group_keys=False).apply(draw, n=2)
Out[268]:
KC    10
JC    10
AD     1
5D     5
5H     5
6H     6
7S     7
KS    10
dtype: int64
```

Example: Group Weighted Average and Correlation

Under the split-apply-combine paradigm of groupby, operations between columns in a DataFrame or two Series, such a group weighted average, become a routine affair. As an example, take this dataset containing group keys, values, and some weights:

```
In [269]: df = DataFrame({'category': ['a', 'a', 'a', 'a', 'b', 'b', 'b', 'b'],
   .....:                  'data': np.random.randn(8),
   .....:                  'weights': np.random.rand(8)})

In [270]: df
Out[270]:
  category      data   weights
0        a  1.561587  0.957515
1        a  1.219984  0.347267
2        a -0.482239  0.581362
3        a  0.315667  0.217091
4        b -0.047852  0.894406
5        b -0.454145  0.918564
6        b -0.556774  0.277825
7        b  0.253321  0.955905
```

The group weighted average by category would then be:

```
In [271]: grouped = df.groupby('category')

In [272]: get_wavg = lambda g: np.average(g['data'], weights=g['weights'])

In [273]: grouped.apply(get_wavg)
Out[273]:
category
a          0.811643
b         -0.122262
dtype: float64
```

As a less trivial example, consider a data set from Yahoo! Finance containing end of day prices for a few stocks and the S&P 500 index (the SPX ticker):

```
In [274]: close_px = pd.read_csv('ch09/stock_px.csv', parse_dates=True, index_col=0)

In [275]: close_px.info()
<class 'pandas.core.frame.DataFrame'>
DatetimeIndex: 2214 entries, 2003-01-02 00:00:00 to 2011-10-14 00:00:00
Data columns (total 4 columns):
AAPL    2214 non-null float64
MSFT    2214 non-null float64
XOM     2214 non-null float64
SPX     2214 non-null float64
dtypes: float64(4)
In [276]: close_px[-4:]
Out[276]:
              AAPL   MSFT    XOM      SPX
2011-10-11  400.29  27.00  76.27  1195.54
2011-10-12  402.19  26.96  77.16  1207.25
2011-10-13  408.43  27.18  76.37  1203.66
2011-10-14  422.00  27.27  78.11  1224.58
```

One task of interest might be to compute a DataFrame consisting of the yearly correlations of daily returns (computed from percent changes) with SPX. Here is one way to do it:

```
In [277]: rets = close_px.pct_change().dropna()

In [278]: spx_corr = lambda x: x.corrwith(x['SPX'])

In [279]: by_year = rets.groupby(lambda x: x.year)

In [280]: by_year.apply(spx_corr)
Out[280]:
          AAPL      MSFT      XOM  SPX
2003  0.541124  0.745174  0.661265    1
2004  0.374283  0.588531  0.557742    1
2005  0.467540  0.562374  0.631010    1
2006  0.428267  0.406126  0.518514    1
2007  0.508118  0.658770  0.786264    1
2008  0.681434  0.804626  0.828303    1
2009  0.707103  0.654902  0.797921    1
2010  0.710105  0.730118  0.839057    1
2011  0.691931  0.800996  0.859975    1
```

There is, of course, nothing to stop you from computing inter-column correlations:

```
# Annual correlation of Apple with Microsoft
In [281]: by_year.apply(lambda g: g['AAPL'].corr(g['MSFT']))
Out[281]:
2003    0.480868
2004    0.259024
2005    0.300093
2006    0.161735
2007    0.417738
2008    0.611901
2009    0.432738
2010    0.571946
2011    0.581987
dtype: float64
```

Example: Group-wise Linear Regression

In the same vein as the previous example, you can use groupby to perform more complex group-wise statistical analysis, as long as the function returns a pandas object or scalar value. For example, I can define the following regress function (using the statsmodels econometrics library) which executes an ordinary least squares (OLS) regression on each chunk of data:

```
import statsmodels.api as sm
def regress(data, yvar, xvars):
    Y = data[yvar]
    X = data[xvars]
    X['intercept'] = 1.
    result = sm.OLS(Y, X).fit()
    return result.params
```

Now, to run a yearly linear regression of AAPL on SPX returns, I execute:

```
In [283]: by_year.apply(regress, 'AAPL', ['SPX'])
Out[283]:
           SPX  intercept
2003  1.195406   0.000710
2004  1.363463   0.004201
2005  1.766415   0.003246
2006  1.645496   0.000080
2007  1.198761   0.003438
2008  0.968016  -0.001110
2009  0.879103   0.002954
2010  1.052608   0.001261
2011  0.806605   0.001514
```

Pivot Tables and Cross-Tabulation

A *pivot table* is a data summarization tool frequently found in spreadsheet programs and other data analysis software. It aggregates a table of data by one or more keys, arranging the data in a rectangle with some of the group keys along the rows and some along the columns. Pivot tables in Python with pandas are made possible using the groupby facility described in this chapter combined with reshape operations utilizing hierarchical indexing. DataFrame has a pivot_table method, and additionally there is a top-level pandas.pivot_table function. In addition to providing a convenience interface to groupby, pivot_table also can add partial totals, also known as *margins*.

Returning to the tipping data set, suppose I wanted to compute a table of group means (the default pivot_table aggregation type) arranged by sex and smoker on the rows:

```
In [284]: tips.pivot_table(index=['sex', 'smoker'])
Out[284]:
                   size       tip   tip_pct   total_bill
sex    smoker
Female No      2.592593  2.773519  0.156921    18.105185
       Yes     2.242424  2.931515  0.182150    17.977879
Male   No      2.711340  3.113402  0.160669    19.791237
       Yes     2.500000  3.051167  0.152771    22.284500
```

This could have been easily produced using groupby. Now, suppose we want to aggregate only tip_pct and size, and additionally group by day. I'll put smoker in the table columns and day in the rows:

```
In [285]: tips.pivot_table(['tip_pct', 'size'], index=['sex', 'day'],
   .....:                   columns='smoker')
Out[285]:
                tip_pct              size
smoker               No       Yes       No       Yes
sex    day
Female Fri    0.165296  0.209129  2.500000  2.000000
       Sat    0.147993  0.163817  2.307692  2.200000
       Sun    0.165710  0.237075  3.071429  2.500000
       Thur   0.155971  0.163073  2.480000  2.428571
Male   Fri    0.138005  0.144730  2.000000  2.125000
```

```
Sat   0.162132  0.139067  2.656250  2.629630
Sun   0.158291  0.173964  2.883721  2.600000
Thur  0.165706  0.164417  2.500000  2.300000
```

This table could be augmented to include partial totals by passing `margins=True`. This has the effect of adding `All` row and column labels, with corresponding values being the group statistics for all the data within a single tier. In this below example, the `All` values are means without taking into account smoker vs. non-smoker (the `All` columns) or any of the two levels of grouping on the rows (the `All` row):

```
In [286]: tips.pivot_table(['tip_pct', 'size'], index=['sex', 'day'],
    .....:                  columns='smoker', margins=True)
Out[286]:
                 tip_pct                        size
smoker                No       Yes       All       No       Yes       All
sex    day
Female Fri     0.165296  0.209129  0.199388  2.500000  2.000000  2.111111
       Sat     0.147993  0.163817  0.156470  2.307692  2.200000  2.250000
       Sun     0.165710  0.237075  0.181569  3.071429  2.500000  2.944444
       Thur    0.155971  0.163073  0.157525  2.480000  2.428571  2.468750
Male   Fri     0.138005  0.144730  0.143385  2.000000  2.125000  2.100000
       Sat     0.162132  0.139067  0.151577  2.656250  2.629630  2.644068
       Sun     0.158291  0.173964  0.162344  2.883721  2.600000  2.810345
       Thur    0.165706  0.164417  0.165276  2.500000  2.300000  2.433333
All            0.159328  0.163196  0.160803  2.668874  2.408602  2.569672
```

To use a different aggregation function, pass it to `aggfunc`. For example, `'count'` or `len` will give you a cross-tabulation (count or frequency) of group sizes:

```
In [287]: tips.pivot_table('tip_pct', index=['sex', 'smoker'], columns='day',
    .....:                  aggfunc=len, margins=True)
Out[287]:
day           Fri  Sat  Sun  Thur  All
sex    smoker
Female No       2   13   14    25   54
       Yes      7   15    4     7   33
Male   No       2   32   43    20   97
       Yes      8   27   15    10   60
All            19   87   76    62  244
```

If some combinations are empty (or otherwise NA), you may wish to pass a `fill_value`:

```
In [288]: tips.pivot_table('size', index=['time', 'sex', 'smoker'],
    .....:                  columns='day', aggfunc='sum', fill_value=0)
Out[288]:
day                   Fri  Sat  Sun  Thur
time   sex    smoker
Dinner Female No        2   30   43     2
              Yes       8   33   10     0
       Male   No        4   85  124     0
              Yes      12   71   39     0
Lunch  Female No        3    0    0    60
              Yes       6    0    0    17
       Male   No        0    0    0    50
              Yes       5    0    0    23
```

See Table 9-2 for a summary of `pivot_table` methods.

Table 9-2. pivot_table options

Function name	Description
values	Column name or names to aggregate. By default aggregates all numeric columns
rows	Column names or other group keys to group on the rows of the resulting pivot table
cols	Column names or other group keys to group on the columns of the resulting pivot table
aggfunc	Aggregation function or list of functions; 'mean' by default. Can be any function valid in a groupby context
fill_value	Replace missing values in result table
margins	Add row/column subtotals and grand total, False by default

Cross-Tabulations: Crosstab

A cross-tabulation (or *crosstab* for short) is a special case of a pivot table that computes group frequencies. Here is a canonical example taken from the Wikipedia page on cross-tabulation:

```
In [292]: data
Out[292]:
   Sample  Gender   Handedness
0       1  Female  Right-handed
1       2    Male   Left-handed
2       3  Female  Right-handed
3       4    Male  Right-handed
4       5    Male   Left-handed
5       6    Male  Right-handed
6       7  Female  Right-handed
7       8  Female   Left-handed
8       9    Male  Right-handed
9      10  Female  Right-handed
```

As part of some survey analysis, we might want to summarize this data by gender and handedness. You could use `pivot_table` to do this, but the `pandas.crosstab` function is very convenient:

```
In [293]: pd.crosstab(data.Gender, data.Handedness, margins=True)
Out[293]:
Handedness  Left-handed  Right-handed  All
Gender
Female                1             4    5
Male                  2             3    5
All                   3             7   10
```

The first two arguments to `crosstab` can each either be an array or Series or a list of arrays. As in the tips data:

```
In [294]: pd.crosstab([tips.time, tips.day], tips.smoker, margins=True)
Out[294]:
smoker           No  Yes  All
time     day
```

```
Dinner Fri      3    9   12
       Sat     45   42   87
       Sun     57   19   76
       Thur     1    0    1
Lunch  Fri      1    6    7
       Thur    44   17   61
All            151  93  244
```

Example: 2012 Federal Election Commission Database

The US Federal Election Commission publishes data on contributions to political campaigns. This includes contributor names, occupation and employer, address, and contribution amount. An interesting dataset is from the 2012 US presidential election (*http://www.fec.gov/disclosurep/PDownload.do*). As of this writing (June 2012), the full dataset for all states is a 150 megabyte CSV file P00000001-ALL.csv, which can be loaded with pandas.read_csv:

```
In [13]: fec = pd.read_csv('ch09/P00000001-ALL.csv')
```

```
In [14]: fec.info()
Out[14]:
<class 'pandas.core.frame.DataFrame'>
Int64Index: 1001731 entries, 0 to 1001730
Data columns:
cmte_id             1001731  non-null values
cand_id             1001731  non-null values
cand_nm             1001731  non-null values
contbr_nm           1001731  non-null values
contbr_city         1001716  non-null values
contbr_st           1001727  non-null values
contbr_zip          1001620  non-null values
contbr_employer     994314  non-null values
contbr_occupation   994433  non-null values
contb_receipt_amt   1001731  non-null values
contb_receipt_dt    1001731  non-null values
receipt_desc        14166  non-null values
memo_cd             92482  non-null values
memo_text           97770  non-null values
form_tp             1001731  non-null values
file_num            1001731  non-null values
dtypes: float64(1), int64(1), object(14)
```

A sample record in the DataFrame looks like this:

```
In [15]: fec.ix[123456]
Out[15]:
cmte_id                           C00431445
cand_id                           P80003338
cand_nm                      Obama, Barack
contbr_nm                      ELLMAN, IRA
contbr_city                           TEMPE
contbr_st                                AZ
contbr_zip                        852816719
contbr_employer    ARIZONA STATE UNIVERSITY
```

```
contbr_occupation              PROFESSOR
contb_receipt_amt                     50
contb_receipt_dt               01-DEC-11
receipt_desc                         NaN
memo_cd                              NaN
memo_text                            NaN
form_tp                            SA17A
file_num                          772372
Name: 123456
```

You can probably think of many ways to start slicing and dicing this data to extract informative statistics about donors and patterns in the campaign contributions. I'll spend the next several pages showing you a number of different analyses that apply techniques you have learned about so far.

You can see that there are no political party affiliations in the data, so this would be useful to add. You can get a list of all the unique political candidates using unique (note that NumPy suppresses the quotes around the strings in the output):

```
In [16]: unique_cands = fec.cand_nm.unique()

In [17]: unique_cands
Out[17]:
array([Bachmann, Michelle, Romney, Mitt, Obama, Barack,
       Roemer, Charles E. 'Buddy' III, Pawlenty, Timothy,
       Johnson, Gary Earl, Paul, Ron, Santorum, Rick, Cain, Herman,
       Gingrich, Newt, McCotter, Thaddeus G, Huntsman, Jon, Perry, Rick], dtype=object)

In [18]: unique_cands[2]
Out[18]: 'Obama, Barack'
```

An easy way to indicate party affiliation is using a dict:[2]

```
parties = {'Bachmann, Michelle': 'Republican',
           'Cain, Herman': 'Republican',
           'Gingrich, Newt': 'Republican',
           'Huntsman, Jon': 'Republican',
           'Johnson, Gary Earl': 'Republican',
           'McCotter, Thaddeus G': 'Republican',
           'Obama, Barack': 'Democrat',
           'Paul, Ron': 'Republican',
           'Pawlenty, Timothy': 'Republican',
           'Perry, Rick': 'Republican',
           "Roemer, Charles E. 'Buddy' III": 'Republican',
           'Romney, Mitt': 'Republican',
           'Santorum, Rick': 'Republican'}
```

Now, using this mapping and the map method on Series objects, you can compute an array of political parties from the candidate names:

```
In [20]: fec.cand_nm[123456:123461]
Out[20]:
```

---

2. This makes the simplifying assumption that Gary Johnson is a Republican even though he later became the Libertarian party candidate.

```
123456     Obama, Barack
123457     Obama, Barack
123458     Obama, Barack
123459     Obama, Barack
123460     Obama, Barack
Name: cand_nm

In [21]: fec.cand_nm[123456:123461].map(parties)
Out[21]:
123456     Democrat
123457     Democrat
123458     Democrat
123459     Democrat
123460     Democrat
Name: cand_nm

# Add it as a column
In [22]: fec['party'] = fec.cand_nm.map(parties)

In [23]: fec['party'].value_counts()
Out[23]:
Democrat      593746
Republican    407985
```

A couple of data preparation points. First, this data includes both contributions and refunds (negative contribution amount):

```
In [24]: (fec.contb_receipt_amt > 0).value_counts()
Out[24]:
True      991475
False      10256
```

To simplify the analysis, I'll restrict the data set to positive contributions:

```
In [25]: fec = fec[fec.contb_receipt_amt > 0]
```

Since Barack Obama and Mitt Romney are the main two candidates, I'll also prepare a subset that just has contributions to their campaigns:

```
In [26]: fec_mrbo = fec[fec.cand_nm.isin(['Obama, Barack', 'Romney, Mitt'])]
```

Donation Statistics by Occupation and Employer

Donations by occupation is another oft-studied statistic. For example, lawyers (attorneys) tend to donate more money to Democrats, while business executives tend to donate more to Republicans. You have no reason to believe me; you can see for yourself in the data. First, the total number of donations by occupation is easy:

```
In [27]: fec.contbr_occupation.value_counts()[:10]
Out[27]:
RETIRED                  233990
INFORMATION REQUESTED     35107
ATTORNEY                  34286
HOMEMAKER                 29931
PHYSICIAN                 23432
```

```
INFORMATION REQUESTED PER BEST EFFORTS      21138
ENGINEER                                    14334
TEACHER                                     13990
CONSULTANT                                  13273
PROFESSOR                                   12555
```

You will notice by looking at the occupations that many refer to the same basic job type, or there are several variants of the same thing. Here is a code snippet illustrates a technique for cleaning up a few of them by mapping from one occupation to another; note the "trick" of using `dict.get` to allow occupations with no mapping to "pass through":

```python
occ_mapping = {
   'INFORMATION REQUESTED PER BEST EFFORTS' : 'NOT PROVIDED',
   'INFORMATION REQUESTED' : 'NOT PROVIDED',
   'INFORMATION REQUESTED (BEST EFFORTS)' : 'NOT PROVIDED',
   'C.E.O.': 'CEO'
}

# If no mapping provided, return x
f = lambda x: occ_mapping.get(x, x)
fec.contbr_occupation = fec.contbr_occupation.map(f)
```

I'll also do the same thing for employers:

```python
emp_mapping = {
   'INFORMATION REQUESTED PER BEST EFFORTS' : 'NOT PROVIDED',
   'INFORMATION REQUESTED' : 'NOT PROVIDED',
   'SELF' : 'SELF-EMPLOYED',
   'SELF EMPLOYED' : 'SELF-EMPLOYED',
}

# If no mapping provided, return x
f = lambda x: emp_mapping.get(x, x)
fec.contbr_employer = fec.contbr_employer.map(f)
```

Now, you can use `pivot_table` to aggregate the data by party and occupation, then filter down to the subset that donated at least $2 million overall:

```python
In [34]: by_occupation = fec.pivot_table('contb_receipt_amt',
   ....:                                  index='contbr_occupation',
   ....:                                  columns='party', aggfunc='sum')

In [35]: over_2mm = by_occupation[by_occupation.sum(1) > 2000000]

In [36]: over_2mm
Out[36]:
party                    Democrat       Republican
contbr_occupation
ATTORNEY              11141982.97     7477194.430000
CEO                    2074974.79     4211040.520000
CONSULTANT             2459912.71     2544725.450000
ENGINEER                951525.55     1818373.700000
EXECUTIVE              1355161.05     4138850.090000
HOMEMAKER              4248875.80    13634275.780000
INVESTOR                884133.00     2431768.920000
```

```
LAWYER              3160478.87     391224.320000
MANAGER              762883.22    1444532.370000
NOT PROVIDED        4866973.96   20565473.010000
OWNER               1001567.36    2408286.920000
PHYSICIAN           3735124.94    3594320.240000
PRESIDENT           1878509.95    4720923.760000
PROFESSOR           2165071.08     296702.730000
REAL ESTATE          528902.09    1625902.250000
RETIRED            25305116.38   23561244.489999
SELF-EMPLOYED        672393.40    1640252.540000
```

It can be easier to look at this data graphically as a bar plot ('barh' means horizontal bar plot, see Figure 9-2):

```
In [38]: over_2mm.plot(kind='barh')
```

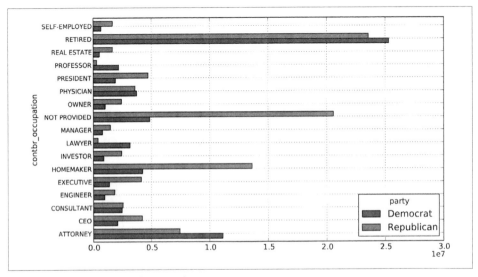

Figure 9-2. Total donations by party for top occupations

You might be interested in the top donor occupations or top companies donating to Obama and Romney. To do this, you can group by candidate name and use a variant of the top method from earlier in the chapter:

```
def get_top_amounts(group, key, n=5):
    totals = group.groupby(key)['contb_receipt_amt'].sum()

    # Order totals by key in descending order
    return totals.order(ascending=False)[-n:]
```

Then aggregated by occupation and employer:

```
In [40]: grouped = fec_mrbo.groupby('cand_nm')

In [41]: grouped.apply(get_top_amounts, 'contbr_occupation', n=7)
Out[41]:
```

```
cand_nm       contbr_occupation
Obama, Barack RETIRED              25305116.38
              ATTORNEY             11141982.97
              NOT PROVIDED          4866973.96
              HOMEMAKER             4248875.80
              PHYSICIAN             3735124.94
              LAWYER                3160478.87
              CONSULTANT            2459912.71
Romney, Mitt  RETIRED             11508473.59
              NOT PROVIDED         11396894.84
              HOMEMAKER             8147446.22
              ATTORNEY              5364718.82
              PRESIDENT             2491244.89
              EXECUTIVE             2300947.03
              C.E.O.                1968386.11
Name: contb_receipt_amt

In [42]: grouped.apply(get_top_amounts, 'contbr_employer', n=10)
Out[42]:
cand_nm       contbr_employer
Obama, Barack RETIRED              22694358.85
              SELF-EMPLOYED        18626807.16
              NOT EMPLOYED          8586308.70
              NOT PROVIDED          5053480.37
              HOMEMAKER             2605408.54
              STUDENT                318831.45
              VOLUNTEER              257104.00
              MICROSOFT              215585.36
              SIDLEY AUSTIN LLP      168254.00
              REFUSED                149516.07
Romney, Mitt  NOT PROVIDED        12059527.24
              RETIRED             11506225.71
              HOMEMAKER             8147196.22
              SELF-EMPLOYED         7414115.22
              STUDENT                496490.94
              CREDIT SUISSE          281150.00
              MORGAN STANLEY         267266.00
              GOLDMAN SACH & CO.     238250.00
              BARCLAYS CAPITAL       162750.00
              H.I.G. CAPITAL         139500.00
Name: contb_receipt_amt
```

Bucketing Donation Amounts

A useful way to analyze this data is to use the cut function to discretize the contributor amounts into buckets by contribution size:

```
In [43]: bins = np.array([0, 1, 10, 100, 1000, 10000, 100000, 1000000, 10000000])

In [44]: labels = pd.cut(fec_mrbo.contb_receipt_amt, bins)

In [45]: labels
Out[45]:
Factor:contb_receipt_amt
array([(10, 100], (100, 1000], (100, 1000], ..., (1, 10], (10, 100],
```

```
                (100, 1000]], dtype=object)
    Levels (8): array([(0, 1], (1, 10], (10, 100], (100, 1000], (1000, 10000],
           (10000, 100000], (100000, 1000000], (1000000, 10000000]], dtype=object)
```

We can then group the data for Obama and Romney by name and bin label to get a histogram by donation size:

```
In [46]: grouped = fec_mrbo.groupby(['cand_nm', labels])

In [47]: grouped.size().unstack(0)
Out[47]:
cand_nm             Obama, Barack  Romney, Mitt
contb_receipt_amt
(0, 1]                        493            77
(1, 10]                     40070          3681
(10, 100]                  372280         31853
(100, 1000]                153991         43357
(1000, 10000]               22284         26186
(10000, 100000]                 2             1
(100000, 1000000]               3           NaN
(1000000, 10000000]             4           NaN
```

This data shows that Obama has received a significantly larger number of small donations than Romney. You can also sum the contribution amounts and normalize within buckets to visualize percentage of total donations of each size by candidate:

```
In [48]: bucket_sums = grouped.contb_receipt_amt.sum().unstack(0)

In [49]: bucket_sums
Out[49]:
cand_nm             Obama, Barack  Romney, Mitt
contb_receipt_amt
(0, 1]                     318.24         77.00
(1, 10]                 337267.62      29819.66
(10, 100]             20288981.41    1987783.76
(100, 1000]           54798531.46   22363381.69
(1000, 10000]         51753705.67   63942145.42
(10000, 100000]          59100.00      12700.00
(100000, 1000000]      1490683.08           NaN
(1000000, 10000000]    7148839.76           NaN

In [50]: normed_sums = bucket_sums.div(bucket_sums.sum(axis=1), axis=0)

In [51]: normed_sums
Out[51]:
cand_nm             Obama, Barack  Romney, Mitt
contb_receipt_amt
(0, 1]                   0.805182      0.194818
(1, 10]                  0.918767      0.081233
(10, 100]                0.910769      0.089231
(100, 1000]              0.710176      0.289824
(1000, 10000]            0.447326      0.552674
(10000, 100000]          0.823120      0.176880
(100000, 1000000]        1.000000           NaN
(1000000, 10000000]      1.000000           NaN
```

```
In [52]: normed_sums[:-2].plot(kind='barh', stacked=True)
```

I excluded the two largest bins as these are not donations by individuals. See Figure 9-3 for the resulting figure.

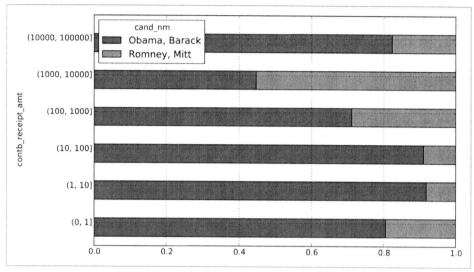

Figure 9-3. Percentage of total donations received by candidates for each donation size

There are of course many refinements and improvements of this analysis. For example, you could aggregate donations by donor name and zip code to adjust for donors who gave many small amounts versus one or more large donations. I encourage you to download it and explore it yourself.

Donation Statistics by State

Aggregating the data by candidate and state is a routine affair:

```
In [53]: grouped = fec_mrbo.groupby(['cand_nm', 'contbr_st'])

In [54]: totals = grouped.contb_receipt_amt.sum().unstack(0).fillna(0)

In [55]: totals = totals[totals.sum(1) > 100000]

In [56]: totals[:10]
Out[56]:
cand_nm    Obama, Barack  Romney, Mitt
contbr_st
AK              281840.15      86204.24
AL              543123.48     527303.51
AR              359247.28     105556.00
AZ             1506476.98    1888436.23
CA            23824984.24   11237636.60
```

```
CO       2132429.49    1506714.12
CT       2068291.26    3499475.45
DC       4373538.80    1025137.50
DE        336669.14      82712.00
FL       7318178.58    8338458.81
```

If you divide each row by the total contribution amount, you get the relative percentage of total donations by state for each candidate:

```
In [57]: percent = totals.div(totals.sum(1), axis=0)

In [58]: percent[:10]
Out[58]:
cand_nm    Obama, Barack   Romney, Mitt
contbr_st
AK              0.765778       0.234222
AL              0.507390       0.492610
AR              0.772902       0.227098
AZ              0.443745       0.556255
CA              0.679498       0.320502
CO              0.585970       0.414030
CT              0.371476       0.628524
DC              0.810113       0.189887
DE              0.802776       0.197224
FL              0.467417       0.532583
```

## CHAPTER 10

Time Series

Time series data is an important form of structured data in many different fields, such as finance, economics, ecology, neuroscience, or physics. Anything that is observed or measured at many points in time forms a time series. Many time series are *fixed frequency*, which is to say that data points occur at regular intervals according to some rule, such as every 15 seconds, every 5 minutes, or once per month. Time series can also be *irregular* without a fixed unit or time or offset between units. How you mark and refer to time series data depends on the application and you may have one of the following:

- *Timestamps*, specific instants in time
- Fixed *periods*, such as the month January 2007 or the full year 2010
- *Intervals* of time, indicated by a start and end timestamp. Periods can be thought of as special cases of intervals
- Experiment or elapsed time; each timestamp is a measure of time relative to a particular start time. For example, the diameter of a cookie baking each second since being placed in the oven

In this chapter, I am mainly concerned with time series in the first 3 categories, though many of the techniques can be applied to experimental time series where the index may be an integer or floating point number indicating elapsed time from the start of the experiment. The simplest and most widely used kind of time series are those indexed by timestamp.

pandas provides a standard set of time series tools and data algorithms. With this, you can efficiently work with very large time series and easily slice and dice, aggregate, and resample irregular and fixed frequency time series. As you might guess, many of these tools are especially useful for financial and economics applications, but you could certainly use them to analyze server log data, too.

Some of the features and code, in particular period logic, presented in this chapter were derived from the now defunct scikits.timeseries library.

Date and Time Data Types and Tools

The Python standard library includes data types for date and time data, as well as calendar-related functionality. The datetime, time, and calendar modules are the main places to start. The datetime.datetime type, or simply datetime, is widely used:

```
In [13]: from datetime import datetime

In [14]: now = datetime.now()

In [15]: now
Out[15]: datetime.datetime(2014, 7, 31, 0, 2, 55, 874995)

In [16]: now.year, now.month, now.day
Out[16]: (2014, 7, 31)
```

datetime stores both the date and time down to the microsecond. datetime.time delta represents the temporal difference between two datetime objects:

```
In [17]: delta = datetime(2011, 1, 7) - datetime(2008, 6, 24, 8, 15)

In [18]: delta
Out[18]: datetime.timedelta(926, 56700)

In [19]: delta.days          In [20]: delta.seconds
Out[19]: 926                 Out[20]: 56700
```

You can add (or subtract) a timedelta or multiple thereof to a datetime object to yield a new shifted object:

```
In [21]: from datetime import timedelta

In [22]: start = datetime(2011, 1, 7)

In [23]: start + timedelta(12)
Out[23]: datetime.datetime(2011, 1, 19, 0, 0)

In [24]: start - 2 * timedelta(12)
Out[24]: datetime.datetime(2010, 12, 14, 0, 0)
```

The data types in the datetime module are summarized in Table 10-1. While this chapter is mainly concerned with the data types in pandas and higher level time series manipulation, you will undoubtedly encounter the datetime-based types in many other places in Python the wild.

Table 10-1. Types in datetime module

Type	Description
date	Store calendar date (year, month, day) using the Gregorian calendar.
time	Store time of day as hours, minutes, seconds, and microseconds
datetime	Stores both date and time
timedelta	Represents the difference between two datetime values (as days, seconds, and microseconds)

Converting between string and datetime

datetime objects and pandas Timestamp objects, which I'll introduce later, can be formatted as strings using str or the strftime method, passing a format specification:

```
In [25]: stamp = datetime(2011, 1, 3)
```

```
In [26]: str(stamp)                    In [27]: stamp.strftime('%Y-%m-%d')
Out[26]: '2011-01-03 00:00:00'         Out[27]: '2011-01-03'
```

See Table 10-2 for a complete list of the format codes. These same format codes can be used to convert strings to dates using datetime.strptime:

```
In [28]: value = '2011-01-03'
```

```
In [29]: datetime.strptime(value, '%Y-%m-%d')
Out[29]: datetime.datetime(2011, 1, 3, 0, 0)
```

```
In [30]: datestrs = ['7/6/2011', '8/6/2011']
```

```
In [31]: [datetime.strptime(x, '%m/%d/%Y') for x in datestrs]
Out[31]: [datetime.datetime(2011, 7, 6, 0, 0), datetime.datetime(2011, 8, 6, 0, 0)]
```

datetime.strptime is the best way to parse a date with a known format. However, it can be a bit annoying to have to write a format spec each time, especially for common date formats. In this case, you can use the parser.parse method in the third party dateutil package:

```
In [32]: from dateutil.parser import parse
```

```
In [33]: parse('2011-01-03')
Out[33]: datetime.datetime(2011, 1, 3, 0, 0)
```

dateutil is capable of parsing almost any human-intelligible date representation:

```
In [34]: parse('Jan 31, 1997 10:45 PM')
Out[34]: datetime.datetime(1997, 1, 31, 22, 45)
```

In international locales, day appearing before month is very common, so you can pass dayfirst=True to indicate this:

```
In [35]: parse('6/12/2011', dayfirst=True)
Out[35]: datetime.datetime(2011, 12, 6, 0, 0)
```

pandas is generally oriented toward working with arrays of dates, whether used as an axis index or a column in a DataFrame. The to_datetime method parses many different kinds of date representations. Standard date formats like ISO8601 can be parsed very quickly.

```
In [36]: datestrs
Out[36]: ['7/6/2011', '8/6/2011']

In [37]: pd.to_datetime(datestrs)
Out[37]:
<class 'pandas.tseries.index.DatetimeIndex'>
[2011-07-06, 2011-08-06]
Length: 2, Freq: None, Timezone: None
```

It also handles values that should be considered missing (None, empty string, etc.):

```
In [38]: idx = pd.to_datetime(datestrs + [None])

In [39]: idx
Out[39]:
<class 'pandas.tseries.index.DatetimeIndex'>
[2011-07-06, ..., NaT]
Length: 3, Freq: None, Timezone: None

In [40]: idx[2]
Out[40]: NaT

In [41]: pd.isnull(idx)
Out[41]: array([False, False,  True], dtype=bool)
```

NaT (Not a Time) is pandas's NA value for timestamp data.

 dateutil.parser is a useful, but not perfect tool. Notably, it will recognize some strings as dates that you might prefer that it didn't, like '42' will be parsed as the year 2042 with today's calendar date.

Table 10-2. Datetime format specification (ISO C89 compatible)

Type	Description
%Y	4-digit year
%y	2-digit year
%m	2-digit month [01, 12]
%d	2-digit day [01, 31]
%H	Hour (24-hour clock) [00, 23]
%I	Hour (12-hour clock) [01, 12]
%M	2-digit minute [00, 59]
%S	Second [00, 61] (seconds 60, 61 account for leap seconds)
%w	Weekday as integer [0 (Sunday), 6]

Type	Description
%U	Week number of the year [00, 53]. Sunday is considered the first day of the week, and days before the first Sunday of the year are "week 0".
%W	Week number of the year [00, 53]. Monday is considered the first day of the week, and days before the first Monday of the year are "week 0".
%z	UTC time zone offset as +HHMM or -HHMM, empty if time zone naive
%F	Shortcut for %Y-%m-%d, for example 2012-4-18
%D	Shortcut for %m/%d/%y, for example 04/18/12

datetime objects also have a number of locale-specific formatting options for systems in other countries or languages. For example, the abbreviated month names will be different on German or French systems compared with English systems.

Table 10-3. Locale-specific date formatting

Type	Description
%a	Abbreviated weekday name
%A	Full weekday name
%b	Abbreviated month name
%B	Full month name
%c	Full date and time, for example 'Tue 01 May 2012 04:20:57 PM'
%p	Locale equivalent of AM or PM
%x	Locale-appropriate formatted date; e.g. in US May 1, 2012 yields '05/01/2012'
%X	Locale-appropriate time, e.g. '04:24:12 PM'

Time Series Basics

The most basic kind of time series object in pandas is a Series indexed by timestamps, which is often represented external to pandas as Python strings or datetime objects:

```
In [42]: from datetime import datetime

In [43]: dates = [datetime(2011, 1, 2), datetime(2011, 1, 5), datetime(2011, 1, 7),
   ....:          datetime(2011, 1, 8), datetime(2011, 1, 10), datetime(2011, 1, 12)]

In [44]: ts = Series(np.random.randn(6), index=dates)

In [45]: ts
Out[45]:
2011-01-02   -0.204708
2011-01-05    0.478943
2011-01-07   -0.519439
2011-01-08   -0.555730
2011-01-10    1.965781
```

```
2011-01-12    1.393406
dtype: float64
```

Under the hood, these `datetime` objects have been put in a `DatetimeIndex`:

```
In [47]: ts.index
Out[47]:
<class 'pandas.tseries.index.DatetimeIndex'>
[2011-01-02, ..., 2011-01-12]
Length: 6, Freq: None, Timezone: None
```

 It's not necessary to use the `TimeSeries` constructor explicitly; when creating a Series with a `DatetimeIndex`, pandas knows that the object is a time series.

Like other Series, arithmetic operations between differently-indexed time series automatically align on the dates:

```
In [48]: ts + ts[::2]
Out[48]:
2011-01-02    -0.409415
2011-01-05          NaN
2011-01-07    -1.038877
2011-01-08          NaN
2011-01-10     3.931561
2011-01-12          NaN
dtype: float64
```

pandas stores timestamps using NumPy's `datetime64` data type at the nanosecond resolution:

```
In [49]: ts.index.dtype
Out[49]: dtype('<M8[ns]')
```

Scalar values from a `DatetimeIndex` are pandas `Timestamp` objects

```
In [50]: stamp = ts.index[0]

In [51]: stamp
Out[51]: Timestamp('2011-01-02 00:00:00')
```

A `Timestamp` can be substituted anywhere you would use a `datetime` object. Additionally, it can store frequency information (if any) and understands how to do time zone conversions and other kinds of manipulations. More on both of these things later.

Indexing, Selection, Subsetting

TimeSeries is a subclass of Series and thus behaves in the same way with regard to indexing and selecting data based on label:

```
In [52]: stamp = ts.index[2]
```

```
In [53]: ts[stamp]
Out[53]: -0.51943871505673822
```

As a convenience, you can also pass a string that is interpretable as a date:

```
In [54]: ts['1/10/2011']          In [55]: ts['20110110']
Out[54]: 1.9657805725027142       Out[55]: 1.9657805725027142
```

For longer time series, a year or only a year and month can be passed to easily select slices of data:

```
In [56]: longer_ts = Series(np.random.randn(1000),
   ....:                    index=pd.date_range('1/1/2000', periods=1000))

In [57]: longer_ts
Out[57]:
2000-01-01     0.092908
2000-01-02     0.281746
2000-01-03     0.769023
2000-01-04     1.246435
...
2002-09-23    -0.811676
2002-09-24    -1.830156
2002-09-25    -0.138730
2002-09-26     0.334088
Freq: D, Length: 1000
```

```
In [58]: longer_ts['2001']          In [59]: longer_ts['2001-05']
Out[58]:                            Out[59]:
2001-01-01     1.599534            2001-05-01    -0.622547
2001-01-02     0.474071            2001-05-02     0.936289
2001-01-03     0.151326            2001-05-03     0.750018
2001-01-04    -0.542173            2001-05-04    -0.056715
...                                ...
2001-12-28    -0.433739            2001-05-28     0.111835
2001-12-29     0.092698            2001-05-29    -1.251504
2001-12-30    -1.397820            2001-05-30    -2.949343
2001-12-31     1.457823            2001-05-31     0.634634
Freq: D, Length: 365               Freq: D, Length: 31
```

Slicing with dates works just like with a regular Series:

```
In [60]: ts[datetime(2011, 1, 7):]
Out[60]:
2011-01-07    -0.519439
2011-01-08    -0.555730
2011-01-10     1.965781
2011-01-12     1.393406
dtype: float64
```

Because most time series data is ordered chronologically, you can slice with timestamps not contained in a time series to perform a range query:

```
In [61]: ts                         In [62]: ts['1/6/2011':'1/11/2011']
Out[61]:                            Out[62]:
2011-01-02    -0.204708            2011-01-07    -0.519439
2011-01-05     0.478943            2011-01-08    -0.555730
```

```
2011-01-07   -0.519439          2011-01-10    1.965781
2011-01-08   -0.555730          dtype: float64
2011-01-10    1.965781
2011-01-12    1.393406
dtype: float64
```

As before you can pass either a string date, datetime, or Timestamp. Remember that slicing in this manner produces views on the source time series just like slicing NumPy arrays. There is an equivalent instance method truncate which slices a TimeSeries between two dates:

```
In [63]: ts.truncate(after='1/9/2011')
Out[63]:
2011-01-02   -0.204708
2011-01-05    0.478943
2011-01-07   -0.519439
2011-01-08   -0.555730
dtype: float64
```

All of the above holds true for DataFrame as well, indexing on its rows:

```
In [64]: dates = pd.date_range('1/1/2000', periods=100, freq='W-WED')

In [65]: long_df = DataFrame(np.random.randn(100, 4),
   ....:                     index=dates,
   ....:                     columns=['Colorado', 'Texas', 'New York', 'Ohio'])

In [66]: long_df.ix['5-2001']
Out[66]:
            Colorado    Texas   New York      Ohio
2001-05-02 -0.006045 0.490094 -0.277186 -0.707213
2001-05-09 -0.560107 2.735527  0.927335  1.513906
2001-05-16  0.538600 1.273768  0.667876 -0.969206
2001-05-23  1.676091 -0.817649 0.050188  1.951312
2001-05-30  3.260383 0.963301  1.201206 -1.852001
```

Time Series with Duplicate Indices

In some applications, there may be multiple data observations falling on a particular timestamp. Here is an example:

```
In [67]: dates = pd.DatetimeIndex(['1/1/2000', '1/2/2000', '1/2/2000', '1/2/2000',
   ....:                           '1/3/2000'])

In [68]: dup_ts = Series(np.arange(5), index=dates)

In [69]: dup_ts
Out[69]:
2000-01-01    0
2000-01-02    1
2000-01-02    2
2000-01-02    3
2000-01-03    4
dtype: int64
```

We can tell that the index is not unique by checking its `is_unique` property:

```
In [70]: dup_ts.index.is_unique
Out[70]: False
```

Indexing into this time series will now either produce scalar values or slices depending on whether a timestamp is duplicated:

```
In [71]: dup_ts['1/3/2000']  # not duplicated
Out[71]: 4

In [72]: dup_ts['1/2/2000']  # duplicated
Out[72]:
2000-01-02    1
2000-01-02    2
2000-01-02    3
dtype: int64
```

Suppose you wanted to aggregate the data having non-unique timestamps. One way to do this is to use `groupby` and pass `level=0` (the only level of indexing!):

```
In [73]: grouped = dup_ts.groupby(level=0)
```

```
In [74]: grouped.mean()        In [75]: grouped.count()
Out[74]:                       Out[75]:
2000-01-01    0                2000-01-01    1
2000-01-02    2                2000-01-02    3
2000-01-03    4                2000-01-03    1
dtype: int64                   dtype: int64
```

Date Ranges, Frequencies, and Shifting

Generic time series in pandas are assumed to be irregular; that is, they have no fixed frequency. For many applications this is sufficient. However, it's often desirable to work relative to a fixed frequency, such as daily, monthly, or every 15 minutes, even if that means introducing missing values into a time series. Fortunately pandas has a full suite of standard time series frequencies and tools for resampling, inferring frequencies, and generating fixed frequency date ranges. For example, in the example time series, converting it to be fixed daily frequency can be accomplished by calling `resample`:

```
In [76]: ts                    In [77]: ts.resample('D')
Out[76]:                       Out[77]:
2011-01-02   -0.204708         2011-01-02   -0.204708
2011-01-05    0.478943         2011-01-03        NaN
2011-01-07   -0.519439         2011-01-04        NaN
2011-01-08   -0.555730         2011-01-05    0.478943
2011-01-10    1.965781         2011-01-06        NaN
2011-01-12    1.393406         2011-01-07   -0.519439
dtype: float64                 2011-01-08   -0.555730
                               2011-01-09        NaN
                               2011-01-10    1.965781
                               2011-01-11        NaN
```

```
                    2011-01-12    1.393406
                    Freq: D, dtype: float64
```

Conversion between frequencies or *resampling* is a big enough topic to have its own section later. Here I'll show you how to use the base frequencies and multiples thereof.

Generating Date Ranges

While I used it previously without explanation, you may have guessed that pan das.date_range is responsible for generating a DatetimeIndex with an indicated length according to a particular frequency:

```
In [78]: index = pd.date_range('4/1/2012', '6/1/2012')

In [79]: index
Out[79]:
<class 'pandas.tseries.index.DatetimeIndex'>
[2012-04-01, ..., 2012-06-01]
Length: 62, Freq: D, Timezone: None
```

By default, date_range generates daily timestamps. If you pass only a start or end date, you must pass a number of periods to generate:

```
In [80]: pd.date_range(start='4/1/2012', periods=20)
Out[80]:
<class 'pandas.tseries.index.DatetimeIndex'>
[2012-04-01, ..., 2012-04-20]
Length: 20, Freq: D, Timezone: None

In [81]: pd.date_range(end='6/1/2012', periods=20)
Out[81]:
<class 'pandas.tseries.index.DatetimeIndex'>
[2012-05-13, ..., 2012-06-01]
Length: 20, Freq: D, Timezone: None
```

The start and end dates define strict boundaries for the generated date index. For example, if you wanted a date index containing the last business day of each month, you would pass the 'BM' frequency (business end of month) and only dates falling on or inside the date interval will be included:

```
In [82]: pd.date_range('1/1/2000', '12/1/2000', freq='BM')
Out[82]:
<class 'pandas.tseries.index.DatetimeIndex'>
[2000-01-31, ..., 2000-11-30]
Length: 11, Freq: BM, Timezone: None
```

date_range by default preserves the time (if any) of the start or end timestamp:

```
In [83]: pd.date_range('5/2/2012 12:56:31', periods=5)
Out[83]:
<class 'pandas.tseries.index.DatetimeIndex'>
[2012-05-02 12:56:31, ..., 2012-05-06 12:56:31]
Length: 5, Freq: D, Timezone: None
```

Sometimes you will have start or end dates with time information but want to generate a set of timestamps *normalized* to midnight as a convention. To do this, there is a normalize option:

```
In [84]: pd.date_range('5/2/2012 12:56:31', periods=5, normalize=True)
Out[84]:
<class 'pandas.tseries.index.DatetimeIndex'>
[2012-05-02, ..., 2012-05-06]
Length: 5, Freq: D, Timezone: None
```

Frequencies and Date Offsets

Frequencies in pandas are composed of a *base frequency* and a multiplier. Base frequencies are typically referred to by a string alias, like 'M' for monthly or 'H' for hourly. For each base frequency, there is an object defined generally referred to as a *date offset*. For example, hourly frequency can be represented with the Hour class:

```
In [85]: from pandas.tseries.offsets import Hour, Minute

In [86]: hour = Hour()

In [87]: hour
Out[87]: <Hour>
```

You can define a multiple of an offset by passing an integer:

```
In [88]: four_hours = Hour(4)

In [89]: four_hours
Out[89]: <4 * Hours>
```

In most applications, you would never need to explicitly create one of these objects, instead using a string alias like 'H' or '4H'. Putting an integer before the base frequency creates a multiple:

```
In [90]: pd.date_range('1/1/2000', '1/3/2000 23:59', freq='4h')
Out[90]:
<class 'pandas.tseries.index.DatetimeIndex'>
[2000-01-01 00:00:00, ..., 2000-01-03 20:00:00]
Length: 18, Freq: 4H, Timezone: None
```

Many offsets can be combined together by addition:

```
In [91]: Hour(2) + Minute(30)
Out[91]: <150 * Minutes>
```

Similarly, you can pass frequency strings like '2h30min' which will effectively be parsed to the same expression:

```
In [92]: pd.date_range('1/1/2000', periods=10, freq='1h30min')
Out[92]:
<class 'pandas.tseries.index.DatetimeIndex'>
[2000-01-01 00:00:00, ..., 2000-01-01 13:30:00]
Length: 10, Freq: 90T, Timezone: None
```

Some frequencies describe points in time that are not evenly spaced. For example, 'M' (calendar month end) and 'BM' (last business/weekday of month) depend on the number of days in a month and, in the latter case, whether the month ends on a weekend or not. For lack of a better term, I call these *anchored* offsets.

See Table 10-4 for a listing of frequency codes and date offset classes available in pandas.

 Users can define their own custom frequency classes to provide date logic not available in pandas, though the full details of that are outside the scope of this book.

Table 10-4. Base Time Series Frequencies

Alias	Offset Type	Description
D	Day	Calendar daily
B	BusinessDay	Business daily
H	Hour	Hourly
T or min	Minute	Minutely
S	Second	Secondly
L or ms	Milli	Millisecond (1/1000th of 1 second)
U	Micro	Microsecond (1/1000000th of 1 second)
M	MonthEnd	Last calendar day of month
BM	BusinessMonthEnd	Last business day (weekday) of month
MS	MonthBegin	First calendar day of month
BMS	BusinessMonthBegin	First weekday of month
W-MON, W-TUE, ...	Week	Weekly on given day of week: MON, TUE, WED, THU, FRI, SAT, or SUN.
WOM-1MON, WOM-2MON, ...	WeekOfMonth	Generate weekly dates in the first, second, third, or fourth week of the month. For example, WOM-3FRI for the 3rd Friday of each month.
Q-JAN, Q-FEB, ...	QuarterEnd	Quarterly dates anchored on last calendar day of each month, for year ending in indicated month: JAN, FEB, MAR, APR, MAY, JUN, JUL, AUG, SEP, OCT, NOV, or DEC.
BQ-JAN, BQ-FEB, ...	BusinessQuarterEnd	Quarterly dates anchored on last weekday day of each month, for year ending in indicated month
QS-JAN, QS-FEB, ...	QuarterBegin	Quarterly dates anchored on first calendar day of each month, for year ending in indicated month
BQS-JAN, BQS-FEB, ...	BusinessQuarterBegin	Quarterly dates anchored on first weekday day of each month, for year ending in indicated month
A-JAN, A-FEB, ...	YearEnd	Annual dates anchored on last calendar day of given month: JAN, FEB, MAR, APR, MAY, JUN, JUL, AUG, SEP, OCT, NOV, or DEC.

Alias	Offset Type	Description
BA-JAN, BA-FEB, ...	BusinessYearEnd	Annual dates anchored on last weekday of given month
AS-JAN, AS-FEB, ...	YearBegin	Annual dates anchored on first day of given month
BAS-JAN, BAS-FEB, ...	BusinessYearBegin	Annual dates anchored on first weekday of given month

Week of month dates

One useful frequency class is "week of month", starting with WOM. This enables you to get dates like the third Friday of each month:

```
In [93]: rng = pd.date_range('1/1/2012', '9/1/2012', freq='WOM-3FRI')

In [94]: list(rng)
Out[94]:
[Timestamp('2012-01-20 00:00:00', offset='WOM-3FRI'),
 Timestamp('2012-02-17 00:00:00', offset='WOM-3FRI'),
 Timestamp('2012-03-16 00:00:00', offset='WOM-3FRI'),
 Timestamp('2012-04-20 00:00:00', offset='WOM-3FRI'),
 Timestamp('2012-05-18 00:00:00', offset='WOM-3FRI'),
 Timestamp('2012-06-15 00:00:00', offset='WOM-3FRI'),
 Timestamp('2012-07-20 00:00:00', offset='WOM-3FRI'),
 Timestamp('2012-08-17 00:00:00', offset='WOM-3FRI')]
```

Traders of US equity options will recognize these dates as the standard dates of monthly expiry.

Shifting (Leading and Lagging) Data

"Shifting" refers to moving data backward and forward through time. Both Series and DataFrame have a shift method for doing naive shifts forward or backward, leaving the index unmodified:

```
In [95]: ts = Series(np.random.randn(4),
   ....:             index=pd.date_range('1/1/2000', periods=4, freq='M'))
```

```
In [96]: ts                    In [97]: ts.shift(2)          In [98]: ts.shift(-2)
Out[96]:                       Out[97]:                      Out[98]:
2000-01-31   -0.066748         2000-01-31        NaN         2000-01-31   -0.117388
2000-02-29    0.838639         2000-02-29        NaN         2000-02-29   -0.517795
2000-03-31   -0.117388         2000-03-31   -0.066748        2000-03-31        NaN
2000-04-30   -0.517795         2000-04-30    0.838639        2000-04-30        NaN
Freq: M, dtype: float64        Freq: M, dtype: float64       Freq: M, dtype: float64
```

A common use of shift is computing percent changes in a time series or multiple time series as DataFrame columns. This is expressed as

```
ts / ts.shift(1) - 1
```

Because naive shifts leave the index unmodified, some data is discarded. Thus if the frequency is known, it can be passed to shift to advance the timestamps instead of simply the data:

```
In [99]: ts.shift(2, freq='M')
Out[99]:
2000-03-31   -0.066748
2000-04-30    0.838639
2000-05-31   -0.117388
2000-06-30   -0.517795
Freq: M, dtype: float64
```

Other frequencies can be passed, too, giving you a lot of flexibility in how to lead and lag the data:

```
In [100]: ts.shift(3, freq='D')        In [101]: ts.shift(1, freq='3D')
Out[100]:                              Out[101]:
2000-02-03   -0.066748                 2000-02-03   -0.066748
2000-03-03    0.838639                 2000-03-03    0.838639
2000-04-03   -0.117388                 2000-04-03   -0.117388
2000-05-03   -0.517795                 2000-05-03   -0.517795
dtype: float64                         dtype: float64
```

```
In [102]: ts.shift(1, freq='90T')
Out[102]:
2000-01-31 01:30:00   -0.066748
2000-02-29 01:30:00    0.838639
2000-03-31 01:30:00   -0.117388
2000-04-30 01:30:00   -0.517795
dtype: float64
```

Shifting dates with offsets

The pandas date offsets can also be used with datetime or Timestamp objects:

```
In [103]: from pandas.tseries.offsets import Day, MonthEnd
```

```
In [104]: now = datetime(2011, 11, 17)
```

```
In [105]: now + 3 * Day()
Out[105]: Timestamp('2011-11-20 00:00:00')
```

If you add an anchored offset like MonthEnd, the first increment will roll forward a date to the next date according to the frequency rule:

```
In [106]: now + MonthEnd()
Out[106]: Timestamp('2011-11-30 00:00:00')
```

```
In [107]: now + MonthEnd(2)
Out[107]: Timestamp('2011-12-31 00:00:00')
```

Anchored offsets can explicitly "roll" dates forward or backward using their rollforward and rollback methods, respectively:

```
In [108]: offset = MonthEnd()
```

```
In [109]: offset.rollforward(now)
Out[109]: Timestamp('2011-11-30 00:00:00')
```

```
In [110]: offset.rollback(now)
Out[110]: Timestamp('2011-10-31 00:00:00')
```

A clever use of date offsets is to use these methods with `groupby`:

```
In [111]: ts = Series(np.random.randn(20),
   .....:             index=pd.date_range('1/15/2000', periods=20, freq='4d'))

In [112]: ts.groupby(offset.rollforward).mean()
Out[112]:
2000-01-31   -0.005833
2000-02-29    0.015894
2000-03-31    0.150209
dtype: float64
```

Of course, an easier and faster way to do this is using `resample` (much more on this later):

```
In [113]: ts.resample('M', how='mean')
Out[113]:
2000-01-31   -0.005833
2000-02-29    0.015894
2000-03-31    0.150209
Freq: M, dtype: float64
```

Time Zone Handling

Working with time zones is generally considered one of the most unpleasant parts of time series manipulation. In particular, daylight savings time (DST) transitions are a common source of complication. As such, many time series users choose to work with time series in *coordinated universal time* or *UTC*, which is the successor to Greenwich Mean Time and is the current international standard. Time zones are expressed as offsets from UTC; for example, New York is four hours behind UTC during daylight savings time and 5 hours the rest of the year.

In Python, time zone information comes from the 3rd party `pytz` library, which exposes the *Olson database*, a compilation of world time zone information. This is especially important for historical data because the DST transition dates (and even UTC offsets) have been changed numerous times depending on the whims of local governments. In the United States,the DST transition times have been changed many times since 1900!

For detailed information about `pytz` library, you'll need to look at that library's documentation. As far as this book is concerned, pandas wraps `pytz`'s functionality so you can ignore its API outside of the time zone names. Time zone names can be found interactively and in the docs:

```
In [114]: import pytz
```

```
In [115]: pytz.common_timezones[-5:]
Out[115]: ['US/Eastern', 'US/Hawaii', 'US/Mountain', 'US/Pacific', 'UTC']
```

To get a time zone object from `pytz`, use `pytz.timezone`:

```
In [116]: tz = pytz.timezone('US/Eastern')

In [117]: tz
Out[117]: <DstTzInfo 'US/Eastern' LMT-1 day, 19:04:00 STD>
```

Methods in pandas will accept either time zone names or these objects. I recommend just using the names.

Localization and Conversion

By default, time series in pandas are *time zone naive*. Consider the following time series:

```
rng = pd.date_range('3/9/2012 9:30', periods=6, freq='D')
ts = Series(np.random.randn(len(rng)), index=rng)
```

The index's tz field is None:

```
In [119]: print(ts.index.tz)
None
```

Date ranges can be generated with a time zone set:

```
In [120]: pd.date_range('3/9/2012 9:30', periods=10, freq='D', tz='UTC')
Out[120]:
<class 'pandas.tseries.index.DatetimeIndex'>
[2012-03-09 09:30:00+00:00, ..., 2012-03-18 09:30:00+00:00]
Length: 10, Freq: D, Timezone: UTC
```

Conversion from naive to *localized* is handled by the tz_localize method:

```
In [121]: ts_utc = ts.tz_localize('UTC')

In [122]: ts_utc
Out[122]:
2012-03-09 09:30:00+00:00   -0.202469
2012-03-10 09:30:00+00:00    0.050718
2012-03-11 09:30:00+00:00    0.639869
2012-03-12 09:30:00+00:00    0.597594
2012-03-13 09:30:00+00:00   -0.797246
2012-03-14 09:30:00+00:00    0.472879
Freq: D, dtype: float64

In [123]: ts_utc.index
Out[123]:
<class 'pandas.tseries.index.DatetimeIndex'>
[2012-03-09 09:30:00+00:00, ..., 2012-03-14 09:30:00+00:00]
Length: 6, Freq: D, Timezone: UTC
```

Once a time series has been localized to a particular time zone, it can be converted to another time zone using tz_convert:

```
In [124]: ts_utc.tz_convert('US/Eastern')
Out[124]:
2012-03-09 04:30:00-05:00   -0.202469
2012-03-10 04:30:00-05:00    0.050718
2012-03-11 05:30:00-04:00    0.639869
2012-03-12 05:30:00-04:00    0.597594
```

```
2012-03-13 05:30:00-04:00    -0.797246
2012-03-14 05:30:00-04:00     0.472879
Freq: D, dtype: float64
```

In the case of the above time series, which straddles a DST transition in the US/Eastern time zone, we could localize to EST and convert to, say, UTC or Berlin time:

```
In [125]: ts_eastern = ts.tz_localize('US/Eastern')

In [126]: ts_eastern.tz_convert('UTC')
Out[126]:
2012-03-09 14:30:00+00:00    -0.202469
2012-03-10 14:30:00+00:00     0.050718
2012-03-11 13:30:00+00:00     0.639869
2012-03-12 13:30:00+00:00     0.597594
2012-03-13 13:30:00+00:00    -0.797246
2012-03-14 13:30:00+00:00     0.472879
Freq: D, dtype: float64

In [127]: ts_eastern.tz_convert('Europe/Berlin')
Out[127]:
2012-03-09 15:30:00+01:00    -0.202469
2012-03-10 15:30:00+01:00     0.050718
2012-03-11 14:30:00+01:00     0.639869
2012-03-12 14:30:00+01:00     0.597594
2012-03-13 14:30:00+01:00    -0.797246
2012-03-14 14:30:00+01:00     0.472879
Freq: D, dtype: float64
```

tz_localize and tz_convert are also instance methods on DatetimeIndex:

```
In [128]: ts.index.tz_localize('Asia/Shanghai')
Out[128]:
<class 'pandas.tseries.index.DatetimeIndex'>
[2012-03-09 09:30:00+08:00, ..., 2012-03-14 09:30:00+08:00]
Length: 6, Freq: D, Timezone: Asia/Shanghai
```

 Localizing naive timestamps also checks for ambiguous or non-existent times around daylight savings time transitions.

Operations with Time Zone–aware Timestamp Objects

Similar to time series and date ranges, individual Timestamp objects similarly can be localized from naive to time zone-aware and converted from one time zone to another:

```
In [129]: stamp = pd.Timestamp('2011-03-12 04:00')

In [130]: stamp_utc = stamp.tz_localize('utc')

In [131]: stamp_utc.tz_convert('US/Eastern')
Out[131]: Timestamp('2011-03-11 23:00:00-0500', tz='US/Eastern')
```

You can also pass a time zone when creating the Timestamp:

```
In [132]: stamp_moscow = pd.Timestamp('2011-03-12 04:00', tz='Europe/Moscow')

In [133]: stamp_moscow
Out[133]: Timestamp('2011-03-12 04:00:00+0300', tz='Europe/Moscow')
```

Time zone-aware Timestamp objects internally store a UTC timestamp value as nanoseconds since the UNIX epoch (January 1, 1970); this UTC value is invariant between time zone conversions:

```
In [134]: stamp_utc.value
Out[134]: 1299902400000000000

In [135]: stamp_utc.tz_convert('US/Eastern').value
Out[135]: 1299902400000000000
```

When performing time arithmetic using pandas's DateOffset objects, daylight savings time transitions are respected where possible:

```
# 30 minutes before DST transition
from pandas.tseries.offsets import Hour
stamp = pd.Timestamp('2012-03-12 01:30', tz='US/Eastern')
stamp
stamp + Hour()

# 90 minutes before DST transition
stamp = pd.Timestamp('2012-11-04 00:30', tz='US/Eastern')
stamp
stamp + 2 * Hour()
```

Operations between Different Time Zones

If two time series with different time zones are combined, the result will be UTC. Since the timestamps are stored under the hood in UTC, this is a straightforward operation and requires no conversion to happen:

```
In [140]: rng = pd.date_range('3/7/2012 9:30', periods=10, freq='B')

In [141]: ts = Series(np.random.randn(len(rng)), index=rng)

In [142]: ts
Out[142]:
2012-03-07 09:30:00     0.522356
2012-03-08 09:30:00    -0.546348
2012-03-09 09:30:00    -0.733537
2012-03-12 09:30:00     1.302736
2012-03-13 09:30:00     0.022199
2012-03-14 09:30:00     0.364287
2012-03-15 09:30:00    -0.922839
2012-03-16 09:30:00     0.312656
2012-03-19 09:30:00    -1.128497
2012-03-20 09:30:00    -0.333488
Freq: B, dtype: float64

In [143]: ts1 = ts[:7].tz_localize('Europe/London')
```

```
In [144]: ts2 = ts1[2:].tz_convert('Europe/Moscow')

In [145]: result = ts1 + ts2

In [146]: result.index
Out[146]:
<class 'pandas.tseries.index.DatetimeIndex'>
[2012-03-07 09:30:00+00:00, ..., 2012-03-15 09:30:00+00:00]
Length: 7, Freq: B, Timezone: UTC
```

Periods and Period Arithmetic

Periods represent time spans, like days, months, quarters, or years. The `Period` class represents this data type, requiring a string or integer and a frequency from the above table:

```
In [147]: p = pd.Period(2007, freq='A-DEC')

In [148]: p
Out[148]: Period('2007', 'A-DEC')
```

In this case, the `Period` object represents the full timespan from January 1, 2007 to December 31, 2007, inclusive. Conveniently, adding and subtracting integers from periods has the effect of shifting by their frequency:

```
In [149]: p + 5                          In [150]: p - 2
Out[149]: Period('2012', 'A-DEC')        Out[150]: Period('2005', 'A-DEC')
```

If two periods have the same frequency, their difference is the number of units between them:

```
In [151]: pd.Period('2014', freq='A-DEC') - p
Out[151]: 7
```

Regular ranges of periods can be constructed using the `period_range` function:

```
In [152]: rng = pd.period_range('1/1/2000', '6/30/2000', freq='M')

In [153]: rng
Out[153]:
<class 'pandas.tseries.period.PeriodIndex'>
[2000-01, ..., 2000-06]
Length: 6, Freq: M
```

The `PeriodIndex` class stores a sequence of periods and can serve as an axis index in any pandas data structure:

```
In [154]: Series(np.random.randn(6), index=rng)
Out[154]:
2000-01   -0.514551
2000-02   -0.559782
2000-03   -0.783408
2000-04   -1.797685
2000-05   -0.172670
```

```
2000-06    0.680215
Freq: M, dtype: float64
```

If you have an array of strings, you can also appeal to the `PeriodIndex` class itself:

```
In [155]: values = ['2001Q3', '2002Q2', '2003Q1']

In [156]: index = pd.PeriodIndex(values, freq='Q-DEC')

In [157]: index
Out[157]:
<class 'pandas.tseries.period.PeriodIndex'>
[2001Q3, ..., 2003Q1]
Length: 3, Freq: Q-DEC
```

Period Frequency Conversion

Periods and `PeriodIndex` objects can be converted to another frequency using their `asfreq` method. As an example, suppose we had an annual period and wanted to convert it into a monthly period either at the start or end of the year. This is fairly straightforward:

```
In [158]: p = pd.Period('2007', freq='A-DEC')
```

```
In [159]: p.asfreq('M', how='start')       In [160]: p.asfreq('M', how='end')
Out[159]: Period('2007-01', 'M')           Out[160]: Period('2007-12', 'M')
```

You can think of `Period('2007', 'A-DEC')` as being a cursor pointing to a span of time, subdivided by monthly periods. See Figure 10-1 for an illustration of this. For a *fiscal year* ending on a month other than December, the monthly subperiods belonging are different:

```
In [161]: p = pd.Period('2007', freq='A-JUN')
```

```
In [162]: p.asfreq('M', 'start')       In [163]: p.asfreq('M', 'end')
Out[162]: Period('2006-07', 'M')       Out[163]: Period('2007-06', 'M')
```

When converting from high to low frequency, the superperiod will be determined depending on where the subperiod "belongs". For example, in `A-JUN` frequency, the month `Aug-2007` is actually part of the 2008 period:

```
In [164]: p = pd.Period('Aug-2007', 'M')
```

```
In [165]: p.asfreq('A-JUN')
Out[165]: Period('2008', 'A-JUN')
```

Whole `PeriodIndex` objects or TimeSeries can be similarly converted with the same semantics:

```
In [166]: rng = pd.period_range('2006', '2009', freq='A-DEC')
```

```
In [167]: ts = Series(np.random.randn(len(rng)), index=rng)
```

```
In [168]: ts
Out[168]:
```

```
2006    1.607578
2007    0.200381
2008   -0.834068
2009   -0.302988
Freq: A-DEC, dtype: float64
```

```
In [169]: ts.asfreq('M', how='start')      In [170]: ts.asfreq('B', how='end')
Out[169]:                                   Out[170]:
2006-01    1.607578                          2006-12-29    1.607578
2007-01    0.200381                          2007-12-31    0.200381
2008-01   -0.834068                          2008-12-31   -0.834068
2009-01   -0.302988                          2009-12-31   -0.302988
Freq: M, dtype: float64                     Freq: B, dtype: float64
```

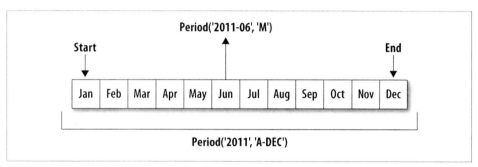

Figure 10-1. Period frequency conversion illustration

Quarterly Period Frequencies

Quarterly data is standard in accounting, finance, and other fields. Much quarterly data is reported relative to a *fiscal year end*, typically the last calendar or business day of one of the 12 months of the year. As such, the period 2012Q4 has a different meaning depending on fiscal year end. pandas supports all 12 possible quarterly frequencies as Q-JAN through Q-DEC:

```
In [171]: p = pd.Period('2012Q4', freq='Q-JAN')
```

```
In [172]: p
Out[172]: Period('2012Q4', 'Q-JAN')
```

In the case of fiscal year ending in January, 2012Q4 runs from November through January, which you can check by converting to daily frequency. See Figure 10-2 for an illustration:

```
In [173]: p.asfreq('D', 'start')      In [174]: p.asfreq('D', 'end')
Out[173]: Period('2011-11-01', 'D')   Out[174]: Period('2012-01-31', 'D')
```

Thus, it's possible to do period arithmetic very easily; for example, to get the timestamp at 4PM on the 2nd to last business day of the quarter, you could do:

```
In [175]: p4pm = (p.asfreq('B', 'e') - 1).asfreq('T', 's') + 16 * 60

In [176]: p4pm
Out[176]: Period('2012-01-30 16:00', 'T')

In [177]: p4pm.to_timestamp()
Out[177]: Timestamp('2012-01-30 16:00:00')
```

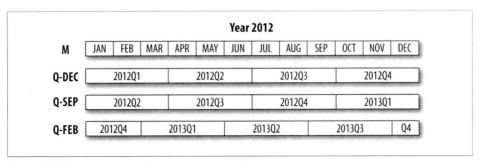

Figure 10-2. Different quarterly frequency conventions

Generating quarterly ranges works as you would expect using period_range. Arithmetic is identical, too:

```
In [178]: rng = pd.period_range('2011Q3', '2012Q4', freq='Q-JAN')

In [179]: ts = Series(np.arange(len(rng)), index=rng)

In [180]: ts
Out[180]:
2011Q3    0
2011Q4    1
2012Q1    2
2012Q2    3
2012Q3    4
2012Q4    5
Freq: Q-JAN, dtype: int64

In [181]: new_rng = (rng.asfreq('B', 'e') - 1).asfreq('T', 's') + 16 * 60

In [182]: ts.index = new_rng.to_timestamp()

In [183]: ts
Out[183]:
2010-10-28 16:00:00    0
2011-01-28 16:00:00    1
2011-04-28 16:00:00    2
2011-07-28 16:00:00    3
2011-10-28 16:00:00    4
2012-01-30 16:00:00    5
dtype: int64
```

Converting Timestamps to Periods (and Back)

Series and DataFrame objects indexed by timestamps can be converted to periods using the to_period method:

```
In [184]: rng = pd.date_range('1/1/2000', periods=3, freq='M')

In [185]: ts = Series(randn(3), index=rng)

In [186]: pts = ts.to_period()

In [187]: ts                       In [188]: pts
Out[187]:                          Out[188]:
2000-01-31    1.663261             2000-01     1.663261
2000-02-29   -0.996206             2000-02    -0.996206
2000-03-31    1.521760             2000-03     1.521760
Freq: M, dtype: float64           Freq: M, dtype: float64
```

Since periods always refer to non-overlapping timespans, a timestamp can only belong to a single period for a given frequency. While the frequency of the new PeriodIndex is inferred from the timestamps by default, you can specify any frequency you want. There is also no problem with having duplicate periods in the result:

```
In [189]: rng = pd.date_range('1/29/2000', periods=6, freq='D')

In [190]: ts2 = Series(randn(6), index=rng)

In [191]: ts2.to_period('M')
Out[191]:
2000-01     0.244175
2000-01     0.423331
2000-01    -0.654040
2000-02     2.089154
2000-02    -0.060220
2000-02    -0.167933
Freq: M, dtype: float64
```

To convert back to timestamps, use to_timestamp:

```
In [192]: pts = ts.to_period()

In [193]: pts
Out[193]:
2000-01     1.663261
2000-02    -0.996206
2000-03     1.521760
Freq: M, dtype: float64

In [194]: pts.to_timestamp(how='end')
Out[194]:
2000-01-31    1.663261
2000-02-29   -0.996206
2000-03-31    1.521760
Freq: M, dtype: float64
```

Creating a PeriodIndex from Arrays

Fixed frequency data sets are sometimes stored with timespan information spread across multiple columns. For example, in this macroeconomic data set, the year and quarter are in different columns:

```
In [195]: data = pd.read_csv('ch08/macrodata.csv')
```

```
In [196]: data.year                      In [197]: data.quarter
Out[196]:                                Out[197]:
0     1959                               0     1
1     1959                               1     2
2     1959                               2     3
3     1959                               3     4
...                                      ...
199   2008                               199   4
200   2009                               200   1
201   2009                               201   2
202   2009                               202   3
Name: year, Length: 203, dtype: float64  Name: quarter, Length: 203, dtype: float64
```

By passing these arrays to PeriodIndex with a frequency, they can be combined to form an index for the DataFrame:

```
In [198]: index = pd.PeriodIndex(year=data.year, quarter=data.quarter, freq='Q-DEC')
```

```
In [199]: index
Out[199]:
<class 'pandas.tseries.period.PeriodIndex'>
[1959Q1, ..., 2009Q3]
Length: 203, Freq: Q-DEC
```

```
In [200]: data.index = index
```

```
In [201]: data.infl
Out[201]:
1959Q1    0.00
1959Q2    2.34
1959Q3    2.74
1959Q4    0.27
...
2008Q4   -8.79
2009Q1    0.94
2009Q2    3.37
2009Q3    3.56
Freq: Q-DEC, Name: infl, Length: 203
```

Resampling and Frequency Conversion

Resampling refers to the process of converting a time series from one frequency to another. Aggregating higher frequency data to lower frequency is called *downsampling*, while converting lower frequency to higher frequency is called *upsampling*. Not all resampling falls into either of these categories; for example, converting W-WED (weekly on Wednesday) to W-FRI is neither upsampling nor downsampling.

pandas objects are equipped with a `resample` method, which is the workhorse function for all frequency conversion:

```
In [202]: rng = pd.date_range('1/1/2000', periods=100, freq='D')

In [203]: ts = Series(randn(len(rng)), index=rng)

In [204]: ts.resample('M', how='mean')
Out[204]:
2000-01-31   -0.165893
2000-02-29    0.078606
2000-03-31    0.223811
2000-04-30   -0.063643
Freq: M, dtype: float64

In [205]: ts.resample('M', how='mean', kind='period')
Out[205]:
2000-01   -0.165893
2000-02    0.078606
2000-03    0.223811
2000-04   -0.063643
Freq: M, dtype: float64
```

`resample` is a flexible and high-performance method that can be used to process very large time series. I'll illustrate its semantics and use through a series of examples.

Table 10-5. Resample method arguments

Argument	Description
freq	String or DateOffset indicating desired resampled frequency, e.g. 'M', '5min', or Second(15)
how='mean'	Function name or array function producing aggregated value, for example 'mean', 'ohlc', np.max. Defaults to 'mean'. Other common values: 'first', 'last', 'median', 'ohlc', 'max', 'min'.
axis=0	Axis to resample on, default axis=0
fill_method=None	How to interpolate when upsampling, as in 'ffill' or 'bfill'. By default does no interpolation.
closed='None'	In downsampling, which end of each interval is closed (inclusive), 'right' or 'left'.
label='None'	In downsampling, how to label the aggregated result, with the 'right' or 'left' bin edge. For example, the 9:30 to 9:35 5-minute interval could be labeled 9:30 or 9:35.

Argument	Description
loffset=None	Time adjustment to the bin labels, such as '-1s' / Second(-1) to shift the aggregate labels one second earlier
limit=None	When forward or backward filling, the maximum number of periods to fill
kind=None	Aggregate to periods ('period') or timestamps ('timestamp'); defaults to kind of index the time series has
convention=None	When resampling periods, the convention ('start' or 'end') for converting the low frequency period to high frequency. Defaults to 'end'

Downsampling

Aggregating data to a regular, lower frequency is a pretty normal time series task. The data you're aggregating doesn't need to be fixed frequently; the desired frequency defines *bin edges* that are used to slice the time series into pieces to aggregate. For example, to convert to monthly, 'M' or 'BM', the data need to be chopped up into one month intervals. Each interval is said to be *half-open*; a data point can only belong to one interval, and the union of the intervals must make up the whole time frame. There are a couple things to think about when using resample to downsample data:

* Which side of each interval is *closed*
* How to label each aggregated bin, either with the start of the interval or the end

To illustrate, let's look at some one-minute data:

```
In [206]: rng = pd.date_range('1/1/2000', periods=12, freq='T')

In [207]: ts = Series(np.arange(12), index=rng)

In [208]: ts
Out[208]:
2000-01-01 00:00:00     0
2000-01-01 00:01:00     1
2000-01-01 00:02:00     2
2000-01-01 00:03:00     3
2000-01-01 00:04:00     4
2000-01-01 00:05:00     5
2000-01-01 00:06:00     6
2000-01-01 00:07:00     7
2000-01-01 00:08:00     8
2000-01-01 00:09:00     9
2000-01-01 00:10:00    10
2000-01-01 00:11:00    11
Freq: T, dtype: int64
```

Suppose you wanted to aggregate this data into five-minute chunks or *bars* by taking the sum of each group:

```
In [209]: ts.resample('5min', how='sum')
Out[209]:
2000-01-01 00:00:00    10
```

```
2000-01-01 00:05:00   35
2000-01-01 00:10:00   21
Freq: 5T, dtype: int64
```

The frequency you pass defines bin edges in five-minute increments. By default, the *left* bin edge is inclusive, so the `00:00` value is included in the `00:00` to `00:05` interval.[1] Passing `closed='right'` changes the interval to be closed on the right:

```
In [210]: ts.resample('5min', how='sum', closed='right')
Out[210]:
1999-12-31 23:55:00    0
2000-01-01 00:00:00   15
2000-01-01 00:05:00   40
2000-01-01 00:10:00   11
Freq: 5T, dtype: int64
```

As you can see, the resulting time series is labeled by the timestamps from the left side of each bin. By passing `label='right'` you can label them with the right bin edge:

```
In [211]: ts.resample('5min', how='sum', closed='right', label='right')
Out[211]:
2000-01-01 00:00:00    0
2000-01-01 00:05:00   15
2000-01-01 00:10:00   40
2000-01-01 00:15:00   11
Freq: 5T, dtype: int64
```

See Figure 10-3 for an illustration of minutely data being resampled to five-minute.

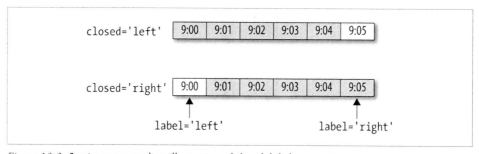

Figure 10-3. 5-minute resampling illustration of closed, label conventions

Lastly, you might want to shift the result index by some amount, say subtracting one second from the right edge to make it more clear which interval the timestamp refers to. To do this, pass a string or date offset to `loffset`:

```
In [212]: ts.resample('5min', how='sum', closed='right', label='right', loffset='-1s')
Out[212]:
1999-12-31 23:59:59    0
```

1. The choice of the default values for `closed` and `label` might seem a bit odd to some users. In practice the choice is somewhat arbitrary; for some target frequencies, `closed='left'` is preferable, while for others `closed='right'` makes more sense. The important thing is that you keep in mind exactly how you are segmenting the data.

```
2000-01-01 00:04:59    15
2000-01-01 00:09:59    40
2000-01-01 00:14:59    11
Freq: 5T, dtype: int64
```

This also could have been accomplished by calling the `shift` method on the result without the `loffset`.

Open-High-Low-Close (OHLC) resampling

In finance, an ubiquitous way to aggregate a time series is to compute four values for each bucket: the first (open), last (close), maximum (high), and minimal (low) values. By passing `how='ohlc'` you will obtain a DataFrame having columns containing these four aggregates, which are efficiently computed in a single sweep of the data:

```
In [213]: ts.resample('5min', how='ohlc')
Out[213]:
                     open  high  low  close
2000-01-01 00:00:00     0     4    0      4
2000-01-01 00:05:00     5     9    5      9
2000-01-01 00:10:00    10    11   10     11
```

Resampling with GroupBy

An alternate way to downsample is to use pandas's groupby functionality. For example, you can group by month or weekday by passing a function that accesses those fields on the time series's index:

```
In [214]: rng = pd.date_range('1/1/2000', periods=100, freq='D')

In [215]: ts = Series(np.arange(100), index=rng)

In [216]: ts.groupby(lambda x: x.month).mean()
Out[216]:
1    15
2    45
3    75
4    95
dtype: int64

In [217]: ts.groupby(lambda x: x.weekday).mean()
Out[217]:
0    47.5
1    48.5
2    49.5
3    50.5
4    51.5
5    49.0
6    50.0
dtype: float64
```

Upsampling and Interpolation

When converting from a low frequency to a higher frequency, no aggregation is needed. Let's consider a DataFrame with some weekly data:

```
In [218]: frame = DataFrame(np.random.randn(2, 4),
   .....:                   index=pd.date_range('1/1/2000', periods=2, freq='W-WED'),
   .....:                   columns=['Colorado', 'Texas', 'New York', 'Ohio'])

In [219]: frame
Out[219]:
            Colorado     Texas  New York      Ohio
2000-01-05 -0.896431  0.677263  0.036503  0.087102
2000-01-12 -0.046662  0.927238  0.482284 -0.867130
```

When resampling this to daily frequency, by default missing values are introduced:

```
In [220]: df_daily = frame.resample('D')

In [221]: df_daily
Out[221]:
            Colorado     Texas  New York      Ohio
2000-01-05 -0.896431  0.677263  0.036503  0.087102
2000-01-06       NaN       NaN       NaN       NaN
2000-01-07       NaN       NaN       NaN       NaN
2000-01-08       NaN       NaN       NaN       NaN
2000-01-09       NaN       NaN       NaN       NaN
2000-01-10       NaN       NaN       NaN       NaN
2000-01-11       NaN       NaN       NaN       NaN
2000-01-12 -0.046662  0.927238  0.482284 -0.867130
```

Suppose you wanted to fill forward each weekly value on the non-Wednesdays. The same filling or interpolation methods available in the `fillna` and `reindex` methods are available for resampling:

```
In [222]: frame.resample('D', fill_method='ffill')
Out[222]:
            Colorado     Texas  New York      Ohio
2000-01-05 -0.896431  0.677263  0.036503  0.087102
2000-01-06 -0.896431  0.677263  0.036503  0.087102
2000-01-07 -0.896431  0.677263  0.036503  0.087102
2000-01-08 -0.896431  0.677263  0.036503  0.087102
2000-01-09 -0.896431  0.677263  0.036503  0.087102
2000-01-10 -0.896431  0.677263  0.036503  0.087102
2000-01-11 -0.896431  0.677263  0.036503  0.087102
2000-01-12 -0.046662  0.927238  0.482284 -0.867130
```

You can similarly choose to only fill a certain number of periods forward to limit how far to continue using an observed value:

```
In [223]: frame.resample('D', fill_method='ffill', limit=2)
Out[223]:
            Colorado     Texas  New York      Ohio
2000-01-05 -0.896431  0.677263  0.036503  0.087102
2000-01-06 -0.896431  0.677263  0.036503  0.087102
2000-01-07 -0.896431  0.677263  0.036503  0.087102
```

```
2000-01-08      NaN       NaN       NaN        NaN
2000-01-09      NaN       NaN       NaN        NaN
2000-01-10      NaN       NaN       NaN        NaN
2000-01-11      NaN       NaN       NaN        NaN
2000-01-12 -0.046662  0.927238  0.482284 -0.867130
```

Notably, the new date index need not overlap with the old one at all:

```
In [224]: frame.resample('W-THU', fill_method='ffill')
Out[224]:
             Colorado     Texas  New York      Ohio
2000-01-06 -0.896431  0.677263  0.036503  0.087102
2000-01-13 -0.046662  0.927238  0.482284 -0.867130
```

Resampling with Periods

Resampling data indexed by periods is reasonably straightforward and works as you would hope:

```
In [225]: frame = DataFrame(np.random.randn(24, 4),
   .....:                   index=pd.period_range('1-2000', '12-2001', freq='M'),
   .....:                   columns=['Colorado', 'Texas', 'New York', 'Ohio'])

In [226]: frame[:5]
Out[226]:
         Colorado     Texas  New York      Ohio
2000-01  0.493841 -0.155434  1.397286  1.507055
2000-02 -1.179442  0.443171  1.395676 -0.529658
2000-03  0.787358  0.248845  0.743239  1.267746
2000-04  1.302395 -0.272154 -0.051532 -0.467740
2000-05 -1.040816  0.426419  0.312945 -1.115689

In [227]: annual_frame = frame.resample('A-DEC', how='mean')

In [228]: annual_frame
Out[228]:
      Colorado     Texas  New York      Ohio
2000  0.556703  0.016631  0.111873 -0.027445
2001  0.046303  0.163344  0.251503 -0.157276
```

Upsampling is more nuanced as you must make a decision about which end of the timespan in the new frequency to place the values before resampling, just like the asfreq method. The convention argument defaults to 'end' but can also be 'start':

```
# Q-DEC: Quarterly, year ending in December
In [229]: annual_frame.resample('Q-DEC', fill_method='ffill')
Out[229]:
        Colorado     Texas  New York      Ohio
2000Q1  0.556703  0.016631  0.111873 -0.027445
2000Q2  0.556703  0.016631  0.111873 -0.027445
2000Q3  0.556703  0.016631  0.111873 -0.027445
2000Q4  0.556703  0.016631  0.111873 -0.027445
2001Q1  0.046303  0.163344  0.251503 -0.157276
2001Q2  0.046303  0.163344  0.251503 -0.157276
2001Q3  0.046303  0.163344  0.251503 -0.157276
```

```
2001Q4  0.046303  0.163344  0.251503 -0.157276

In [230]: annual_frame.resample('Q-DEC', fill_method='ffill', convention='start')
Out[230]:
        Colorado    Texas  New York      Ohio
2000Q1  0.556703  0.016631  0.111873 -0.027445
2000Q2  0.556703  0.016631  0.111873 -0.027445
2000Q3  0.556703  0.016631  0.111873 -0.027445
2000Q4  0.556703  0.016631  0.111873 -0.027445
2001Q1  0.046303  0.163344  0.251503 -0.157276
2001Q2  0.046303  0.163344  0.251503 -0.157276
2001Q3  0.046303  0.163344  0.251503 -0.157276
2001Q4  0.046303  0.163344  0.251503 -0.157276
```

Since periods refer to timespans, the rules about upsampling and downsampling are more rigid:

- In downsampling, the target frequency must be a *subperiod* of the source frequency.
- In upsampling, the target frequency must be a *superperiod* of the source frequency.

If these rules are not satisfied, an exception will be raised. This mainly affects the quarterly, annual, and weekly frequencies; for example, the timespans defined by Q-MAR only line up with A-MAR, A-JUN, A-SEP, and A-DEC:

```
In [231]: annual_frame.resample('Q-MAR', fill_method='ffill')
Out[231]:
        Colorado    Texas  New York      Ohio
2000Q4  0.556703  0.016631  0.111873 -0.027445
2001Q1  0.556703  0.016631  0.111873 -0.027445
2001Q2  0.556703  0.016631  0.111873 -0.027445
2001Q3  0.556703  0.016631  0.111873 -0.027445
2001Q4  0.046303  0.163344  0.251503 -0.157276
2002Q1  0.046303  0.163344  0.251503 -0.157276
2002Q2  0.046303  0.163344  0.251503 -0.157276
2002Q3  0.046303  0.163344  0.251503 -0.157276
```

Time Series Plotting

Plots with pandas time series have improved date formatting compared with matplotlib out of the box. As an example, I downloaded some stock price data on a few common US stock from Yahoo! Finance:

```
In [232]: close_px_all = pd.read_csv('ch09/stock_px.csv', parse_dates=True, index_col=0)

In [233]: close_px = close_px_all[['AAPL', 'MSFT', 'XOM']]

In [234]: close_px = close_px.resample('B', fill_method='ffill')

In [235]: close_px.info()
<class 'pandas.core.frame.DataFrame'>
DatetimeIndex: 2292 entries, 2003-01-02 00:00:00 to 2011-10-14 00:00:00
Freq: B
Data columns (total 3 columns):
```

```
AAPL    2292 non-null float64
MSFT    2292 non-null float64
XOM     2292 non-null float64
dtypes: float64(3)
```

Calling `plot` on one of the columns grenerates a simple plot, seen in Figure 10-4.

```
In [237]: close_px['AAPL'].plot()
```

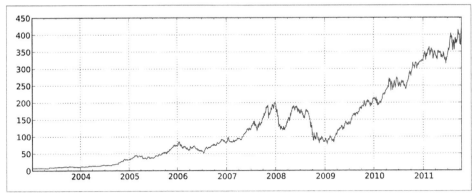

Figure 10-4. AAPL Daily Price

When called on a DataFrame, as you would expect, all of the time series are drawn on a single subplot with a legend indicating which is which. I'll plot only the year 2009 data so you can see how both months and years are formatted on the X axis; see Figure 10-5.

```
In [239]: close_px.ix['2009'].plot()
```

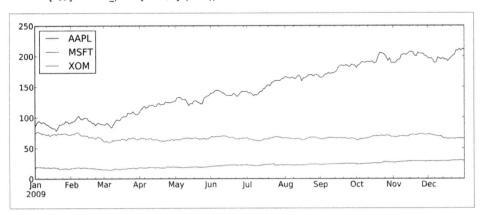

Figure 10-5. Stock Prices in 2009

```
In [241]: close_px['AAPL'].ix['01-2011':'03-2011'].plot()
```

Quarterly frequency data is also more nicely formatted with quarterly markers, something that would be quite a bit more work to do by hand. See Figure 10-7.

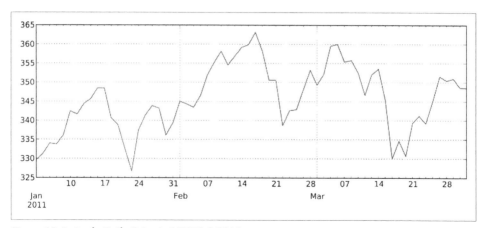

Figure 10-6. Apple Daily Price in 1/2011-3/2011

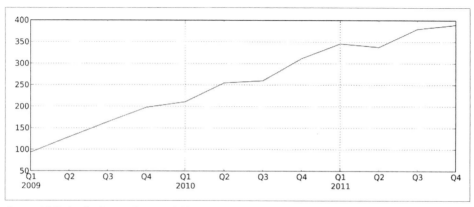

Figure 10-7. Apple Quarterly Price 2009-2011

```
In [243]: appl_q = close_px['AAPL'].resample('Q-DEC', fill_method='ffill')

In [244]: appl_q.ix['2009':].plot()
```

A last feature of time series plotting in pandas is that by right-clicking and dragging to zoom in and out, the dates will be dynamically expanded or contracted and reformatting depending on the timespan contained in the plot view. This is of course only true when using matplotlib in interactive mode.

Moving Window Functions

A common class of array transformations intended for time series operations are statistics and other functions evaluated over a sliding window or with exponentially decaying weights. I call these *moving window functions*, even though it includes functions without a fixed-length window like exponentially-weighted moving average. Like other statistical functions, these also automatically exclude missing data.

`rolling_mean` is one of the simplest such functions. It takes a TimeSeries or DataFrame along with a `window` (expressed as a number of periods):

```
In [248]: close_px.AAPL.plot()
Out[248]: <matplotlib.axes.AxesSubplot at 0xb392ff0c>

In [249]: pd.rolling_mean(close_px.AAPL, 250).plot()
```

See Figure 10-8 for the plot. By default functions like `rolling_mean` require the indicated number of non-NA observations. This behavior can be changed to account for missing data and, in particular, the fact that you will have fewer than `window` periods of data at the beginning of the time series (see Figure 10-9):

```
In [251]: appl_std250 = pd.rolling_std(close_px.AAPL, 250, min_periods=10)

In [252]: appl_std250[5:12]
Out[252]:
2003-01-09         NaN
2003-01-10         NaN
2003-01-13         NaN
2003-01-14         NaN
2003-01-15    0.077496
2003-01-16    0.074760
2003-01-17    0.112368
Freq: B, dtype: float64

In [253]: appl_std250.plot()
```

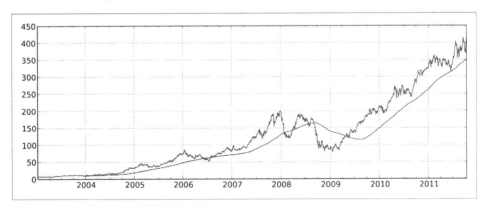

Figure 10-8. Apple Price with 250-day MA

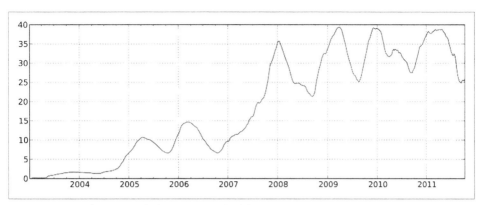

Figure 10-9. Apple 250-day daily return standard deviation

To compute an *expanding window mean*, you can see that an expanding window is just a special case where the window is the length of the time series, but only one or more periods is required to compute a value:

```
# Define expanding mean in terms of rolling_mean
In [254]: expanding_mean = lambda x: rolling_mean(x, len(x), min_periods=1)
```

Calling `rolling_mean` and friends on a DataFrame applies the transformation to each column (see Figure 10-10):

```
In [256]: pd.rolling_mean(close_px, 60).plot(logy=True)
```

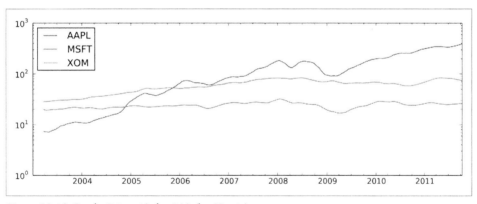

Figure 10-10. Stocks Prices 60-day MA (log Y-axis)

See Table 10-6 for a listing of related functions in pandas.

Table 10-6. Moving window and exponentially-weighted functions

Function	Description
`rolling_count`	Returns number of non-NA observations in each trailing window.
`rolling_sum`	Moving window sum.
`rolling_mean`	Moving window mean.
`rolling_median`	Moving window median.
`rolling_var, rolling_std`	Moving window variance and standard deviation, respectively. Uses n - 1 denominator.
`rolling_skew, rolling_kurt`	Moving window skewness (3rd moment) and kurtosis (4th moment), respectively.
`rolling_min, rolling_max`	Moving window minimum and maximum.
`rolling_quantile`	Moving window score at percentile/sample quantile.
`rolling_corr, rolling_cov`	Moving window correlation and covariance.
`rolling_apply`	Apply generic array function over a moving window.
`ewma`	Exponentially-weighted moving average.
`ewmvar, ewmstd`	Exponentially-weighted moving variance and standard deviation.
`ewmcorr, ewmcov`	Exponentially-weighted moving correlation and covariance.

`bottleneck`, a Python library by Keith Goodman, provides an alternate implementation of NaN-friendly moving window functions and may be worth looking at depending on your application.

Exponentially-weighted functions

An alternative to using a static window size with equally-weighted observations is to specify a constant *decay factor* to give more weight to more recent observations. In mathematical terms, if ma_t is the moving average result at time t and x is the time series in question, each value in the result is computed as $ma_t = a * ma_{t-1} + (1 - a) * x_t$, where a is the decay factor. There are a couple of ways to specify the decay factor, a popular one is using a *span*, which makes the result comparable to a simple moving window function with window size equal to the span.

Since an exponentially-weighted statistic places more weight on more recent observations, it "adapts" faster to changes compared with the equal-weighted version. Here's an example comparing a 60-day moving average of Apple's stock price with an EW moving average with `span=60` (see Figure 10-11):

```
fig, axes = plt.subplots(nrows=2, ncols=1, sharex=True, sharey=True,
                         figsize=(12, 7))

aapl_px = close_px.AAPL['2005':'2009']

ma60 = pd.rolling_mean(aapl_px, 60, min_periods=50)
```

Figure 10-11. Simple moving average versus exponentially-weighted

```
ewma60 = pd.ewma(aapl_px, span=60)

aapl_px.plot(style='k-', ax=axes[0])
ma60.plot(style='k--', ax=axes[0])
aapl_px.plot(style='k-', ax=axes[1])
ewma60.plot(style='k--', ax=axes[1])
axes[0].set_title('Simple MA')
axes[1].set_title('Exponentially-weighted MA')
```

Binary Moving Window Functions

Some statistical operators, like correlation and covariance, need to operate on two time series. As an example, financial analysts are often interested in a stock's correlation to a benchmark index like the S&P 500. We can compute that by computing the percent changes and using `rolling_corr` (see Figure 10-12):

```
In [263]: spx_rets = spx_px / spx_px.shift(1) - 1

In [264]: returns = close_px.pct_change()

In [265]: corr = pd.rolling_corr(returns.AAPL, spx_rets, 125, min_periods=100)

In [266]: corr.plot()
```

Suppose you wanted to compute the correlation of the S&P 500 index with many stocks at once. Writing a loop and creating a new DataFrame would be easy but maybe get repetitive, so if you pass a TimeSeries and a DataFrame, a function like `rolling_corr` will compute the correlation of the TimeSeries (`spx_rets` in this case) with each column in the DataFrame. See Figure 10-13 for the plot of the result:

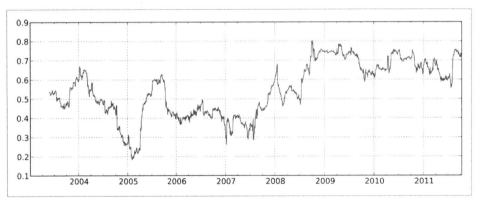

Figure 10-12. Six-month AAPL return correlation to S&P 500

```
In [268]: corr = pd.rolling_corr(returns, spx_rets, 125, min_periods=100)
```

```
In [269]: corr.plot()
```

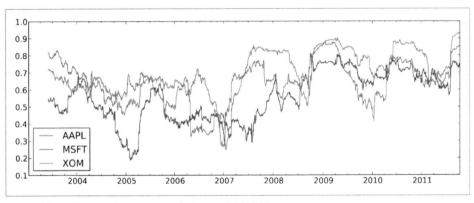

Figure 10-13. Six-month return correlations to S&P 500

User-Defined Moving Window Functions

The `rolling_apply` function provides a means to apply an array function of your own devising over a moving window. The only requirement is that the function produce a single value (a reduction) from each piece of the array. For example, while we can compute sample quantiles using `rolling_quantile`, we might be interested in the percentile rank of a particular value over the sample. The `scipy.stats.percentileof score` function does just this:

```
In [271]: from scipy.stats import percentileofscore
```

```
In [272]: score_at_2percent = lambda x: percentileofscore(x, 0.02)
```

```
In [273]: result = pd.rolling_apply(returns.AAPL, 250, score_at_2percent)
```

```
In [274]: result.plot()
```

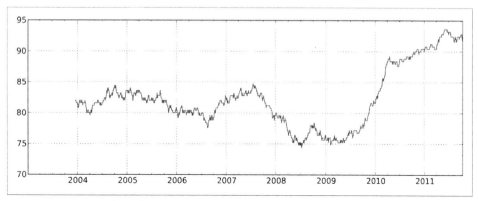

Figure 10-14. Percentile rank of 2% AAPL return over 1 year window

Performance and Memory Usage Notes

Timestamps and periods are represented as 64-bit integers using NumPy's date time64 dtype. This means that for each data point, there is an associated 8 bytes of memory per timestamp. Thus, a time series with 1 million float64 data points has a memory footprint of approximately 16 megabytes. Since pandas makes every effort to share indexes among time series, creating views on existing time series do not cause any more memory to be used. Additionally, indexes for lower frequencies (daily and up) are stored in a central cache, so that any fixed-frequency index is a view on the date cache. Thus, if you have a large collection of low-frequency time series, the memory footprint of the indexes will not be as significant.

Performance-wise, pandas has been highly optimized for data alignment operations (the behind-the-scenes work of differently indexed ts1 + ts2) and resampling. Here is an example of aggregating 10MM data points to OHLC:

```
In [275]: rng = pd.date_range('1/1/2000', periods=10000000, freq='10ms')

In [276]: ts = Series(np.random.randn(len(rng)), index=rng)

In [277]: ts
Out[277]:
2000-01-01 00:00:00              1.543222
2000-01-01 00:00:00.010000       0.887621
2000-01-01 00:00:00.020000      -2.043524
2000-01-01 00:00:00.030000      -0.809157
...
2000-01-02 03:46:39.960000      -1.489348
2000-01-02 03:46:39.970000      -0.194531
2000-01-02 03:46:39.980000       0.967617
2000-01-02 03:46:39.990000       1.605598
```

```
Freq: 10, Length: 10000000

In [278]: ts.resample('15min', how='ohlc').info()
<class 'pandas.core.frame.DataFrame'>
DatetimeIndex: 112 entries, 2000-01-01 00:00:00 to 2000-01-02 03:45:00
Freq: 15T
Data columns (total 4 columns):
open     112 non-null float64
high     112 non-null float64
low      112 non-null float64
close    112 non-null float64
dtypes: float64(4)
In [279]: %timeit ts.resample('15min', how='ohlc')
10 loops, best of 3: 102 ms per loop
```

The runtime may depend slightly on the relative size of the aggregated result; higher frequency aggregates unsurprisingly take longer to compute:

```
In [280]: rng = pd.date_range('1/1/2000', periods=10000000, freq='1s')

In [281]: ts = Series(np.random.randn(len(rng)), index=rng)

In [282]: %timeit ts.resample('15s', how='ohlc')
1 loops, best of 3: 171 ms per loop
```

It's possible that by the time you read this, the performance of these algorithms may be even further improved. As an example, there are currently no optimizations for conversions between regular frequencies, but that would be fairly straightforward to do.

## CHAPTER 11

Financial and Economic Data Applications

The use of Python in the financial industry has been increasing rapidly since 2005, led largely by the maturation of libraries (like NumPy and pandas) and the availability of skilled Python programmers. Institutions have found that Python is well-suited both as an interactive analysis environment as well as enabling robust systems to be developed often in a fraction of the time it would have taken in Java or C++. Python is also an ideal glue layer; it is easy to build Python interfaces to legacy libraries built in C or C++.

While the field of financial analysis is broad enough to fill an entire book, I hope to show you how the tools in this book can be applied to a number of specific problems in finance. As with other research and analysis domains, too much programming effort is often spent wrangling data rather than solving the core modeling and research problems. I personally got started building pandas in 2008 while grappling with inadequate data tools.

In these examples, I'll use the term *cross-section* to refer to data at a fixed point in time. For example, the closing prices of all the stocks in the S&P 500 index on a particular date form a cross-section. Cross-sectional data at multiple points in time over multiple data items (for example, prices together with volume) form a *panel*. Panel data can either be represented as a hierarchically-indexed DataFrame or using the three-dimensional Panel pandas object.

Data Munging Topics

Many helpful data munging tools for financial applications are spread across the earlier chapters. Here I'll highlight a number of topics as they relate to this problem domain.

Time Series and Cross-Section Alignment

One of the most time-consuming issues in working with financial data is the so-called *data alignment* problem. Two related time series may have indexes that don't line up perfectly, or two DataFrame objects might have columns or row labels that don't match. Users of MATLAB, R, and other matrix-programming languages often invest significant effort in wrangling data into perfectly aligned forms. In my experience, having to align data by hand (and worse, having to verify that data is aligned) is a far too rigid and tedious way to work. It is also rife with potential for bugs due to combining misaligned data.

pandas take an alternate approach by automatically aligning data in arithmetic operations. In practice, this grants immense freedom and enhances your productivity. As an example, let's consider a couple of DataFrames containing time series of stock prices and volume:

```
In [16]: prices
Out[16]:
              AAPL    JNJ      SPX    XOM
2011-09-06  379.74  64.64  1165.24  71.15
2011-09-07  383.93  65.43  1198.62  73.65
2011-09-08  384.14  64.95  1185.90  72.82
2011-09-09  377.48  63.64  1154.23  71.01
2011-09-12  379.94  63.59  1162.27  71.84
2011-09-13  384.62  63.61  1172.87  71.65
2011-09-14  389.30  63.73  1188.68  72.64

In [17]: volume
Out[17]:
               AAPL       JNJ       XOM
2011-09-06  18173500  15848300  25416300
2011-09-07  12492000  10759700  23108400
2011-09-08  14839800  15551500  22434800
2011-09-09  20171900  17008200  27969100
2011-09-12  16697300  13448200  26205800
```

Suppose you wanted to compute a volume-weighted average price using all available data (and making the simplifying assumption that the volume data is a subset of the price data). Since pandas aligns the data automatically in arithmetic and excludes missing data in functions like sum, we can express this concisely as:

```
In [18]: prices * volume
Out[18]:
                  AAPL         JNJ  SPX         XOM
2011-09-06  6901204890  1024434112  NaN  1808369745
2011-09-07  4796053560   704007171  NaN  1701933660
2011-09-08  5700560772  1010069925  NaN  1633702136
2011-09-09  7614488812  1082401848  NaN  1986085791
2011-09-12  6343972162   855171038  NaN  1882624672
2011-09-13         NaN         NaN  NaN         NaN
2011-09-14         NaN         NaN  NaN         NaN

In [19]: vwap = (prices * volume).sum() / volume.sum()
```

```
In [20]: vwap                    In [21]: vwap.dropna()
Out[20]:                         Out[21]:
AAPL      380.655181             AAPL      380.655181
JNJ        64.394769             JNJ        64.394769
SPX              NaN             XOM        72.024288
XOM        72.024288             dtype: float64
dtype: float64
```

Since SPX wasn't found in volume, you can choose to explicitly discard that at any point. Should you wish to align by hand, you can use DataFrame's `align` method, which returns a tuple of reindexed versions of the two objects:

```
In [22]: prices.align(volume, join='inner')
Out[22]:
(             AAPL     JNJ    XOM
 2011-09-06  379.74  64.64  71.15
 2011-09-07  383.93  65.43  73.65
 2011-09-08  384.14  64.95  72.82
 2011-09-09  377.48  63.64  71.01
 2011-09-12  379.94  63.59  71.84,              AAPL       JNJ       XOM
 2011-09-06  18173500  15848300  25416300
 2011-09-07  12492000  10759700  23108400
 2011-09-08  14839800  15551500  22434800
 2011-09-09  20171900  17008200  27969100
 2011-09-12  16697300  13448200  26205800)
```

Another indispensable feature is constructing a DataFrame from a collection of potentially differently indexed Series:

```
In [23]: s1 = Series(range(3), index=['a', 'b', 'c'])

In [24]: s2 = Series(range(4), index=['d', 'b', 'c', 'e'])

In [25]: s3 = Series(range(3), index=['f', 'a', 'c'])

In [26]: DataFrame({'one': s1, 'two': s2, 'three': s3})
Out[26]:
   one  three  two
a    0      1  NaN
b    1    NaN    1
c    2      2    2
d  NaN    NaN    0
e  NaN    NaN    3
f  NaN      0  NaN
```

As you have seen earlier, you can of course specify explicitly the index of the result, discarding the rest of the data:

```
In [27]: DataFrame({'one': s1, 'two': s2, 'three': s3}, index=list('face'))
Out[27]:
   one  three  two
f  NaN      0  NaN
a    0      1  NaN
c    2      2    2
e  NaN    NaN    3
```

Operations with Time Series of Different Frequencies

Economic time series are often of annual, quarterly, monthly, daily, or some other more specialized frequency. Some are completely irregular; for example, earnings revisions for a stock may arrive at any time. The two main tools for frequency conversion and realignment are the `resample` and `reindex` methods. `resample` converts data to a fixed frequency while `reindex` conforms data to a new index. Both support optional interpolation (such as forward filling) logic.

Let's consider a small weekly time series:

```
In [28]: ts1 = Series(np.random.randn(3),
   ....:                index=pd.date_range('2012-6-13', periods=3, freq='W-WED'))

In [29]: ts1
Out[29]:
2012-06-13     0.694283
2012-06-20    -2.669195
2012-06-27     0.245842
Freq: W-WED, dtype: float64
```

If you resample this to business daily (Monday-Friday) frequency, you get holes on the days where there is no data:

```
In [30]: ts1.resample('B')
Out[30]:
2012-06-13     0.694283
2012-06-14          NaN
2012-06-15          NaN
2012-06-18          NaN
2012-06-19          NaN
2012-06-20    -2.669195
2012-06-21          NaN
2012-06-22          NaN
2012-06-25          NaN
2012-06-26          NaN
2012-06-27     0.245842
Freq: B, dtype: float64
```

Of course, using `'ffill'` as the `fill_method` forward fills values in those gaps. This is a common practice with lower frequency data as you compute a time series of values on each timestamp having the latest valid or *"as of"* value:

```
In [31]: ts1.resample('B', fill_method='ffill')
Out[31]:
2012-06-13     0.694283
2012-06-14     0.694283
2012-06-15     0.694283
2012-06-18     0.694283
2012-06-19     0.694283
2012-06-20    -2.669195
2012-06-21    -2.669195
2012-06-22    -2.669195
2012-06-25    -2.669195
2012-06-26    -2.669195
```

```
2012-06-27    0.245842
Freq: B, dtype: float64
```

In practice, upsampling lower frequency data to a higher, regular frequency is a fine solution, but in the more general irregular time series case it may be a poor fit. Consider an irregularly sampled time series from the same general time period:

```
In [32]: dates = pd.DatetimeIndex(['2012-6-12', '2012-6-17', '2012-6-18',
   ....:                            '2012-6-21', '2012-6-22', '2012-6-29'])

In [33]: ts2 = Series(np.random.randn(6), index=dates)

In [34]: ts2
Out[34]:
2012-06-12   -0.852518
2012-06-17   -0.961712
2012-06-18    1.062945
2012-06-21    1.338952
2012-06-22   -0.668290
2012-06-29    1.455157
dtype: float64
```

If you wanted to add the "as of" values in ts1 (forward filling) to ts2. One option would be to resample both to a regular frequency then add, but if you want to maintain the date index in ts2, using reindex is a more precise solution:

```
In [35]: ts1.reindex(ts2.index, method='ffill')
Out[35]:
2012-06-12         NaN
2012-06-17    0.694283
2012-06-18    0.694283
2012-06-21   -2.669195
2012-06-22   -2.669195
2012-06-29    0.245842
dtype: float64

In [36]: ts2 + ts1.reindex(ts2.index, method='ffill')
Out[36]:
2012-06-12         NaN
2012-06-17   -0.267430
2012-06-18    1.757228
2012-06-21   -1.330243
2012-06-22   -3.337486
2012-06-29    1.700999
dtype: float64
```

Using periods instead of timestamps

Periods (representing time spans) provide an alternate means of working with different frequency time series, especially financial or economic series with annual or quarterly frequency having a particular reporting convention. For example, a company might announce its quarterly earnings with fiscal year ending in June, thus having Q-JUN frequency. Consider a pair of macroeconomic time series related to GDP and inflation:

```
In [37]: gdp = Series([1.78, 1.94, 2.08, 2.01, 2.15, 2.31, 2.46],
   ....:              index=pd.period_range('1984Q2', periods=7, freq='Q-SEP'))

In [38]: infl = Series([0.025, 0.045, 0.037, 0.04],
   ....:               index=pd.period_range('1982', periods=4, freq='A-DEC'))

In [39]: gdp                          In [40]: infl
Out[39]:                              Out[40]:
1984Q2    1.78                        1982    0.025
1984Q3    1.94                        1983    0.045
1984Q4    2.08                        1984    0.037
1985Q1    2.01                        1985    0.040
1985Q2    2.15                        Freq: A-DEC, dtype: float64
1985Q3    2.31
1985Q4    2.46
Freq: Q-SEP, dtype: float64
```

Unlike time series with timestamps, operations between different-frequency time series indexed by periods are not possible without explicit conversions. In this case, if we know that infl values were observed at the end of each year, we can then convert to Q-SEP to get the right periods in that frequency:

```
In [41]: infl_q = infl.asfreq('Q-SEP', how='end')

In [42]: infl_q
Out[42]:
1983Q1    0.025
1984Q1    0.045
1985Q1    0.037
1986Q1    0.040
Freq: Q-SEP, dtype: float64
```

That time series can then be reindexed with forward-filling to match gdp:

```
In [43]: infl_q.reindex(gdp.index, method='ffill')
Out[43]:
1984Q2    0.045
1984Q3    0.045
1984Q4    0.045
1985Q1    0.037
1985Q2    0.037
1985Q3    0.037
1985Q4    0.037
Freq: Q-SEP, dtype: float64
```

Time of Day and "as of" Data Selection

Suppose you have a long time series containing intraday market data and you want to extract the prices at a particular time of day on each day of the data. What if the data are irregular such that observations do not fall exactly on the desired time? In practice this task can make for error-prone data munging if you are not careful. Here is an example for illustration purposes:

```
# Make an intraday date range and time series
In [44]: rng = pd.date_range('2012-06-01 09:30', '2012-06-01 15:59', freq='T')

# Make a 5-day series of 9:30-15:59 values
In [45]: rng = rng.append([rng + pd.offsets.BDay(i) for i in range(1, 4)])

In [46]: ts = Series(np.arange(len(rng), dtype=float), index=rng)

In [47]: ts
Out[47]:
2012-06-01 09:30:00    0
2012-06-01 09:31:00    1
2012-06-01 09:32:00    2
2012-06-01 09:33:00    3
...
2012-06-06 15:56:00    1556
2012-06-06 15:57:00    1557
2012-06-06 15:58:00    1558
2012-06-06 15:59:00    1559
Length: 1560
```

Indexing with a Python `datetime.time` object will extract values at those times:

```
In [48]: from datetime import time

In [49]: ts[time(10, 0)]
Out[49]:
2012-06-01 10:00:00      30
2012-06-04 10:00:00     420
2012-06-05 10:00:00     810
2012-06-06 10:00:00    1200
dtype: float64
```

Under the hood, this uses an instance method `at_time` (available on individual time series and DataFrame objects alike):

```
In [50]: ts.at_time(time(10, 0))
Out[50]:
2012-06-01 10:00:00      30
2012-06-04 10:00:00     420
2012-06-05 10:00:00     810
2012-06-06 10:00:00    1200
dtype: float64
```

You can select values between two times using the related `between_time` method:

```
In [51]: ts.between_time(time(10, 0), time(10, 1))
Out[51]:
2012-06-01 10:00:00      30
2012-06-01 10:01:00      31
2012-06-04 10:00:00     420
2012-06-04 10:01:00     421
2012-06-05 10:00:00     810
2012-06-05 10:01:00     811
2012-06-06 10:00:00    1200
2012-06-06 10:01:00    1201
dtype: float64
```

As mentioned above, it might be the case that no data actually fall exactly at a time like 10 AM, but you might want to know the last known value at 10 AM:

```
# Set most of the time series randomly to NA
In [53]: indexer = np.sort(np.random.permutation(len(ts))[700:])

In [54]: irr_ts = ts.copy()

In [55]: irr_ts[indexer] = np.nan

In [56]: irr_ts['2012-06-01 09:50':'2012-06-01 10:00']
Out[56]:
2012-06-01 09:50:00     20
2012-06-01 09:51:00    NaN
2012-06-01 09:52:00     22
2012-06-01 09:53:00     23
2012-06-01 09:54:00    NaN
2012-06-01 09:55:00     25
2012-06-01 09:56:00    NaN
2012-06-01 09:57:00    NaN
2012-06-01 09:58:00    NaN
2012-06-01 09:59:00    NaN
2012-06-01 10:00:00    NaN
dtype: float64
```

By passing an array of timestamps to the asof method, you will obtain an array of the last valid (non-NA) values at or before each timestamp. So we construct a date range at 10 AM for each day and pass that to asof:

```
In [57]: selection = pd.date_range('2012-06-01 10:00', periods=4, freq='B')

In [58]: irr_ts.asof(selection)
Out[58]:
2012-06-01 10:00:00      25
2012-06-04 10:00:00     420
2012-06-05 10:00:00     810
2012-06-06 10:00:00    1197
Freq: B, dtype: float64
```

Splicing Together Data Sources

In Chapter 7, I described a number of strategies for merging together two related data sets. In a financial or economic context, there are a few widely occurring use cases:

- Switching from one data source (a time series or collection of time series) to another at a specific point in time
- "Patching" missing values in a time series at the beginning, middle, or end using another time series
- Completely replacing the data for a subset of symbols (countries, asset tickers, and so on)

In the first case, switching from one set of time series to another at a specific instant, it is a matter of splicing together two TimeSeries or DataFrame objects using `pandas.con cat`:

```
In [59]: data1 = DataFrame(np.ones((6, 3), dtype=float),
   ....:                    columns=['a', 'b', 'c'],
   ....:                    index=pd.date_range('6/12/2012', periods=6))

In [60]: data2 = DataFrame(np.ones((6, 3), dtype=float) * 2,
   ....:                    columns=['a', 'b', 'c'],
   ....:                    index=pd.date_range('6/13/2012', periods=6))

In [61]: spliced = pd.concat([data1.ix[:'2012-06-14'], data2.ix['2012-06-15':]])

In [62]: spliced
Out[62]:
            a  b  c
2012-06-12  1  1  1
2012-06-13  1  1  1
2012-06-14  1  1  1
2012-06-15  2  2  2
2012-06-16  2  2  2
2012-06-17  2  2  2
2012-06-18  2  2  2
```

Suppose in a similar example that `data1` was missing a time series present in `data2`:

```
In [63]: data2 = DataFrame(np.ones((6, 4), dtype=float) * 2,
   ....:                    columns=['a', 'b', 'c', 'd'],
   ....:                    index=pd.date_range('6/13/2012', periods=6))

In [64]: spliced = pd.concat([data1.ix[:'2012-06-14'], data2.ix['2012-06-15':]])

In [65]: spliced
Out[65]:
            a  b  c    d
2012-06-12  1  1  1  NaN
2012-06-13  1  1  1  NaN
2012-06-14  1  1  1  NaN
2012-06-15  2  2  2    2
2012-06-16  2  2  2    2
2012-06-17  2  2  2    2
2012-06-18  2  2  2    2
```

Using `combine_first`, you can bring in data from before the splice point to extend the history for `'d'` item:

```
In [66]: spliced_filled = spliced.combine_first(data2)

In [67]: spliced_filled
Out[67]:
            a  b  c    d
2012-06-12  1  1  1  NaN
2012-06-13  1  1  1    2
2012-06-14  1  1  1    2
2012-06-15  2  2  2    2
```

```
2012-06-16  2  2  2    2
2012-06-17  2  2  2    2
2012-06-18  2  2  2    2
```

Since `data2` does not have any values for `2012-06-12`, no values are filled on that day.

DataFrame has a related method `update` for performing in-place updates. You have to pass `overwrite=False` to make it only fill the holes:

```
In [68]: spliced.update(data2, overwrite=False)

In [69]: spliced
Out[69]:
            a  b  c    d
2012-06-12  1  1  1  NaN
2012-06-13  1  1  1    2
2012-06-14  1  1  1    2
2012-06-15  2  2  2    2
2012-06-16  2  2  2    2
2012-06-17  2  2  2    2
2012-06-18  2  2  2    2
```

To replace the data for a subset of symbols, you can use any of the above techniques, but sometimes it's simpler to just set the columns directly with DataFrame indexing:

```
In [70]: cp_spliced = spliced.copy()

In [71]: cp_spliced[['a', 'c']] = data1[['a', 'c']]

In [72]: cp_spliced
Out[72]:
              a  b    c    d
2012-06-12    1  1    1  NaN
2012-06-13    1  1    1    2
2012-06-14    1  1    1    2
2012-06-15    1  2    1    2
2012-06-16    1  2    1    2
2012-06-17    1  2    1    2
2012-06-18  NaN  2  NaN    2
```

Return Indexes and Cumulative Returns

In a financial context, *returns* usually refer to percent changes in the price of an asset. Let's consider price data for Apple in 2011 and 2012:

```
In [73]: import pandas.io.data as web

In [74]: price = web.get_data_yahoo('AAPL', '2011-01-01')['Adj Close']

In [75]: price[-5:]
Out[75]:
Date
2014-07-15    95.32
2014-07-16    94.78
2014-07-17    93.09
```

```
2014-07-18    94.43
2014-07-21    93.94
Name: Adj Close, dtype: float64
```

For Apple, which has no dividends, computing the cumulative percent return between two points in time requires computing only the percent change in the price:

```
In [76]: price['2011-10-03'] / price['2011-3-01'] - 1
Out[76]: 0.072327044025157106
```

For other stocks with dividend payouts, computing how much money you make from holding a stock can be more complicated. The adjusted close values used here have been adjusted for splits and dividends, however. In all cases, it's quite common to derive a *return index*, which is a time series indicating the value of a unit investment (one dollar, say). Many assumptions can underlie the return index; for example, some will choose to reinvest profit and others not. In the case of Apple, we can compute a simple return index using cumprod:

```
In [77]: returns = price.pct_change()

In [78]: ret_index = (1 + returns).cumprod()

In [79]: ret_index[0] = 1  # Set first value to 1

In [80]: ret_index
Out[80]:
Date
2011-01-03    1.000000
2011-01-04    1.005333
2011-01-05    1.013556
2011-01-06    1.012667
...
2014-07-16    2.106222
2014-07-17    2.068667
2014-07-18    2.098444
2014-07-21    2.087556
Name: Adj Close, Length: 892
```

With a return index in hand, computing cumulative returns at a particular resolution is simple:

```
In [81]: m_returns = ret_index.resample('BM', how='last').pct_change()

In [82]: m_returns['2012']
Out[82]:
Date
2012-01-31    0.127125
2012-02-29    0.188352
2012-03-30    0.105306
2012-04-30   -0.026017
2012-05-31   -0.010660
2012-06-29    0.010774
2012-07-31    0.045899
2012-08-31    0.093885
2012-09-28    0.002740
```

```
2012-10-31    -0.107564
2012-11-30    -0.012371
2012-12-31    -0.090785
Freq: BM, Name: Adj Close, dtype: float64
```

Of course, in this simple case (no dividends or other adjustments to take into account) these could have been computed from the daily percent changed by resampling with aggregation (here, to periods):

```
In [83]: m_rets = (1 + returns).resample('M', how='prod', kind='period') - 1

In [84]: m_rets['2012']
Out[84]:
Date
2012-01     0.127125
2012-02     0.188352
2012-03     0.105306
2012-04    -0.026017
2012-05    -0.010660
2012-06     0.010774
2012-07     0.045899
2012-08     0.093885
2012-09     0.002740
2012-10    -0.107564
2012-11    -0.012371
2012-12    -0.090785
Freq: M, Name: Adj Close, dtype: float64
```

If you had dividend dates and percentages, including them in the total return per day would look like:

```
returns[dividend_dates] += dividend_pcts
```

Group Transforms and Analysis

In Chapter 9, you learned the basics of computing group statistics and applying your own transformations to groups in a dataset.

Let's consider a collection of hypothetical stock portfolios. I first randomly generate a broad *universe* of 2000 tickers:

```
import random; random.seed(0)
import string

N = 1000
def rands(n):
    choices = string.ascii_uppercase
    return ''.join([random.choice(choices) for _ in xrange(n)])
tickers = np.array([rands(5) for _ in xrange(N)])
```

I then create a DataFrame containing 3 columns representing hypothetical, but random portfolios for a subset of tickers:

```
M = 500
df = DataFrame({'Momentum' : np.random.randn(M) / 200 + 0.03,
```

```
'Value' : np.random.randn(M) / 200 + 0.08,
'ShortInterest' : np.random.randn(M) / 200 - 0.02},
index=tickers[:M])
```

Next, let's create a random industry classification for the tickers. To keep things simple, I'll just keep it to 2 industries, storing the mapping in a Series:

```
ind_names = np.array(['FINANCIAL', 'TECH'])
sampler = np.random.randint(0, len(ind_names), N)
industries = Series(ind_names[sampler], index=tickers,
                    name='industry')
```

Now we can group by industries and carry out group aggregation and transformations:

```
In [91]: by_industry = df.groupby(industries)

In [92]: by_industry.mean()
Out[92]:
          Momentum  ShortInterest     Value
industry
FINANCIAL  0.029485      -0.020739  0.079929
TECH       0.030407      -0.019609  0.080113

In [93]: by_industry.describe()
Out[93]:
                   Momentum  ShortInterest       Value
industry
FINANCIAL count  246.000000     246.000000  246.000000
          mean     0.029485      -0.020739    0.079929
          std      0.004802       0.004986    0.004548
          min      0.017210      -0.036997    0.067025
          25%      0.026263      -0.024138    0.076638
          50%      0.029261      -0.020833    0.079804
          75%      0.032806      -0.017345    0.082718
          max      0.045884      -0.006322    0.093334
TECH      count  254.000000     254.000000  254.000000
          mean     0.030407      -0.019609    0.080113
          std      0.005303       0.005074    0.004886
          min      0.016778      -0.032682    0.065253
          25%      0.026456      -0.022779    0.076737
          50%      0.030650      -0.019829    0.080296
          75%      0.033602      -0.016923    0.083353
          max      0.049638      -0.003698    0.093081
```

By defining transformation functions, it's easy to transform these portfolios by industry. For example, standardizing within industry is widely used in equity portfolio construction:

```
# Within-Industry Standardize
def zscore(group):
    return (group - group.mean()) / group.std()

df_stand = by_industry.apply(zscore)
```

You can verify that each industry has mean 0 and standard deviation 1:

```
In [95]: df_stand.groupby(industries).agg(['mean', 'std'])
Out[95]:
                Momentum          ShortInterest              Value
                  mean  std           mean  std              mean  std
industry
FINANCIAL  1.121054e-15    1   3.083577e-15    1   7.996765e-15    1
TECH      -2.893573e-16    1  -1.879511e-15    1  -7.141269e-15    1
```

Other, built-in kinds of transformations, like rank, can be used more concisely:

```
# Within-industry rank descending
In [96]: ind_rank = by_industry.rank(ascending=False)

In [97]: ind_rank.groupby(industries).agg(['min', 'max'])
Out[97]:
                Momentum      ShortInterest       Value
              min   max         min   max       min   max
industry
FINANCIAL       1   246           1   246         1   246
TECH            1   254           1   254         1   254
```

In quantitative equity, "rank and standardize" is a common sequence of transforms. You could do this by chaining together rank and zscore like so:

```
# Industry rank and standardize
In [98]: by_industry.apply(lambda x: zscore(x.rank())).info()
<class 'pandas.core.frame.DataFrame'>
Index: 500 entries, VTKGN to PTDQE
Data columns (total 3 columns):
Momentum         500 non-null float64
ShortInterest    500 non-null float64
Value            500 non-null float64
dtypes: float64(3)
```

Group Factor Exposures

Factor analysis is a technique in quantitative portfolio management. Portfolio holdings and performance (profit and less) are decomposed using one or more *factors* (risk factors are one example) represented as a portfolio of weights. For example, a stock price's co-movement with a benchmark (like S&P 500 index) is known as its *beta*, a common risk factor. Let's consider a contrived example of a portfolio constructed from 3 randomly-generated factors (usually called the *factor loadings*) and some weights:

```
from numpy.random import rand
fac1, fac2, fac3 = np.random.rand(3, 1000)

ticker_subset = tickers.take(np.random.permutation(N)[:1000])

# Weighted sum of factors plus noise
port = Series(0.7 * fac1 - 1.2 * fac2 + 0.3 * fac3 + rand(1000),
              index=ticker_subset)
factors = DataFrame({'f1': fac1, 'f2': fac2, 'f3': fac3},
                    index=ticker_subset)
```

Vector correlations between each factor and the portfolio may not indicate too much:

```
In [100]: factors.corrwith(port)
Out[100]:
f1    0.402377
f2   -0.680980
f3    0.168083
dtype: float64
```

The standard way to compute the factor exposures is by least squares regression; using `pandas.ols` with `factors` as the explanatory variables we can compute exposures over the entire set of tickers:

```
In [101]: pd.ols(y=port, x=factors).beta
Out[101]:
f1           0.761789
f2          -1.208760
f3           0.289865
intercept    0.484477
dtype: float64
```

As you can see, the original factor weights can nearly be recovered since there was not too much additional random noise added to the portfolio. Using `groupby` you can compute exposures industry by industry. To do so, write a function like so:

```
def beta_exposure(chunk, factors=None):
    return pd.ols(y=chunk, x=factors).beta
```

Then, group by `industries` and apply that function, passing the DataFrame of factor loadings:

```
In [103]: by_ind = port.groupby(industries)

In [104]: exposures = by_ind.apply(beta_exposure, factors=factors)

In [105]: exposures.unstack()
Out[105]:
                 f1         f2        f3    intercept
industry
FINANCIAL  0.790329  -1.182970  0.275624   0.455569
TECH       0.740857  -1.232882  0.303811   0.508188
```

Decile and Quartile Analysis

Analyzing data based on sample quantiles is another important tool for financial analysts. For example, the performance of a stock portfolio could be broken down into quartiles (four equal-sized chunks) based on each stock's price-to-earnings. Using `pandas.qcut` combined with `groupby` makes quantile analysis reasonably straightforward.

As an example, let's consider a simple trend following or *momentum* strategy trading the S&P 500 index via the SPY exchange-traded fund. You can download the price history from Yahoo! Finance:

```
In [106]: import pandas.io.data as web

In [107]: data = web.get_data_yahoo('SPY', '2006-01-01')

In [108]: data.info()
<class 'pandas.core.frame.DataFrame'>
DatetimeIndex: 2151 entries, 2006-01-03 00:00:00 to 2014-07-21 00:00:00
Data columns (total 6 columns):
Open        2151 non-null float64
High        2151 non-null float64
Low         2151 non-null float64
Close       2151 non-null float64
Volume      2151 non-null int64
Adj Close   2151 non-null float64
dtypes: float64(5), int64(1)
```

Now, we'll compute daily returns and a function for transforming the returns into a trend signal formed from a lagged moving sum:

```
px = data['Adj Close']
returns = px.pct_change()

def to_index(rets):
    index = (1 + rets).cumprod()
    first_loc = max(index.index.get_loc(index.idxmax()) - 1, 0)
    index.values[first_loc] = 1
    return index

def trend_signal(rets, lookback, lag):
    signal = pd.rolling_sum(rets, lookback, min_periods=lookback - 5)
    return signal.shift(lag)
```

Using this function, we can (naively) create and test a trading strategy that trades this momentum signal every Friday:

```
In [110]: signal = trend_signal(returns, 100, 3)

In [111]: trade_friday = signal.resample('W-FRI').resample('B', fill_method='ffill')

In [112]: trade_rets = trade_friday.shift(1) * returns

In [113]: trade_rets = trade_rets[:len(returns)]
```

We can then convert the strategy returns to a return index and plot them (see Figure 11-1):

```
In [114]: to_index(trade_rets).plot()
```

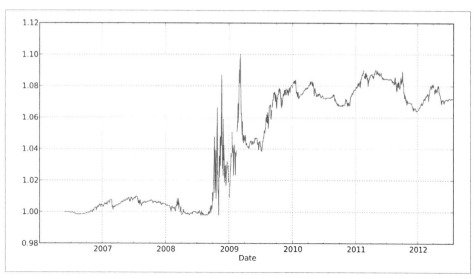

Figure 11-1. SPY momentum strategy return index

Suppose you wanted to decompose the strategy performance into more and less volatile periods of trading. Trailing one-year annualized standard deviation is a simple measure of volatility, and we can compute Sharpe ratios to assess the reward-to-risk ratio in various volatility regimes:

```
vol = pd.rolling_std(returns, 250, min_periods=200) * np.sqrt(250)

def sharpe(rets, ann=250):
    return rets.mean() / rets.std()  * np.sqrt(ann)
```

Now, dividing `vol` into quartiles with `qcut` and aggregating with `sharpe` we obtain:

```
In [116]: trade_rets.groupby(pd.qcut(vol, 4)).agg(sharpe)
Out[116]:
[0.0954, 0.122]    1.119797
(0.122, 0.177]     0.662405
(0.177, 0.227]    -0.707900
(0.227, 0.457]     0.467419
dtype: float64
```

These results show that the strategy performed the best during the period when the volatility was the highest.

More Example Applications

Here is a small set of additional examples.

Signal Frontier Analysis

In this section, I'll describe a simplified cross-sectional mean reversion portfolio and show how you might explore a grid of model parameterizations. First, I'll load historical prices for a portfolio of financial and technology stocks:

```
names = ['AAPL', 'GOOG', 'MSFT', 'DELL', 'GS', 'MS', 'BAC', 'C']
def get_px(stock, start, end):
    return web.get_data_yahoo(stock, start, end)['Adj Close']
px = DataFrame({n: get_px(n, '1/1/2009', '6/1/2012') for n in names})
```

We can easily plot the cumulative returns of each stock (see Figure 11-2):

```
In [119]: px = px.asfreq('B').fillna(method='pad')

In [120]: rets = px.pct_change()

In [121]: ((1 + rets).cumprod() - 1).plot()
```

For the portfolio construction, we'll compute mean reversion over a certain lookback, then rank in descending order and standardize:

```
def calc_mom(price, lookback, lag):
    mom_ret = price.shift(lag).pct_change(lookback)
    ranks = mom_ret.rank(axis=1, ascending=False)
    demeaned = ranks.subtract(ranks.mean(axis=1), axis=0)
    return demeaned.divide(demeaned.std(axis=1), axis=0)
```

With this transform function in hand, we can set up a strategy backtesting function that computes a portfolio for a particular lookback and holding period (days between trading), returning the overall Sharpe ratio:

```
compound = lambda x : (1 + x).prod() - 1
daily_sr = lambda x: x.mean() / x.std()

def strat_sr(prices, lb, hold):
    # Compute portfolio weights
    freq = '%dB' % hold
    port = calc_mom(prices, lb, lag=1)

    daily_rets = prices.pct_change()

    # Compute portfolio returns
    port = port.shift(1).resample(freq, how='first')
    returns = daily_rets.resample(freq, how=compound)
    port_rets = (port * returns).sum(axis=1)

    return daily_sr(port_rets) * np.sqrt(252 / hold)
```

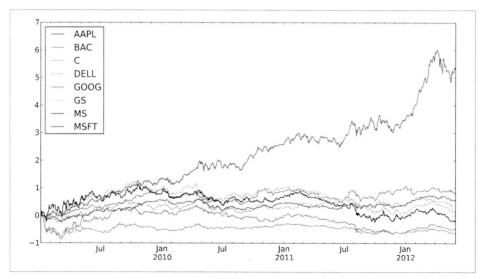

Figure 11-2. Cumulative returns for each of the stocks

When called with the prices and a parameter combination, this function returns a scalar value:

```
In [124]: strat_sr(px, 70, 30)
Out[124]: 0.32217663506235655
```

From there, you can evaluate the **strat_sr** function over a grid of parameters, storing them as you go in a `defaultdict` and finally putting the results in a DataFrame:

```
from collections import defaultdict

lookbacks = range(20, 90, 5)
holdings = range(20, 90, 5)
dd = defaultdict(dict)
for lb in lookbacks:
    for hold in holdings:
        dd[lb][hold] = strat_sr(px, lb, hold)

ddf = DataFrame(dd)
ddf.index.name = 'Holding Period'
ddf.columns.name = 'Lookback Period'
```

To visualize the results and get an idea of what's going on, here is a function that uses matplotlib to produce a heatmap with some adornments:

```
import matplotlib.pyplot as plt

def heatmap(df, cmap=plt.cm.gray_r):
    fig = plt.figure()
    ax = fig.add_subplot(111)
    axim = ax.imshow(df.values, cmap=cmap, interpolation='nearest')
    ax.set_xlabel(df.columns.name)
```

```
ax.set_xticks(np.arange(len(df.columns)))
ax.set_xticklabels(list(df.columns))
ax.set_ylabel(df.index.name)
ax.set_yticks(np.arange(len(df.index)))
ax.set_yticklabels(list(df.index))
plt.colorbar(axim)
```

Calling this function on the backtest results, we get Figure 11-3:

```
In [127]: heatmap(ddf)
```

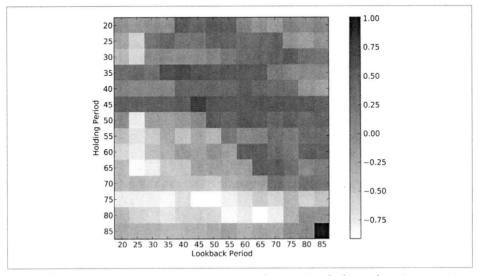

Figure 11-3. Heatmap of mean reversion strategy Sharpe ratio (higher is better) over various lookbacks and holding periods

Future Contract Rolling

A *future* is an ubiquitous form of derivative contract; it is an agreement to take delivery of a certain asset (such as oil, gold, or shares of the FTSE 100 index) on a particular date. In practice, modeling and trading futures contracts on equities, currencies, commodities, bonds, and other asset classes is complicated by the time-limited nature of each contract. For example, at any given time for a type of future (say silver or copper futures) multiple contracts with different *expiration dates* may be traded. In many cases, the future contract expiring next (the *near* contract) will be the most liquid (highest volume and lowest bid-ask spread).

For the purposes of modeling and forecasting, it can be much easier to work with a *continuous* return index indicating the profit and loss associated with always holding the near contract. Transitioning from an expiring contract to the next (or *far*) contract is referred to as *rolling*. Computing a continuous future series from the individual contract data is not necessarily a straightforward exercise and typically requires a deeper understanding of the market and how the instruments are traded. For example, in practice when and how quickly would you trade out of an expiring contract and into the next contract? Here I describe one such process.

First, I'll use scaled prices for the SPY exchange-traded fund as a proxy for the S&P 500 index:

```
In [129]: import pandas.io.data as web

# Approximate price of S&P 500 index
In [130]: px = web.get_data_yahoo('SPY')['Adj Close'] * 10

In [131]: px
Out[131]:
Date
2010-01-04    1034.4
2010-01-05    1037.1
2010-01-06    1037.9
...
2014-07-17    1957.1
2014-07-18    1977.1
2014-07-21    1973.4
Name: Adj Close, Length: 1144
```

Now, a little bit of setup. I put a couple of S&P 500 future contracts and expiry dates in a Series:

```
from datetime import datetime
expiry = {'ESU2': datetime(2012, 9, 21),
          'ESZ2': datetime(2012, 12, 21)}
expiry = Series(expiry).order()
```

expiry then looks like:

```
In [133]: expiry
Out[133]:
ESU2    2012-09-21
ESZ2    2012-12-21
dtype: datetime64[ns]
```

Then, I use the Yahoo! Finance prices along with a random walk and some noise to simulate the two contracts into the future:

```
np.random.seed(12347)
N = 200
walk = (np.random.randint(0, 200, size=N) - 100) * 0.25
perturb = (np.random.randint(0, 20, size=N) - 10) * 0.25
walk = walk.cumsum()

rng = pd.date_range(px.index[0], periods=len(px) + N, freq='B')
near = np.concatenate([px.values, px.values[-1] + walk])
far = np.concatenate([px.values, px.values[-1] + walk + perturb])
prices = DataFrame({'ESU2': near, 'ESZ2': far}, index=rng)
```

prices then has two time series for the contracts that differ from each other by a random amount:

```
In [135]: prices.tail()
Out[135]:
              ESU2     ESZ2
2015-02-20  2002.65  2004.40
2015-02-23  1988.90  1991.15
2015-02-24  1996.90  1998.65
2015-02-25  2013.40  2012.65
2015-02-26  1993.40  1991.15
```

One way to splice time series together into a single continuous series is to construct a weighting matrix. Active contracts would have a weight of 1 until the expiry date approaches. At that point you have to decide on a roll convention. Here is a function that computes a weighting matrix with linear decay over a number of periods leading up to expiry:

```
def get_roll_weights(start, expiry, items, roll_periods=5):
    # start : first date to compute weighting DataFrame
    # expiry : Series of ticker -> expiration dates
    # items : sequence of contract names

    dates = pd.date_range(start, expiry[-1], freq='B')
    weights = DataFrame(np.zeros((len(dates), len(items))),
                        index=dates, columns=items)

    prev_date = weights.index[0]
    for i, (item, ex_date) in enumerate(expiry.iteritems()):
        if i < len(expiry) - 1:
            weights.ix[prev_date:ex_date - pd.offsets.BDay(), item] = 1
            roll_rng = pd.date_range(end=ex_date - pd.offsets.BDay(),
                                     periods=roll_periods + 1, freq='B')

            decay_weights = np.linspace(0, 1, roll_periods + 1)
            weights.ix[roll_rng, item] = 1 - decay_weights
            weights.ix[roll_rng, expiry.index[i + 1]] = decay_weights
        else:
            weights.ix[prev_date:, item] = 1

        prev_date = ex_date

    return weights
```

The weights look like this around the ESU2 expiry:

```
In [137]: weights = get_roll_weights('6/1/2012', expiry, prices.columns)
```

```
In [138]: weights.ix['2012-09-12':'2012-09-21']
Out[138]:
             ESU2  ESZ2
2012-09-12   1.0   0.0
2012-09-13   1.0   0.0
2012-09-14   0.8   0.2
2012-09-17   0.6   0.4
2012-09-18   0.4   0.6
2012-09-19   0.2   0.8
```

```
2012-09-20   0.0   1.0
2012-09-21   0.0   1.0
```

Finally, the rolled future returns are just a weighted sum of the contract returns:

```
In [139]: rolled_returns = (prices.pct_change() * weights).sum(1)
```

Rolling Correlation and Linear Regression

Dynamic models play an important role in financial modeling as they can be used to simulate trading decisions over a historical period. Moving window and exponentially-weighted time series functions are an example of tools that are used for dynamic models.

Correlation is one way to look at the co-movement between the changes in two asset time series. pandas's `rolling_corr` function can be called with two return series to compute the moving window correlation. First, I load some price series from Yahoo! Finance and compute daily returns:

```
aapl = web.get_data_yahoo('AAPL', '2000-01-01')['Adj Close']
msft = web.get_data_yahoo('MSFT', '2000-01-01')['Adj Close']

aapl_rets = aapl.pct_change()
msft_rets = msft.pct_change()
```

Then, I compute and plot the one-year moving correlation (see Figure 11-4):

```
In [142]: pd.rolling_corr(aapl_rets, msft_rets, 250).plot()
```

One issue with correlation between two assets is that it does not capture differences in volatility. Least-squares regression provides another means for modeling the dynamic relationship between a variable and one or more other predictor variables.

```
In [144]: model = pd.ols(y=aapl_rets, x={'MSFT': msft_rets}, window=250)

In [145]: model.beta
Out[145]:
                  MSFT    intercept
Date
2000-12-28   0.432848   -0.002112
2000-12-29   0.424561   -0.001777
2001-01-02   0.424072   -0.001817
2001-01-03   0.435653   -0.001280
2001-01-04   0.434781   -0.001332
...               ...         ...
2014-07-15   0.087899    0.001879
2014-07-16   0.081518    0.001834
2014-07-17   0.057425    0.001824
2014-07-18   0.057862    0.001872
2014-07-21   0.054647    0.001923
[3409 rows x 2 columns]

In [146]: model.beta['MSFT'].plot()
```

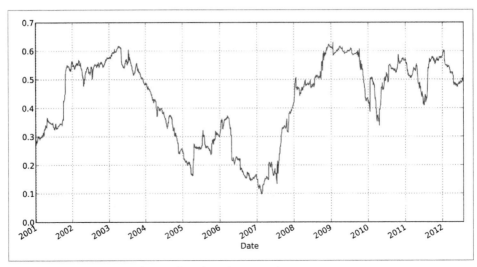

Figure 11-4. One-year correlation of Apple with Microsoft

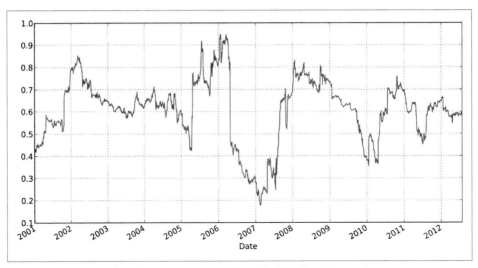

Figure 11-5. One-year beta (OLS regression coefficient) of Apple to Microsoft

pandas's `ols` function implements static and dynamic (expanding or rolling window) least squares regressions. For more sophisticated statistical and econometrics models, see the statsmodels project (*http://statsmodels.sourceforge.net*).

## CHAPTER 12

Advanced NumPy

ndarray Object Internals

The NumPy ndarray provides a means to interpret a block of homogeneous data (either contiguous or strided, more on this later) as a multidimensional array object. As you've seen, the data type, or *dtype*, determines how the data is interpreted as being floating point, integer, boolean, or any of the other types we've been looking at.

Part of what makes ndarray powerful is that every array object is a *strided* view on a block of data. You might wonder, for example, how the array view arr[::2, ::-1] does not copy any data. Simply put, the ndarray is more than just a chunk of memory and a dtype; it also has striding information which enables the array to move through memory with varying step sizes. More precisely, the ndarray internally consists of the following:

- A *pointer to data*, that is a block of system memory
- The *data type* or dtype
- A tuple indicating the array's *shape*; For example, a 10 by 5 array would have shape (10, 5)

```
In [8]: np.ones((10, 5)).shape
Out[8]: (10, 5)
```

- A tuple of *strides*, integers indicating the number of bytes to "step" in order to advance one element along a dimension; For example, a typical (C order, more on this later) 3 x 4 x 5 array of float64 (8-byte) values has strides (160, 40, 8)

```
In [9]: np.ones((3, 4, 5), dtype=np.float64).strides
Out[9]: (160, 40, 8)
```

While it is rare that a typical NumPy user would be interested in the array strides, they are the critical ingredient in constructing copyless array views. Strides can even be negative which enables an array to move *backward* through memory, which would be the case in a slice like obj[::-1] or obj[:, ::-1].

See Figure 12-1 for a simple mockup the ndarray innards.

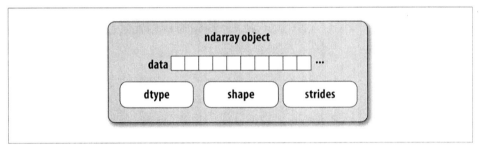

Figure 12-1. The NumPy ndarray object

NumPy dtype Hierarchy

You may occasionally have code which needs to check whether an array contains integers, floating point numbers, strings, or Python objects. Because there are many types of floating point numbers (float16 through float128), checking that the dtype is among a list of types would be very verbose. Fortunately, the dtypes have superclasses such as np.integer and np.floating which can be used in conjunction with the np.issubd type function:

```
In [10]: ints = np.ones(10, dtype=np.uint16)

In [11]: floats = np.ones(10, dtype=np.float32)

In [12]: np.issubdtype(ints.dtype, np.integer)
Out[12]: True

In [13]: np.issubdtype(floats.dtype, np.floating)
Out[13]: True
```

You can see all of the parent classes of a specific dtype by calling the type's mro method:

```
In [14]: np.float64.mro()
Out[14]:
[numpy.float64,
 numpy.floating,
 numpy.inexact,
 numpy.number,
 numpy.generic,
 float,
 object]
```

Most NumPy users will never have to know about this, but it occasionally comes in handy. See Figure 12-2 for a graph of the dtype hierarchy and parent-subclass relationships [1].

---

1. Some of the dtypes have trailing underscores in their names. These are there to avoid variable name conflicts between the NumPy-specific types and the Python built-in ones.

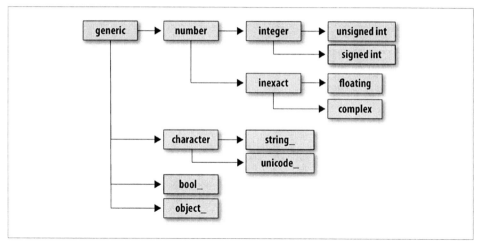

Figure 12-2. The NumPy dtype class hierarchy

Advanced Array Manipulation

There are many ways to work with arrays beyond fancy indexing, slicing, and boolean subsetting. While much of the heavy lifting for data analysis applications is handled by higher level functions in pandas, you may at some point need to write a data algorithm that is not found in one of the existing libraries.

Reshaping Arrays

Given what we know about NumPy arrays, it should come as little surprise that you can convert an array from one shape to another without copying any data. To do this, pass a tuple indicating the new shape to the reshape array instance method. For example, suppose we had a one-dimensional array of values that we wished to rearrange into a matrix:

```
In [15]: arr = np.arange(8)

In [16]: arr
Out[16]: array([0, 1, 2, 3, 4, 5, 6, 7])

In [17]: arr.reshape((4, 2))
Out[17]:
array([[0, 1],
       [2, 3],
       [4, 5],
       [6, 7]])
```

A multidimensional array can also be reshaped:

```
In [18]: arr.reshape((4, 2)).reshape((2, 4))
Out[18]:
```

```
array([[0, 1, 2, 3],
       [4, 5, 6, 7]])
```

One of the passed shape dimensions can be -1, in which case the value used for that dimension will be inferred from the data:

```
In [19]: arr = np.arange(15)      In [20]: arr.reshape((5, -1))
                                  Out[20]:
                                  array([[ 0,  1,  2],
                                         [ 3,  4,  5],
                                         [ 6,  7,  8],
                                         [ 9, 10, 11],
                                         [12, 13, 14]])
```

Since an array's shape attribute is a tuple, it can be passed to reshape, too:

```
In [21]: other_arr = np.ones((3, 5))
```

```
In [22]: other_arr.shape
Out[22]: (3, 5)
```

```
In [23]: arr.reshape(other_arr.shape)
Out[23]:
array([[ 0,  1,  2,  3,  4],
       [ 5,  6,  7,  8,  9],
       [10, 11, 12, 13, 14]])
```

The opposite operation of reshape from one-dimensional to a higher dimension is typically known as *flattening* or *raveling*:

```
In [24]: arr = np.arange(15).reshape((5, 3))      In [25]: arr
                                                  Out[25]:
                                                  array([[ 0,  1,  2],
                                                         [ 3,  4,  5],
                                                         [ 6,  7,  8],
                                                         [ 9, 10, 11],
                                                         [12, 13, 14]])
```

```
In [26]: arr.ravel()
Out[26]: array([ 0,  1,  2,  3,  4,  5,  6,  7,  8,  9, 10, 11, 12, 13, 14])
```

ravel does not produce a copy of the underlying data if it does not have to (more on this below). The flatten method behaves like ravel except it always returns a copy of the data:

```
In [27]: arr.flatten()
Out[27]: array([ 0,  1,  2,  3,  4,  5,  6,  7,  8,  9, 10, 11, 12, 13, 14])
```

The data can be reshaped or raveled in different orders. This is a slightly nuanced topic for new NumPy users and is therefore the next subtopic.

C versus Fortran Order

Contrary to some other scientific computing environments like R and MATLAB, NumPy gives you much more control and flexibility over the layout of your data in memory. By default, NumPy arrays are created in *row major* order. Spatially this means that if you have a two-dimensional array of data, the items in each row of the array are stored in adjacent memory locations. The alternative to row major ordering is *column major* order, which means that (you guessed it) values within each column of data are stored in adjacent memory locations.

For historical reasons, row and column major order are also know as C and Fortran order, respectively. In FORTRAN 77, the language of our forebears, matrices were all column major.

Functions like `reshape` and `ravel`, accept an `order` argument indicating the order to use the data in the array. This can be `'C'` or `'F'` in most cases (there are also less commonly-used options `'A'` and `'K'`; see the NumPy documentation). These are illustrated in Figure 12-3.

```
In [28]: arr = np.arange(12).reshape((3, 4))

In [29]: arr
Out[29]:
array([[ 0,  1,  2,  3],
       [ 4,  5,  6,  7],
       [ 8,  9, 10, 11]])

In [30]: arr.ravel()
Out[30]: array([ 0,  1,  2,  3,  4,  5,  6,  7,  8,  9, 10, 11])

In [31]: arr.ravel('F')
Out[31]: array([ 0,  4,  8,  1,  5,  9,  2,  6, 10,  3,  7, 11])
```

Reshaping arrays with more than two dimensions can be a bit mind-bending. The key difference between C and Fortran order is the order in which the dimensions are walked:

- *C / row major order:* traverse higher dimensions *first* (e.g. axis 1 before advancing on axis 0).
- *Fortran / column major order:* traverse higher dimensions *last* (e.g. axis 0 before advancing on axis 1).

Concatenating and Splitting Arrays

`numpy.concatenate` takes a sequence (tuple, list, etc.) of arrays and joins them together in order along the input axis.

```
In [32]: arr1 = np.array([[1, 2, 3], [4, 5, 6]])

In [33]: arr2 = np.array([[7, 8, 9], [10, 11, 12]])

In [34]: np.concatenate([arr1, arr2], axis=0)
Out[34]:
array([[ 1,  2,  3],
       [ 4,  5,  6],
```

```
         [ 7,  8,  9],
         [10, 11, 12]])

In [35]: np.concatenate([arr1, arr2], axis=1)
Out[35]:
array([[ 1,  2,  3,  7,  8,  9],
       [ 4,  5,  6, 10, 11, 12]])
```

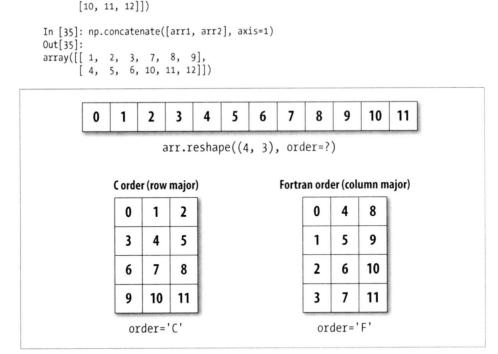

Figure 12-3. Reshaping in C (row major) or Fortran (column major) order

There are some convenience functions, like vstack and hstack, for common kinds of concatenation. The above operations could have been expressed as:

```
In [36]: np.vstack((arr1, arr2))    In [37]: np.hstack((arr1, arr2))
Out[36]:                            Out[37]:
array([[ 1,  2,  3],                array([[ 1,  2,  3,  7,  8,  9],
       [ 4,  5,  6],                       [ 4,  5,  6, 10, 11, 12]])
       [ 7,  8,  9],
       [10, 11, 12]])
```

split, on the other hand, slices apart an array into multiple arrays along an axis:

```
In [38]: from numpy.random import randn

In [39]: arr = randn(5, 2)     In [40]: arr
                               Out[40]:
                               array([[ 0.1689,  0.3287],
                                      [ 0.4703,  0.8989],
                                      [ 0.1535,  0.0243],
                                      [-0.2832,  1.1536],
                                      [ 0.2707,  0.8075]])

In [41]: first, second, third = np.split(arr, [1, 3])

In [42]: first
```

```
Out[42]: array([[ 0.1689,  0.3287]])
```

```
In [43]: second                In [44]: third
Out[43]:                       Out[44]:
array([[ 0.4703,  0.8989],     array([[-0.2832,  1.1536],
       [ 0.1535,  0.0243]])            [ 0.2707,  0.8075]])
```

See Table 12-1 for a list of all relevant concatenation and splitting functions, some of which are provided only as a convenience of the very general purpose concatenate.

Table 12-1. Array concatenation functions

Function	Description
concatenate	Most general function, concatenates collection of arrays along one axis
vstack, row_stack	Stack arrays row-wise (along axis 0)
hstack	Stack arrays column-wise (along axis 1)
column_stack	Like hstack, but converts 1D arrays to 2D column vectors first
dstack	Stack arrays "depth"-wise (along axis 2)
split	Split array at passed locations along a particular axis
hsplit / vsplit / dsplit	Convenience functions for splitting on axis 0, 1, and 2, respectively.

Stacking helpers: r_ and c_

There are two special objects in the NumPy namespace, r_ and c_, that make stacking arrays more concise:

```
In [45]: arr = np.arange(6)
```

```
In [46]: arr1 = arr.reshape((3, 2))
```

```
In [47]: arr2 = randn(3, 2)
```

```
In [48]: np.r_[arr1, arr2]       In [49]: np.c_[np.r_[arr1, arr2], arr]
Out[48]:                         Out[49]:
array([[ 0.    ,  1.    ],       array([[ 0.    ,  1.    ,  0.    ],
       [ 2.    ,  3.    ],              [ 2.    ,  3.    ,  1.    ],
       [ 4.    ,  5.    ],              [ 4.    ,  5.    ,  2.    ],
       [ 0.7258, -1.5325],              [ 0.7258, -1.5325,  3.    ],
       [-0.4696, -0.2127],              [-0.4696, -0.2127,  4.    ],
       [-0.1072,  1.2871]])            [-0.1072,  1.2871,  5.    ]])
```

These additionally can translate slices to arrays:

```
In [50]: np.c_[1:6, -10:-5]
Out[50]:
array([[ 1, -10],
       [ 2,  -9],
       [ 3,  -8],
       [ 4,  -7],
       [ 5,  -6]])
```

See the docstring for more on what you can do with c_ and r_.

Repeating Elements: Tile and Repeat

 The need to replicate or repeat arrays is less common with NumPy than it is with other popular array programming languages like MATLAB. The main reason for this is that *broadcasting* fulfills this need better, which is the subject of the next section.

The two main tools for repeating or replicating arrays to produce larger arrays are the repeat and `tile` functions. repeat replicates each element in an array some number of times, producing a larger array:

```
In [51]: arr = np.arange(3)
```

```
In [52]: arr.repeat(3)
Out[52]: array([0, 0, 0, 1, 1, 1, 2, 2, 2])
```

By default, if you pass an integer, each element will be repeated that number of times. If you pass an array of integers, each element can be repeated a different number of times:

```
In [53]: arr.repeat([2, 3, 4])
Out[53]: array([0, 0, 1, 1, 1, 2, 2, 2, 2])
```

Multidimensional arrays can have their elements repeated along a particular axis.

```
In [54]: arr = randn(2, 2)
```

```
In [55]: arr                      In [56]: arr.repeat(2, axis=0)
Out[55]:                          Out[56]:
array([[ 0.7157, -0.6387],        array([[ 0.7157, -0.6387],
       [ 0.3626,  0.849 ]])              [ 0.7157, -0.6387],
                                         [ 0.3626,  0.849 ],
                                         [ 0.3626,  0.849 ]])
```

Note that if no axis is passed, the array will be flattened first, which is likely not what you want. Similarly you can pass an array of integers when repeating a multidimensional array to repeat a given slice a different number of times:

```
In [57]: arr.repeat([2, 3], axis=0)
Out[57]:
array([[ 0.7157, -0.6387],
       [ 0.7157, -0.6387],
       [ 0.3626,  0.849 ],
       [ 0.3626,  0.849 ],
       [ 0.3626,  0.849 ]])
```

```
In [58]: arr.repeat([2, 3], axis=1)
Out[58]:
array([[ 0.7157,  0.7157, -0.6387, -0.6387, -0.6387],
       [ 0.3626,  0.3626,  0.849 ,  0.849 ,  0.849 ]])
```

tile, on the other hand, is a shortcut for stacking copies of an array along an axis. You can visually think about it as like "laying down tiles":

```
In [59]: arr
Out[59]:
array([[ 0.7157, -0.6387],
       [ 0.3626,  0.849 ]])

In [60]: np.tile(arr, 2)
Out[60]:
array([[ 0.7157, -0.6387,  0.7157, -0.6387],
       [ 0.3626,  0.849 ,  0.3626,  0.849 ]])
```

The second argument is the number of tiles; with a scalar, the tiling is made row-by-row, rather than column by column: The second argument to `tile` can be a tuple indicating the layout of the "tiling":

```
In [61]: arr
Out[61]:
array([[ 0.7157, -0.6387],
       [ 0.3626,  0.849 ]])
```

```
In [62]: np.tile(arr, (2, 1))      In [63]: np.tile(arr, (3, 2))
Out[62]:                           Out[63]:
array([[ 0.7157, -0.6387],         array([[ 0.7157, -0.6387,  0.7157, -0.6387],
       [ 0.3626,  0.849 ],                [ 0.3626,  0.849 ,  0.3626,  0.849 ],
       [ 0.7157, -0.6387],                [ 0.7157, -0.6387,  0.7157, -0.6387],
       [ 0.3626,  0.849 ]])                [ 0.3626,  0.849 ,  0.3626,  0.849 ],
                                           [ 0.7157, -0.6387,  0.7157, -0.6387],
                                           [ 0.3626,  0.849 ,  0.3626,  0.849 ]])
```

Fancy Indexing Equivalents: Take and Put

As you may recall from Chapter 4, one way to get and set subsets of arrays is by *fancy* indexing using integer arrays:

```
In [64]: arr = np.arange(10) * 100
```

```
In [65]: inds = [7, 1, 2, 6]        In [66]: arr[inds]
                                    Out[66]: array([700, 100, 200, 600])
```

There are alternate ndarray methods that are useful in the special case of only making a selection on a single axis:

```
In [67]: arr.take(inds)
Out[67]: array([700, 100, 200, 600])

In [68]: arr.put(inds, 42)

In [69]: arr
Out[69]: array([  0,  42,  42, 300, 400, 500,  42,  42, 800, 900])

In [70]: arr.put(inds, [40, 41, 42, 43])
```

```
In [71]: arr
Out[71]: array([  0,  41,  42, 300, 400, 500,  43,  40, 800, 900])
```

To use take along other axes, you can pass the axis keyword:

```
In [72]: inds = [2, 0, 2, 1]

In [73]: arr = randn(2, 4)

In [74]: arr
Out[74]:
array([[-0.8237,  2.6047, -0.4578, -1.    ],
       [ 2.3198, -1.0792,  0.518 ,  0.2527]])

In [75]: arr.take(inds, axis=1)
Out[75]:
array([[-0.4578, -0.8237, -0.4578,  2.6047],
       [ 0.518 ,  2.3198,  0.518 , -1.0792]])
```

put does not accept an axis argument but rather indexes into the flattened (one-dimensional, C order) version of the array (this could be changed in principle). Thus, when you need to set elements using an index array on other axes, you will want to use fancy indexing.

 As of this writing, the take and put functions in general have better performance than their fancy indexing equivalents by a significant margin. I regard this as a "bug" and something to be fixed in NumPy, but it's something worth keeping in mind if you're selecting subsets of large arrays using integer arrays:

```
In [76]: arr = randn(1000, 50)

# Random sample of 500 rows
In [77]: inds = np.random.permutation(1000)[:500]

In [78]: %timeit arr[inds]
1000 loops, best of 3: 356 us per loop

In [79]: %timeit arr.take(inds, axis=0)
10000 loops, best of 3: 34 us per loop
```

Broadcasting

Broadcasting describes how arithmetic works between arrays of different shapes. It is a very powerful feature, but one that can be easily misunderstood, even by experienced users. The simplest example of broadcasting occurs when combining a scalar value with an array:

```
In [80]: arr = np.arange(5)

In [81]: arr                          In [82]: arr * 4
Out[81]: array([0, 1, 2, 3, 4])       Out[82]: array([ 0,  4,  8, 12, 16])
```

Here we say that the scalar value 4 has been *broadcast* to all of the other elements in the multiplication operation.

For example, we can demean each column of an array by subtracting the column means. In this case, it is very simple:

```
In [83]: arr = randn(4, 3)

In [84]: arr.mean(0)
Out[84]: array([ 0.1321,  0.552 ,  0.8571])

In [85]: demeaned = arr - arr.mean(0)
```

```
In [86]: demeaned                            In [87]: demeaned.mean(0)
Out[86]:                                     Out[87]: array([ 0., -0., -0.])
array([[ 0.1718, -0.1972, -1.3669],
       [-0.1292,  1.6529, -0.3429],
       [-0.2891, -0.0435,  1.2322],
       [ 0.2465, -1.4122,  0.4776]])
```

See Figure 12-4 for an illustration of this operation. Demeaning the rows as a broadcast operation requires a bit more care. Fortunately, broadcasting potentially lower dimensional values across any dimension of an array (like subtracting the row means from each column of a two-dimensional array) is possible as long as you follow the rules. This brings us to:

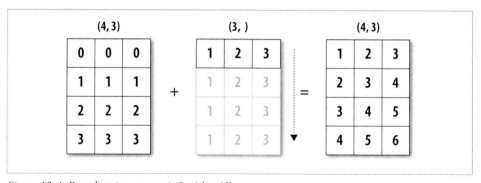

Figure 12-4. Broadcasting over axis 0 with a 1D array

The Broadcasting Rule

Two arrays are compatible for broadcasting if for each *trailing dimension* (that is, starting from the end), the axis lengths match or if either of the lengths is 1. Broadcasting is then performed over the missing and / or length 1 dimensions.

Even as an experienced NumPy user, I often must stop to draw pictures and think about the broadcasting rule. Consider the last example and suppose we wished instead to subtract the mean value from each row. Since `arr.mean(0)` has length 3, it is compatible for broadcasting across axis 0 because the trailing dimension in `arr` is 3 and therefore matches. According to the rules, to subtract over axis 1 (that is, subtract the row mean from each row), the smaller array must have shape (4, 1):

```
In [88]: arr
Out[88]:
array([[ 0.3039,  0.3548, -0.5097],
       [ 0.0029,  2.2049,  0.5142],
       [-0.1571,  0.5085,  2.0893],
       [ 0.3786, -0.8602,  1.3347]])

In [89]: row_means = arr.mean(1)        In [90]: row_means.reshape((4, 1))
                                        Out[90]:
                                        array([[ 0.0496],
                                               [ 0.9073],
                                               [ 0.8136],
                                               [ 0.2844]])

In [91]: demeaned = arr - row_means.reshape((4, 1))

In [92]: demeaned.mean(1)
Out[92]: array([ 0.,  0.,  0.,  0.])
```

Has your head exploded yet? See Figure 12-5 for an illustration of this operation.

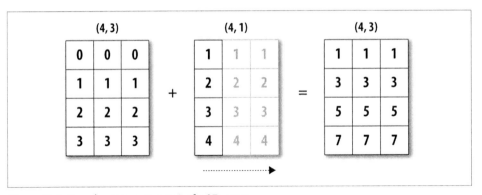

Figure 12-5. Broadcasting over axis 1 of a 2D array

See Figure 12-6 for another illustration, this time adding a two-dimensional array to a three-dimensional one across axis 0.

Broadcasting Over Other Axes

Broadcasting with higher dimensional arrays can seem even more mind-bending, but it is really a matter of following the rules. If you don't, you'll get an error like this:

```
In [93]: arr - arr.mean(1)
---------------------------------------------------------------
ValueError                                Traceback (most recent call last)
<ipython-input-93-7b87b85a20b2> in <module>()
```

```
----> 1 arr - arr.mean(1)
ValueError: operands could not be broadcast together with shapes (4,3) (4)
```

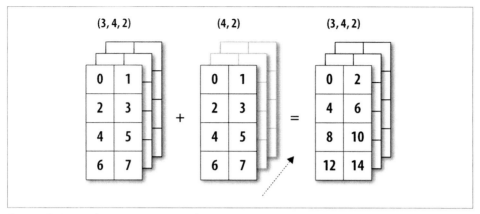

Figure 12-6. Broadcasting over axis 0 of a 3D array

It's quite common to want to perform an arithmetic operation with a lower dimensional array across axes other than axis 0. According to the broadcasting rule, the "broadcast dimensions" must be 1 in the smaller array. In the example of row demeaning above this meant reshaping the row means to be shape (4, 1) instead of (4,):

```
In [94]: arr - arr.mean(1).reshape((4, 1))
Out[94]:
array([[ 0.2542,  0.3051, -0.5594],
       [-0.9044,  1.2976, -0.3931],
       [-0.9707, -0.3051,  1.2757],
       [ 0.0942, -1.1446,  1.0503]])
```

In the three-dimensional case, broadcasting over any of the three dimensions is only a matter of reshaping the data to be shape-compatible. See Figure 12-7 for a nice visualization of the shapes required to broadcast over each axis of a three-dimensional array.

A very common problem, therefore, is needing to add a new axis with length 1 specifically for broadcasting purposes, especially in generic algorithms. Using reshape is one option, but inserting an axis requires constructing a tuple indicating the new shape. This can often be a tedious exercise. Thus, NumPy arrays offer a special syntax for inserting new axes by indexing. We use the special np.newaxis attribute along with "full" slices to insert the new axis:

```
In [95]: arr = np.zeros((4, 4))

In [96]: arr_3d = arr[:, np.newaxis, :]      In [97]: arr_3d.shape
                                             Out[97]: (4, 1, 4)

In [98]: arr_1d = np.random.normal(size=3)

In [99]: arr_1d[:, np.newaxis]        In [100]: arr_1d[np.newaxis, :]
Out[99]:                              Out[100]: array([[-0.3899,  0.396 , -0.1852]])
```

```
array([[-0.3899],
       [ 0.396 ],
       [-0.1852]])
```

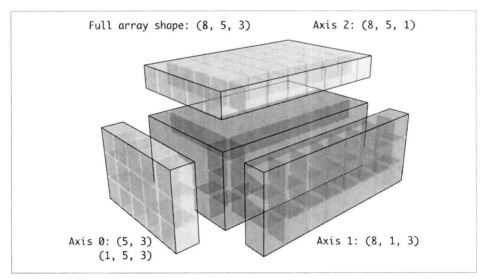

Figure 12-7. Compatible 2D array shapes for broadcasting over a 3D array

Thus, if we had a three-dimensional array and wanted to demean axis 2, say, we would only need to write:

```
In [101]: arr = randn(3, 4, 5)

In [102]: depth_means = arr.mean(2)

In [103]: depth_means
Out[103]:
array([[ 0.1097,  0.3118, -0.5473,  0.2663],
       [ 0.1747,  0.1379,  0.1146, -0.4224],
       [ 0.0217,  0.3686, -0.0468,  1.3026]])

In [104]: demeaned = arr - depth_means[:, :, np.newaxis]

In [105]: demeaned.mean(2)
Out[105]:
array([[ 0.,  0., -0.,  0.],
       [ 0., -0., -0.,  0.],
       [-0., -0.,  0.,  0.]])
```

If you're completely confused by this, don't worry. With practice you will get the hang of it!

Some readers might wonder if there's a way to generalize demeaning over an axis without sacrificing performance. There is, in fact, but it requires some indexing gymnastics:

```
def demean_axis(arr, axis=0):
    means = arr.mean(axis)

    # This generalized things like [:, :, np.newaxis] to N dimensions
    indexer = [slice(None)] * arr.ndim
    indexer[axis] = np.newaxis
    return arr - means[indexer]
```

Setting Array Values by Broadcasting

The same broadcasting rule governing arithmetic operations also applies to setting values via array indexing. In the simplest case, we can do things like:

```
In [106]: arr = np.zeros((4, 3))
```

```
In [107]: arr[:] = 5          In [108]: arr
                              Out[108]:
                              array([[ 5.,  5.,  5.],
                                     [ 5.,  5.,  5.],
                                     [ 5.,  5.,  5.],
                                     [ 5.,  5.,  5.]])
```

However, if we had a one-dimensional array of values we wanted to set into the columns of the array, we can do that as long as the shape is compatible:

```
In [109]: col = np.array([1.28, -0.42, 0.44, 1.6])
```

```
In [110]: arr[:] = col[:, np.newaxis]      In [111]: arr
                                           Out[111]:
                                           array([[ 1.28,  1.28,  1.28],
                                                  [-0.42, -0.42, -0.42],
                                                  [ 0.44,  0.44,  0.44],
                                                  [ 1.6 ,  1.6 ,  1.6 ]])
```

```
In [112]: arr[:2] = [[-1.37], [0.509]]     In [113]: arr
                                           Out[113]:
                                           array([[-1.37 , -1.37 , -1.37 ],
                                                  [ 0.509,  0.509,  0.509],
                                                  [ 0.44 ,  0.44 ,  0.44 ],
                                                  [ 1.6 ,  1.6 ,  1.6 ]])
```

Advanced ufunc Usage

While many NumPy users will only make use of the fast element-wise operations provided by the universal functions, there are a number of additional features that occasionally can help you write more concise code without loops.

ufunc Instance Methods

Each of NumPy's binary ufuncs has special methods for performing certain kinds of special vectorized operations. These are summarized in Table 12-2, but I'll give a few concrete examples to illustrate how they work.

`reduce` takes a single array and aggregates its values, optionally along an axis, by performing a sequence of binary operations. For example, an alternate way to sum elements in an array is to use `np.add.reduce`:

```
In [114]: arr = np.arange(10)

In [115]: np.add.reduce(arr)
Out[115]: 45

In [116]: arr.sum()
Out[116]: 45
```

The starting value (0 for `add`) depends on the ufunc. If an axis is passed, the reduction is performed along that axis. This allows you to answer certain kinds of questions in a concise way. As a less trivial example, we can use `np.logical_and` to check whether the values in each row of an array are sorted:

```
In [118]: arr = randn(5, 5)

In [119]: arr[::2].sort(1) # sort a few rows

In [120]: arr[:, :-1] < arr[:, 1:]
Out[120]:
array([[ True,  True,  True,  True],
       [False,  True, False, False],
       [ True,  True,  True,  True],
       [ True, False,  True,  True],
       [ True,  True,  True,  True]], dtype=bool)

In [121]: np.logical_and.reduce(arr[:, :-1] < arr[:, 1:], axis=1)
Out[121]: array([ True, False,  True, False,  True], dtype=bool)
```

Of course, `logical_and.reduce` is equivalent to the `all` method.

`accumulate` is related to `reduce` like `cumsum` is related to `sum`. It produces an array of the same size with the intermediate "accumulated" values:

```
In [122]: arr = np.arange(15).reshape((3, 5))

In [123]: np.add.accumulate(arr, axis=1)
Out[123]:
array([[ 0,  1,  3,  6, 10],
       [ 5, 11, 18, 26, 35],
       [10, 21, 33, 46, 60]])
```

`outer` performs a pairwise cross-product between two arrays:

```
In [124]: arr = np.arange(3).repeat([1, 2, 2])
```

```
In [125]: arr
Out[125]: array([0, 1, 1, 2, 2])

In [126]: np.multiply.outer(arr, np.arange(5))
Out[126]:
array([[0, 0, 0, 0, 0],
       [0, 1, 2, 3, 4],
       [0, 1, 2, 3, 4],
       [0, 2, 4, 6, 8],
       [0, 2, 4, 6, 8]])
```

The output of outer will have a dimension that is the sum of the dimensions of the inputs:

```
In [127]: result = np.subtract.outer(randn(3, 4), randn(5))

In [128]: result.shape
Out[128]: (3, 4, 5)
```

The last method, reduceat, performs a "local reduce", in essence an array groupby operation in which slices of the array are aggregated together. While it's less flexible than the GroupBy capabilities in pandas, it can be very fast and powerful in the right circumstances. It accepts a sequence of "bin edges" which indicate how to split and aggregate the values:

```
In [129]: arr = np.arange(10)

In [130]: np.add.reduceat(arr, [0, 5, 8])
Out[130]: array([10, 18, 17])
```

The results are the reductions (here, sums) performed over arr[0:5], arr[5:8], and arr[8:]. Like the other methods, you can pass an axis argument:

```
In [131]: arr = np.multiply.outer(np.arange(4), np.arange(5))
```

```
In [132]: arr                          In [133]: np.add.reduceat(arr, [0, 2, 4], axis=1)
Out[132]:                              Out[133]:
array([[ 0,  0,  0,  0,  0],           array([[ 0,  0,  0],
       [ 0,  1,  2,  3,  4],                  [ 1,  5,  4],
       [ 0,  2,  4,  6,  8],                  [ 2, 10,  8],
       [ 0,  3,  6,  9, 12]])                 [ 3, 15, 12]])
```

Table 12-2. ufunc methods

Method	Description
reduce(x)	Aggregate values by successive applications of the operation
accumulate(x)	Aggregate values, preserving all partial aggregates
reduceat(x, bins)	"Local" reduce or "group by". Reduce contiguous slices of data to produce aggregated array.
outer(x, y)	Apply operation to all pairs of elements in x and y. Result array has shape x.shape + y.shape

Custom ufuncs

There are a couple facilities for creating your own functions with ufunc-like semantics. numpy.frompyfunc accepts a Python function along with a specification for the number of inputs and outputs. For example, a simple function that adds element-wise would be specified as:

```
In [134]: def add_elements(x, y):
   .....:     return x + y

In [135]: add_them = np.frompyfunc(add_elements, 2, 1)

In [136]: add_them(np.arange(8), np.arange(8))
Out[136]: array([0, 2, 4, 6, 8, 10, 12, 14], dtype=object)
```

Functions created using frompyfunc always return arrays of Python objects which isn't very convenient. Fortunately, there is an alternate, but slightly less featureful function numpy.vectorize that is a bit more intelligent about type inference:

```
In [137]: add_them = np.vectorize(add_elements, otypes=[np.float64])

In [138]: add_them(np.arange(8), np.arange(8))
Out[138]: array([ 0.,  2.,  4.,  6.,  8., 10., 12., 14.])
```

These functions provide a way to create ufunc-like functions, but they are very slow because they require a Python function call to compute each element, which is a lot slower than NumPy's C-based ufunc loops:

```
In [139]: arr = randn(10000)

In [140]: %timeit add_them(arr, arr)
100 loops, best of 3: 2.12 ms per loop

In [141]: %timeit np.add(arr, arr)
100000 loops, best of 3: 11.6 us per loop
```

There are a number of projects under way in the scientific Python community to make it easier to define new ufuncs whose performance is closer to that of the built-in ones.

Structured and Record Arrays

You may have noticed up until now that ndarray is a *homogeneous* data container; that is, it represents a block of memory in which each element takes up the same number of bytes, determined by the dtype. On the surface, this would appear to not allow you to represent heterogeneous or tabular-like data. A *structured* array is an ndarray in which each element can be thought of as representing a *struct* in C (hence the "structured" name) or a row in a SQL table with multiple named fields:

```
In [142]: dtype = [('x', np.float64), ('y', np.int32)]

In [143]: sarr = np.array([(1.5, 6), (np.pi, -2)], dtype=dtype)
```

```
In [144]: sarr
Out[144]:
array([(1.5, 6), (3.141592653589793, -2)],
      dtype=[('x', '<f8'), ('y', '<i4')])
```

There are several ways to specify a structured dtype (see the online NumPy documentation). One typical way is as a list of tuples with (field_name, field_data_type). Now, the elements of the array are tuple-like objects whose elements can be accessed like a dictionary:

```
In [145]: sarr[0]
Out[145]: (1.5, 6)

In [146]: sarr[0]['y']
Out[146]: 6
```

The field names are stored in the dtype.names attribute. On accessing a field on the structured array, a strided view on the data is returned thus copying nothing:

```
In [147]: sarr['x']
Out[147]: array([ 1.5   ,  3.1416])
```

Nested dtypes and Multidimensional Fields

When specifying a structured dtype, you can additionally pass a shape (as an int or tuple):

```
In [148]: dtype = [('x', np.int64, 3), ('y', np.int32)]

In [149]: arr = np.zeros(4, dtype=dtype)

In [150]: arr
Out[150]:
array([([0, 0, 0], 0), ([0, 0, 0], 0), ([0, 0, 0], 0), ([0, 0, 0], 0)],
      dtype=[('x', '<i8', (3,)), ('y', '<i4')])
```

In this case, the x field now refers to an array of length three for each record:

```
In [151]: arr[0]['x']
Out[151]: array([0, 0, 0])
```

Conveniently, accessing arr['x'] then returns a two-dimensional array instead of a one-dimensional array as in prior examples:

```
In [152]: arr['x']
Out[152]:
array([[0, 0, 0],
       [0, 0, 0],
       [0, 0, 0],
       [0, 0, 0]])
```

This enables you to express more complicated, nested structures as a single block of memory in an array. Though, since dtypes can be arbitrarily complex, why not nested dtypes? Here is a simple example:

```
In [153]: dtype = [('x', [('a', 'f8'), ('b', 'f4')]), ('y', np.int32)]

In [154]: data = np.array([(((1, 2), 5), ((3, 4), 6)], dtype=dtype)

In [155]: data['x']
Out[155]:
array([[(1.0, 2.0), (3.0, 4.0)],
       dtype=[('a', '<f8'), ('b', '<f4')])

In [156]: data['y']
Out[156]: array([5, 6], dtype=int32)

In [157]: data['x']['a']
Out[157]: array([ 1.,  3.])
```

As you can see, variable-shape fields and nested records is a very rich feature that can be the right tool in certain circumstances. A DataFrame from pandas, by contrast, does not support this feature directly, though it is similar to hierarchical indexing.

Why Use Structured Arrays?

Compared with, say, a DataFrame from pandas, NumPy structured arrays are a comparatively low-level tool. They provide a means to interpreting a block of memory as a tabular structure with arbitrarily complex nested columns. Since each element in the array is represented in memory as a fixed number of bytes, structured arrays provide a very fast and efficient way of writing data to and from disk (including memory maps, more on this later), transporting it over the network, and other such use.

As another common use for structured arrays, writing data files as fixed length record byte streams is a common way to serialize data in C and C++ code, which is commonly found in legacy systems in industry. As long as the format of the file is known (the size of each record and the order, byte size, and data type of each element), the data can be read into memory using np.fromfile. Specialized uses like this are beyond the scope of this book, but it's worth knowing that such things are possible.

Structured Array Manipulations: numpy.lib.recfunctions

While there is not as much functionality available for structured arrays as for Data-Frames, the NumPy module numpy.lib.recfunctions has some helpful tools for adding and dropping fields or doing basic join-like operations. The thing to remember with these tools is that it is typically necessary to create a new array to make any modifications to the dtype (like adding or dropping a column). These functions are left to the interested reader to explore as I do not use them anywhere in this book.

More About Sorting

Like Python's built-in list, the ndarray **sort** instance method is an *in-place* sort, meaning that the array contents are rearranged without producing a new array:

```
In [158]: arr = randn(6)

In [159]: arr.sort()

In [160]: arr
Out[160]: array([-1.082 ,  0.3759,  0.8014,  1.1397,  1.2888,  1.8413])
```

When sorting arrays in-place, remember that if the array is a view on a different ndarray, the original array will be modified:

```
In [161]: arr = randn(3, 5)

In [162]: arr
Out[162]:
array([[-0.3318, -1.4711,  0.8705, -0.0847, -1.1329],
       [-1.0111, -0.3436,  2.1714,  0.1234, -0.0189],
       [ 0.1773,  0.7424,  0.8548,  1.038 , -0.329 ]])

In [163]: arr[:, 0].sort()  # Sort first column values in-place

In [164]: arr
Out[164]:
array([[-1.0111, -1.4711,  0.8705, -0.0847, -1.1329],
       [-0.3318, -0.3436,  2.1714,  0.1234, -0.0189],
       [ 0.1773,  0.7424,  0.8548,  1.038 , -0.329 ]])
```

On the other hand, numpy.sort creates a new, sorted copy of an array. Otherwise it accepts the same arguments (such as kind, more on this below) as ndarray.sort:

```
In [165]: arr = randn(5)

In [166]: arr
Out[166]: array([-1.1181, -0.2415, -2.0051,  0.7379, -1.0614])

In [167]: np.sort(arr)
Out[167]: array([-2.0051, -1.1181, -1.0614, -0.2415,  0.7379])

In [168]: arr
Out[168]: array([-1.1181, -0.2415, -2.0051,  0.7379, -1.0614])
```

All of these sort methods take an axis argument for sorting the sections of data along the passed axis independently:

```
In [169]: arr = randn(3, 5)

In [170]: arr
Out[170]:
array([[ 0.5955, -0.2682,  1.3389, -0.1872,  0.9111],
       [-0.3215,  1.0054, -0.5168,  1.1925, -0.1989],
       [ 0.3969, -1.7638,  0.6071, -0.2222, -0.2171]])
```

```
In [171]: arr.sort(axis=1)

In [172]: arr
Out[172]:
array([[-0.2682, -0.1872,  0.5955,  0.9111,  1.3389],
       [-0.5168, -0.3215, -0.1989,  1.0054,  1.1925],
       [-1.7638, -0.2222, -0.2171,  0.3969,  0.6071]])
```

You may notice that none of the sort methods have an option to sort in descending order. This is not actually a big deal because array slicing produces views, thus not producing a copy or requiring any computational work. Many Python users are familiar with the "trick" that for a list `values`, `values[::-1]` returns a list in reverse order. The same is true for ndarrays:

```
In [173]: arr[:, ::-1]
Out[173]:
array([[ 1.3389,  0.9111,  0.5955, -0.1872, -0.2682],
       [ 1.1925,  1.0054, -0.1989, -0.3215, -0.5168],
       [ 0.6071,  0.3969, -0.2171, -0.2222, -1.7638]])
```

Indirect Sorts: argsort and lexsort

In data analysis it's very common to need to reorder data sets by one or more keys. For example, a table of data about some students might need to be sorted by last name then by first name. This is an example of an *indirect* sort, and if you've read the pandas-related chapters you have already seen many higher-level examples. Given a key or keys (an array or values or multiple arrays of values), you wish to obtain an array of integer *indices* (I refer to them colloquially as *indexers*) that tells you how to reorder the data to be in sorted order. The two main methods for this are `argsort` and `numpy.lexsort`. As a trivial example:

```
In [174]: values = np.array([5, 0, 1, 3, 2])

In [175]: indexer = values.argsort()

In [176]: indexer
Out[176]: array([1, 2, 4, 3, 0])

In [177]: values[indexer]
Out[177]: array([0, 1, 2, 3, 5])
```

As a less trivial example, this code reorders a 2D array by its first row:

```
In [178]: arr = randn(3, 5)

In [179]: arr[0] = values

In [180]: arr
Out[180]:
array([[ 5.    ,  0.    ,  1.    ,  3.    ,  2.    ],
       [-0.3636, -0.1378,  2.1777, -0.4728,  0.8356],
       [-0.2089,  0.2316,  0.728 , -1.3918,  1.9956]])
```

```
In [181]: arr[:, arr[0].argsort()]
Out[181]:
array([[ 0.    , 1.    , 2.    , 3.    , 5.    ],
       [-0.1378, 2.1777, 0.8356, -0.4728, -0.3636],
       [ 0.2316, 0.728 , 1.9956, -1.3918, -0.2089]])
```

lexsort is similar to argsort, but it performs an indirect *lexicographical* sort on multiple key arrays. Suppose we wanted to sort some data identified by first and last names:

```
In [182]: first_name = np.array(['Bob', 'Jane', 'Steve', 'Bill', 'Barbara'])

In [183]: last_name = np.array(['Jones', 'Arnold', 'Arnold', 'Jones', 'Walters'])

In [184]: sorter = np.lexsort((first_name, last_name))

In [185]: zip(last_name[sorter], first_name[sorter])
Out[185]:
[('Arnold', 'Jane'),
 ('Arnold', 'Steve'),
 ('Jones', 'Bill'),
 ('Jones', 'Bob'),
 ('Walters', 'Barbara')]
```

lexsort can be a bit confusing the first time you use it because the order in which the keys are used to order the data starts with the *last* array passed. As you can see, last_name was used before first_name.

> pandas methods like Series's and DataFrame's sort_index methods and the Series order method are implemented with variants of these functions (which also must take into account missing values)

Alternate Sort Algorithms

A *stable* sorting algorithm preserves the relative position of equal elements. This can be especially important in indirect sorts where the relative ordering is meaningful:

```
In [186]: values = np.array(['2:first', '2:second', '1:first', '1:second', '1:third'])

In [187]: key = np.array([2, 2, 1, 1, 1])

In [188]: indexer = key.argsort(kind='mergesort')

In [189]: indexer
Out[189]: array([2, 3, 4, 0, 1])

In [190]: values.take(indexer)
Out[190]:
array(['1:first', '1:second', '1:third', '2:first', '2:second'],
      dtype='|S8')
```

The only stable sort available is *mergesort* which has guaranteed O(n log n) performance (for complexity buffs), but its performance is on average worse than the default quicksort method. See Table 12-3 for a summary of available methods and their relative performance (and performance guarantees). This is not something that most users will ever have to think about but useful to know that it's there.

Table 12-3. Array sorting methods

Kind	Speed	Stable	Work space	Worst-case
'quicksort'	1	No	0	$O(n^2)$
'mergesort'	2	Yes	n / 2	$O(n \log n)$
'heapsort'	3	No	0	$O(n \log n)$

 At the time of this writing, sort algorithms other than quicksort are not available on arrays of Python objects (dtype=object). This means occasionally that algorithms requiring stable sorting will require workarounds when dealing with Python objects.

numpy.searchsorted: Finding elements in a Sorted Array

searchsorted is an array method that performs a binary search on a sorted array, returning the location in the array where the value would need to be inserted to maintain sortedness:

```
In [191]: arr = np.array([0, 1, 7, 12, 15])

In [192]: arr.searchsorted(9)
Out[192]: 3
```

As you might expect, you can also pass an array of values to get an array of indices back:

```
In [193]: arr.searchsorted([0, 8, 11, 16])
Out[193]: array([0, 3, 3, 5])
```

You might have noticed that searchsorted returned 0 for the 0 element. This is because the default behavior is to return the index at the left side of a group of equal values:

```
In [194]: arr = np.array([0, 0, 0, 1, 1, 1, 1])

In [195]: arr.searchsorted([0, 1])
Out[195]: array([0, 3])

In [196]: arr.searchsorted([0, 1], side='right')
Out[196]: array([3, 7])
```

As another application of searchsorted, suppose we had an array of values between 0 and 10,000) and a separate array of "bucket edges" that we wanted to use to bin the data:

```
In [197]: data = np.floor(np.random.uniform(0, 10000, size=50))

In [198]: bins = np.array([0, 100, 1000, 5000, 10000])

In [199]: data
```

```
Out[199]:
array([ 8304.,  4181.,  9352.,  4907.,  3250.,  8546.,  2673.,  6152.,
        2774.,  5130.,  9553.,  4997.,  1794.,  9688.,   426.,  1612.,
         651.,  8653.,  1695.,  4764.,  1052.,  4836.,  8020.,  3479.,
        1513.,  5872.,  8992.,  7656.,  4764.,  5383.,  2319.,  4280.,
        4150.,  8601.,  3946.,  9904.,  7286.,  9969.,  6032.,  4574.,
        8480.,  4298.,  2708.,  7358.,  6439.,  7916.,  3899.,  9182.,
         871.,  7973.])
```

To then get a labeling of which interval each data point belongs to (where 1 would mean the bucket [0, 100)), we can simply use searchsorted:

```
In [200]: labels = bins.searchsorted(data)
```

```
In [201]: labels
Out[201]:
array([4, 3, 4, 3, 3, 4, 3, 4, 3, 4, 4, 3, 3, 4, 2, 3, 2, 4, 3, 3, 3, 3, 4,
       3, 3, 4, 4, 4, 3, 4, 3, 3, 3, 4, 3, 4, 4, 4, 4, 3, 4, 3, 3, 4, 4, 4,
       3, 4, 2, 4])
```

This, combined with pandas's groupby, can be used to easily bin data:

```
In [202]: Series(data).groupby(labels).mean()
Out[202]:
2    649.333333
3   3411.521739
4   7935.041667
```

Note that NumPy actually has a function digitize that computes this bin labeling:

```
In [203]: np.digitize(data, bins)
Out[203]:
array([4, 3, 4, 3, 3, 4, 3, 4, 3, 4, 4, 3, 3, 4, 2, 3, 2, 4, 3, 3, 3, 3, 4,
       3, 3, 4, 4, 4, 3, 4, 3, 3, 3, 4, 3, 4, 4, 4, 4, 3, 4, 3, 3, 4, 4, 4,
       3, 4, 2, 4])
```

NumPy Matrix Class

Compared with other languages for matrix operations and linear algebra, like MAT-LAB, Julia, and GAUSS, NumPy's linear algebra syntax can often be quite verbose. One reason is that matrix multiplication requires using numpy.dot. Also NumPy's indexing semantics are different, which makes porting code to Python less straightforward at times. Selecting a single row (e.g. X[1, :]) or column (e.g. X[:, 1]) from a 2D array yields a 1D array compared with a 2D array as in, say, MATLAB.

```
In [204]: X = np.array([[ 8.82768214,  3.82222409, -1.14276475,  2.04411587],
   .....:               [ 3.82222409,  6.75272284,  0.83909108,  2.08293758],
   .....:               [-1.14276475,  0.83909108,  5.01690521,  0.79573241],
   .....:               [ 2.04411587,  2.08293758,  0.79573241,  6.24095859]])
```

```
In [205]: X[:, 0]  # one-dimensional
Out[205]: array([ 8.8277,  3.8222, -1.1428,  2.0441])
```

```
In [206]: y = X[:, :1]  # two-dimensional by slicing
```

```
In [207]: X
Out[207]:
array([[ 8.8277,  3.8222, -1.1428,  2.0441],
       [ 3.8222,  6.7527,  0.8391,  2.0829],
       [-1.1428,  0.8391,  5.0169,  0.7957],
       [ 2.0441,  2.0829,  0.7957,  6.241 ]])

In [208]: y
Out[208]:
array([[ 8.8277],
       [ 3.8222],
       [-1.1428],
       [ 2.0441]])
```

In this case, the product $y^T X y$ would be expressed like so:

```
In [209]: np.dot(y.T, np.dot(X, y))
Out[209]: array([[ 1195.468]])
```

To aid in writing code with a lot of matrix operations, NumPy has a `matrix` class which has modified indexing behavior to make it more MATLAB-like: single rows and columns come back two-dimensional and multiplication with * is matrix multiplication. The above operation with `numpy.matrix` would look like:

```
In [210]: Xm = np.matrix(X)

In [211]: ym = Xm[:, 0]

In [212]: Xm
Out[212]:
matrix([[ 8.8277,  3.8222, -1.1428,  2.0441],
        [ 3.8222,  6.7527,  0.8391,  2.0829],
        [-1.1428,  0.8391,  5.0169,  0.7957],
        [ 2.0441,  2.0829,  0.7957,  6.241 ]])

In [213]: ym
Out[213]:
matrix([[ 8.8277],
        [ 3.8222],
        [-1.1428],
        [ 2.0441]])

In [214]: ym.T * Xm * ym
Out[214]: matrix([[ 1195.468]])
```

`matrix` also has a special attribute I which returns the matrix inverse:

```
In [215]: Xm.I * X
Out[215]:
matrix([[ 1., -0., -0., -0.],
        [ 0.,  1.,  0.,  0.],
        [ 0.,  0.,  1.,  0.],
        [ 0.,  0.,  0.,  1.]])
```

I do not recommend using `numpy.matrix` as a replacement for regular ndarrays because they are generally more seldom used. In individual functions with lots of linear algebra, it may be helpful to convert the function argument to `matrix` type, then cast back to regular arrays with `np.asarray` (which does not copy any data) before returning them.

Advanced Array Input and Output

In Chapter 4, I introduced you to `np.save` and `np.load` for storing arrays in binary format on disk. There are a number of additional options to consider for more sophisticated use. In particular, memory maps have the additional benefit of enabling you to work with data sets that do not fit into RAM.

Memory-mapped Files

A *memory-mapped* file is a method for treating potentially very large binary data on disk as an in-memory array. NumPy implements a `memmap` object that is ndarray-like, enabling small segments of a large file to be read and written without reading the whole array into memory. Additionally, a `memmap` has the same methods as an in-memory array and thus can be substituted into many algorithms where an ndarray would be expected.

To create a new `memmap`, use the function `np.memmap` and pass a file path, dtype, shape, and file mode:

```
In [216]: mmap = np.memmap('mymmap', dtype='float64', mode='w+', shape=(10000, 10000))
```

```
In [217]: mmap
Out[217]:
memmap([[ 0.,  0.,  0., ...,  0.,  0.,  0.],
        [ 0.,  0.,  0., ...,  0.,  0.,  0.],
        [ 0.,  0.,  0., ...,  0.,  0.,  0.],
        ...,
        [ 0.,  0.,  0., ...,  0.,  0.,  0.],
        [ 0.,  0.,  0., ...,  0.,  0.,  0.],
        [ 0.,  0.,  0., ...,  0.,  0.,  0.]])
```

Slicing a `memmap` returns views on the data on disk:

```
In [218]: section = mmap[:5]
```

If you assign data to these, it will be buffered in memory (like a Python file object), but can be written to disk by calling `flush`:

```
In [219]: section[:] = np.random.randn(5, 10000)
```

```
In [220]: mmap.flush()
```

```
In [221]: mmap
Out[221]:
memmap([[-0.1614, -0.1768,  0.422 , ..., -0.2195, -0.1256, -0.4012],
        [ 0.4898, -2.2219, -0.7684, ..., -2.3517, -1.0782,  1.3208],
        [-0.6875,  1.6901, -0.7444, ..., -1.4218, -0.0509,  1.2224],
```

```
      ...,
      [ 0.   , 0.   , 0.   , ..., 0.   , 0.   , 0.   ],
      [ 0.   , 0.   , 0.   , ..., 0.   , 0.   , 0.   ],
      [ 0.   , 0.   , 0.   , ..., 0.   , 0.   , 0.   ]])

In [222]: del mmap
```

Whenever a memory map falls out of scope and is garbage-collected, any changes will be flushed to disk also. When *opening an existing memory map*, you still have to specify the dtype and shape as the file is just a block of binary data with no metadata on disk:

```
In [223]: mmap = np.memmap('mymmap', dtype='float64', shape=(10000, 10000))

In [224]: mmap
Out[224]:
memmap([[-0.1614, -0.1768,  0.422 , ..., -0.2195, -0.1256, -0.4012],
        [ 0.4898, -2.2219, -0.7684, ..., -2.3517, -1.0782,  1.3208],
        [-0.6875,  1.6901, -0.7444, ..., -1.4218, -0.0509,  1.2224],
        ...,
        [ 0.   , 0.   , 0.   , ..., 0.   , 0.   , 0.   ],
        [ 0.   , 0.   , 0.   , ..., 0.   , 0.   , 0.   ],
        [ 0.   , 0.   , 0.   , ..., 0.   , 0.   , 0.   ]])
```

Since a memory map is just an on-disk ndarray, there are no issues using a structured dtype as described above.

HDF5 and Other Array Storage Options

PyTables and h5py are two Python projects providing NumPy-friendly interfaces for storing array data in the efficient and compressible HDF5 format (HDF stands for *hierarchical data format*). You can safely store hundreds of gigabytes or even terabytes of data in HDF5 format. The use of these libraries is unfortunately outside the scope of the book.

PyTables provides a rich facility for working with structured arrays with advanced querying features and the ability to add column indexes to accelerate queries. This is very similar to the table indexing capabilities provided by relational databases.

Performance Tips

Getting good performance out of code utilizing NumPy is often straightforward, as array operations typically replace otherwise comparatively extremely slow pure Python loops. Here is a brief list of some of the things to keep in mind:

- Convert Python loops and conditional logic to array operations and boolean array operations
- Use broadcasting whenever possible
- Avoid copying data using array views (slicing)
- Utilize ufuncs and ufunc methods

If you can't get the performance you require after exhausting the capabilities provided by NumPy alone, writing code in C, Fortran, or especially Cython (see a bit more on this below) may be in order. I personally use Cython (*http://cython.org*) heavily in my own work as an easy way to get C-like performance with minimal development.

The Importance of Contiguous Memory

While the full extent of this topic is a bit outside the scope of this book, in some applications the memory layout of an array can significantly affect the speed of computations. This is based partly on performance differences having to do with the cache hierarchy of the CPU; operations accessing contiguous blocks of memory (for example, summing the rows of a C order array) will generally be the fastest because the memory subsystem will buffer the appropriate blocks of memory into the ultrafast L1 or L2 CPU cache. Also, certain code paths inside NumPy's C codebase have been optimized for the contiguous case in which generic strided memory access can be avoided.

To say that an array's memory layout is *contiguous* means that the elements are stored in memory in the order that they appear in the array with respect to Fortran (column major) or C (row major) ordering. By default, NumPy arrays are created as *C-contiguous* or just simply contiguous. A column major array, such as the transpose of a C-contiguous array, is thus said to be Fortran-contiguous. These properties can be explicitly checked via the `flags` attribute on the `ndarray`:

```
In [227]: arr_c = np.ones((1000, 1000), order='C')

In [228]: arr_f = np.ones((1000, 1000), order='F')

In [229]: arr_c.flags          In [230]: arr_f.flags
Out[229]:                      Out[230]:
  C_CONTIGUOUS : True            C_CONTIGUOUS : False
  F_CONTIGUOUS : False           F_CONTIGUOUS : True
  OWNDATA : True                 OWNDATA : True
  WRITEABLE : True               WRITEABLE : True
  ALIGNED : True                 ALIGNED : True
  UPDATEIFCOPY : False           UPDATEIFCOPY : False

In [231]: arr_f.flags.f_contiguous
Out[231]: True
```

In this example, summing the rows of these arrays should, in theory, be faster for arr_c than arr_f since the rows are contiguous in memory. Here I check for sure using %timeit in IPython:

```
In [232]: %timeit arr_c.sum(1)
1000 loops, best of 3: 1.33 ms per loop

In [233]: %timeit arr_f.sum(1)
100 loops, best of 3: 8.75 ms per loop
```

When looking to squeeze more performance out of NumPy, this is often a place to invest some effort. If you have an array that does not have the desired memory order, you can use copy and pass either 'C' or 'F':

```
In [234]: arr_f.copy('C').flags
Out[234]:
  C_CONTIGUOUS : True
  F_CONTIGUOUS : False
  OWNDATA : True
  WRITEABLE : True
  ALIGNED : True
  UPDATEIFCOPY : False
```

When constructing a view on an array, keep in mind that the result is not guaranteed to be contiguous:

```
In [235]: arr_c[:50].flags.contiguous
Out[235]: True
```

```
In [236]: arr_c[:, :50].flags
Out[236]:
  C_CONTIGUOUS : False
  F_CONTIGUOUS : False
  OWNDATA : False
  WRITEABLE : True
  ALIGNED : True
  UPDATEIFCOPY : False
```

Other Speed Options: Cython, f2py, C

In recent years, the Cython project ((*http://cython.org*) has become the tool of choice for many scientific Python programmers for implementing fast code that may need to interact with C or C++ libraries, but without having to write pure C code. You can think of Cython as Python with static types and the ability to interleave functions implemented in C into Python-like code. For example, a simple Cython function to sum the elements of a one-dimensional array might look like:

```
from numpy cimport ndarray, float64_t

def sum_elements(ndarray[float64_t] arr):
    cdef Py_ssize_t i, n = len(arr)
    cdef float64_t result = 0

    for i in range(n):
        result += arr[i]

    return result
```

Cython takes this code, translates it to C, then compiles the generated C code to create a Python extension. Cython is an attractive option for performance computing because the code is only slightly more time-consuming to write than pure Python code and it integrates closely with NumPy. A common workflow is to get an algorithm working in Python, then translate it to Cython by adding type declarations and a handful of other tweaks. For more, see the project documentation.

Some other options for writing high performance code with NumPy include f2py, a wrapper generator for Fortran 77 and 90 code, and writing pure C extensions.

Python Language Essentials

Knowledge is a treasure, but practice is the key to it.

—Thomas Fuller

People often ask me about good resources for learning Python for data-centric applications. While there are many excellent Python language books, I am usually hesitant to recommend some of them as they are intended for a general audience rather than tailored for someone who wants to load in some data sets, do some computations, and plot some of the results. There are actually a couple of books on "scientific programming in Python", but they are geared toward numerical computing and engineering applications: solving differential equations, computing integrals, doing Monte Carlo simulations, and various topics that are more mathematically-oriented rather than being about data analysis and statistics. As this is a book about becoming proficient at working with data in Python, I think it is valuable to spend some time highlighting the most important features of Python's built-in data structures and libraries from the perspective of processing and manipulating structured and unstructured data. As such, I will only present roughly enough information to enable you to follow along with the rest of the book.

This chapter is not intended to be an exhaustive introduction to the Python language but rather a biased, no-frills overview of features which are used repeatedly throughout this book. For new Python programmers, I recommend that you supplement this chapter with the official Python tutorial (*http://docs.python.org*) and potentially one of the many excellent (and much longer) books on general purpose Python programming. In my opinion, it is *not* necessary to become proficient at building good software in Python to be able to productively do data analysis. I encourage you to use IPython to experiment with the code examples and to explore the documentation for the various types, functions, and methods. Note that some of the code used in the examples may not necessarily be fully-introduced at this point.

Much of this book focuses on high performance array-based computing tools for working with large data sets. In order to use those tools you must often first do some munging to corral messy data into a more nicely structured form. Fortunately, Python is one of the easiest-to-use languages for rapidly whipping your data into shape. The greater your facility with Python, the language, the easier it will be for you to prepare new data sets for analysis.

The Python Interpreter

Python is an *interpreted* language. The Python interpreter runs a program by executing one statement at a time. The standard interactive Python interpreter can be invoked on the command line with the python command:

```
$ python
Python 2.7.2 (default, Oct  4 2011, 20:06:09)
[GCC 4.6.1] on linux2
Type "help", "copyright", "credits" or "license" for more information.
>>> a = 5
>>> print(a)
5
```

The >>> you see is the *prompt* where you'll type expressions. To exit the Python interpreter and return to the command prompt, you can either type exit() or press Ctrl-D.

Running Python programs is as simple as calling python with a .py file as its first argument. Suppose we had created hello_world.py with these contents:

```
print 'Hello world'
```

This can be run from the terminal simply as:

```
$ python hello_world.py
Hello world
```

While many Python programmers execute all of their Python code in this way, many *scientific* Python programmers make use of IPython, an enhanced interactive Python interpreter. Chapter 3 is dedicated to the IPython system. By using the %run command, IPython executes the code in the specified file in the same process, enabling you to explore the results interactively when it's done.

```
$ ipython
Python 2.7.2 |EPD 7.1-2 (64-bit)| (default, Jul  3 2011, 15:17:51)
Type "copyright", "credits" or "license" for more information.

IPython 0.12 -- An enhanced Interactive Python.
?         -> Introduction and overview of IPython's features.
%quickref -> Quick reference.
help      -> Python's own help system.
object?   -> Details about 'object', use 'object??' for extra details.

In [1]: %run hello_world.py
Hello world

In [2]:
```

The default IPython prompt adopts the numbered In [2]: style compared with the standard >>> prompt.

The Basics

Language Semantics

The Python language design is distinguished by its emphasis on readability, simplicity, and explicitness. Some people go so far as to liken it to "executable pseudocode".

Indentation, not braces

Python uses whitespace (tabs or spaces) to structure code instead of using braces as in many other languages like R, C++, Java, and Perl. Take the for loop in the above quicksort algorithm:

```
for x in array:
    if x < pivot:
        less.append(x)
    else:
        greater.append(x)
```

A colon denotes the start of an indented code block after which all of the code must be indented by the same amount until the end of the block. In another language, you might instead have something like:

```
for x in array {
        if x < pivot {
            less.append(x)
        } else {
            greater.append(x)
        }
    }
```

One major reason that whitespace matters is that it results in most Python code looking cosmetically similar, which means less cognitive dissonance when you read a piece of code that you didn't write yourself (or wrote in a hurry a year ago!). In a language without significant whitespace, you might stumble on some differently formatted code like:

```
for x in array
    {
      if x < pivot
      {
        less.append(x)
      }
      else
      {
        greater.append(x)
```

```
    }
  }
```

Love it or hate it, significant whitespace is a fact of life for Python programmers, and in my experience it helps make Python code a lot more readable than other languages I've used. While it may seem foreign at first, I suspect that it will grow on you after a while.

 I strongly recommend that you use *4 spaces* to as your default indentation and that your editor replace tabs with 4 spaces. Many text editors have a setting that will replace tab stops with spaces automatically (do this!). Some people use tabs or a different number of spaces, with 2 spaces not being terribly uncommon. 4 spaces is by and large the standard adopted by the vast majority of Python programmers, so I recommend doing that in the absence of a compelling reason otherwise.

As you can see by now, Python statements also do not need to be terminated by semicolons. Semicolons can be used, however, to separate multiple statements on a single line:

```
a = 5; b = 6; c = 7
```

Putting multiple statements on one line is generally discouraged in Python as it often makes code less readable.

Everything is an object

An important characteristic of the Python language is the consistency of its *object model*. Every number, string, data structure, function, class, module, and so on exists in the Python interpreter in its own "box" which is referred to as a *Python object*. Each object has an associated *type* (for example, *string* or *function*) and internal data. In practice this makes the language very flexible, as even functions can be treated just like any other object.

Comments

Any text preceded by the hash mark (pound sign) # is ignored by the Python interpreter. This is often used to add comments to code. At times you may also want to exclude certain blocks of code without deleting them. An easy solution is to *comment out* the code:

```
results = []
for line in file_handle:
    # keep the empty lines for now
    # if len(line) == 0:
    #   continue
    results.append(line.replace('foo', 'bar'))
```

Function and object method calls

Functions are called using parentheses and passing zero or more arguments, optionally assigning the returned value to a variable:

```
result = f(x, y, z)
g()
```

Almost every object in Python has attached functions, known as *methods*, that have access to the object's internal contents. They can be called using the syntax:

```
obj.some_method(x, y, z)
```

Functions can take both *positional* and *keyword* arguments:

```
result = f(a, b, c, d=5, e='foo')
```

More on this later.

Variables and pass-by-reference

When assigning a variable (or *name*) in Python, you are creating a *reference* to the object on the right hand side of the equals sign. In practical terms, consider a list of integers:

```
In [241]: a = [1, 2, 3]
```

Suppose we assign a to a new variable b:

```
In [242]: b = a
```

In some languages, this assignment would cause the data [1, 2, 3] to be copied. In Python, a and b actually now refer to the same object, the original list [1, 2, 3] (see Figure A-1 for a mockup). You can prove this to yourself by appending an element to a and then examining b:

```
In [243]: a.append(4)

In [244]: b
Out[244]: [1, 2, 3, 4]
```

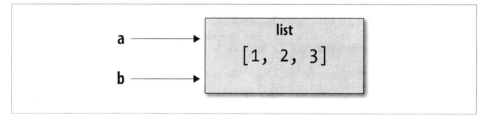

Figure A-1. Two references for the same object

Understanding the semantics of references in Python and when, how, and why data is copied is especially critical when working with larger data sets in Python.

Assignment is also referred to as *binding*, as we are binding a name to an object. Variable names that have been assigned may occasionally be referred to as bound variables.

When you pass objects as arguments to a function, you are only passing references; no copying occurs. Thus, Python is said to *pass by reference*, whereas some other languages support both pass by value (creating copies) and pass by reference. This means that a function can mutate the internals of its arguments. Suppose we had the following function:

```
def append_element(some_list, element):
    some_list.append(element)
```

Then given what's been said, this should not come as a surprise:

```
In [2]: data = [1, 2, 3]

In [3]: append_element(data, 4)

In [4]: data
Out[4]: [1, 2, 3, 4]
```

Dynamic references, strong types

In contrast with many compiled languages, such as Java and C++, object *references* in Python have no type associated with them. There is no problem with the following:

```
In [245]: a = 5        In [246]: type(a)
                       Out[246]: int

In [247]: a = 'foo'    In [248]: type(a)
                       Out[248]: str
```

Variables are names for objects within a particular namespace; the type information is stored in the object itself. Some observers might hastily conclude that Python is not a "typed language". This is not true; consider this example:

```
In [249]: '5' + 5
---------------------------------------------------------------------------
TypeError                                 Traceback (most recent call last)
<ipython-input-249-f9dbf5f0b234> in <module>()
----> 1 '5' + 5
TypeError: cannot concatenate 'str' and 'int' objects
```

In some languages, such as Visual Basic, the string '5' might get implicitly converted (or *casted*) to an integer, thus yielding 10. Yet in other languages, such as JavaScript, the integer 5 might be casted to a string, yielding the concatenated string '55'. In this regard Python is considered a *strongly-typed* language, which means that every object has a specific type (or *class*), and implicit conversions will occur only in certain obvious circumstances, such as the following:

```
In [250]: a = 4.5

In [251]: b = 2

# String formatting, to be visited later
In [252]: print 'a is %s, b is %s' % (type(a), type(b))
a is <type 'float'>, b is <type 'int'>

In [253]: a / b
Out[253]: 2.25
```

Knowing the type of an object is important, and it's useful to be able to write functions that can handle many different kinds of input. You can check that an object is an instance of a particular type using the isinstance function:

```
In [254]: a = 5        In [255]: isinstance(a, int)
                       Out[255]: True
```

isinstance can accept a tuple of types if you want to check that an object's type is among those present in the tuple:

```
In [256]: a = 5; b = 4.5

In [257]: isinstance(a, (int, float))      In [258]: isinstance(b, (int, float))
Out[257]: True                             Out[258]: True
```

Attributes and methods

Objects in Python typically have both attributes, other Python objects stored "inside" the object, and methods, functions associated with an object which can have access to the object's internal data. Both of them are accessed via the syntax obj.attribute_name:

```
In [1]: a = 'foo'

In [2]: a.<Tab>
a.capitalize  a.format     a.isupper    a.rindex      a.strip
a.center      a.index      a.join       a.rjust       a.swapcase
a.count       a.isalnum    a.ljust      a.rpartition  a.title
a.decode      a.isalpha    a.lower      a.rsplit      a.translate
a.encode      a.isdigit    a.lstrip     a.rstrip      a.upper
a.endswith    a.islower    a.partition  a.split       a.zfill
a.expandtabs  a.isspace    a.replace    a.splitlines
a.find        a.istitle    a.rfind      a.startswith
```

Attributes and methods can also be accessed by name using the getattr function:

```
>>> getattr(a, 'split')
<function split>
```

While we will not extensively use the functions getattr and related functions hasattr and setattr in this book, they can be used very effectively to write generic, reusable code.

"Duck" typing

Often you may not care about the type of an object but rather only whether it has certain methods or behavior. For example, you can verify that an object is iterable if it implemented the *iterator protocol*. For many objects, this means it has a __iter__ "magic method", though an alternative and better way to check is to try using the iter function:

```
def isiterable(obj):
    try:
        iter(obj)
        return True
    except TypeError: # not iterable
        return False
```

This function would return True for strings as well as most Python collection types:

```
In [260]: isiterable('a string')        In [261]: isiterable([1, 2, 3])
Out[260]: True                          Out[261]: True

In [262]: isiterable(5)
Out[262]: False
```

A place where I use this functionality all the time is to write functions that can accept multiple kinds of input. A common case is writing a function that can accept any kind of sequence (list, tuple, ndarray) or even an iterator. You can first check if the object is a list (or a NumPy array) and, if it is not, convert it to be one:

```
if not isinstance(x, list) and isiterable(x):
    x = list(x)
```

Imports

In Python a *module* is simply a .py file containing function and variable definitions along with such things imported from other .py files. Suppose that we had the following module:

```
# some_module.py
PI = 3.14159

def f(x):
    return x + 2

def g(a, b):
    return a + b
```

If we wanted to access the variables and functions defined in some_module.py, from another file in the same directory we could do:

```
import some_module
result = some_module.f(5)
pi = some_module.PI
```

Or equivalently:

```
from some_module import f, g, PI
result = g(5, PI)
```

By using the as keyword you can give imports different variable names:

```
import some_module as sm
from some_module import PI as pi, g as gf

r1 = sm.f(pi)
r2 = gf(6, pi)
```

Binary operators and comparisons

Most of the binary math operations and comparisons are as you might expect:

```
In [263]: 5 - 7          In [264]: 12 + 21.5
Out[263]: -2             Out[264]: 33.5

In [265]: 5 <= 2
Out[265]: False
```

See Table A-1 for all of the available binary operators.

To check if two references refer to the same object, use the is keyword. is not is also perfectly valid if you want to check that two objects are not the same:

```
In [266]: a = [1, 2, 3]

In [267]: b = a

# Note, the list function always creates a new list
In [268]: c = list(a)

In [269]: a is b          In [270]: a is not c
Out[269]: True           Out[270]: True
```

Note this is not the same thing is comparing with ==, because in this case we have:

```
In [271]: a == c
Out[271]: True
```

A very common use of is and is not is to check if a variable is None, since there is only one instance of None:

```
In [272]: a = None

In [273]: a is None
Out[273]: True
```

Table A-1. Binary operators

Operation	Description
a + b	Add a and b
a - b	Subtract b from a
a * b	Multiply a by b
a / b	Divide a by b
a // b	Floor-divide a by b, dropping any fractional remainder

Operation	Description
a ** b	Raise a to the b power
a & b	True if both a and b are True. For integers, take the bitwise AND.
a | b	True if either a or b is True. For integers, take the bitwise OR.
a ^ b	For booleans, True if a or b is True, but not both. For integers, take the bitwise EXCLUSIVE-OR.
a == b	True if a equals b
a != b	True if a is not equal to b
a <= b, a < b	True if a is less than (less than or equal) to b
a > b, a >= b	True if a is greater than (greater than or equal) to b
a is b	True if a and b reference same Python object
a is not b	True if a and b reference different Python objects

Strictness versus laziness

When using any programming language, it's important to understand *when* expressions are evaluated. Consider the simple expression:

```
a = b = c = 5
d = a + b * c
```

In Python, once these statements are evaluated, the calculation is immediately (or *strictly*) carried out, setting the value of d to 30. In another programming paradigm, such as in a pure functional programming language like Haskell, the value of d might not be evaluated until it is actually used elsewhere. The idea of deferring computations in this way is commonly known as *lazy evaluation*. Python, on the other hand, is a very strict (or eager) language. Nearly all of the time, computations and expressions are evaluated immediately. Even in the above simple expression, the result of b * c is computed as a separate step before adding it to a.

There are Python techniques, especially using iterators and generators, which can be used to achieve laziness. When performing very expensive computations which are only necessary some of the time, this can be an important technique in data-intensive applications.

Mutable and immutable objects

Most objects in Python are mutable, such as lists, dicts, NumPy arrays, or most user-defined types (classes). This means that the object or values that they contain can be modified.

```
In [274]: a_list = ['foo', 2, [4, 5]]

In [275]: a_list[2] = (3, 4)

In [276]: a_list
Out[276]: ['foo', 2, (3, 4)]
```

Others, like strings and tuples, are immutable:

```
In [277]: a_tuple = (3, 5, (4, 5))

In [278]: a_tuple[1] = 'four'
---------------------------------------------------------------------------
TypeError                                 Traceback (most recent call last)
<ipython-input-278-b7966a9ae0f1> in <module>()
----> 1 a_tuple[1] = 'four'
TypeError: 'tuple' object does not support item assignment
```

Remember that just because you *can* mutate an object does not mean that you always *should*. Such actions are known in programming as *side effects*. For example, when writing a function, any side effects should be explicitly communicated to the user in the function's documentation or comments. If possible, I recommend trying to avoid side effects and *favor immutability*, even though there may be mutable objects involved.

Scalar Types

Python has a small set of built-in types for handling numerical data, strings, boolean (True or False) values, and dates and time. See Table A-2 for a list of the main scalar types. Date and time handling will be discussed separately as these are provided by the datetime module in the standard library.

Table A-2. Standard Python Scalar Types

Type	Description
None	The Python "null" value (only one instance of the None object exists)
str	String type. ASCII-valued only in Python 2.x and Unicode in Python 3
unicode	Unicode string type
float	Double-precision (64-bit) floating point number. Note there is no separate double type.
bool	A True or False value
int	Signed integer with maximum value determined by the platform.
long	Arbitrary precision signed integer. Large int values are automatically converted to long.

Numeric types

The primary Python types for numbers are int and float. The size of the integer which can be stored as an int is dependent on your platform (whether 32 or 64-bit), but Python will transparently convert a very large integer to long, which can store arbitrarily large integers.

```
In [279]: ival = 17239871

In [280]: ival ** 6
Out[280]: 26254519291092456596965462913230729701102721L
```

Floating point numbers are represented with the Python `float` type. Under the hood each one is a double-precision (64 bits) value. They can also be expressed using scientific notation:

```
In [281]: fval = 7.243

In [282]: fval2 = 6.78e-5
```

In Python 3, integer division not resulting in a whole number will always yield a floating point number:

```
In [284]: 3 / 2
Out[284]: 1.5
```

In Python 2.7 and below (which some readers will likely be using), you can enable this behavior by default by putting the following cryptic-looking statement at the top of your module:

```
from __future__ import division
```

Without this in place, you can always explicitly convert the denominator into a floating point number:

```
In [285]: 3 / float(2)
Out[285]: 1.5
```

To get C-style integer division (which drops the fractional part if the result is not a whole number), use the floor division operator `//`:

```
In [286]: 3 // 2
Out[286]: 1
```

Complex numbers are written using j for the imaginary part:

```
In [287]: cval = 1 + 2j

In [288]: cval * (1 - 2j)
Out[288]: (5+0j)
```

Strings

Many people use Python for its powerful and flexible built-in string processing capabilities. You can write *string literal* using either single quotes `'` or double quotes `"`:

```
a = 'one way of writing a string'
b = "another way"
```

For multiline strings with line breaks, you can use triple quotes, either `'''` or `"""`:

```
c = """
This is a longer string that
spans multiple lines
"""
```

Python strings are immutable; you cannot modify a string without creating a new string:

```
In [289]: a = 'this is a string'

In [290]: a[10] = 'f'
---------------------------------------------------------------------
TypeError                                 Traceback (most recent call last)
<ipython-input-290-5ca625d1e504> in <module>()
----> 1 a[10] = 'f'
TypeError: 'str' object does not support item assignment

In [291]: b = a.replace('string', 'longer string')

In [292]: b
Out[292]: 'this is a longer string'
```

Many Python objects can be converted to a string using the str function:

```
In [293]: a = 5.6       In [294]: s = str(a)

In [295]: s
Out[295]: '5.6'
```

Strings are a sequence of characters and therefore can be treated like other sequences, such as lists and tuples:

```
In [296]: s = 'python'     In [297]: list(s)
                           Out[297]: ['p', 'y', 't', 'h', 'o', 'n']

In [298]: s[:3]
Out[298]: 'pyt'
```

The backslash character \ is an *escape character*, meaning that it is used to specify special characters like newline \n or unicode characters. To write a string literal with backslashes, you need to escape them:

```
In [299]: s = '12\\34'

In [300]: print s
12\34
```

If you have a string with a lot of backslashes and no special characters, you might find this a bit annoying. Fortunately you can preface the leading quote of the string with r which means that the characters should be interpreted as is:

```
In [301]: s = r'this\has\no\special\characters'

In [302]: s
Out[302]: 'this\\has\\no\\special\\characters'
```

Adding two strings together concatenates them and produces a new string:

```
In [303]: a = 'this is the first half '

In [304]: b = 'and this is the second half'

In [305]: a + b
Out[305]: 'this is the first half and this is the second half'
```

String templating or formatting is another important topic. The number of ways to do so has expanded with the advent of Python 3, here I will briefly describe the mechanics of one of the main interfaces. Strings with a % followed by one or more format characters is a target for inserting a value into that string (this is quite similar to the printf function in C). As an example, consider this string:

```
In [306]: template = '%.2f %s are worth $%d'
```

In this string, %s means to format an argument as a string, %.2f a number with 2 decimal places, and %d an integer. To substitute arguments for these format parameters, use the binary operator % with a tuple of values:

```
In [307]: template % (4.5560, 'Argentine Pesos', 1)
Out[307]: '4.56 Argentine Pesos are worth $1'
```

String formatting is a broad topic; there are multiple methods and numerous options and tweaks available to control how values are formatted in the resulting string. To learn more, I recommend you seek out more information on the web.

I discuss general string processing as it relates to data analysis in more detail in Chapter 7.

Booleans

The two boolean values in Python are written as True and False. Comparisons and other conditional expressions evaluate to either True or False. Boolean values are combined with the and and or keywords:

```
In [308]: True and True
Out[308]: True

In [309]: False or True
Out[309]: True
```

Almost all built-in Python tops and any class defining the __nonzero__ magic method have a True or False interpretation in an if statement:

```
In [310]: a = [1, 2, 3]
   .....: if a:
   .....:     print 'I found something!'
   .....:
I found something!

In [311]: b = []
   .....: if not b:
   .....:     print 'Empty!'
   .....:
Empty!
```

Most objects in Python have a notion of true- or falseness. For example, empty sequences (lists, dicts, tuples, etc.) are treated as False if used in control flow (as above with the empty list b). You can see exactly what boolean value an object coerces to by invoking bool on it:

```
In [312]: bool([]), bool([1, 2, 3])
Out[312]: (False, True)

In [313]: bool('Hello world!'), bool('')
Out[313]: (True, False)

In [314]: bool(0), bool(1)
Out[314]: (False, True)
```

Type casting

The str, bool, int and float types are also functions which can be used to cast values to those types:

```
In [315]: s = '3.14159'
```

```
In [316]: fval = float(s)        In [317]: type(fval)
                                 Out[317]: float
```

```
In [318]: int(fval)       In [319]: bool(fval)        In [320]: bool(0)
Out[318]: 3               Out[319]: True              Out[320]: False
```

None

None is the Python null value type. If a function does not explicitly return a value, it implicitly returns None.

```
In [321]: a = None       In [322]: a is None
                         Out[322]: True
```

```
In [323]: b = 5          In [324]: b is not None
                         Out[324]: True
```

None is also a common default value for optional function arguments:

```
def add_and_maybe_multiply(a, b, c=None):
    result = a + b

    if c is not None:
        result = result * c

    return result
```

While a technical point, it's worth bearing in mind that None is not a reserved keyword but rather a unique instance of NoneType.

Dates and times

The built-in Python datetime module provides datetime, date, and time types. The datetime type as you may imagine combines the information stored in date and time and is the most commonly used:

```
In [325]: from datetime import datetime, date, time
```

```
In [326]: dt = datetime(2011, 10, 29, 20, 30, 21)
```

```
In [327]: dt.day      In [328]: dt.minute
Out[327]: 29          Out[328]: 30
```

Given a datetime instance, you can extract the equivalent date and time objects by calling methods on the datetime of the same name:

```
In [329]: dt.date()                    In [330]: dt.time()
Out[329]: datetime.date(2011, 10, 29)  Out[330]: datetime.time(20, 30, 21)
```

The strftime method formats a datetime as a string:

```
In [331]: dt.strftime('%m/%d/%Y %H:%M')
Out[331]: '10/29/2011 20:30'
```

Strings can be converted (parsed) into datetime objects using the strptime function:

```
In [332]: datetime.strptime('20091031', '%Y%m%d')
Out[332]: datetime.datetime(2009, 10, 31, 0, 0)
```

See Table 10-2 for a full list of format specifications.

When aggregating or otherwise grouping time series data, it will occasionally be useful to replace fields of a series of datetimes, for example replacing the minute and second fields with zero, producing a new object:

```
In [333]: dt.replace(minute=0, second=0)
Out[333]: datetime.datetime(2011, 10, 29, 20, 0)
```

The difference of two datetime objects produces a datetime.timedelta type:

```
In [334]: dt2 = datetime(2011, 11, 15, 22, 30)

In [335]: delta = dt2 - dt

In [336]: delta                             In [337]: type(delta)
Out[336]: datetime.timedelta(17, 7179)      Out[337]: datetime.timedelta
```

Adding a timedelta to a datetime produces a new shifted datetime:

```
In [338]: dt
Out[338]: datetime.datetime(2011, 10, 29, 20, 30, 21)

In [339]: dt + delta
Out[339]: datetime.datetime(2011, 11, 15, 22, 30)
```

Control Flow

if, elif, and else

The if statement is one of the most well-known control flow statement types. It checks a condition which, if True, evaluates the code in the block that follows:

```
if x < 0:
    print 'It's negative'
```

An if statement can be optionally followed by one or more elif blocks and a catch-all else block if all of the conditions are False:

```
if x < 0:
    print 'It's negative'
elif x == 0:
    print 'Equal to zero'
elif 0 < x < 5:
    print 'Positive but smaller than 5'
else:
    print 'Positive and larger than or equal to 5'
```

If any of the conditions is True, no further elif or else blocks will be reached. With a compound condition using and or or, conditions are evaluated left-to-right and will short circuit:

```
In [340]: a = 5; b = 7

In [341]: c = 8; d = 4

In [342]: if a < b or c > d:
   .....:     print 'Made it'
Made it
```

In this example, the comparison c > d never gets evaluated because the first comparison was True.

for loops

for loops are for iterating over a collection (like a list or tuple) or an iterater. The standard syntax for a for loop is:

```
for value in collection:
    # do something with value
```

A for loop can be advanced to the next iteration, skipping the remainder of the block, using the continue keyword. Consider this code which sums up integers in a list and skips None values:

```
sequence = [1, 2, None, 4, None, 5]
total = 0
for value in sequence:
    if value is None:
        continue
    total += value
```

A for loop can be exited altogether using the break keyword. This code sums elements of the list until a 5 is reached:

```
sequence = [1, 2, 0, 4, 6, 5, 2, 1]
total_until_5 = 0
for value in sequence:
    if value == 5:
        break
    total_until_5 += value
```

As we will see in more detail, if the elements in the collection or iterator are sequences (tuples or lists, say), they can be conveniently *unpacked* into variables in the for loop statement:

```
for a, b, c in iterator:
    # do something
```

while loops

A while loop specifies a condition and a block of code that is to be executed until the condition evaluates to False or the loop is explicitly ended with break:

```
x = 256
total = 0
while x > 0:
    if total > 500:
        break
    total += x
    x = x // 2
```

pass

pass is the "no-op" statement in Python. It can be used in blocks where no action is to be taken; it is only required because Python uses whitespace to delimit blocks:

```
if x < 0:
    print 'negative!'
elif x == 0:
    # TODO: put something smart here
    pass
else:
    print 'positive!'
```

It's common to use pass as a place-holder in code while working on a new piece of functionality:

```
def f(x, y, z):
    # TODO: implement this function!
    pass
```

Exception handling

Handling Python errors or *exceptions* gracefully is an important part of building robust programs. In data analysis applications, many functions only work on certain kinds of input. As an example, Python's float function is capable of casting a string to a floating point number, but fails with ValueError on improper inputs:

```
In [343]: float('1.2345')
Out[343]: 1.2345

In [344]: float('something')
---------------------------------------------------------------------------
ValueError                                Traceback (most recent call last)
<ipython-input-344-439904410854> in <module>()
```

```
----> 1 float('something')
ValueError: could not convert string to float: something
```

Suppose we wanted a version of **float** that fails gracefully, returning the input argument. We can do this by writing a function that encloses the call to **float** in a try/except block:

```
def attempt_float(x):
    try:
        return float(x)
    except:
        return x
```

The code in the **except** part of the block will only be executed if **float(x)** raises an exception:

```
In [346]: attempt_float('1.2345')
Out[346]: 1.2345

In [347]: attempt_float('something')
Out[347]: 'something'
```

You might notice that **float** can raise exceptions other than **ValueError**:

```
In [348]: float((1, 2))
---------------------------------------------------------------------
TypeError                                 Traceback (most recent call last)
<ipython-input-348-842079ebb635> in <module>()
----> 1 float((1, 2))
TypeError: float() argument must be a string or a number
```

You might want to only suppress **ValueError**, since a **TypeError** (the input was not a string or numeric value) might indicate a legitimate bug in your program. To do that, write the exception type after **except**:

```
def attempt_float(x):
    try:
        return float(x)
    except ValueError:
        return x
```

We have then:

```
In [350]: attempt_float((1, 2))
---------------------------------------------------------------------
TypeError                                 Traceback (most recent call last)
<ipython-input-350-9bdfd730cead> in <module>()
----> 1 attempt_float((1, 2))
<ipython-input-349-3e06b8379b6b> in attempt_float(x)
      1 def attempt_float(x):
      2     try:
----> 3         return float(x)
      4     except ValueError:
      5         return x
TypeError: float() argument must be a string or a number
```

You can catch multiple exception types by writing a tuple of exception types instead (the parentheses are required):

```
def attempt_float(x):
    try:
        return float(x)
    except (TypeError, ValueError):
        return x
```

In some cases, you may not want to suppress an exception, but you want some code to be executed regardless of whether the code in the try block succeeds or not. To do this, use finally:

```
f = open(path, 'w')

try:
    write_to_file(f)
finally:
    f.close()
```

Here, the file handle f will *always* get closed. Similarly, you can have code that executes only if the try: block succeeds using else:

```
f = open(path, 'w')

try:
    write_to_file(f)
except:
    print 'Failed'
else:
    print 'Succeeded'
finally:
    f.close()
```

range and xrange

The range function produces a list of evenly-spaced integers:

```
In [352]: range(10)
Out[352]: [0, 1, 2, 3, 4, 5, 6, 7, 8, 9]
```

Both a start, end, and step can be given:

```
In [353]: range(0, 20, 2)
Out[353]: [0, 2, 4, 6, 8, 10, 12, 14, 16, 18]
```

As you can see, range produces integers up to but not including the endpoint. A common use of range is for iterating through sequences by index:

```
seq = [1, 2, 3, 4]
for i in range(len(seq)):
    val = seq[i]
```

For very long ranges, it's recommended to use xrange, which takes the same arguments as range but returns an iterator that generates integers one by one rather than generating all of them up-front and storing them in a (potentially very large) list. This snippet sums all numbers from 0 to 9999 that are multiples of 3 or 5:

```
sum = 0
for i in xrange(10000):
    # % is the modulo operator
    if i % 3 == 0 or i % 5 == 0:
        sum += i
```

 In Python 3, range always returns an iterator, and thus it is not necessary to use the xrange function

Ternary Expressions

A *ternary expression* in Python allows you combine an if-else block which produces a value into a single line or expression. The syntax for this in Python is

```
value = true-expr if condition else
    false-expr
```

Here, *true-expr* and *false-expr* can be any Python expressions. It has the identical effect as the more verbose

```
if condition:
    value = true-expr
else:
    value = false-expr
```

This is a more concrete example:

```
In [354]: x = 5

In [355]: 'Non-negative' if x >= 0 else 'Negative'
Out[355]: 'Non-negative'
```

As with if-else blocks, only one of the expressions will be evaluated. While it may be tempting to always use ternary expressions to condense your code, realize that you may sacrifice readability if the condition as well and the true and false expressions are very complex.

Data Structures and Sequences

Python's data structures are simple, but powerful. Mastering their use is a critical part of becoming a proficient Python programmer.

Tuple

A tuple is a one-dimensional, fixed-length, *immutable* sequence of Python objects. The easiest way to create one is with a comma-separated sequence of values:

```
In [356]: tup = 4, 5, 6

In [357]: tup
Out[357]: (4, 5, 6)
```

When defining tuples in more complicated expressions, it's often necessary to enclose the values in parentheses, as in this example of creating a tuple of tuples:

```
In [358]: nested_tup = (4, 5, 6), (7, 8)

In [359]: nested_tup
Out[359]: ((4, 5, 6), (7, 8))
```

Any sequence or iterator can be converted to a tuple by invoking tuple:

```
In [360]: tuple([4, 0, 2])
Out[360]: (4, 0, 2)

In [361]: tup = tuple('string')

In [362]: tup
Out[362]: ('s', 't', 'r', 'i', 'n', 'g')
```

Elements can be accessed with square brackets [] as with most other sequence types. Like C, C++, Java, and many other languages, sequences are 0-indexed in Python:

```
In [363]: tup[0]
Out[363]: 's'
```

While the objects stored in a tuple may be mutable themselves, once created it's not possible to modify which object is stored in each slot:

```
In [364]: tup = tuple(['foo', [1, 2], True])

In [365]: tup[2] = False
---------------------------------------------------------------------------
TypeError                                 Traceback (most recent call last)
<ipython-input-365-c7308343b841> in <module>()
----> 1 tup[2] = False
TypeError: 'tuple' object does not support item assignment

# however
In [366]: tup[1].append(3)

In [367]: tup
Out[367]: ('foo', [1, 2, 3], True)
```

Tuples can be concatenated using the + operator to produce longer tuples:

```
In [368]: (4, None, 'foo') + (6, 0) + ('bar',)
Out[368]: (4, None, 'foo', 6, 0, 'bar')
```

Multiplying a tuple by an integer, as with lists, has the effect of concatenating together that many copies of the tuple.

```
In [369]: ('foo', 'bar') * 4
Out[369]: ('foo', 'bar', 'foo', 'bar', 'foo', 'bar', 'foo', 'bar')
```

Note that the objects themselves are not copied, only the references to them.

Unpacking tuples

If you try to *assign* to a tuple-like expression of variables, Python will attempt to *unpack* the value on the right-hand side of the equals sign:

```
In [370]: tup = (4, 5, 6)

In [371]: a, b, c = tup

In [372]: b
Out[372]: 5
```

Even sequences with nested tuples can be unpacked:

```
In [373]: tup = 4, 5, (6, 7)

In [374]: a, b, (c, d) = tup

In [375]: d
Out[375]: 7
```

Using this functionality it's easy to swap variable names, a task which in many languages might look like:

```
tmp = a
a = b
b = tmp

b, a = a, b
```

One of the most common uses of variable unpacking when iterating over sequences of tuples or lists:

```
seq = [(1, 2, 3), (4, 5, 6), (7, 8, 9)]
for a, b, c in seq:
    pass
```

Another common use is for returning multiple values from a function. More on this later.

Tuple methods

Since the size and contents of a tuple cannot be modified, it is very light on instance methods. One particularly useful one (also available on lists) is count, which counts the number of occurrences of a value:

```
In [376]: a = (1, 2, 2, 2, 3, 4, 2)
```

```
In [377]: a.count(2)
Out[377]: 4
```

List

In contrast with tuples, lists are variable-length and their contents can be modified. They can be defined using square brackets [] or using the list type function:

```
In [378]: a_list = [2, 3, 7, None]

In [379]: tup = ('foo', 'bar', 'baz')

In [380]: b_list = list(tup)          In [381]: b_list
                                      Out[381]: ['foo', 'bar', 'baz']

In [382]: b_list[1] = 'peekaboo'      In [383]: b_list
                                      Out[383]: ['foo', 'peekaboo', 'baz']
```

Lists and tuples are semantically similar as one-dimensional sequences of objects and thus can be used interchangeably in many functions.

Adding and removing elements

Elements can be appended to the end of the list with the append method:

```
In [384]: b_list.append('dwarf')

In [385]: b_list
Out[385]: ['foo', 'peekaboo', 'baz', 'dwarf']
```

Using insert you can insert an element at a specific location in the list:

```
In [386]: b_list.insert(1, 'red')

In [387]: b_list
Out[387]: ['foo', 'red', 'peekaboo', 'baz', 'dwarf']
```

 insert is computationally expensive compared with append as references to subsequent elements have to be shifted internally to make room for the new element.

The inverse operation to insert is pop, which removes and returns an element at a particular index:

```
In [388]: b_list.pop(2)
Out[388]: 'peekaboo'

In [389]: b_list
Out[389]: ['foo', 'red', 'baz', 'dwarf']
```

Elements can be removed by value using remove, which locates the first such value and removes it from the last:

```
In [390]: b_list.append('foo')

In [391]: b_list.remove('foo')

In [392]: b_list
Out[392]: ['red', 'baz', 'dwarf', 'foo']
```

If performance is not a concern, by using append and remove, a Python list can be used as a perfectly suitable "multi-set" data structure.

You can check if a list contains a value using the in keyword:

```
In [393]: 'dwarf' in b_list
Out[393]: True
```

Note that checking whether a list contains a value is a lot slower than dicts and sets as Python makes a linear scan across the values of the list, whereas the others (based on hash tables) can make the check in constant time.

Concatenating and combining lists

Similar to tuples, adding two lists together with + concatenates them:

```
In [394]: [4, None, 'foo'] + [7, 8, (2, 3)]
Out[394]: [4, None, 'foo', 7, 8, (2, 3)]
```

If you have a list already defined, you can append multiple elements to it using the extend method:

```
In [395]: x = [4, None, 'foo']

In [396]: x.extend([7, 8, (2, 3)])

In [397]: x
Out[397]: [4, None, 'foo', 7, 8, (2, 3)]
```

Note that list concatenation is a compartively expensive operation since a new list must be created and the objects copied over. Using extend to append elements to an existing list, especially if you are building up a large list, is usually preferable. Thus,

```
everything = []
for chunk in list_of_lists:
    everything.extend(chunk)
```

is faster than than the concatenative alternative

```
everything = []
for chunk in list_of_lists:
    everything = everything + chunk
```

Sorting

A list can be sorted in-place (without creating a new object) by calling its sort function:

```
In [398]: a = [7, 2, 5, 1, 3]
```

```
In [399]: a.sort()

In [400]: a
Out[400]: [1, 2, 3, 5, 7]
```

sort has a few options that will occasionally come in handy. One is the ability to pass a secondary *sort key*, i.e. a function that produces a value to use to sort the objects. For example, we could sort a collection of strings by their lengths:

```
In [401]: b = ['saw', 'small', 'He', 'foxes', 'six']

In [402]: b.sort(key=len)

In [403]: b
Out[403]: ['He', 'saw', 'six', 'small', 'foxes']
```

Binary search and maintaining a sorted list

The built-in bisect module implements binary-search and insertion into a sorted list. bisect.bisect finds the location where an element should be inserted to keep it sorted, while bisect.insort actually inserts the element into that location:

```
In [404]: import bisect

In [405]: c = [1, 2, 2, 2, 3, 4, 7]

In [406]: bisect.bisect(c, 2)      In [407]: bisect.bisect(c, 5)
Out[406]: 4                        Out[407]: 6

In [408]: bisect.insort(c, 6)

In [409]: c
Out[409]: [1, 2, 2, 2, 3, 4, 6, 7]
```

 The bisect module functions do not check whether the list is sorted as doing so would be computationally expensive. Thus, using them with an unsorted list will succeed without error but may lead to incorrect results.

Slicing

You can select sections of list-like types (arrays, tuples, NumPy arrays) by using slice notation, which in its basic form consists of start:stop passed to the indexing operator []:

```
In [410]: seq = [7, 2, 3, 7, 5, 6, 0, 1]

In [411]: seq[1:5]
Out[411]: [2, 3, 7, 5]
```

Slices can also be assigned to with a sequence:

```
In [412]: seq[3:4] = [6, 3]
```

```
In [413]: seq
Out[413]: [7, 2, 3, 6, 3, 5, 6, 0, 1]
```

While element at the start index is included, the stop index is not included, so that the number of elements in the result is stop - start.

Either the start or stop can be omitted in which case they default to the start of the sequence and the end of the sequence, respectively:

```
In [414]: seq[:5]          In [415]: seq[3:]
Out[414]: [7, 2, 3, 6, 3]   Out[415]: [6, 3, 5, 6, 0, 1]
```

Negative indices slice the sequence relative to the end:

```
In [416]: seq[-4:]          In [417]: seq[-6:-2]
Out[416]: [5, 6, 0, 1]      Out[417]: [6, 3, 5, 6]
```

Slicing semantics takes a bit of getting used to, especially if you're coming from R or MATLAB. See Figure A-2 for a helpful illustrating of slicing with positive and negative integers.

A step can also be used after a second colon to, say, take every other element:

```
In [418]: seq[::2]
Out[418]: [7, 3, 3, 6, 1]
```

A clever use of this is to pass -1 which has the useful effect of reversing a list or tuple:

```
In [419]: seq[::-1]
Out[419]: [1, 0, 6, 5, 3, 6, 3, 2, 7]
```

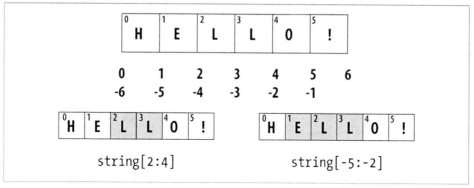

Figure A-2. Illustration of Python slicing conventions

Built-in Sequence Functions

Python has a handful of useful sequence functions that you should familiarize yourself with and use at any opportunity.

enumerate

It's common when iterating over a sequence to want to keep track of the index of the
current item. A do-it-yourself approach would look like:

```
i = 0
for value in collection:
    # do something with value
    i += 1
```

Since this is so common, Python has a built-in function enumerate which returns a
sequence of (i, value) tuples:

```
for i, value in enumerate(collection):
    # do something with value
```

When indexing data, a useful pattern that uses enumerate is computing a dict mapping
the values of a sequence (which are assumed to be unique) to their locations in the
sequence:

```
In [420]: some_list = ['foo', 'bar', 'baz']

In [421]: mapping = dict((v, i) for i, v in enumerate(some_list))

In [422]: mapping
Out[422]: {'bar': 1, 'baz': 2, 'foo': 0}
```

sorted

The sorted function returns a new sorted list from the elements of any sequence:

```
In [423]: sorted([7, 1, 2, 6, 0, 3, 2])
Out[423]: [0, 1, 2, 2, 3, 6, 7]

In [424]: sorted('horse race')
Out[424]: [' ', 'a', 'c', 'e', 'e', 'h', 'o', 'r', 'r', 's']
```

A common pattern for getting a sorted list of the unique elements in a sequence is to
combine sorted with set:

```
In [425]: sorted(set('this is just some string'))
Out[425]: [' ', 'e', 'g', 'h', 'i', 'j', 'm', 'n', 'o', 'r', 's', 't', 'u']
```

zip

zip "pairs" up the elements of a number of lists, tuples, or other sequences, to create
a list of tuples:

```
In [426]: seq1 = ['foo', 'bar', 'baz']

In [427]: seq2 = ['one', 'two', 'three']

In [428]: zip(seq1, seq2)
Out[428]: [('foo', 'one'), ('bar', 'two'), ('baz', 'three')]
```

zip can take an arbitrary number of sequences, and the number of elements it produces is determined by the *shortest* sequence:

```
In [429]: seq3 = [False, True]

In [430]: zip(seq1, seq2, seq3)
Out[430]: [('foo', 'one', False), ('bar', 'two', True)]
```

A very common use of `zip` is for simultaneously iterating over multiple sequences, possibly also combined with enumerate:

```
In [431]: for i, (a, b) in enumerate(zip(seq1, seq2)):
   .....:     print('%d: %s, %s' % (i, a, b))
   .....:
0: foo, one
1: bar, two
2: baz, three
```

Given a "zipped" sequence, `zip` can be applied in a clever way to "unzip" the sequence. Another way to think about this is converting a list of *rows* into a list of *columns*. The syntax, which looks a bit magical, is:

```
In [432]: pitchers = [('Nolan', 'Ryan'), ('Roger', 'Clemens'),
   .....:             ('Schilling', 'Curt')]

In [433]: first_names, last_names = zip(*pitchers)

In [434]: first_names
Out[434]: ('Nolan', 'Roger', 'Schilling')

In [435]: last_names
Out[435]: ('Ryan', 'Clemens', 'Curt')
```

We'll look in more detail at the use of * in a function call. It is equivalent to the following:

```
zip(seq[0], seq[1], ..., seq[len(seq) - 1])
```

reversed

reversed iterates over the elements of a sequence in reverse order:

```
In [436]: list(reversed(range(10)))
Out[436]: [9, 8, 7, 6, 5, 4, 3, 2, 1, 0]
```

Dict

dict is likely the most important built-in Python data structure. A more common name for it is *hash map* or *associative array*. It is a flexibly-sized collection of *key-value* pairs, where *key* and *value* are Python objects. One way to create one is by using curly braces {} and using colons to separate keys and values:

```
In [437]: empty_dict = {}

In [438]: d1 = {'a' : 'some value', 'b' : [1, 2, 3, 4]}
```

```
In [439]: d1
Out[439]: {'a': 'some value', 'b': [1, 2, 3, 4]}
```

Elements can be accessed and inserted or set using the same syntax as accessing elements of a list or tuple:

```
In [440]: d1[7] = 'an integer'
```

```
In [441]: d1
Out[441]: {7: 'an integer', 'a': 'some value', 'b': [1, 2, 3, 4]}
```

```
In [442]: d1['b']
Out[442]: [1, 2, 3, 4]
```

You can check if a dict contains a key using the same syntax as with checking whether a list or tuple contains a value:

```
In [443]: 'b' in d1
Out[443]: True
```

Values can be deleted either using the del keyword or the pop method (which simultaneously returns the value and deletes the key):

```
In [444]: d1[5] = 'some value'
```

```
In [445]: d1['dummy'] = 'another value'
```

```
In [446]: del d1[5]
```

```
In [447]: ret = d1.pop('dummy')        In [448]: ret
                                        Out[448]: 'another value'
```

The keys and values method give you lists of the keys and values, respectively. While the key-value pairs are not in any particular order, these functions output the keys and values in the same order:

```
In [449]: d1.keys()           In [450]: d1.values()
Out[449]: ['a', 'b', 7]       Out[450]: ['some value', [1, 2, 3, 4], 'an integer']
```

 If you're using Python 3, dict.keys() and dict.values() are iterators instead of lists.

One dict can be merged into another using the update method:

```
In [451]: d1.update({'b' : 'foo', 'c' : 12})
```

```
In [452]: d1
Out[452]: {7: 'an integer', 'a': 'some value', 'b': 'foo', 'c': 12}
```

Creating dicts from sequences

It's common to occasionally end up with two sequences that you want to pair up element-wise in a dict. As a first cut, you might write code like this:

```
mapping = {}
for key, value in zip(key_list, value_list):
    mapping[key] = value
```

Since a dict is essentially a collection of 2-tuples, it should be no shock that the dict type function accepts a list of 2-tuples:

```
In [453]: mapping = dict(zip(range(5), reversed(range(5))))
```

```
In [454]: mapping
Out[454]: {0: 4, 1: 3, 2: 2, 3: 1, 4: 0}
```

In a later section we'll talk about *dict comprehensions*, another elegant way to construct dicts.

Default values

It's very common to have logic like:

```
if key in some_dict:
    value = some_dict[key]
else:
    value = default_value
```

Thus, the dict methods get and pop can take a default value to be returned, so that the above if-else block can be written simply as:

```
value = some_dict.get(key, default_value)
```

get by default will return None if the key is not present, while pop will raise an exception. With *setting* values, a common case is for the values in a dict to be other collections, like lists. For example, you could imagine categorizing a list of words by their first letters as a dict of lists:

```
In [455]: words = ['apple', 'bat', 'bar', 'atom', 'book']
```

```
In [456]: by_letter = {}
```

```
In [457]: for word in words:
   .....:     letter = word[0]
   .....:     if letter not in by_letter:
   .....:         by_letter[letter] = [word]
   .....:     else:
   .....:         by_letter[letter].append(word)
   .....:
```

```
In [458]: by_letter
Out[458]: {'a': ['apple', 'atom'], 'b': ['bat', 'bar', 'book']}
```

The setdefault dict method is for precisely this purpose. The if-else block above can be rewritten as:

```
        by_letter.setdefault(letter, []).append(word)
```

The built-in `collections` module has a useful class, `defaultdict`, which makes this even easier. One is created by passing a type or function for generating the default value for each slot in the dict:

```
from collections import defaultdict
by_letter = defaultdict(list)
for word in words:
    by_letter[word[0]].append(word)
```

The initializer to `defaultdict` only needs to be a callable object (e.g. any function), not necessarily a type. Thus, if you wanted the default value to be 4 you could pass a function returning 4

```
counts = defaultdict(lambda: 4)
```

Valid dict key types

While the values of a dict can be any Python object, the keys have to be immutable objects like scalar types (int, float, string) or tuples (all the objects in the tuple need to be immutable, too). The technical term here is *hashability*. You can check whether an object is hashable (can be used as a key in a dict) with the `hash` function:

```
In [459]: hash('string')
Out[459]: -9167918882415130555

In [460]: hash((1, 2, (2, 3)))
Out[460]: 1097636502276347782

In [461]: hash((1, 2, [2, 3])) # fails because lists are mutable
---------------------------------------------------------------------------
TypeError                                 Traceback (most recent call last)
<ipython-input-461-800cd14ba8be> in <module>()
----> 1 hash((1, 2, [2, 3])) # fails because lists are mutable
TypeError: unhashable type: 'list'
```

To use a list as a key, an easy fix is to convert it to a tuple:

```
In [462]: d = {}

In [463]: d[tuple([1, 2, 3])] = 5

In [464]: d
Out[464]: {(1, 2, 3): 5}
```

Set

A set is an unordered collection of unique elements. You can think of them like dicts, but keys only, no values. A set can be created in two ways: via the `set` function or using a *set literal* with curly braces:

```
In [465]: set([2, 2, 2, 1, 3, 3])
Out[465]: set([1, 2, 3])
```

```
In [466]: {2, 2, 2, 1, 3, 3}
Out[466]: set([1, 2, 3])
```

Sets support mathematical *set operations* like union, intersection, difference, and symmetric difference. See Table A-3 for a list of commonly used set methods.

```
In [467]: a = {1, 2, 3, 4, 5}
```

```
In [468]: b = {3, 4, 5, 6, 7, 8}
```

```
In [469]: a | b  # union (or)
Out[469]: set([1, 2, 3, 4, 5, 6, 7, 8])
```

```
In [470]: a & b  # intersection (and)
Out[470]: set([3, 4, 5])
```

```
In [471]: a - b  # difference
Out[471]: set([1, 2])
```

```
In [472]: a ^ b  # symmetric difference (xor)
Out[472]: set([1, 2, 6, 7, 8])
```

You can also check if a set is a subset of (is contained in) or a superset of (contains all elements of) another set:

```
In [473]: a_set = {1, 2, 3, 4, 5}
```

```
In [474]: {1, 2, 3}.issubset(a_set)
Out[474]: True
```

```
In [475]: a_set.issuperset({1, 2, 3})
Out[475]: True
```

As you might guess, sets are equal if their contents are equal:

```
In [476]: {1, 2, 3} == {3, 2, 1}
Out[476]: True
```

Table A-3. Python Set Operations

Function	Alternate Syntax	Description
a.add(x)	N/A	Add element x to the set a
a.remove(x)	N/A	Remove element x from the set a
a.union(b)	a | b	All of the unique elements in a and b.
a.intersection(b)	a & b	All of the elements in *both* a and b.
a.difference(b)	a - b	The elements in a that are not in b.
a.symmetric_difference(b)	a ^ b	All of the elements in a or b but *not both*.
a.issubset(b)	N/A	True if the elements of a are all contained in b.
a.issuperset(b)	N/A	True if the elements of b are all contained in a.
a.isdisjoint(b)	N/A	True if a and b have no elements in common.

List, Set, and Dict Comprehensions

List comprehensions are one of the most-loved Python language features. They allow you to concisely form a new list by filtering the elements of a collection and transforming the elements passing the filter in one concise expression. They take the basic form:

```
[expr for val in collection if condition]
```

This is equivalent to the following for loop:

```
result = []
for val in collection:
    if condition:
        result.append(expr)
```

The filter condition can be omitted, leaving only the expression. For example, given a list of strings, we could filter out strings with length 2 or less and also convert them to uppercase like this:

```
In [477]: strings = ['a', 'as', 'bat', 'car', 'dove', 'python']

In [478]: [x.upper() for x in strings if len(x) > 2]
Out[478]: ['BAT', 'CAR', 'DOVE', 'PYTHON']
```

Set and dict comprehensions are a natural extension, producing sets and dicts in a idiomatically similar way instead of lists. A dict comprehension looks like this:

```
dict_comp = {key-expr : value-expr for value in collection
             if condition}
```

A set comprehension looks like the equivalent list comprehension except with curly braces instead of square brackets:

```
set_comp = {expr for value in collection if condition}
```

Like list comprehensions, set and dict comprehensions are just syntactic sugar, but they similarly can make code both easier to write and read. Consider the list of strings above. Suppose we wanted a set containing just the lengths of the strings contained in the collection; this could be easily computed using a set comprehension:

```
In [479]: unique_lengths = {len(x) for x in strings}

In [480]: unique_lengths
Out[480]: set([1, 2, 3, 4, 6])
```

As a simple dict comprehension example, we could create a lookup map of these strings to their locations in the list:

```
In [481]: loc_mapping = {val : index for index, val in enumerate(strings)}

In [482]: loc_mapping
Out[482]: {'a': 0, 'as': 1, 'bat': 2, 'car': 3, 'dove': 4, 'python': 5}
```

Note that this dict could be equivalently constructed by:

```
loc_mapping = dict((val, idx) for idx, val in enumerate(strings))
```

The dict comprehension version is shorter and cleaner in my opinion.

 Dict and set comprehensions were added to Python fairly recently in Python 2.7 and Python 3.1+.

Nested list comprehensions

Suppose we have a list of lists containing some boy and girl names:

```
In [483]: all_data = [['Tom', 'Billy', 'Jefferson', 'Andrew', 'Wesley', 'Steven', 'Joe'],
     .....:           ['Susie', 'Casey', 'Jill', 'Ana', 'Eva', 'Jennifer', 'Stephanie']]
```

You might have gotten these names from a couple of files and decided to keep the boy and girl names separate. Now, suppose we wanted to get a single list containing all names with two or more e's in them. We could certainly do this with a simple for loop:

```
names_of_interest = []
for names in all_data:
    enough_es = [name for name in names if name.count('e') >= 2]
    names_of_interest.extend(enough_es)
```

You can actually wrap this whole operation up in a single *nested list comprehension*, which will look like:

```
In [484]: result = [name for names in all_data for name in names
     .....:           if name.count('e') >= 2]

In [485]: result
Out[485]: ['Jefferson', 'Wesley', 'Steven', 'Jennifer', 'Stephanie']
```

At first, nested list comprehensions are a bit hard to wrap your head around. The for parts of the list comprehension are arranged according to the order of nesting, and any filter condition is put at the end as before. Here is another example where we "flatten" a list of tuples of integers into a simple list of integers:

```
In [486]: some_tuples = [(1, 2, 3), (4, 5, 6), (7, 8, 9)]

In [487]: flattened = [x for tup in some_tuples for x in tup]

In [488]: flattened
Out[488]: [1, 2, 3, 4, 5, 6, 7, 8, 9]
```

Keep in mind that the order of the for expressions would be the same if you wrote a nested for loop instead of a list comprehension:

```
flattened = []

for tup in some_tuples:
    for x in tup:
        flattened.append(x)
```

You can have arbitrarily many levels of nesting, though if you have more than two or three levels of nesting you should probably start to question your data structure design. It's important to distinguish the above syntax from a list comprehension inside a list comprehension, which is also perfectly valid:

```
In [229]: [[x for x in tup] for tup in some_tuples]
```

Functions

Functions are the primary and most important method of code organization and reuse in Python. There may not be such a thing as having too many functions. In fact, I would argue that most programmers doing data analysis don't write enough functions! As you have likely inferred from prior examples, functions are declared using the def keyword and returned from using the return keyword:

```
def my_function(x, y, z=1.5):
    if z > 1:
        return z * (x + y)
    else:
        return z / (x + y)
```

There is no issue with having multiple return statements. If the end of a function is reached without encountering a return statement, None is returned.

Each function can have some number of *positional* arguments and some number of *keyword* arguments. Keyword arguments are most commonly used to specify default values or optional arguments. In the above function, x and y are positional arguments while z is a keyword argument. This means that it can be called in either of these equivalent ways:

```
my_function(5, 6, z=0.7)
my_function(3.14, 7, 3.5)
```

The main restriction on function arguments is that the keyword arguments *must* follow the positional arguments (if any). You can specify keyword arguments in any order; this frees you from having to remember which order the function arguments were specified in and only what their names are.

Namespaces, Scope, and Local Functions

Functions can access variables in two different scopes: *global* and *local*. An alternate and more descriptive name describing a variable scope in Python is a *namespace*. Any variables that are assigned within a function by default are assigned to the local namespace. The local namespace is created when the function is called and immediately populated by the function's arguments. After the function is finished, the local namespace is destroyed (with some exceptions, see section on closures below). Consider the following function:

```
def func():
    a = []
    for i in range(5):
        a.append(i)
```

Upon calling func(), the empty list a is created, 5 elements are appended, then a is destroyed when the function exits. Suppose instead we had declared a

```
a = []
def func():
    for i in range(5):
        a.append(i)
```

Assigning global variables within a function is possible, but those variables must be declared as global using the global keyword:

```
In [489]: a = None

In [490]: def bind_a_variable():
   .....:     global a
   .....:     a = []
   .....: bind_a_variable()
   .....:

In [491]: print a
[]
```

 I generally discourage people from using the global keyword frequently. Typically global variables are used to store some kind of state in a system. If you find yourself using a lot of them, it's probably a sign that some object-oriented programming (using classes) is in order.

Functions can be declared anywhere, and there is no problem with having *local* functions that are dynamically created when a function is called:

```
def outer_function(x, y, z):
    def inner_function(a, b, c):
        pass
    pass
```

In the above code, the inner_function will not exist until outer_function is called. As soon as outer_function is done executing, the inner_function is destroyed.

Nested inner functions can access the local namespace of the enclosing function, but they cannot bind new variables in it. I'll talk a bit more about this in the section on closures.

In a strict sense, all functions are local to some scope, that scope may just be the module level scope.

Returning Multiple Values

When I first programmed in Python after having programmed in Java and C++, one of my favorite features was the ability to return multiple values from a function. Here's a simple example:

```
def f():
    a = 5
    b = 6
    c = 7
    return a, b, c

a, b, c = f()
```

In data analysis and other scientific applications, you will likely find yourself doing this very often as many functions may have multiple outputs, whether those are data structures or other auxiliary data computed inside the function. If you think about tuple packing and unpacking from earlier in this chapter, you may realize that what's happening here is that the function is actually just returning *one* object, namely a tuple, which is then being unpacked into the result variables. In the above example, we could have done instead:

```
return_value = f()
```

In this case, `return_value` would be, as you may guess, a 3-tuple with the three returned variables. A potentially attractive alternative to returning multiple values like above might be to return a dict instead:

```
def f():
    a = 5
    b = 6
    c = 7
    return {'a' : a, 'b' : b, 'c' : c}
```

Functions Are Objects

Since Python functions are objects, many constructs can be easily expressed that are difficult to do in other languages. Suppose we were doing some data cleaning and needed to apply a bunch of transformations to the following list of strings:

```
states = ['   Alabama ', 'Georgia!', 'Georgia', 'georgia', 'FlOrIda',
          'south   carolina##', 'West virginia?']
```

Anyone who has ever worked with user-submitted survey data can expect messy results like these. Lots of things need to happen to make this list of strings uniform and ready for analysis: whitespace stripping, removing punctuation symbols, and proper capitalization. As a first pass, we might write some code like:

```
import re  # Regular expression module

def clean_strings(strings):
    result = []
```

```
    for value in strings:
        value = value.strip()
        value = re.sub('[!#?]', '', value) # remove punctuation
        value = value.title()
        result.append(value)
    return result
```

The result looks like this:

```
In [15]: clean_strings(states)
Out[15]:
['Alabama',
 'Georgia',
 'Georgia',
 'Georgia',
 'Florida',
 'South Carolina',
 'West Virginia']
```

An alternate approach that you may find useful is to make a list of the operations you want to apply to a particular set of strings:

```
def remove_punctuation(value):
    return re.sub('[!#?]', '', value)

clean_ops = [str.strip, remove_punctuation, str.title]

def clean_strings(strings, ops):
    result = []
    for value in strings:
        for function in ops:
            value = function(value)
        result.append(value)
    return result
```

Then we have

```
In [22]: clean_strings(states, clean_ops)
Out[22]:
['Alabama',
 'Georgia',
 'Georgia',
 'Georgia',
 'Florida',
 'South Carolina',
 'West Virginia']
```

A more *functional* pattern like this enables you to easily modify how the strings are transformed at a very high level. The clean_strings function is also now more reusable!

You can naturally use functions as arguments to other functions like the built-in map function, which applies a function to a collection of some kind:

```
In [23]: map(remove_punctuation, states)
Out[23]:
['   Alabama ',
 'Georgia',
```

```
      'Georgia',
      'georgia',
      'FlOrIda',
      'south   carolina',
      'West virginia']
```

Anonymous (lambda) Functions

Python has support for so-called *anonymous* or *lambda* functions, which are really just simple functions consisting of a single statement, the result of which is the return value. They are defined using the lambda keyword, which has no meaning other than "we are declaring an anonymous function."

```
def short_function(x):
    return x * 2

equiv_anon = lambda x: x * 2
```

I usually refer to these as lambda functions in the rest of the book. They are especially convenient in data analysis because, as you'll see, there are many cases where data transformation functions will take functions as arguments. It's often less typing (and clearer) to pass a lambda function as opposed to writing a full-out function declaration or even assigning the lambda function to a local variable. For example, consider this silly example:

```
def apply_to_list(some_list, f):
    return [f(x) for x in some_list]

ints = [4, 0, 1, 5, 6]
apply_to_list(ints, lambda x: x * 2)
```

You could also have written [x * 2 for x in ints], but here we were able to succinctly pass a custom operator to the apply_to_list function.

As another example, suppose you wanted to sort a collection of strings by the number of distinct letters in each string:

```
In [492]: strings = ['foo', 'card', 'bar', 'aaaa', 'abab']
```

Here we could pass a lambda function to the list's **sort** method:

```
In [493]: strings.sort(key=lambda x: len(set(list(x))))

In [494]: strings
Out[494]: ['aaaa', 'foo', 'abab', 'bar', 'card']
```

 One reason lambda functions are called anonymous functions is that the function object itself is never given a name attribute.

Closures: Functions that Return Functions

Closures are nothing to fear. They can actually be a very useful and powerful tool in the right circumstance! In a nutshell, a closure is any *dynamically-generated* function returned by another function. The key property is that the returned function has access to the variables in the local namespace where it was created. Here is a very simple example:

```
def make_closure(a):
    def closure():
        print('I know the secret: %d' % a)
    return closure

closure = make_closure(5)
```

The difference between a closure and a regular Python function is that the closure continues to have access to the namespace (the function) where it was created, even though that function is done executing. So in the above case, the returned closure will always print I know the secret: 5 whenever you call it. While it's common to create closures whose internal state (in this example, only the value of a) is static, you can just as easily have a mutable object like a dict, set, or list that can be modified. For example, here's a function that returns a function that keeps track of arguments it has been called with:

```
def make_watcher():
    have_seen = {}

    def has_been_seen(x):
        if x in have_seen:
            return True
        else:
            have_seen[x] = True
            return False

    return has_been_seen
```

Using this on a sequence of integers I obtain:

```
In [496]: watcher = make_watcher()

In [497]: vals = [5, 6, 1, 5, 1, 6, 3, 5]

In [498]: [watcher(x) for x in vals]
Out[498]: [False, False, False, True, True, True, False, True]
```

However, one technical limitation to keep in mind is that while you can mutate any internal state objects (like adding key-value pairs to a dict), you cannot *bind* variables in the enclosing function scope. One way to work around this is to modify a dict or list rather than binding variables:

```
def make_counter():
    count = [0]
    def counter():
```

```
            # increment and return the current count
            count[0] += 1
            return count[0]
        return counter

    counter = make_counter()
```

You might be wondering why this is useful. In practice, you can write very general functions with lots of options, then fabricate simpler, more specialized functions. Here's an example of creating a string formatting function:

```
    def format_and_pad(template, space):
        def formatter(x):
            return (template % x).rjust(space)

        return formatter
```

You could then create a floating point formatter that always returns a length-15 string like so:

```
    In [500]: fmt = format_and_pad('%.4f', 15)

    In [501]: fmt(1.756)
    Out[501]: '         1.7560'
```

If you learn more about object-oriented programming in Python, you might observe that these patterns also could be implemented (albeit more verbosely) using classes.

Extended Call Syntax with *args, **kwargs

The way that function arguments work under the hood in Python is actually very simple. When you write func(a, b, c, d=some, e=value), the positional and keyword arguments are actually packed up into a tuple and dict, respectively. So the internal function receives a tuple args and dict kwargs and internally does the equivalent of:

```
    a, b, c = args
    d = kwargs.get('d', d_default_value)
    e = kwargs.get('e', e_default_value)
```

This all happens nicely behind the scenes. Of course, it also does some error checking and allows you to specify some of the positional arguments as keywords also (even if they aren't keyword in the function declaration!).

```
    def say_hello_then_call_f(f, *args, **kwargs):
        print 'args is', args
        print 'kwargs is', kwargs
        print("Hello! Now I'm going to call %s" % f)
        return f(*args, **kwargs)

    def g(x, y, z=1):
        return (x + y) / z
```

Then if we call g with say_hello_then_call_f we get:

```
In [8]: say_hello_then_call_f(g, 1, 2, z=5.)
args is (1, 2)
kwargs is {'z': 5.0}
Hello! Now I'm going to call <function g at 0x2dd5cf8>
Out[8]: 0.6
```

Currying: Partial Argument Application

Currying is a fun computer science term which means deriving new functions from existing ones by *partial argument application*. For example, suppose we had a trivial function that adds two numbers together:

```
def add_numbers(x, y):
    return x + y
```

Using this function, we could derive a new function of one variable, add_five, that adds 5 to its argument:

```
add_five = lambda y: add_numbers(5, y)
```

The second argument to add_numbers is said to be *curried*. There's nothing very fancy here as we really only have defined a new function that calls an existing function. The built-in functools module can simplify this process using the partial function:

```
from functools import partial
add_five = partial(add_numbers, 5)
```

When discussing pandas and time series data, we'll use this technique to create specialized functions for transforming data series

```
# compute 60-day moving average of time series x
ma60 = lambda x: pandas.rolling_mean(x, 60)

# Take the 60-day moving average of all time series in data
data.apply(ma60)
```

Generators

Having a consistent way to iterate over sequences, like objects in a list or lines in a file, is an important Python feature. This is accomplished by means of the *iterator protocol*, a generic way to make objects iterable. For example, iterating over a dict yields the dict keys:

```
In [502]: some_dict = {'a': 1, 'b': 2, 'c': 3}

In [503]: for key in some_dict:
   .....:     print key,
a c b
```

When you write for key in some_dict, the Python interpreter first attempts to create an iterator out of some_dict:

```
In [504]: dict_iterator = iter(some_dict)
```

```
In [505]: dict_iterator
Out[505]: <dictionary-keyiterator at 0x10a0a1578>
```

Any iterator is any object that will yield objects to the Python interpreter when used in a context like a for loop. Most methods expecting a list or list-like object will also accept any iterable object. This includes built-in methods such as min, max, and sum, and type constructors like list and tuple:

```
In [506]: list(dict_iterator)
Out[506]: ['a', 'c', 'b']
```

A *generator* is a simple way to construct a new iterable object. Whereas normal functions execute and return a single value, generators return a sequence of values lazily, pausing after each one until the next one is requested. To create a generator, use the yield keyword instead of return in a function:

```
def squares(n=10):
    print 'Generating squares from 1 to %d' % (n ** 2)
    for i in xrange(1, n + 1):
        yield i ** 2
```

When you actually call the generator, no code is immediately executed:

```
In [2]: gen = squares()

In [3]: gen
Out[3]: <generator object squares at 0x34c8280>
```

It is not until you request elements from the generator that it begins executing its code:

```
In [4]: for x in gen:
   ...:     print x,
   ...:
Generating squares from 0 to 100
1 4 9 16 25 36 49 64 81 100
```

As a less trivial example, suppose we wished to find all unique ways to make change for $1 (100 cents) using an arbitrary set of coins. You can probably think of various ways to implement this and how to store the unique combinations as you come up with them. One way is to write a generator that yields lists of coins (represented as integers):

```
def make_change(amount, coins=[1, 5, 10, 25], hand=None):
    hand = [] if hand is None else hand
    if amount == 0:
        yield hand
    for coin in coins:
        # ensures we don't give too much change, and combinations are unique
        if coin > amount or (len(hand) > 0 and hand[-1] < coin):
            continue

        for result in make_change(amount - coin, coins=coins,
                                   hand=hand + [coin]):
            yield result
```

The details of the algorithm are not that important (can you think of a shorter way?). Then we can write:

```
In [508]: for way in make_change(100, coins=[10, 25, 50]):
   .....:     print way
[10, 10, 10, 10, 10, 10, 10, 10, 10, 10]
[25, 25, 10, 10, 10, 10, 10]
[25, 25, 25, 25]
[50, 10, 10, 10, 10, 10]
[50, 25, 25]
[50, 50]

In [509]: len(list(make_change(100)))
Out[509]: 242
```

Generator expresssions

A simple way to make a generator is by using a *generator expression*. This is a generator analogue to list, dict and set comprehensions; to create one, enclose what would otherwise be a list comprehension with parenthesis instead of brackets:

```
In [510]: gen = (x ** 2 for x in xrange(100))
```

```
In [511]: gen
Out[511]: <generator object <genexpr> at 0x10a0a31e0>
```

This is completely equivalent to the following more verbose generator:

```
def _make_gen():
    for x in xrange(100):
        yield x ** 2
gen = _make_gen()
```

Generator expressions can be used inside any Python function that will accept a generator:

```
In [512]: sum(x ** 2 for x in xrange(100))
Out[512]: 328350
```

```
In [513]: dict((i, i **2) for i in xrange(5))
Out[513]: {0: 0, 1: 1, 2: 4, 3: 9, 4: 16}
```

itertools module

The standard library itertools module has a collection of generators for many common data algorithms. For example, groupby takes any sequence and a function; this groups consecutive elements in the sequence by return value of the function. Here's an example:

```
In [514]: import itertools
```

```
In [515]: first_letter = lambda x: x[0]
```

```
In [516]: names = ['Alan', 'Adam', 'Wes', 'Will', 'Albert', 'Steven']
```

```
In [517]: for letter, names in itertools.groupby(names, first_letter):
   .....:     print letter, list(names) # names is a generator
A ['Alan', 'Adam']
```

```
W ['Wes', 'Will']
A ['Albert']
S ['Steven']
```

See Table A-4 for a list of a few other itertools functions I've frequently found useful.

Table A-4. Some useful itertools functions

Function	Description
`imap(func, *iterables)`	Generator version of the built-in `map`; applies `func` to each zipped tuple of the passed sequences.
`ifilter(func, iterable)`	Generator version of the built-in `filter`; yields elements x for which `func(x)` is True.
`combinations(iterable, k)`	Generates a sequence of all possible k-tuples of elements in the iterable, ignoring order.
`permutations(iterable, k)`	Generates a sequence of all possible k-tuples of elements in the iterable, respecting order.
`groupby(iterable[, keyfunc])`	Generates (key, `sub-iterator`) for each unique key

 In Python 3, several built-in functions (`zip`, `map`, `filter`) producing lists have been replaced by their generator versions found in `itertools` in Python 2.

Files and the operating system

Most of this book uses high-level tools like `pandas.read_csv` to read data files from disk into Python data structures. However, it's important to understand the basics of how to work with files in Python. Fortunately, it's very simple, which is part of why Python is so popular for text and file munging.

To open a file for reading or writing, use the built-in `open` function with either a relative or absolute file path:

```
In [518]: path = 'ch13/segismundo.txt'

In [519]: f = open(path)
```

By default, the file is opened in read-only mode `'r'`. We can then treat the file handle f like a list and iterate over the lines like so

```
for line in f:
    pass
```

The lines come out of the file with the end-of-line (EOL) markers intact, so you'll often see code to get an EOL-free list of lines in a file like

```
In [520]: lines = [x.rstrip() for x in open(path)]

In [521]: lines
```

```
Out[521]:
['Sue\xc3\xb1a el rico en su riqueza,',
 'que m\xc3\xa1s cuidados le ofrece;',
 '',
 'sue\xc3\xb1a el pobre que padece',
 'su miseria y su pobreza;',
 '',
 'sue\xc3\xb1a el que a medrar empieza,',
 'sue\xc3\xb1a el que afana y pretende,',
 'sue\xc3\xb1a el que agravia y ofende,',
 '',
 'y en el mundo, en conclusi\xc3\xb3n,',
 'todos sue\xc3\xb1an lo que son,',
 'aunque ninguno lo entiende.',
 '']
```

If we had typed f = open(path, 'w'), a *new file* at ch13/segismundo.txt would have been created, overwriting any one in its place. See below for a list of all valid file read/write modes.

Table A-5. Python file modes

Mode	Description
r	Read-only mode
w	Write-only mode. Creates a new file (deleting any file with the same name)
a	Append to existing file (create it if it does not exist)
r+	Read and write
b	Add to mode for binary files, that is 'rb' or 'wb'
U	Use universal newline mode. Pass by itself 'U' or appended to one of the read modes like 'rU'

To write text to a file, you can use either the file's write or writelines methods. For example, we could create a version of prof_mod.py with no blank lines like so:

```
In [522]: with open('tmp.txt', 'w') as handle:
   .....:     handle.writelines(x for x in open(path) if len(x) > 1)

In [523]: open('tmp.txt').readlines()
Out[523]:
['Sue\xc3\xb1a el rico en su riqueza,\n',
 'que m\xc3\xa1s cuidados le ofrece;\n',
 'sue\xc3\xb1a el pobre que padece\n',
 'su miseria y su pobreza;\n',
 'sue\xc3\xb1a el que a medrar empieza,\n',
 'sue\xc3\xb1a el que afana y pretende,\n',
 'sue\xc3\xb1a el que agravia y ofende,\n',
 'y en el mundo, en conclusi\xc3\xb3n,\n',
 'todos sue\xc3\xb1an lo que son,\n',
 'aunque ninguno lo entiende.\n']
```

See Table A-6 for many of the most commonly-used file methods.

Table A-6. *Important Python file methods or attributes*

Method	Description
read([size])	Return data from file as a string, with optional size argument indicating the number of bytes to read
readlines([size])	Return list of lines in the file, with optional size argument
readlines([size])	Return list of lines (as strings) in the file
write(str)	Write passed string to file.
writelines(strings)	Write passed sequence of strings to the file.
close()	Close the handle
flush()	Flush the internal I/O buffer to disk
seek(pos)	Move to indicated file position (integer).
tell()	Return current file position as integer.
closed	True if the file is closed.

Index

Symbols

! character, 56, 57, 60
!= operator, 87
!cmd command, 56
"two-language" problem, 2–3
(hash mark), 384
$PATH variable, 8
% character, 394
%a datetime format, 289
%A datetime format, 289
%alias magic function, 57
%automagic magic function, 51
%b datetime format, 289
%B datetime format, 289
%bookmark magic function, 56, 58
%c datetime format, 289
%cd magic function, 56
%cpaste magic function, 47–48, 51
%d datetime format, 288
%D datetime format, 289
%d format character, 394
%debug magic function, 50–51, 58
%dhist magic function, 56
%dirs magic function, 56
%env magic function, 56
%F datetime format, 289
%gui magic function, 53
%H datetime format, 288
%hist magic function, 51, 55
%I datetime format, 288
%logstart magic function, 56
%logstop magic function, 56
%lprun magic function, 66, 68
%m datetime format, 288

%M datetime format, 288
%magic magic function, 51
%p datetime format, 289
%page magic function, 51
%paste magic function, 47, 51
%pdb magic function, 50, 59
%popd magic function, 56
%prun magic function, 51, 66
%pushd magic function, 56
%pwd magic function, 56
%quickref magic function, 51
%reset magic function, 51, 55
%run magic function, 45–46, 51, 382
%S datetime format, 288
%s format character, 394
%time magic function, 51, 63
%timeit magic function, 50, 63, 64
%U datetime format, 289
%w datetime format, 288
%W datetime format, 289
%who magic function, 51
%whos magic function, 51
%who_ls magic function, 51
%x datetime format, 289
%X datetime format, 289
%xdel magic function, 51, 55
%xmode magic function, 50
%Y datetime format, 288
%y datetime format, 288
%z datetime format, 289
& operator, 87
* operator, 101
+ operator, 402, 405
2012 Federal Election Commission database example, 276–284

defined, 382

Python interpreter, 382

interrupting code, 46, 49

intersect1d method, 99

intersection method, 118, 413

intervals of time, 285

inv function, 102

inverse trigonometric functions, 92

.ipynb files, 68

IPython, 5

  bookmarking directories, 58

  command history in, 54–56

    input and output variables, 54–55

    logging of, 55–56

    reusing command history, 54

  design tips, 70–72

    flat is better than nested, 71

    keeping relevant objects and data alive, 71

    overcoming fear of longer files, 71–72

  development tools, 58–68

    debugger, 58–62

    profiling code, 64–66

    profiling function line-by-line, 66–68

    timing code, 63–64

  executing code from clipboard, 46–48

  HTML Notebook in, 68

  integration with IDEs and editors, 48

  integration with mathplotlib, 52–53

  keyboard shortcuts for, 48

  magic commands in, 50–51

  making classes output correctly, 72

  object introspection in, 44–45

  profiles for, 73–74

  Qt console for, 51–52

  Quick Reference Card for, 51

  reloading module dependencies, 70

  %run command in, 45–46

  shell commands in, 56–57

  tab completion in, 43–44

  tracebacks in, 49–50

ipython_config.py file, 73

irow method, 124, 149

is keyword, 389

isdisjoint method, 413

isfinite function, 92

isin method, 137–139

isinf function, 92

isinstance function, 387

isnull method, 92, 110, 140

issubdtype function, 350

issubset method, 413

issuperset method, 413

is_monotonic method, 118

is_unique method, 118

iter function, 388

iterating over groups, 253–254

iterator argument, 158

iterator protocol, 388, 423

itertools module, 425–426, 425

ix_ function, 89

J

join method, 182, 205, 210

JSON (JavaScript Object Notation), 14, 163–164, 212

K

KDE (kernel density estimate) plots, 237

keep_date_col argument, 158

kernels, 237

key-value pairs, 409

keyboard shortcuts, 49

  for deleting text, 49

  for IPython, 48

KeyboardInterrupt event, 46

keys

  argument, 186

  for dicts, 412

  method, 410

keyword arguments, 385, 416

kind argument, 232, 310

kurt method, 136

L

label argument, 231, 309, 311

lambda functions, 209, 260, 420

last method, 259

layout of arrays in memory, 352–353

left argument, 179

left_index argument, 179

left_on argument, 179

legends in matplotlib, 226

len function, 210, 257

less function, 92

less_equal function, 92

level keyword, 257

on index, 180–182
meshgrid function, 93
methods
    defined, 385
    for tuples, 403
    in Python, 385
    starting with underscore, 44
Microsoft Excel files, 170
.mil domain, 14
min method, 97, 132, 135, 259, 424
minimum function, 92
missing data, 139–143
    filling in, 142–143
    filtering out, 140–141
mod function, 92
modf function, 91
modules, 388
momentum, 339
MongoDB, 173–174
MovieLens 1M data set example, 22–28
moving window functions, 317–322
    binary moving window functions, 321
    exponentially-weighted functions, 320
    user-defined, 322
mro method, 350
mul method, 127
MultiIndex Index object, 117, 144, 146
multiple profiles, 73
multiply function, 92
munging, 11
mutable objects, 390–391

N

NA data type, 140
names argument, 158, 186
namespaces
    defined, 416
    in Python, 416–417
naming trends
    in US baby names 1880-2010 example, 33–40
        boy names that became girl names, 39–40
        measuring increase in diversity, 34–37
        revolution of last letter, 37–38
NaN (not a number), 97, 110, 139
na_values argument, 158
ncols option, 221
ndarray, 76

Boolean indexing, 85–88
creating arrays, 77–78
data types for, 79–81
fancy indexing, 88–89
indexes for, 82–85
operations between arrays, 81–82
slicing arrays, 82–85
swapping axes in, 89–90
transposing, 89–90
nested code, 71
nested data types, 367–368
nested list comprehensions, 415–416
New York MTA (Metropolitan Transportation Authority), 167
None data type, 391, 395
normal function, 103, 106
normalized timestamps, 295
NoSQL databases, 173
not a number (NaN), 97, 110, 139
NotebookCloud, 68
notnull method, 110, 140
not_equal function, 92
.npy files, 99
.npz files, 100
nrows argument, 158, 221
nuisance column, 253
numeric data types, 391–392
NumPy, 4
    arrays in, 351–358
        concatenating, 353–355
        c_ object, 355
        layout of in memory, 352–353
        replicating, 356–357
        reshaping, 351–352
        r_ object, 355
        saving to file, 375–376
        splitting, 353–355
        subsets for, 357–358
    broadcasting, 358–363
        over other axes, 360–363
        setting array values by, 363
    data processing using
        where function, 94–96
    data processing using arrays, 93–99
        conditional logic as array operation, 94–96
        methods for boolean arrays, 97
        sorting arrays, 97–98
        statistical methods, 96

unique function, 98–99
data types for, 349–350
file input and output with arrays, 99–101
    saving and loading text files, 100–101
    storing on disk in binary format, 99–100
linear algebra, 101–102
matrix operations in, 373–375
ndarray arrays, 76
    Boolean indexing, 85–88
    creating, 77–78
    data types for, 79–81
    fancy indexing, 88–89
    indexes for, 82–85
    operations between arrays, 81–82
    slicing arrays, 82–85
    swapping axes in, 89–90
    transposing, 89–90
numpy-discussion (mailing list), 9
performance of, 376–379
    contiguous memory, 377–378
    Cython project, 378–379
random number generation, 102–103
random walks example, 104–106
sorting, 369–373
    algorithms for, 371–372
    finding elements in sorted array, 372–373
    indirect sorts, 370–371
structured arrays in, 366–368
    benefits of, 368
    mainpulating, 368
    nested data types, 367–368
universal functions for, 91–92, 363–366
    custom, 366
    in pandas, 128–129
    instance methods for, 364–365

0

object introspection, 44–45
object model, 384
object type, 80
objectify function, 164, 167
objs argument, 186
offsets for time series data, 298–299
OHLC (Open-High-Low-Close) resampling, 312
ols function, 348
Olson database, 299
on argument, 179
ones function, 78
open function, 426
Open-High-Low-Close (OHLC) resampling, 312
operators in Python, 389
or keyword, 397
order method, 371
OS X, setting up Python on, 7
outer method, 364, 365
outliers, filtering, 200–201
output variables, 54–55

P

pad method, 211
pairs plot, 239
pandas, 4–5
    arithmetic and data alignment, 125–128
        arithmetic methods with fill values, 126
        operations between DataFrame and Series, 127–128
    data structures for, 108–117
        DataFrame, 111–116
        Index objects, 116–117
        Panel, 149–151
        Series, 108–111
    drop function, 121
    filtering in, 122–124
    handling missing data, 139–143
        filling in, 142–143
        filtering out, 140–141
    hierarchical indexing in, 143–148
        sorting levels, 146–147
        summary statistics by level, 147
        with DataFrame columns, 147–148
    indexes in, 132–133
    indexing options, 122–124
    integer indexing, 148–149
    NumPy universal functions with, 128–129
    plotting with, 230
        bar plots, 233–236
        density plots, 236–237
        histograms, 236–237
        line plots, 230–233
        scatter plots, 237–239
    ranking data in, 130–132
    reductions in, 133–139
    reindex function, 118–121
    selecting in objects, 122–124

rolling_quantile function, 320, 322
rolling_skew function, 320
rolling_std function, 320
rolling_sum function, 320
rolling_var function, 320
rot argument, 232
rows option, 275
row_stack function, 355
rstrip method, 206, 211
r_ object, 355

S

save function, 99, 375
save method, 169, 173
savefig method, 229
savez function, 100
saving text files, 100–101
scatter method, 237
scatter plots, 237–239
scatter_matrix function, 239
SciPy library, 6
scipy-user (mailing list), 9
scope, 416–417
screen, clearing, 49
scripting languages, 2
scripts, 2
search method, 207, 209
searchsorted method, 372
seed function, 103
seek method, 428
semantics, 383–391
    attributes in, 387
    comments in, 384
    "duck" typing, 388
    functions in, 385
    import directive, 388–389
    indentation, 383–384
    methods in, 385
    mutable objects in, 390–391
    object model, 384
    operators for, 389
    references in, 385–386
    strict evaluation, 390
    strongly-typed language, 386–387
    variables in, 385–386
semicolons, 384
sentinels, 139, 157
sep argument, 158
sequence functions, 407–409

    enumerate function, 408
    reversed function, 409
    sorted function, 408
    zip function, 408–409
Series data structure, 108–111
    arithmetic operations between DataFrame and, 127–128
    grouping with, 255–256
set comprehensions, 414–416
set function, 412
setattr function, 387
setdefault method, 411
setdiff1d method, 99
sets/set comprehensions, 412–413
setxor1d method, 99
set_index function, 148
set_index method, 192
set_title method, 224
set_trace function, 61
set_value method, 124
set_xlabel method, 224
set_xlim method, 224
set_xticklabels method, 224
set_xticks method, 224
shapefiles, 244
shapes, 76, 349
sharex option, 221, 232
sharey option, 221, 232
shell commands in IPython, 56–57
shifting in time series data, 297–299
shortcuts, keyboard, 49
    for deleting text, 49
    for IPython, 48
shuffle function, 103
sign function, 92, 201
signal frontier analysis, 342–344
sin function, 92
sinh function, 92
size method, 253
skew method, 136
skipinitialspace option, 163
skipna method, 134
skipna option, 134
skiprows argument, 158
skip_footer argument, 158
slice method, 211
slicing
    arrays, 82–85
    lists, 406–407

underscore (_), 44, 54
unicode type, 15, 80, 391
uniform function, 103
union method, 99, 118, 203, 413
unique method, 98–99, 118, 137–139, 277
universal functions, 91–92, 363–366
    custom, 366
    in pandas, 128–129
    instance methods for, 364–365
universal newline mode, 427
unpacking tuples, 403
unstack function, 145
update method, 334
upper method, 206, 210, 211
upsampling, 309, 313–314
US baby names 1880-2010 example, 28–40
    boy names that became girl names, 39–40
    measuring increase in diversity, 34–37
    revolution of last letter, 37–38
usa.gov data from bit.ly example, 14–22
USDA (US Department of Agriculture) food
        database example, 211–215
use_index argument, 232
UTC (coordinated universal time), 299

V

ValueError event, 398, 399
values method, 410
value_counts method, 137–139
var method, 97, 135, 259
variables, 51
    (see also environment variables)
    deleting, 51
    displaying, 51
    in Python, 385–386
Varoquaux, Gaël, 247
vectorization, 81
    defined, 93
vectorize function, 366
vectorized string methods, 209–210
verbose argument, 158
verify_integrity argument, 186
views, 82, 114
visualization tools
    Chaco, 246
    mayavi, 247
vsplit function, 355
vstack function, 354

W

w file mode, 427
Wattenberg, Laura, 37
Web APIs, file input/output with, 171
week of month dates, 297
when expressions, 390
where function, 94–96, 187
while loops, 398
whitespace, structuring code with, 383–384
Wickham, Hadley, 250
Williams, Ashley, 211
Windows, setting up Python on, 7
working directory
    changing to passed directory, 56
    of current system, returning, 56
wrangling (see data wrangling)
write method, 427
write-only mode, 427
writelines method, 427
writer method, 163
writing
    to databases, 172–174
    to text files, 160–161

X

xlim method, 223, 224
XML (extensible markup language) files, 167–
        168
xrange function, 400–401
xs method, 124
xticklabels method, 223

Y

yield keyword, 424
ylim argument, 232
yticks argument, 232

Z

zeros function, 78
zip function, 408–409

About the Author

Wes McKinney is a New York–based data hacker and entrepreneur. After finishing his undergraduate degree in mathematics at MIT in 2007, he went on to do quantitative finance work at AQR Capital Management in Greenwich, CT. Frustrated by cumbersome data analysis tools, he learned Python and in 2008, started building what would later become the pandas project. He's now an active member of the scientific Python community and is an advocate for the use of Python in data analysis, finance, and statistical computing applications.

Colophon

The animal on the cover of *Python for Data Analysis* is a golden-tailed, or pen-tailed, tree shrew (*Ptilocercus lowii*). The golden-tailed tree shrew is the only one of its species in the genus *Ptilocercus* and family *Ptilocercidae*; all the other tree shrews are of the family *Tupaiidae*. Tree shrews are identified by their long tails and soft red-brown fur. As nicknamed, the golden-tailed tree shrew has a tail that resembles the feather on a quill pen. Tree shrews are omnivores, feeding primarily on insects, fruit, seeds, and small vertebrates.

Found predominantly in Indonesia, Malaysia, and Thailand, these wild mammals are known for their chronic consumption of alcohol. Malaysian tree shrews were found to spend several hours consuming the naturally fermented nectar of the bertam palm, equalling about 10 to 12 glasses of wine with 3.8% alcohol content. Despite this, no golden-tailed tree shrew has ever been intoxicated, thanks largely to their impressive ethanol breakdown, which includes metabolizing the alcohol in a way not used by humans. Also more impressive than any of their mammal counterparts, including humans? Brain to body mass ratio.

Despite these mammals' name, the golden-tailed shrew is not a true shrew, instead more closely related to primates. Because of their close relation, tree shrews have become an alternative to primates in medical experimentation for myopia, psychosocial stress, and hepatitis.

The cover image is from *Cassel's Natural History*. The cover font is Adobe ITC Garamond. The text font is Linotype Birka; the heading font is Adobe Myriad Condensed; and the code font is LucasFont's TheSansMonoCondensed.

Have it your way.

Get even more for your money.

Join the O'Reilly Community, and register the O'Reilly books you own. It's free, and you'll get:

- $4.99 ebook upgrade offer
- 40% upgrade offer on O'Reilly print books
- Membership discounts on books and events
- Free lifetime updates to ebooks and videos
- Multiple ebook formats, DRM FREE
- Participation in the O'Reilly community
- Newsletters
- Account management
- 100% Satisfaction Guarantee

Signing up is easy:

1. Go to: oreilly.com/go/register
2. Create an O'Reilly login.
3. Provide your address.
4. Register your books.

Note: English-language books only

To order books online:
oreilly.com/store

For questions about products or an order:
orders@oreilly.com

To sign up to get topic-specific email announcements and/or news about upcoming books, conferences, special offers, and new technologies:
elists@oreilly.com

For technical questions about book content:
booktech@oreilly.com

To submit new book proposals to our editors:
proposals@oreilly.com

O'Reilly books are available in multiple DRM-free ebook formats. For more information:
oreilly.com/ebooks

CPSIA information can be obtained at www.ICGtesting.com
Printed in the USA
BVOW02s1158180315

392275BV00003B/4/P